T0231947

Algorithmic Regimes

Digital Studies

The *Digital Studies* book series aims to provide a space for social and cultural research with and about the digital. In particular, it focuses on ambitious and experimental works which explore and critically engage with the roles of digital data, methods, devices and infrastructures in collective life as well as the issues, challenges and troubles that accompany them.

The series invites proposals for monographs and edited collections which attend to the dynamics, politics, economics and social lives of digital technologies and techniques, informed by and in conversation with fields such as science and technology studies and new media studies.

The series welcomes works which conceptualize, rethink and/or intervene around digitally mediated practices and cultures. It is open to a range of contributions including thoughtful interpretive work, analytical artefacts, creative code, speculative design and/or inventive repurposing of digital objects and methods of the medium.

Series editors
Tobias Blanke, University of Amsterdam
Liliana Bounegru, King's College London
Carolin Gerlitz, University of Siegen
Jonathan Gray, King's College London
Sabine Niederer, Amsterdam University of Applied Sciences
Richard Rogers, University of Amsterdam

Algorithmic Regimes

Methods, Interactions, and Politics

Edited by
Juliane Jarke,
Bianca Prietl,
Simon Egbert,
Yana Boeva,
Hendrik Heuer,
and Maike Arnold

Amsterdam University Press

We acknowledge support for the publication costs by the Open Access Publication Fund of Bielefeld University, the State and University Library Bremen (SuUB), the Deutsche Forschungsgemeinschaft (DFG), and the Publication Fund of the University of Basel for Open Access.

Cover illustration: Collage by Maja-Lee Voigt
Images used:
Foucault123 (2021): English: French philosopher and author Michel Foucault. [https://commons.wikimedia.org/wiki/File:685aee19dcc45fbdf325c1ce74738c87v1_max_755x425_b3535db-83dc50e27c1bb1392364c95a2.jpg, last accessed 08/22/2023]. CC-BY-SA-4.0. Changes were made.
Gaetgeaw, Yutthana (2021): A silhouette of a flock of birds taking flight. The concept of... iStock. https://www.istockphoto.com/de/vektor/eine-silhouette-eines-vogelschwarms-der-die-flucht-ergreift-der-begriff-der-gm1355957895-430264699 [last accessed 08/22/2023]. Changes were made.
Grabolle, Anton (o.J.): Classification Cupboard. Better Images of AI. www.instagram.com/antongrabolle [last accessed 08/22/2023]. CC-BY-4.0. Changes were made.
Heuer, H. (2023). Scikit-Learn Example in Python. Permission granted by the authors.

Cover design: Coördesign, Leiden
Lay-out: Crius Group, Hulshout

ISBN	978 94 6372 848 5
e-ISBN	978 90 4855 690 8
DOI	10.5117/9789463728485
NUR	670

Table of Contents

III. POLITICS

1. Knowing in Algorithmic Regimes: An Introduction

Juliane Jarke, Bianca Prietl, Simon Egbert, Yana Boeva, and Hendrik Heuer

Algorithms have risen to become one of the—if not *the*—central technology for creating, circulating, and evaluating knowledge in multiple societal arenas. In this volume, we argue that this shift has, and will continue to have, profound implications for how knowledge is produced and what and whose knowledge is valued and deemed valid. Ultimately, it will transform the epistemological, methodological, and political foundations of knowledge production, sense-making, and decision-making in contemporary societies. To attend to this fundamental change, we propose the concept of *algorithmic regimes*. It draws our attention to the transformation in today's "regime[s] of truth" (Foucault, 1977, p. 13), in particular to the socio-material "apparatuses" (Barad, 2007), cultures, and practices that configure and regulate how (valid) knowledge is produced and by which means truth claims can be made. Knowledge production in algorithmic regimes refers to the ways in which people as well as algorithms gain access to the world, how "reality" is made intelligible and subsequently constructed, and how power and agency are redistributed across human and non-human actors. In algorithmic regimes, the role of human subjects for knowledge production and circulation is decentred, because algorithmic systems are co-shaping ways of knowing and being in the world.

This knowledge transformation has fuelled—and been fuelled by—utopian visions of open and transparent societies and science that lend strength to democratic processes and grassroots movements. Algorithmic systems indeed allow for *new modes of participatory and collaborative knowledge-making and knowledge circulation.* As a result, new modes of knowledge creation and transparency are emerging that may counter official narratives, monitor policy-making, and allow for collective action by engaging civil society organizations or individuals (Milan, 2013; D'Ignazio & Klein, 2020;

Jarke, J., B. Prietl, S. Egbert, Y. Boeva, H. Heuer, and M. Arnold (eds.), *Algorithmic Regimes: Methods, Interactions, and Politics*. Amsterdam: Amsterdam University Press, 2024
DOI 10.5117/9789463728485_CH01

Rajão & Jarke, 2018). The participation of citizens in collaborative knowledge-making is also actively sought by governments and public administrations (e.g., civic tech, participatory urban planning, or participatory budgeting) and research institutions (e.g., citizen science).

However, knowledge production within algorithmic regimes has also proven to be "violent" (McQuillan, 2022) or "harmful" (Noble, 2018; Eubanks, 2018). Over the past two decades, we have witnessed increased surveillance and control through corporate- and government-run algorithmic systems, along with the reinforcement of structural inequalities and systemic discrimination (O'Neil, 2016; Noble, 2018; Gebru, 2019; Prietl, 2019; D'Ignazio & Klein, 2020; Weber & Prietl, 2022; Chun, 2021; on how the bias discourse unfolded around Twitter's cropping algorithm, see Lopez, in this volume; on how the notion of bias and possible solutions are negotiated "within" the computer science community, see Kinder-Kurlanda & Fahimi, in this volume; on empowering everyday users in understanding and detecting potentially harmful algorithmic behaviours, see Eslami & Heuer, in this volume). Vast amounts of online data, for example, have become an increasingly important source of information for state security and, in particular, intelligence services (Lyon, 2014, 2015; on how data use and non-use informs German police, see Büchner et al., in this volume). Economic systems worldwide have likewise become centred around the collection and exploitation of personal data, leading to what Shoshana Zuboff (2019) has termed "surveillance capitalism." Importantly, pervasive and integrated algorithmic systems not only allow state and corporate actors to produce increasingly detailed knowledge about individuals or groups of people, but these systems also afford unprecedented power and control over individuals and groups (Véliz, 2021; McQuillan, 2022; on knowledge requirements to shape recommendation algorithms and power redistribution, see Poechhacker et al., in this volume).

In this volume, we use the term "regime" to conceptualize this transformation of knowledge production as more or less stable socio-material assemblages which surface as coherent patterns of thinking and acting in the world (Deleuze & Guattari, 1987, pp. 503; Bröckling et al., 2011, p. 17; Dean, 1999, p. 21). Any discussion of such regimes must address questions of knowledge and power, in particular, the capacity of social actors to govern both others and themselves by controlling truth claims (Foucault, 1977, p. 13; Foucault, 1980, p. 93; on how predictive systems allow rendering the future governable, see Egbert, in this volume; on how fake news produce new trust regimes, see Wiengarn & Arnold, in this volume; on how sensitizing activities with everyday users subtly foregrounds algorithms and establishes a shared understanding, see Storms & Alvarado, in this volume; on how scientific truth claims are made within algorithmic regimes, see Gramelsberger et al., in this volume): "There can be no possible exercise of power without a certain economy of discourses of truth which operates through and on the basis of this association" (Foucault, 1980, p. 93).

In *algorithmic* regimes "the techniques and procedures which are valorized for obtaining truth" (ibid.) are transformed due to the widespread deployment of algorithms and algorithmic systems. Algorithmic truth claims neglect or even oppose concepts of situated or partial knowledge (Haraway, 1988). Rather, truth claims put forth by algorithmic systems suggest not only that the knowledge produced by and through these systems provides "optimal solution[s] but that other possibilities are suboptimal by definition" (McQuillan, 2022, p. 109; on the epistemic positioning of academic data science, see Prietl & Raible, in this volume).

Hence, the ongoing transformation of society through algorithmic systems is not a mere technology-induced shift in social and scientific knowledge production, but instead leads to an "epistemic colonization" (Gillespie, 2014; see also Beer, 2018; Kitchin, 2014, 2022) and *new knowledge regimes*. To grasp the complexity and momentousness of this shift, it is necessary to look beyond the technical nature of algorithms to acknowledge the wider social, political, cultural, economic, and material entanglements of algorithmic systems as they apply to the generation, accumulation, storage, and connection of (big) data (Seaver, 2017, 2019; on how different framings of machine learning as black boxes produce different socio-technical boundaries within and of algorithmic regimes, see Jarke & Heuer, in this volume; on how algorithmic interactions are constantly reconfigured by different socio-technical, economic, and political drivers, see Boeva & Kropp, in this volume). Powerful discourses purport that algorithms are not only the key to objective and universal knowledge production but also "fixes" for social problems. These discourses are just as relevant to understanding current shifts in society's truth regime as the multiple economic and political drivers that are pushing to integrate algorithms across civic, social, economic, industrial, administrative, and academic arenas of knowledge production.

Three interconnected aspects are crucial for understanding algorithmic regimes and their importance to how people produce knowledge and thus make sense of the world: (1) the *methods* of designing and researching algorithmic systems; (2) *interactions* and how algorithmic systems reconfigure them; and (3) the *politics* and power relations engrained in algorithmic regimes. Although we discuss these three perspectives on algorithmic regimes separately, they are closely related to one another in reality, making their distinction foremost an analytical one. For example, the question of which methods to use for studying and designing algorithmic systems is a highly political one, because different methods allow us to attend to different aspects of algorithmic systems. Interactions within algorithmic regimes take different forms depending on the power relations underpinning specific interactional settings.

To shed light on algorithmic regimes as proposed above, this volume brings together interdisciplinary perspectives that explore each aspect in a dedicated section. Contributions in Section I, "Methods," review and *propose methods for algorithmic systems research and design*. We start with a general review of how algorithms and algorithmic systems have been conceptualized and understood in critical algorithm studies and wider social science and humanities discourses, followed by methodological implications for researching and designing algorithmic systems. Section II, "Interactions," offers insights into *how algorithmic regimes reconfigure interactions*. Multiple ways of interacting with data, algorithms, and algorithmic systems are discussed, illustrating how these interactions not only produce personal, interpersonal, or public knowledge, but also generate trust in algorithmic truth claims. Further complicating the matter, interactions with algorithmic regimes are not consistently obvious to actors, an insight that suggests a variation in issues that may emerge depending on individual algorithmic understandings. Contributions in Section III, "Politics," consider *how power relations are engrained in algorithmic regimes*. By viewing questions of knowledge (production) as inextricably intertwined with questions of power, this section starts by reviewing the literature on algorithmic bias, considers research into the capitalist, sexist, as well as (post)colonial structuring of algorithmic regimes, and then turns to approaches to tackling these problems through artificial intelligence (AI) ethics and initiatives for fair and trustworthy algorithmic systems.

Each section consists of four chapters followed by a commentary. We introduce each section in greater detail and summarize the chapters and commentaries below. Finally, we close this introduction with a reflection on what it means to know (and come to know) in algorithmic regimes.

Methods: What Are Algorithmic Systems and How Can We Study Them?

Considering the literature on critical algorithm studies and the wider discourse on algorithms and algorithmic systems in the social sciences and humanities, a central question that repeatedly arises is what scholars

```python
def bubble_sort(seq):
    changed = True
    while changed:
        changed = False
        for i in range(len(seq) - 1):
            if seq[i] > seq[i+1]:
                seq[i], seq[i+1] = seq[i+1], seq[i]
                changed = True
    return seq
```

Figure 1.1. Bubble sort algorithm in Python. Source: Rosetta Code (2023).

mean when referring to "algorithms" or "algorithmic systems." The concept of algorithms, it seems, has travelled far and wide from its technical roots in computer science and mathematics to encompass a broad variety of phenomena that now captivate critical social science and humanity scholars. All "[t]his talk about algorithms" in the social sciences has been criticized, though, as not speaking about "*actual* algorithm[s]" (Seaver, 2017, p. 1, emphasis in original) but rather about algorithms as ephemeral and intangible phenomena (Burke, 2019; Dourish, 2016). Many social science studies about algorithmic systems tend to explore spatiotemporal processes of their design, use, and application (Dahlman et al., 2021). So the question remains: What exactly do we mean when we talk about algorithms and algorithmic systems?

In computing, an algorithm is a finite, definite, effective procedure that applies a computational rule to transform an input into an output (Knuth, 1968–2022). Cormen et al. (2000) define an algorithm as any clearly circumscribed computational procedure that takes some value, or set of values, as an input and produces some other value, or set of values, as the output. Canonical examples of algorithms include search algorithms or sorting algorithms such as bubble sort (Figure 1.1) or quicksort. A classic example of an algorithm is Euclid's algorithm, which is used to find the greatest common divisor of two integers. Dijkstra's algorithm, a famous algorithm used to determine the shortest path between two nodes in a graph, is applied in some form today by Google Maps and other geo-services.

In the above definitions, algorithms are characterized technically as being comprised of an input, an output, states of computation, and a computational rule. Specifically, an algorithm may be defined as consisting of a logical component (knowledge about the problem) and a control component (strategies for solving the problem) (Kowalski, 1979). Introna (2016) used those two components as the starting point to consider not what algorithms *are* but what constitutes their *doing*. There are multiple ways to characterize what algorithms "do." Considering the bubble sort algorithm or Google's page rank, we could say that they *sort* or *rank*. Following Introna, however, this definition is of limited utility, "as it conceals the implicit operations or assumptions that are necessary for such an answer to make sense" (2016, p. 21). What we could also say is that an algorithm such as bubble sort *compares* two values (Figure 1.1, line 6) in order to decide whether to *swap* them (Figure 1.1, line 7). Comparison serves the goal of sorting. This, Introna holds, is the action (or doing), the *temporal flow* of the code that enacts the sorting process. In these technical definitions of algorithms, the "programming subject" (Mackenzie, 2013) defines the *logical conditions* by rendering a problem in a particular way (e.g., that social entities need to be ranked) and the *structures of control* by implementing computational rules for solving the problem (e.g., specific sorting algorithms). Hence, those who program algorithmic systems inscribe certain understandings, assumptions, and ideas about the social world, including how (social) problems can or should be technically solved. This possibility to read and analyse what software code does is limited, however, to classic imperative programming. A programmer (or a team of programmers) explicitly programmes an algorithm in a programming language, meaning they write the instructions and computational rules that constitute said algorithm. But even in this case, the following should be acknowledged:

> The longer the system has been running, the greater the number of programmers who have worked on it, and the less any one person understands it. As years pass and untold numbers of programmers and analysts come and go, the system takes on a life of its own. It runs. That is its claim to existence: it does useful work. However badly, however buggy, however obsolete—it runs. And no one individual completely understands how. (Ullman, 1997, pp. 116–117, cited in Introna, 2016, pp. 25–26)

Circumscribing "the algorithm" can become nearly impossible, as it may not even exist within one computer, network, or organization (Dourish, 2016).

With the rise of machine learning (ML), we are witnessing a fundamental shift in how computational rules come to be. In ML, computational rules (the strategies for solving a problem) are not explicitly written in any programming language but inferred from data using an ML algorithm—a fact which makes ML-based systems fundamentally opaque. To illustrate: when applying the bubble sort algorithm, the specific computational rule is clear at each step. For an ML-based algorithmic system, the rule merely specifies how the input is transformed to infer the model, but not *how* the model is inferred. This is a crucial difference. On the one hand, it allows ML-based algorithmic systems to solve complex tasks like recognizing objects in images and translating languages. On the other hand, it increases the complexity and difficulty of studying ML-based algorithmic systems' logical conditions and structures of control (see Mackenzie, in this volume).

Hence, the methods for researching algorithmic systems depend on the programming paradigms used in their development. Algorithmic systems based on imperative programming can be explored through an analysis of their code, as has been shown by software studies or critical code studies (Mackenzie, 2017; Fuller, 2008). In contrast, algorithmic systems which are "trained" and based on ML escape these traditional methods. For such systems that infer rules from data, it is important to consider critically the data used to train them, the data providers, the practitioners who train and evaluate such systems, and the communities and collectives which use and (re)appropriate them (Costanza-Chock, 2020; D'Ignazio & Klein, 2020). Axel Meunier, Jonathan Gray, and Donato Ricci (2021) have suggested attending to "troublesome encounters" with algorithms, for example, "when things go wrong" or unexpected to attend to explore algorithms beyond computational processes.

The methods-related contributions in this volume provide inter-disciplinary perspectives spanning the fields of computer science and human–computer interaction, philosophy, sociology, and science and technology studies (STS). They critically engage with ML in the interest of a deeper understanding and more transparent design of these systems. Taken together, the methods discussed empower researchers to explore the implicit and explicit assumptions "inscribed" into algorithmic systems (boyd & Crawford, 2012). As documented by Rieder (2017), algorithmic techniques travel between different scientific and non-scientific applications. Overall, contributions in this section consider how algorithmic systems may be evaluated, audited, and designed in ways that engender trust, fairness, and accountability.

Motahhare Eslami and Hendrik Heuer open Section I, "Methods," with their chapter, "Revisiting Transparency Efforts in Algorithmic Regimes," in which they discuss and evaluate existing human-computer interaction methods to study, research, and design algorithmic systems through the lens of transparency. Eslami and Heuer provide an overview of such approaches, point out where they fall short, and explore where new methodological designs are needed. Their review of folk theories and user beliefs suggests that when not designed carefully, interventions for algorithmic transparency can cause more harm than good. Based on these insights, the two authors call for widespread algorithmic literacy to help people make more informed decisions in their day-to-day encounters with algorithmic systems.

Chapter 3, "Understanding and Analysing Science's Algorithmic Regimes: A Primer in Computational Science Code Studies," by Gabriele Gramelsberger, Daniel Wenz, and Dawid Kasprowicz, provides a perspective from philosophy of science and technology. The authors propose computational science code studies (CSS) as a novel method for understanding the role of algorithmic systems in scientific knowledge production. In a case study involving computational astrophysics, they demonstrate how CSS can be used to analyse data structures, code layers, and code genealogies. The authors' method allows science studies scholars without a background in software development to study knowledge artefacts of scientific programming and reconstruct how scientific concepts and models are integrated into computational science models.

Chapter 4, by Elias Storms, a cultural sociologist, and Oscar Alvarado, a human–computer interaction scholar, is entitled "Sensitizing for Algorithms: Foregrounding Experience in the Interpretive Study of Algorithmic Regimes." In it, the authors address the question of how to involve people without technical expertise in participatory algorithmic systems research and design. Motivated by the complexity of the term "algorithm" and the low awareness of algorithms among most people, they propose and evaluate sensitizing activities that subtly foreground the presence of algorithms, thus raising algorithmic awareness and establishing a shared understanding without influencing the experiences or expectations of research participants.

In Chapter 5, "Reassembling the Black Box of Machine Learning: Of Monsters and the Reversibility of Foldings," Juliane Jarke and Hendrik Heuer explore the different ways in which we encounter machine learning as a black box. The contribution offers a critical reflection on machine learning grounded in STS. Jarke and Heuer identify three different understandings of ML-based systems as black boxes and demonstrate how the metaphor of the black box as a mode of inquiry permits the construction of different understandings as to what is considered a legitimate and constitutive element of an algorithmic system and what is not. In so doing, they draw attention to the ways in which black boxing serves as specific knowledge- and boundary-making practices in the emergence and stabilization of algorithmic regimes.

Chapter 6, "Commentary: Methods in Algorithmic Regimes," by Adrian Mackenzie, is a comment on this section. Mackenzie reflects on the four contributions and his own ways of knowing and coming to know algorithms and algorithmic systems. He wonders "whether all interest in algorithms stems from the deep unease occasioned by technical action" and asks whether living in an algorithmic regime produces (inevitably) methodological ambivalence. In highlighting that many things become infrastructural in algorithmic regimes, Mackenzie also offers advice for investigating algorithms and their effects. The author encourages fellow scholars to attend to breakdowns, follow the detours, and find "paths around corners and ways of opening doors." The difficulties inherent in embarking on these new and untrodden paths are demonstrated in how these four contributions wrestle with questions of knowing in algorithmic regimes.

Overall, this section demonstrates that calls for transparency, fairness, and accountability are only of limited utility (see also Lopez and Kinder-Kurlanda & Fahimi, in this volume). Algorithmic literacy is needed both to empower users in their everyday experience and to enable designers and researchers to critically question how such systems come to be configured. This includes awareness as to how algorithmic systems "solve" or address (social) problems, for example, about *logical conditions* that render a (social) problem in a particular way and *structures of control* that implement computational rules for solving it. Hence, in line with feminist STS and new materialism, algorithmic systems are best understood not as technologies that respond to existing problems, but rather as "apparatuses" (Barad, 2007) that produce reality through specific ways of configuring and framing problems in the first place. The knowledge produced through these systems therefore does not merely depict reality but produces it. In other words, how people engage with and come to know about algorithmic systems matters (Zakharova, 2022).

Interactions: How Do Algorithmic Regimes Reconfigure Interactions?

Section II, "Interactions," attends to some of the intended as well as un-intended reconfigurations of social relations and trust in truth claims brought forth by algorithmic regimes. The chapters highlight how different forms of interactions, whether human–algorithm, human–human, or more-than-human, simultaneously configure and are configured by algorithmic systems. As illustrated by the burgeoning research in critical algorithm studies, data studies, and software studies, interactions with algorithmic systems happen both implicitly and explicitly.

First, human–algorithm interactions *transform everyday knowledge-making practices*, as has been exemplified by studies on self-tracking devices (Duttweiler et al., 2016; Lupton, 2016; Neff, 2016). People interact purposefully with algorithmic systems built into wearables like fitness trackers and apps, as well as with their physical data, to produce new empirical self-knowledge (Lupton, 2018), thereby creating an "algorithmic self" (Pasquale, 2015) and developing new forms of human–algorithm communication (Hepp, 2020). For example, Katrin Amelang (2022) considers how period-tracking apps produce forms of self-knowledge that go beyond traditional pen-and-paper practices. Now, though, tools previously viewed as enabling women to gain control over their bodies have become a source of increasing insecurity due to changing abortion legislation and fears of third-party access by the state or health insurance providers.

Algorithmic regimes also *transform how professionals come to know about key aspects of their work*. One social domain in which this currently applies is crowd work and platform labour. When platform users understand how their interactions with apps, platforms, and technologies affect them, typically in an unfavourable manner, they attempt to "game" these algorithmic systems (Irani, 2015; Rosenblat & Stark, 2016; Schaupp, 2021). Another example is education: algorithmic systems have also become central to how educators produce and implement knowledge about schooling and learning (Jarke & Breiter, 2019; Hartong & Förschler, 2019; Grant, 2022). In educational algorithmic regimes, teachers learn about students and their performance through algorithmic systems (Jarke & Macgilchrist, 2021). This leads to what Alice Bradbury (2019) has described as "data-driven subjectivities" and Neil Selwyn, Luci Pangrazio, and Bronwyn Cumbo (2022) termed "knowing the (datafied) student": both teachers and children make sense of learning successes and failures based on how they are computed and displayed in algorithmic systems.

In other more explicit instances of human–machine interactions such as coding, approaches such as visual programming languages aim to democratize computer programming and make it more accessible to a broader public (Alt, 2011; Noone & Mooney, 2018; Vee, 2017). Such accessible forms of programming that aim to improve coding literacy can be quickly learned and digested through online tutorials and the reuse of code, thereby propagating an algorithmic regime that retains a near-to-black box state (Heuer et al., 2021). Users mainly interact with inputs and outputs by reusing and recombining modularized algorithmic components in a graphical user interface (Chun, 2005; Eischen, 2003). The modularization and segmentation of algorithms as reusable and distributed components as part of the epistemic culture of computer science and software engineering drives an algorithmic regime of ignorance with unforeseeable consequences (Burke, 2019; Malazita & Resetar, 2019).

Second, and concerning human–human interaction, *algorithmic systems and their role in producing knowledge* relevant to these interactions *often remain inaccessible, or even invisible, to human understanding.* This applies, for example, to presumptive human-to-human interactions such as hiring, school admissions processes, or credit scoring. In these situations, algorithmic systems such as automated decision-making systems produce (discriminatory) truth claims that are often inaccessible to humans (Chiusi et al., 2020; Eubanks, 2018; Noble, 2018; O'Neil, 2016; see also the "Politics" section in this volume). Looking beyond such relatively privileged situations, attending to such epistemic transformations is particularly relevant in social arenas that are supposed to serve and support marginalized and minoritized populations. For example, Virginia Eubanks (2018) explored how algorithmic systems surveil, control, and disproportionately disadvantage families receiving social benefits. Paola Lopez (2019, 2021), Stefanie Büchner and Henrik Dosdall (2021), as well as Doris Allhutter and colleagues (2020), researched the algorithmic system employed by the Austrian Job Centre to determine the likelihood of a jobseeker finding a new job and receiving further job training. These case studies question the agency afforded to civil servants to challenge knowledge produced by algorithmic systems while simultaneously warning against the risks of algorithmic regimes.

Third, algorithmic systems reconfigure *relations and interactions on more-than-human and planetary scales* (Crawford, 2021; Gabrys, 2020). Using the visual and analytical metaphor of the atlas for their study of voice assistants such as Amazon Echo and others, Kate Crawford and Vladan Joler (2018) argue that personal interactions with these algorithmic devices are always also interactions between data, human labour, and earthly resources. Rarely do these interactions happen in real time, as human and planetary time differ in their pace. Instead, they serve to connect the digital and the physical, the natural and the artificial, humans and environments, to support computational power. For the various human actors involved, interactions with AI-based virtual assistants are increasingly becoming instantaneous acts. Furthermore, users and micro-workers are prompted to perform tasks such as data cleaning and labelling, thereby "impersonating" AI to overcome technology's shortcomings (Burrell & Fourcade, 2021; Shestakofsky, 2017; Tubaro & Casilli, 2022). By doing so, not only the algorithmic systems but also the human knowledge practices behind them become opaque in order to increase trust in their truth claims.

In sum, it is important to consider how and through which interfaces different users as well as producers and developers interact with algorithmic systems. This section asks which kinds of knowledge are produced through these practices, and which forms of interactions emerge in and through algorithmic regimes.

The first contribution to this section is Chapter 7, "Buildings in the Algorithmic Regime: Infrastructuring Processes in Computational Design," by Yana Boeva and Cordula Kropp. In it they present an empirical case study of human–algorithmic interactions in architectural practice from an STS, infrastructure, and software studies perspective. They examine ongoing changes in the production of buildings and built environments as algorithms, coding, and AI reconfigure design practice and knowledge. The chapter illustrates how the integration of algorithms into design software becomes a continuous "infrastructuring" process that happens through multiple social, technological, and politico-economic decisions. Infrastructuring, they argue, not only conceals algorithms and automation in software systems, thus making them unintelligible to architects, engineers, and urban developers even as they interact with them in design work, but it also reconfigures knowledge about and the design of the built environment.

In Chapter 8, "The Organization in the Loop: Exploring Organizations as Complex Elements of Algorithmic Assemblages," Stefanie Büchner, Henrik Dosdall, and Ioanna Constantiou introduce the role of organizations in shaping algorithmic regimes. Through interactions with different algorithmic assemblages, they argue that algorithmic regimes emerge within organizations—for knowledge production and integration. Presenting a cross-case comparison between predictive policing in Germany and algorithmic decision support systems in healthcare, the chapter foregrounds the role of organizations in producing algorithmic regimes, taking the conversation beyond the more broadly discussed roles of users and developers and into the field of organization studies.

Jörn Wiengarn and Maike Arnold's philosophical perspective focuses on the social-epistemic effects of the algorithmic regime of fake news. In Chapter 9, "Algorithm-Driven Reconfigurations of Trust Regimes: An Analysis of the Potentiality of Fake News," they present a taxonomy of potentially disrupting and far-reaching effects of interacting with—or, as they write, confronting—fake news. In their analysis of the impact of fake news on a person's trust network, they introduce three scenarios: a person interacting with fake news remaining robust towards a disinformation's source, a person becoming disoriented by it, or beginning to fully trust fake news and mistrust any other news sources. Given these findings, the growing and increasingly opaque presence of ML-based algorithmic systems in news and information creation and our everyday interactions with them call for closer examination.

Chapter 10, "Recommender Systems beyond the Filter Bubble: Algorithmic Media and the Fabrication of Publics," by Nikolaus Poechhacker, Marcus Burkhardt, and Jan-Hendrik Passoth, examines different algorithmic systems for information recommendation and how interactions with them construct publics. Following Bernhard Rieder (2017), the authors analyse two ideal-typical recommender systems used in well-known digital media systems, particularly by public broadcasters, and how those systems mediate between databases, interfaces, and practices in the formation of digital publics. Publics, they argue, drawing upon Dewey's pragmatist concept of "issue publics" (Dewey, 2006), are reconfigured by different algorithmic recommender systems by mediating between different practices within a wider algorithmic regime. How democratic societies are informed and develop knowledge depends on the recommendation approach employed and, more specifically, the interactions with it defined by those empowered to shape it.

Finally, Chapter 11, "Commentary: Taking to Machines: Knowledge Production and Social Relations in the Age of Governance *by* Data Infrastructure," by Stefania Milan, rounds off the section by reflecting on the four contributions and how algorithmic regimes affect social interactions. As algorithmic developments take over critical social decisions, for Milan, a continuous activity of "taking to machines," algorithmic regimes manifest modes of "governance *by* data infrastructure." These modes of governance transform our social interactions, which she encourages us to consider carefully as they increasingly begin to dominate knowledge production and publicly relevant decisions. The opaque state of algorithmic regimes and their data infrastructures has the potential to shift "agency, control, and sovereignty away" from the public to algorithmic agents (and the tech industry), depending on interests and also on interactions, as the four contributions emphasize.

Overall, this section and its contributions highlight how existing forms of knowledge are reconfigured while new ones are created as people interact with algorithmic systems and take part in algorithmic regimes. Algorithmic interactions, as the contributions illustrate, can impact individuals even in situations where they might not be deploying an algorithmic system directly, as in the case of public servants using automated decision-making systems. When users have to rely on these systems, such as public servants, professionals, and news producers and the multiple organizations they belong to, the result is a reshaping, not only of the practices and structures of knowledge legitimation but also the grounds upon which current and future societies exist. Accordingly, turning our attention to interactions with algorithmic systems allows us to see how algorithmic regimes emerge.

Politics: How Are Power Relations Engrained in Algorithmic Regimes?

Studying the politics of algorithmic regimes often reveals the strong linkage of regulatory, technological, and economic issues within knowledge production and the opaque ways in which institutions and companies distribute and standardize knowledge. Section III, "Politics," largely follows the Foucauldian understanding of the term politics, thus, looking at the ways that knowledge and power are co-constitutive. The chapters in this section, therefore, zero in on this claim by focusing on different dimensions of the power/knowledge nexus in algorithmic regimes.

In recent years, the politics of algorithmic systems have gained increasing attention, especially when it comes to instances of bias in AI and algorithmic discrimination (Noble, 2018; Gebru, 2019; Prietl, 2019; D'Ignazio & Klein, 2020; Weber & Prietl, 2022; Chun, 2021). This research argues that discriminatory results should be considered less as "bugs"—implying a quick-fix mentality—but instead should be seen as pervasive to algorithmic systems' design and execution, starting with the epistemological assumptions that inform them. One important gateway for discrimination is the (training) data sets upon which ML algorithms are based. These often mirror historically established asymmetries of in/visibility, for instance, under-representing already marginalized social groups (with regards to a gender data gap Criado-Perez, 2019; see also Lopez, 2021). Data, however, are only one aspect of the problem. Other aspects include epistemological and/or ontological assumptions such as the belief that data can speak for itself (termed "data fundamentalism" by Crawford, 2013), an attitude of "technosolutionism" according to which all (social) problems can ultimately be solved through technologies (Morozov, 2013), or the premise that knowledge derived from historical data can be used to predict and *nota bene* even shape the future (cf. Rona-Tas, 2020; Esposito, 2021; Eyert & Lopez, 2023). Given the growing awareness of algorithmic discrimination, the politics of digital technologies are also increasingly being acknowledged as a serious societal challenge.

Current efforts to tackle connected problems predominantly either take the form of calls for ethics (Floridi et al., 2018; Dignum, 2018; Hagendorff, 2020; Prietl, 2021) or organizing workshops and conferences under the headings FAccT and FAT/ML to debate how fairness, accountability, and transparency in machine learning can be achieved.

In grappling with the question of how the new modes of algorithmic knowledge production and decision-making are connected to social relations of power, scholars have also problematized the structuring of AI and digital platforms more fundamentally, pointing to the political economy of digitalization and datafication. Some have stressed their capitalist nature (Zuboff, 2019; Srnicek, 2016, 2018), pointing out that a handful of private corporations seek to dominate the development of AI and other algorithmic technologies by controlling vast amounts of data plus the technological infrastructure for generating, storing, and processing these data (boyd & Crawford, 2012; Lyon, 2004). Others have highlighted the military background and governmental use of AI for surveillance and warfare technologies (Lyon, 2004; Weber, 2016; Eubanks, 2018). Considering that most influential (corporate and government) actors are located in the Global North, algorithmic regimes are also described as situated within (post)colonial structures (Hagerty & Rubinov, 2019). This is especially visible when it comes to the workforce required for developing algorithmic systems. Whereas those responsible for conceptualizing, designing, and developing algorithmic technologies constitute a rather homogenous group of predominantly "white," well-educated, and socio-economically privileged men, the largely invisible, less glamorous, low-skilled, and low-paying work of content moderation or simple data handling is done by a mostly anonymous (online) crowd of workers located in the Global South (Qiu, 2022; Gray & Suri, 2019).

Focusing on the socio-material effects of algorithmic systems, Stefania Milan and Emiliano Treré (2019) have further argued against "universalist" interpretations of the increasing importance of algorithmic systems and digital data, thus challenging predominant narratives of algorithmic systems in the sciences. Rather, scholars need to consider how communities and people live with and experience algorithmic regimes differently depending on where they are situated. These experiences take many different forms: from the border control of migrant bodies that are detected and governed differently through algorithmic systems (Gundhus, 2021) to the ways in which knowledge about algorithmic systems enables or disables social and economic advancement in underprivileged communities (Rangaswamy & Narasimhan, 2022).

As these works demonstrate, studying the political nature and impact of algorithmic regimes is not limited to questions of algorithmic bias. It is also about who configures and shapes algorithmic regimes, to what ends and for whose benefit, what are the dominant ideas and imaginaries underpinning this development, how are they negotiated, institutionalized, and materialized, and which realities do algorithmic regimes enact. Put differently, and as feminist and other critical perspectives in STS have long argued, technical artefacts and the epistemological and methodological premises of knowledge production are inextricably linked to questions of politics and power; they are neither neutral nor objective (Haraway, 1988; Barad, 2003; Weber, 2016; Beer, 2018).

Chapter 12, "The Politics of Data Science: Institutionalizing Algorithmic Regimes of Knowledge Production," by Bianca Prietl and Stefanie Raible, presents an empirical study of the academic institutionalization of data science in Germany, Austria, and Switzerland that draws on the tradition of Foucauldian discourse analysis as power analysis. By analysing how data science is structurally implemented, epistemologically positioned, and discursively legitimized, the authors aim to capture the power dynamics incorporated in the establishment of a specific regime of knowledge production, one that is based on algorithmic big data analysis. The chapter offers a critical engagement with data science as a crucial actor in professionalizing, promoting, and legitimizing algorithmic modes of knowledge production.

In Chapter 13, "Algorithmic Futures: Governmentality and Prediction Regimes," Simon Egbert proposes to analyse predictive analytics and the corresponding applications as "prediction regimes," understood as a subtype of algorithmic regimes. Drawing on the Foucauldian notion of truth regimes and the close nexus of power and knowledge, he highlights the important role of predictive algorithms when it comes to deciding in the present based on algorithmically produced knowledge about the future. Drawing on works from governmentality studies, he argues that (predictive) algorithms are "rendering devices," making the future calculable and, hence, governable in the present, ultimately demonstrating the inherently political character of algorithmic regimes.

In Chapter 14, "Power and Resistance in the Twitter Bias Discourse," Paola Lopez discusses the case of the cropping algorithm from the microblogging and social networking service Twitter, which was heavily criticized in the autumn of 2020, as users observed that the machine learning-based cropping tool for preview pictures discriminated against Black people, systematically cutting their faces from preview pictures more often than for White people.

Combining a Foucauldian perspective on the power/knowledge nexus with a mathematical perspective that examines the mathematics of algorithmic systems, Lopez discusses the problems and underlying questions of machine bias, fairness, and transparency that become salient in Twitter's "biased" cropping tool and the company's reaction to this critique.

Chapter 15, "Making Algorithms Fair: Ethnographic Insights from Machine Learning Interventions," by Katharina Kinder-Kurlanda and Miriam Fahimi, offers an (auto)ethnographic analysis of how an interdisciplinary project consortium (NoBIAS) grapples with making algorithms less biased and, hence, fairer. Bringing a cultural anthropology approach to STS, they focus on the importance of computer science experts as key "intellectuals" in algorithmic regimes and reconstruct the negotiation of different understandings of algorithms, on the one hand, and fairness and bias, on the other. In doing so, they point to the fact that, all technical complexities aside, actually making an algorithm fair is often not a straightforward undertaking.

The section concludes with Chapter 16, "Commentary: The Entanglements, Experiments, and Uncertainties of Algorithmic Regimes," a comment by Nanna Bonde Thylstrup that reflects upon the chapters of this section, arguing that in engaging with the politics of algorithmic systems it is necessary not only to attend to the ways in which they generate new modes of control, organization, and knowledge production, but also to how these new modes of knowledge production are constituted by messes, failures, and uncertainties.

As the chapters in this section demonstrate, there are no easy answers to questions of power and politics in algorithmic regimes. This is especially true when taking bias, discrimination, and fairness as starting points that remain properties of algorithmic systems and hence often seen as in need of a techno-fix (for a critique of such supposedly ready to implement "solutions," and the proposition of an "ethics of doubt," see Amoore, 2020). Throughout the contributions in this section, the power/knowledge nexus reveals itself to be closely connected to forms and practices of in/visibility. Whenever there is opaqueness in an algorithmic regime, those obscured issues are not likely to become part of discourses or practices—whatever is kept in the dark will probably not join the ranks of public knowledge. This insight underlines the importance of taking a (self-)reflexive stance towards algorithms, considering them from an inside-out perspective by researching key actors but also by establishing a broad, open, and participatory societal discussion about algorithmic regimes, their relationship to power, and their practical limits. This means, as McQuillan (2022) argues, that we not only need algorithmic literacy but also feminist literacy that allows us to uncover systemic and structural power imbalances and inequalities in our contemporary algorithmic regimes.

Conclusion: Re-imagining Algorithmic Futures

How different social actors come to know about and make sense of the world has been transformed profoundly through the deployment of algorithms and algorithmic systems of knowledge production. This volume explores how the epistemological, methodological, and political foundations of knowledge production, sense-making, and decision-making change in contemporary societies by focusing on three distinct but highly interrelated aspects of what we propose to analyse as *algorithmic regimes*: (1) the *methods* to research and design algorithmic regimes; (2) how algorithmic regimes reconfigure *interactions*; and (3) the *politics* engrained in algorithmic regimes. The contributions in this volume demonstrate that algorithmic systems now operate as constitutive parts of knowledge creation about social processes and social interactions as well as constitutive parts of knowledge circulation within them. The related applications are highly diverse: algorithmic decision-making systems decide on eligibility for social welfare, (pre)select job applicants, or even establish new research paradigms based on so-called data science methods. Concluding this introduction, we would like to take a step back and consider the implications of our endeavour on a broader scale and what it might mean for re-imagining algorithmic futures.

This volume and other critical works serve as a warning against algorithmic systems that claim to provide universal answers to complex social problems and simple truths about social reality based on the claim of "optimization" (McQuillan, 2022; D'Ignazio & Klein, 2020; Hepp et al., 2022). In algorithmic regimes, validation is emphasized over verification processes and scientific concepts of truth and probability are replaced with trust and reliability (e.g., Weber & Prietl, 2022). As a result, an "ontology of association" (Amoore, 2011) starts to dominate, which privileges correlation over causation. In many instances, complex social and structural problems (such as equal access to education) come to be configured as individual. This framing shifts our attention and scope of action from structural barriers to educational equity to a responsibilization of individuals (Macgilchrist, 2019). Hence, knowledge produced by and through algorithmic systems is in many instances reductionist and even harmful.

In light of increasing uncertainty about humanity's future and questions about the basic values on which our societies stand, it seems more important than ever to consider which kinds of knowledge we value and which knowledge regimes we look to for answers to multiple collective uncertainties and challenges—including climate disaster, racial injustice, the care crisis, war, or displacement. Feminist scholars have long argued that all knowledge is situated and partial (e.g., Haraway, 1988). This also holds for algorithmic systems. Even though they strive to appear otherwise, algorithmic systems are not value-neutral. They configure algorithmic regimes through optimization, exclusion, colonization, and a positivist reproduction of existing social orders. In so doing,

> [c]urrent AI overlooks the work of care that underpins the world, and replaces it with datafied models of reality that are disconnected and domineering.... Adopting AI as our prosthetic, as our extended means of knowing the world, brings certain consequences in how the world becomes objectified.... If we are aiming instead for an alternative based on care and repair, it matters what we ground our knowledge on. (McQuillan, 2022, pp. 107–110)

Algorithmic regimes devalue and invisibilize the work and knowledge practices of caregivers (D'Ignazio & Klein, 2020; Zakharova & Jarke, 2022). It is our collective responsibility (and hope) to consider how algorithmic systems can be (re)configured to serve the common good. This requires, as many of the contributions in this volume show, algorithmic literacy and transparency into how algorithmic systems define (social) problems and come to be configured as sites of knowledge production (and truth claims) about social processes and relations. This is not merely a technical challenge that might involve "ethics checklists" being applied by software engineers, but instead requires a broader dialogue about the algorithmic future(s) we want to live in. Considering new modes of knowledge production as algorithmic regimes provides a critical lens through which it is possible to question the objectivity and validity of algorithmic truth claims and connect them to how power becomes manifest.

Ultimately, this leads to the question of what kind of society we want to live in. Which socio-technical futures do we desire? How can we imagine futures of social justice, social cohesion, and caring communities in (opposition to) algorithmic regimes? At the core of these questions lies the realization that algorithmic systems do not operate separately from the social world, but as part of its ongoing becoming.

Acknowledgements

This volume is the result of several years' long, loose, but highly focused interdisciplinary dialogue between scholars at all stages of their careers interested in questions of how the spread of algorithms transforms how we know and exist in this world. Many of us first met at the EASST conference in 2018 in Lancaster, UK, and have remained in contact ever since. Our special thanks go to Gabriele Gramelsberger and Jutta Weber, who organized the panel on "The Power of Correlation and the Promises of Auto-Management: On the Epistemological and Societal Dimension of Data-Based Algorithms" at the EASST conference in 2018. A first attempt at further pursuing that dialogue happened in the form of a proposal for a German Research Council network—for which we are indebted to Dawid Kasprowicz for taking on the lion's share of the proposal work. Unfortunately, that proposal was not accepted but, due to the disruptions caused by the COVID-19 pandemic and the resulting wildfire of digitally mediated communication, including in academia, that dialogue could be maintained, deepened in several online workshops, and opened to other researchers. Our interdisciplinary exchange was challenging, instructive, productive, and rewarding for us all, which is why we thank all authors and commentators for their willingness to engage in it. We would like to thank Vanessa Komar for her help in preparing the final manuscript. In addition, we would like to thank the Institute for Information Management Bremen (ifib) at the University of Bremen for their support in creating the index of this book. Last but not least, we would like to thank the University of Bielefeld, the University of Basel, and the University of Bremen for their open-access funding of this volume.

References

Allhutter, D., Cech, F., Fischer, F., Grill, G., & Mager, A. (2020). Algorithmic profiling of job seekers in Austria: How austerity politics are made effective. *Frontiers in Big Data, 3*, article 5. https://doi.org/10.3389/fdata.2020.00005

Alt, C. (2011). Objects of our affection: How object orientation made computation a medium. In E. Huhtamo & J. Parikka (Eds.), *Media archaeology: Approaches, applications, and implications* (pp. 278–301). University of California Press.

Alvarado, O., Heuer, H., Vanden Abeele, V., Breiter, A., & Verbert, K. (2020). Middle-aged video consumers' beliefs about algorithmic recommendations on YouTube. In *Proceedings of the ACM on Human–Computer Interaction, 4*(CSCW2), article no. 121. https://doi.org/10.1145/3415192

Amelang, K. (2022). (Not) safe to use: Insecurities in everyday data practices with period-tracking apps. In A. Hepp, J. Jarke, & L. Kramp (Eds.), *New perspectives in critical data studies* (pp. 297–321). Palgrave. https://doi.org/10.1007/978-3-030-96180-0_13

Amoore, L. (2011). Data derivatives: On the emergence of a security risk calculus for our times. *Theory, Culture & Society, 28*(6), 24–43. https://doi.org/10.1177/0263276411417430

Amoore, L. (2020). *Cloud ethics: Algorithms and the attributes of ourselves and others*. Duke University Press.

Barad, K. (2003). Posthumanist performativity: Toward an understanding of how matter comes to matter. *Signs: Journal of Women in Culture and Society, 28*(3), 801–831. https://doi.org/10.1086/345321

Barad, K. (2007). *Meeting the universe halfway: Quantum physics and the entanglement of matter and meaning*. Duke University Press.

Beer, D. (2018). *The data gaze: Capitalism, power and perception*. Sage.

boyd, d., & Crawford, K. (2012). Critical questions for big data: Provocations for a cultural, technological, and scholarly phenomenon. *Information, Communication & Society, 15*(5), 662–679.

Bradbury, A. (2019). Datafied at four: The role of data in the "schoolification" of early childhood education in England. *Learning, Media and Technology, 44*(1), 7–21.

Bröckling, U., Krasmann, S., & Lemke, T. (Eds.). (2011). *Governmentality: Current issues and future challenges*. Routledge.

Büchner, S., & Dosdall, H. (2021). Organisation und Algorithmus: Wie algorithmische Kategorien, Vergleiche und Bewertungen durch Organisationen relevant gemacht werden. *KZfSS Kölner Zeitschrift für Soziologie und Sozialpsychologie, 73*(S1), 333–357. https://doi.org/10.1007/s11577-021-00752-0

Burke, A. (2019). Occluded algorithms. *Big Data & Society, 6*(2). https://doi.org/10.1177/2053951719858743

Burrell, J., & Fourcade, M. (2021). The society of algorithms. *Annual Review of Sociology, 47*(1), 213–237. https://doi.org/10.1146/annurev-soc-090820-020800

Chiusi, F., Fischer, S., Kayser-Bril, N., & Spielkamp, M. (2020). *Automating society report 2020*. AlgorithmWatch. https://automatingsociety.algorithmwatch.org/

Chun, W. (2005). On software, or the persistence of visual knowledge. *Grey Room, 18*, 26–51.

Chun, W. (2021). *Discriminating data: Correlation, neighborhoods, and the new politics of recognition*. MIT Press.

Cormen, T. H., Leiserson, C. E., Rivest, R. L., Leiserson, C. E., & Rivest, R. L. (2000). *Introduction to algorithms*. MIT Press.

Costanza-Chock, S. (2020). *Design justice: Community-led practices to build the worlds we need*. MIT Press.

Crawford, K. (2013, April 1). The hidden bias in big data. *Harvard Business Review.* https://hbr.org/2013/04/the-hidden-biases-in-big-data

Crawford, K. (2021). *Atlas of AI: Power, politics, and the planetary costs of artificial intelligence.* Yale University Press.

Crawford, K., & Joler, V. (2018). *Anatomy of an AI system.* http://www.anatomyof.ai

Criado-Perez, C. (2019). *Invisible women: Exposing data bias in a world designed for men.* Vintage.

Dahlman, S., Gulbrandsen, I. T., & Just, S. N. (2021). Algorithms as organizational figuration: The sociotechnical arrangements of a fintech start-up. *Big Data & Society, 8*(1). https://doi.org/10.1177/20539517211026702

Dean, M. (1999). *Governmentality: Power and rule in modern society.* Sage.

Deleuze, G., & Guattari, F. (1987). *A thousand plateaus: Capitalism and schizophrenia.* University of Minnesota Press.

Dewey, J. (2006). *The public & its problems.* Combined Academic Publ. (Original work published 1927).

D'Ignazio, C., & Klein, L. F. (2020). *Data feminism.* MIT Press.

Dignum, V. (2018). Ethics in artificial intelligence: Introduction to the special issue. *Ethics and Information Technology, 20,* 1–3. https://doi.org/10.1007/s10676-018-9450-z

Dourish, P. (2016). Algorithms and their others: Algorithmic culture in context. *Big Data & Society, 3*(2). https://doi.org/10.1177/2053951716665128

Duttweiler, S., Gugutzer, R., Passoth, J., & Strübing, J. (Eds.). (2016). *Leben nach Zahlen. Self-Tracking als Optimierungsprojekt?* Transcript.

Eischen, K. (2003). Opening the "black box" of software: The micro-foundations of informational technologies, practices and environments. *Information, Communication & Society, 6*(1), 57–81. https://doi.org/10.1080/1369118032000068769

Esposito, E. (2021). Unpredictability. In N. B. Thylstrup, D. Agostinho, A. Ring, C. D'Ignazio, & K. Veel (Eds.), *Uncertain archives: Critical keywords for big data* (pp. 533–539). MIT Press.

Eubanks, V. (2018). *Automating inequality: How high-tech tools profile, police, and punish the poor.* St. Martin's Press.

Eyert, F., & Lopez, P. (2023). Rethinking transparency as a communicative constellation. In *FAccT '23: Proceedings of the 2023 ACM Conference on Fairness, Accountability, and Transparency* (pp. 444–454). https://doi.org/10.1145/3593013.3594010

Foucault, M. (1977). The political function of the intellectual. *Radical Philosophy, 17*(13), 12–14.

Foucault, M. (1980). Two lectures. In M. Foucault, *Power/knowledge: Selected interviews and other writings 1972–1977* (pp. 78–108). Pantheon.

Floridi, L., Cowls, J., Beltrametti, M., Chatila, R., Chazerand, P., Dignum, V., Luetge, C., Madelin, R., Pagallo, U., Rossi, F., Schafer, B., Valcke, P., & Vayena, E. (2018).

AI4People—An ethical framework for a good AI society. *Minds and Machines,* *28*, 689–707.

Fuller, M. (Ed.). (2008). *Software studies: A lexicon*. MIT Press.

Gabrys, J. (2020). Smart forests and data practices: From the internet of trees to planetary governance. *Big Data & Society, 7*(1). https://doi.org/10.1177/2053951720904871

Gebru, T. (2019). Race and gender. In M. Dubber, F. Pasquale, & S. Das (Eds.), *The Oxford handbook on AI ethics* (pp. 253–269). Oxford University Press.

Gillespie, T. (2014). The relevance of algorithms. In T. Gillespie, P. J. Boczkowski, & K. A. Foot (Eds.), *Media technologies: Essays on communication, materiality, and society* (pp. 167–193). MIT Press.

Grant, L. (2022). Reconfiguring education through data: How data practices reconfigure teacher professionalism and curriculum. In A. Hepp, J. Jarke, & L. Kramp (Eds.), *New perspectives in critical data studies* (pp. 217–241). https://doi.org/10.1007/978-3-030-96180-0_10

Gray, M. L., & Suri, S. (2019). *Ghost work: How to stop Silicon Valley from building a new global underclass*. Eamon Dolan Books.

Gundhus, H. O. I. (2021). Shaping migrants as threats: Multilayered discretion, criminalization, and risk assessment tools. *International Journal for Crime, Justice and Social Democracy, 10*(3), 56–71. https://doi.org/10.5204/ijcjsd.2041

Hagendorff, T. (2020). The ethics of AI ethics: An evaluation of guidelines. *Minds & Machines, 30*, 99–120.

Hagerty, A., & Rubinov, I. (2019). Global AI ethics: A review of the social impacts and ethical implications of artificial intelligence. https://arxiv.org/abs/1907.07892

Haraway, D. (1988). Situated knowledges: The science question in feminism and the privilege of partial perspective. *Feminist Studies, 14*(3), 575–599. https://doi.org/10.2307/3178066

Hartong, S., & Förschler, A. (2019). Opening the black box of data-based school monitoring: Data infrastructures, flows and practices in state education agencies. *Big Data & Society, 6*(1). https://doi.org/10.1177/2053951719853311

Hepp, A. (2020). Artificial companions, social bots and work bots: communicative robots as research objects of media and communication studies. *Media, Culture & Society, 42*(7–8), 1410–1426.

Hepp, A., Jarke, J., & Kramp, L. (Eds.). (2022). *New perspectives in critical data studies: The ambivalences of data power*. Palgrave. https://doi.org/10.1007/978-3-030-96180-0_1

Heuer, H., Jarke, J., & Breiter, A. (2021). Machine learning in tutorials: Universal applicability, underinformed application, and other misconceptions. *Big Data & Society, 8*(1), 1–13. https://doi.org/10.1177/20539517211017593

Introna, L. D. (2016). Algorithms, governance, and governmentality: On governing academic writing. *Science, Technology, & Human Values, 41*(1), 17–49. https://doi.org/10.1177/0162243915587360

Irani, L. (2015). Difference and dependence among digital workers: The case of Amazon Mechanical Turk. *South Atlantic Quarterly, 114*(1), 225–234. https://doi.org/10.1215/00382876-2831665

Jarke, J., & Breiter, A. (2019). Editorial: The datafication of education. *Learning, Media and Technology, 44*(1), 1–6. https://doi.org/10.1080/17439884.2019.1573833

Jarke, J., & Macgilchrist, F. (2021). Dashboard stories: How narratives told by predictive analytics reconfigure roles, risk and sociality in education. *Big Data & Society, 8*(1). https://doi.org/10.1177/20539517211025561

Kitchin, R. (2014). *The data revolution: Big data, open data, data infrastructures & their consequences.* Sage.

Kitchin, R. (2022). *The data revolution: A critical analysis of big data, open data & infrastructure* (2nd ed.). Sage.

Knuth, D. E. (1968–2022). *The art of computer programming* (5 vols.). Addison-Wesley.

Kowalski, R. (1979). Algorithm = logic + control. *Communications of the ACM, 22*(7), 424–436.

Lopez, P. (2019). Reinforcing Intersectional Inequality via the AMS Algorithm in Austria. In G. Getzinger & M. Jahrbacher (Eds.), *Critical issues in science, technology and society studies: Conference proceedings of the STS conference Graz 2019, May 6th–7th* (pp. 289–309). https://doi.org/10.3217/978-3-85125-668-0-16

Lopez, P. (2021). Bias does not equal bias: A socio-technical typology of bias in data-based algorithmic systems. *Internet Policy Review, 10*(4). https://doi.org/10.14763/2021.4.1598

Lupton, D. (2016). *The quantified self: A sociology of self-tracking.* Polity.

Lupton, D. (2018). How do data come to matter? Living and becoming with personal data. *Big Data & Society, 5*(2), 1–11. https://doi.org/10.1177/2053951718786314

Lyon, D. (2004). Globalizing surveillance: Comparative and sociological perspectives. *International Sociology, 19*(2), 135–149. https://doi.org/10.1177/0268580904042897

Lyon, D. (2014). Surveillance, Snowden, and big data: Capacities, consequences, critique. *Big Data & Society, 1*(2). https://doi.org/10.1177/2053951714541861

Lyon, D. (2015). *Surveillance after Snowden.* Polity.

Macgilchrist, F. (2019). Cruel optimism in edtech: When the digital data practices of educational technology providers inadvertently hinder educational equity. *Learning, Media and Technology, 44*(1), 77–86. https://doi.org/10.1080/17439884.2018.1556217

Mackenzie, A. (2013). Programming subjects in the regime of anticipation: Software studies and subjectivity. *Subjectivity: International Journal of Critical Philosophy, 6*(4), 391–405. https://doi.org/10.1057/sub.2013.12

Mackenzie, A. (2017). *Machine learners: Archaeology of a data practice.* MIT Press.

Malazita, J. W., & Resetar, K. (2019). Infrastructures of abstraction: How computer science education produces anti-political subjects. *Digital Creativity, 30*(4), 300–312. https://doi.org/10.1080/14626268.2019.1682616

McQuillan, D. (2022). *Resisting AI: An anti-fascist approach to artificial intelligence.* Policy Press.

Meunier, A., Gray, J., & Ricci, D. (2021, December 16). A new AI lexicon: Algorithm trouble—Troublesome encounters with algorithms that go beyond computational processes. *AI Now.* https://ainowinstitute.org/publication/a-new-ai-lexicon-algorithm-trouble

Milan, S. (2013). *Social movements and their technologies: Wiring social change.* Palgrave Macmillan.

Milan, S., & Treré, E. (2019). Big data from the South(s): Beyond data universalism. *Television & New Media, 20*(4), 319–335. https://doi.org/10.1177/1527476419837739

Morozov, E. (2013). *To save everything, click here: The folly of technological solutionism.* PublicAffairs.

Neff, G., & Nafus, D. (2016). *Self-tracking.* MIT Press.

Noble, S. U. (2018). *Algorithms of oppression: How search engines reinforce racism.* New York University Press.

Noone, M., & Mooney, A. (2018). Visual and textual programming languages: A systematic review of the literature. *Journal of Computer Education, 5*, 149–174. https://doi.org/10.1007/s40692-018-0101-5

O'Neil, C. (2016). *Weapons of math destruction: How big data increases inequality and threatens democracy.* Crown.

Pasquale, F. (2015). The algorithmic self. *The Hedgehog Review, 17*(1), 30–45.

Prietl, B. (2019). Algorithmische Entscheidungssysteme revisited: Wie Maschinen gesellschaftliche Herrschaftsverhältnisse reproduzieren können. *Feministische Studien, 37*(2), 303–319. https://doi.org/10.1515/fs-2019-0029

Prietl, B. (2021). Warum Ethikstandards nicht alles sind: zu den herrschaftskonservierenden Effekten aktueller Digitalisierungskritik. *Behemoth: A Journal on Civilization, 14*(2), 19–30. https://freidok.uni-freiburg.de/fedora/objects/freidok:218966/datastreams/FILE1/content

Qiu, J. L. (2022). Data power and counter-power with Chinese characteristics. In A. Hepp, J. Jarke, & L. Kramp (Eds.), *New perspectives in critical data studies: The ambivalences of data power* (pp. 27–46). Palgrave Macmillan. https://doi.org/10.1007/978-3-030-96180-0_2

Rajão, R., & Jarke, J. (2018). The materiality of data transparency and the (re)configuration of environmental activism in the Brazilian Amazon. *Social Movement Studies, 17*(3), 318–332. https://doi.org/10.1080/14742837.2018.1459297

Rangaswamy, N., & Narasimhan, H. (2022). The power of data science ontogeny: Thick data studies on the Indian IT skill tutoring microcosm. In A. Hepp, J. Jarke, & L. Kramp (Eds.), *New perspectives in critical data studies: The ambivalences of data power* (pp. 75–96). Palgrave Macmillan. https://doi.org/10.1007/978-3-030-96180-0_4

Rieder, B. (2017). Beyond surveillance: How do markets and algorithms "think"? *Le Foucaldien, 3*(1), 1–20. https://doi.org/10.16995/lefou.30

Rona-Tas, A. (2020). Predicting the future: Art and algorithms. *Socio-Economic Review, 18*(3), 893–911. https://doi.org/10.1093/ser/mwaa040

Rosenblat, A., & Stark, L. (2016). Algorithmic labor and information asymmetries: A case study of Uber's drivers. *International Journal of Communication, 10*(0), 3758–3784.

Rosetta Code. (2023, May 28). Sorting algorithms/bubble sort. https://rosettacode.org/w/index.php?title=Sorting_algorithms/Bubble_sort&oldid=343389

Schaupp, S. (2021). Algorithmic integration and precarious (dis)obedience: On the co-constitution of migration regime and workplace regime in digitalised manufacturing and logistics. *Work, Employment and Society, 36*(2), 310–327. https://doi.org/10.1177/09500170211031458

Seaver, N. (2017). Algorithms as culture: Some tactics for the ethnography of algorithmic systems. *Big Data & Society, 4*(2). https://doi.org/10.1177/2053951717738104

Seaver, N. (2019). Knowing algorithms. In J. Vertesi & D. Ribes (Eds.), *digitalSTS: A field guide for science & technology studies* (pp. 412–422). Princeton University Press.

Selwyn, N., Pangrazio, L., & Cumbo, B. (2022). Knowing the (datafied) student: The production of the student subject through school data. *British Journal of Educational Studies, 70*(3), 345–361.

Shestakofsky, B. (2017). Working algorithms: Software automation and the future of work. *Work and Occupations, 44*(4), 376–423. https://doi.org/10.1177/0730888417726119

Srnicek, N. (2016). *Platform capitalism.* Polity.

Srnicek, N. (2018). Platform monopolies and the political economy of AI. In J. McDonnell (Ed.), *Economics for the many* (pp. 152–163). Verso.

Tubaro, P., & Casilli, A. A. (2022). Human listeners and virtual assistants: Privacy and labor arbitrage in the production of smart technologies. In M. Graham & F. Ferrari (Eds.), *Digital work in the planetary market* (pp. 175–190). MIT Press.

Vee, A. (2017). *Coding literacy: How computer programming is changing writing.* MIT Press.

Véliz, C. (2021). *Privacy is power.* Melville House.

Weber, J. (2016). Keep adding. On kill lists, drone warfare and the politics of databases. *Environment and Planning D: Society and Space, 34*(1), 107–125. https://doi.org/10.1177/0263775815623537

Weber, J., & Prietl, B. (2022). AI in the age of technoscience: On the rise of data-driven AI and its epistem-ontological foundations. In A. Elliot (Ed.), *The Routledge social science handbook of AI* (pp. 58–73). Routledge.

Zakharova, I. (2022). *Understanding data studies: A methodological and conceptual inquiry into research on datafication.* PhD thesis, University of Bremen. https://doi.org/10.26092/elib/1675

Zakharova, I., & Jarke, J. (2022). Educational technologies as matters of care. *Learning, Media and Technology, 47*(1), 95–108. https://doi.org/10.1080/174398 84.2021.2018605

Zuboff, S. (2019). *The age of surveillance capitalism: The fight for a human future at the new frontier of power.* PublicAffairs.

About the Authors

Juliane Jarke is Professor of Digital Societies at the University of Graz, Austria. Her research attends to the increasing importance of digital data and algorithmic systems in the public sector, in education, and for ageing populations. She received her PhD in organisation, work and technology from Lancaster University, UK, and has a background in computer science, philosophy, and science and technology studies (STS).

Bianca Prietl is Professor for Gender Studies with a Focus on Digitalization at the University of Basel in Switzerland. Her main area of expertise is feminist technoscience studies, with her more recent work focusing on the interrelations of knowledge, power, and gender in the context of (digital) datafication.

Simon Egbert, PhD, is a postdoctoral researcher in the Faculty of Sociology of Bielefeld University, in Germany, working in the research project "The Social Consequences of Algorithmic Forecast in Insurance, Medicine and Policing" (ERC grant agreement no. 833749). His research interests are science and technology studies (STS), algorithm studies, sociology of testing, and the sociology of the future.

Yana Boeva is a postdoctoral researcher at the Institute for Social Sciences and the Cluster of Excellence "Integrative Computational Design and Construction for Architecture (IntCDC)" at the University of Stuttgart, Germany. Her research explores the transformation of design, architectural practice, and different user expectations of computation and automation.

Dr. **Hendrik Heuer** is a senior researcher at the University of Bremen and the Institute for Information Management Bremen (ifib) in Germany. His research focuses on human–computer interaction and machine learning. Currently, he is working on ways to fight misinformation. He studied and worked in Bremen, Stockholm, Helsinki, and Amsterdam, and was a visiting postdoctoral research fellow at Harvard University.

I.

METHODS

2. Revisiting Transparency Efforts in Algorithmic Regimes

Motahhare Eslami and Hendrik Heuer

Abstract

In this chapter, we evaluate research methods aimed at bringing transparency and accountability to opaque, potentially biased algorithmic systems. We critically review methods that promote transparency through awareness, correctness, interpretability, and accountability, probing into users' perceptions and interactions with these systems. These methods, while valuable, can fall short when improperly designed, overwhelming users rather than providing actionable information. This situation underscores the importance of algorithmic literacy and public education, which can empower users in their interactions with algorithmic systems. We conclude with a discussion on strategies to foster such literacy in schools and public spaces, as well as empowering everyday users in understanding and detecting potentially harmful algorithmic behaviours, thereby facilitating informed and transparent interactions with these systems.

Keywords: algorithm auditing; algorithmic literacy; awareness; interpretability; public interest technology; user auditing

Introduction

Artificial intelligence (AI) and machine learning (ML) algorithms are powerful: They tell us what content to read, what movie to watch, what product to buy, and even whom to date. But the scope of algorithmic influence doesn't end here; the deployment of AI systems has rewritten the rules in many high-stakes domains: algorithms are now judges of the

Jarke, J., B. Prietl, S. Egbert, Y. Boeva, H. Heuer, and M. Arnold (eds.), *Algorithmic Regimes: Methods, Interactions, and Politics*. Amsterdam: Amsterdam University Press, 2024
DOI 10.5117/9789463728485_CH02

criminal justice system, social workers of child welfare organizations, and recruiters of hiring companies. The potential for algorithmic decision-making across all these domains is extraordinary: the ability to consume and analyse data at scale and recognize patterns beyond the scope of an individual's capacity, layered with the professional expertise of human decision-makers, can be transformative. Yet, as is consistently documented, reports of AI-driven decision-making are not all good. These reports have raised a number of accountability issues, including opacity and bias in AI systems which can have a devastating impact on many groups of users, particularly marginalized communities. Some examples, out of many, include predictive policing tools being biased against Black people (Angwin et al., 2016) and welfare resource distribution systems taking away already established and deserved benefits from poor or working-class individuals (Eubanks, 2018).

The power of algorithmic systems, along with their opacity and bias, have opened up new research areas for bringing accountability into these systems. Chief among these accountability efforts are introducing transparency into AI systems. Transparency focuses on how to provide visibility into different aspects of algorithmic systems. While the current efforts in bringing transparency have had a significant impact on making AI systems more accountable, they still fall short in many cases. For example, social media feeds have started providing "transparency" into why an ad is shown to a user; yet, previous work has shown that users are not usually able to find those transparency products (e.g., finding the menu of "Why am I seeing this ad?") in the first place (Eslami et al., 2018).

This chapter provides a review of existing motivations for algorithmic transparency, different audiences of transparency, and some of the existing methods that provide transparency into users' interactions with algorithmic systems. The methodological breadth of this chapter allows understanding the implicit and explicit assumptions that are inscribed into algorithmic systems. We do, however, also highlight the limitations of methods to study algorithmic systems. We introduce fresh perspectives to the concepts of transparency techniques that empower everyday users of algorithmic systems in the design, development, and, later, evaluation of algorithmic systems. Our recommendation is to educate users of algorithmic systems about these systems, their challenges, and potential biases and provide users with algorithmic literacy to provide them with an informed interaction with algorithmic regimes. Such methods can complement the existing transparency efforts by equipping users with the knowledge they need in interacting with algorithmic systems.

Transparency and the Need for It in Algorithmic Regimes

We operationalize the term "transparency" as a way of providing visibility into different aspects of algorithmic systems and how it can impact users' interaction with the system. A lot of important scholarly work has focused on issues around the opacity and transparency of algorithmic systems. For Blanco et al. (2012), transparency is "the disclosure of how the system really works." Diakopoulos and Koliska (2017) defined the term "algorithmic transparency" as "the disclosure of information about algorithms to enable monitoring, checking, criticism, or intervention by interested parties." In the context of recommender systems, Jannach et al. (2016) distinguish two kinds of transparency: the transparency of the data that a system is trained on and the transparency of the algorithm that is used to process the data. In their survey of explanations in recommender systems, Tintarev and Masthoff (2012) recognize transparency as one of three important motivations for explanations in recommender systems (alongside trust and scrutability).

Transparency is frequently presented as a solution to the complexity and the lack of explainability of algorithmic systems. Kroll (2015), a legal scholar, criticized the belief that transparency can solve the legal fairness challenges associated with algorithmic systems and automated decisions. He argues that transparency may even be a problem because it could help adversaries exploit a system. Transparency could, for example, help people avoid paying taxes. If the algorithm used to recognize tax avoidance is available, people may start using ways of avoiding taxes that are not recognized by the algorithm. Kroll argues that transparency is neither necessary nor sufficient to ensure fairness. Opacity, as the complement to transparency, has also been investigated in depth. Burrell (2016), for instance, distinguished between three forms of opacity: (1) intentional corporate or state secrecy, (2) technical illiteracy, and (3) an opacity that arises from the characteristics of machine learning algorithms and the scale.

Accountability as a Motivation for Transparency

As described, during the past few years, algorithmic systems are used in various domains including education, policing, and social services. Algorithms promise to support departments in the public and private sector and increase the speed with which users' needs and concerns are addressed. Yet, recent years have seen many cases of risks introduced by biased yet opaque algorithms. Below, we describe some examples of the accountability challenges in algorithmic systems which have resulted in calls for transparency to mitigate some of these challenges.

In the United States, many cities employ algorithms to increase efficiency in service provision to citizens. However, many of these systems have inflicted harm on marginalized and minoritized communities. For example, predictive policing tools have been shown to be racially biased (Angwin et al., 2016), resulting in protests and communities' resistance (Murray & Giammarise, 2020). As Eubanks (2018) states, these algorithms automate the existing inequities in the societal structure at scale. This is highly problematic as many countries increasingly rely on ML-based systems. For example, the German government cites three "great hopes" that artificial intelligence is associated with: (1) accelerated administrative processes, (2) smooth road traffic without traffic jams, and (3) improved medical diagnostics, for example, in cancer therapy. This interest in machine learning motivated the NGO AlgorithmWatch to compile the *Automating Society Report 2020*. In the report, they analyse where automated decision-making systems are used in practice in Germany and what accountability challenges are associated with these systems (Chiusi et al., 2020). Their analysis of such systems in Germany showed that algorithmic systems are used for predictive policing to sort "militant Salafists" into three threat levels (high, conspicuous, and moderate) and to calculate the level of risk a person has of causing violence due to Islamic extremism. Such tools are also applied to identify child pornography, to check the identity of migrants, and to administer cases and automate payments in welfare or social security administrations. The report documents a number of transparency challenges associated with such systems, including a lack of adequate auditing, enforcement, skills, and explanations regarding such automated decision-making systems. They also find that hastily deployed systems negatively impact the rights of citizens and that the EU member states that have deployed such systems witness an increasing number of legal challenges and defeats. All these challenges have given rise to calls for transparency to hold algorithmic systems more accountable. In the following sections, we discuss different aspects of transparency in algorithmic systems, identify when they fall short, and provide recommendations that can improve the existing transparency efforts.

Transparency for Who?

An important question in this context is who transparency and awareness are for. As our review showed, the awareness of algorithmic systems and explanations of how the systems work require human action and, in most cases, both a high level of knowledge about technology and domain expertise. This means that a lot of effort is required to effectively use any transparency intervention in the interface. However, considering automation as one of the reasons why people rely on algorithmic systems, the following tension has to be addressed: the more users have to be involved, the less useful the algorithmic systems are. This poses the question: Who benefits from transparency? This connects to Kemper and Kolkman (2019), who pose the question: If transparency is a primary concern, then to whom should algorithms be transparent? They argue that without a critical audience, the socio-technical assemblages around algorithms cannot be held account-able. They discuss the 2050 calculator, a tool used by the UK government that models energy and emissions. The tool maximized transparency by open-sourcing the source code of the tool, however the developers of the tool found that few people actually engaged with the source code. The developers believe that since the model was open source, the users were less inclined to contest its outcomes. Based on this example, Kemper and Kolkman (2019) warn that transparency can be an empty signifier rather than a helpful tool. They argue that it is important to consider both how transparency takes shape and who it is likely to be engaged with.

Informed by Kemper and Kolkman (2019), we examine the different kinds of stakeholders that are distinguished in the literature. In Sharp et al. (2019), the authors distinguish between novice, expert, casual, or frequent users. The issue of transparency becomes even more challenging when considering other ways of distinguishing between users. Eason (1989), among others, distinguishes between primary, secondary, and tertiary users. Like frequent users, primary users use the system frequently and interact with the system directly. Secondary users are those who use a system occasionally or through an intermediary. Tertiary users can be those who buy a system, i.e., those responsible for operating it, as well as those who are affected by the system. To illustrate how different the needs of these different kinds of stakeholders are and to show how challenging it is to make an algorithmic system transparent to them, we will consider COMPAS as a concrete example.

COMPAS is a case management and decision support tool that predicts how likely a defendant is to commit a crime again. The system was famously shown to enact systematic ethnic and gender biases. The primary users of a system like COMPAS are those who use the system directly. This, for instance, includes case workers, who prepare the documents and dossiers for judges and others. Secondary users of a system are those who use the system through intermediaries like case workers. This includes judges and other people who are involved in the decision-making around the likelihood of the recidivism of a defendant. The defendants themselves are tertiary users, i.e., they may not even be aware that the COMPAS system is affecting their chance of being free. This makes it clear that transparency means different things to different users. First and foremost, for many users of algorithmic systems, the different users may not even be aware that a system exists. Secondary and tertiary users in particular may not be aware of how decisions about them are made and what kind of systems are involved. Albeit not the primary focus, especially in the COMPAS example, it could even be argued that the data about the defendants is collected under false pretense in that they may not know what the data about themselves is used for.

In this section, we discuss who transparency is for. Considering this is crucial because opening up the black boxes of machine learning is very challenging. We argue that even if developers try to make certain aspects of algorithmic systems transparent, those who need that information the most would likely not benefit because interpreting what the features of an algorithmic system represent is a challenging task. For algorithmic systems to make decisions, data needs to be preprocessed so that complex information is represented as numbers. This is a highly complex task that can have important repercussions on the predictions of a system. The way that ethnicity is transformed into numbers can, for instance, affect the system. A system may not be able to recognize anything beyond the categories "male" and "female," thus not capturing the full spectrum of biological sex and gender identities. The last example highlights that while algorithmic regimes may try to enact stable and distinct categories, these may not exist in reality. In "Principles of Categorization," Rosch (2002) writes that the "most interesting aspect of this classification system is that it does not exist." She argues that certain types of categorizations "may appear in the imagination of poets, but they are never found in the practical or linguistic classes of organisms or of man-made objects used by any of the cultures of the world." Considering the concept of categorization in the context of algorithmic regimes and transparency is crucial. Due to the ways that contemporary machine learning-based systems work, they inevitably will make a prediction, even in situations where the categories may be inappropriate, misdefined, or non-existing. In such cases, transparency is necessary to help people understand the shortcomings of machine learning. Consider a medical imaging system trained to segment uteruses in medical scans. Based on our own experience with such systems, we know that contemporary systems inevitably identify pixels in an image as a uterus, even if the person in the image does not have a uterus (if no extra precautions are taken). To identify these mistakes, transparency is needed.

The insight that transparency is needed due to the complexity of algorithmic regimes does, however, pose the question: Who does this transparency help? Specifically related to the COMPAS example, transparency regarding explainability and the traceability of the decisions of these systems is challenging. Take the scores produced by COMPAS as an example. The COMPAS system scores defendants on a 10-point scale from 1 to 10, with scores between 1 to 4 as "low," 5 to 7 as "medium"; and 8 to 10 as "high." It remains unspecified how these numbers are determined and how they can be compared. Is the difference from 7 to 8 the same as the one from 8 to 9? If not, how do they account for the fact that the score of 8 and the difference between 7 and 8 can have a massive impact on people's lives? Considering the rating scale used by COMPAS and the goal of transparency, those who create and study algorithmic regimes need to attend to who transparency is for and how the output and the workings of algorithmic regimes can be made meaningful for people. As described in the previous paragraphs, this not only includes transparency for primary users. Algorithmic regimes also need to be made transparent to secondary and tertiary users. This, however, is challenging since secondary and tertiary users may even lack basic algorithmic awareness. In addition to that, the peculiarities of different domains make the study of algorithmic regimes even more complex. Social media platforms are one important example of this. These platforms employ machine learning-based systems to curate their content. On platforms like YouTube and TikTok, the videos that a user watches are selected by an algorithmic system. This poses questions for the scientific study of such systems. For a TV news broadcaster like the BBC, an intersubjective agreement on what the BBC stands for can be reached. While this assessment does, of course, depend on a number of factors—e.g., whether the person is from Britain, how frequently they watch the programme, and whether they have never watched it—most people will still be able to agree on what kinds of programmes the BBC is known for. In addition to that, regardless of where people live, they can still watch the programme to get an idea about what the BBC stands for. With machine learning-based curation systems on platforms like YouTube and TikTok, this is more challenging. Even though the website and its layout are the same for all users, the algorithmic personalization leads to vastly different recommendations for each user. As such, it is impossible to compare what one user sees to what another user sees. Therefore, the algorithmic system is not even the same for all primary users. This increases the difficulty of making the system transparent to secondary and tertiary users as well as to the researchers that study the algorithmic regimes. This has important consequences for how valid knowledge about such systems can be produced and how truth claims can be made.

Existing Transparency Methods in Algorithmic Regimes

Considering the importance of transparency, a large body of scholarly work has contributed different ways of increasing the transparency of algorithmic systems. While in this chapter we will not be able to provide a comprehensive overview, we would still like to highlight a number of contributions and discuss how they relate to transparency efforts. For this, we distinguish different dimensions that are relevant to the study of transparency. These dimensions are based on Rader et al.'s (2018) distinction between awareness, correctness, interpretability, and accountability. Awareness relates to users knowing that algorithmic systems exist and recognizing the agency of such systems. Correctness describes how well the outputs of algorithm system align with users' expectations. Interpretability is concerned with how sensible the performance of system is. Accountability relates to the perceived fairness and control. Examples of awareness, i.e., users knowing that an algorithmic exists and users being able to recognize the agency of algorithms, has been studied in many contexts, including Facebook's News Feed (Rader & Gray, 2015; Eslami et al., 2015; Alvarado & Waern, 2018; Rader et al., 2018), YouTube recommendations (Alvarado et al., 2020), and Netflix recommendations (Alvarado et al., 2019). Other relevant examples include ads on Facebook (Eslami et al., 2018), Yelp reviews (Eslami et al., 2019), as well as spam filters (Cramer et al., 2009) and student grading algorithms (Kizilcec, 2016). All these contributions have in common that they examine whether users know that an algorithm exists and whether they can recognize the agency of algorithms.

Correctness is another dimension that Rader et al. (2018) recognize. They characterize this as how well the output of ML systems aligns with users' expectations. Prior work has engaged with this in several contexts, including Facebook's News Feed (Rader & Gray, 2015; Eslami et al., 2015; Eslami et al., 2016; Rader et al., 2018), YouTube recommendations (Alvarado et al., 2020), Yelp reviews (Eslami et al., 2019), student grading (Kizilcec, 2016), and news recommendations in general (Heuer, 2021). In this context, some solutions are applicable to all kinds of algorithms, either through explanations (Ribeiro et al., 2016) or systematic audits (Sandvig et al., 2014).

Interpretability is the third dimension that is relevant and that focuses on how sensible the performance of a system is. Here, again, several researchers have investigated Facebook's News Feed (Eslami et al., 2016; Rader et al., 2018), Facebook ads (Eslami et al., 2018), student grading (Kizilcec, 2016), as well as movie recommendations and digital camera shopping (Tintarev & Masthoff, 2012). Regarding interpretability, there are also more generic approaches that support people visualizing the models (Ribeiro et al., 2016; Heuer, 2021).

Accountability, which relates to perceived fairness and control, is the fourth dimension discussed by Rader et al. (2018). In this context, Shen et al. (2021) discuss a number of application examples. The audits (Sandvig et al., 2014) and explanations (Ribeiro et al., 2016) are important tools to make sure that users feel in control and that they think that the recommendations are fair.

In addition to papers that evaluate such tools, there are also investigations that focus on folk theories and user beliefs about ML-based systems. However, the overview of the literature shows that even when transparency tools are available, they may not actually make a system more transparent. Users may, for instance, not be aware that transparency tools exist or the transparency tools may not be easy to find by users. The transparency tools may also be intentionally hidden or hard to find for people without experience. Eslami et al. (2018), for instance, demonstrated this in the context of Facebook's ad transparency tools. They found that only 5 of the 32 internet users that they consulted were aware of the existence of ad explanations on Facebook. Their investigation also revealed that the explanations are vague and of limited use for users. This poses the question of whether these explanations are indeed meant to empower users or whether they are merely added to satisfy some transparency regulations or to respond to public pressure. All in all, the investigation implies that there could be shortcomings on both sides. On the one hand, users may lack awareness that transparency tools exist and they may lack the capabilities to fully leverage the transparency tools. On the other hand, the platforms may not be incentivized to provide effective tools to users.

Explainable or interpretable machine learning systems are frequently proposed as a solution to the problem of black box systems that increasingly make decisions. Such explanation tools are frequently designed and developed for expert users like ML industry practitioners, who can use these tools to evaluate systems (Ribeiro et al., 2016). However, as investigations like Heuer (2021) showed in the context of recommendation systems, even domain experts like journalists are unable to use explanations of ML systems to understand the recommendations they receive. Heuer identified an explanatory gap between what is available to explain ML-based curation systems and what users need to understand such systems.

There have been a number of efforts to increase the transparency of algorithmic systems. In the context of algorithmic systems that provide recommendations on social media, Rader et al. (2018) examined several explanation styles. The four styles examined by them include "how," "why," "what," and "objective" explanations. "How" explanations describe inputs and outputs and the steps in between (i.e., a white box scenario). "Why" descriptions explain the motivations and reasons behind outcomes, but not how the system works (i.e., a black box scenario). "What" explanations only reveal the existence and main purpose of the algorithm. "Objective" explanations highlight that a system serves the interests of users. In their empirical study, Rader et al. evaluated how well the explanations support users in identifying biases in a system. Their investigation showed that such explanations increased participants' awareness of how a system works. All explanations also helped people detect biases. At the same time, explanations did not support users in gauging the correctness of the output of a system. This connects to the important problem of a potential feedback loop that Rader and Gray (2015) described in the context of machine learning-based curation systems like Facebook. This feedback loop describes: (1) how users' behaviour is influenced by beliefs about a platform, (2) how this potentially affects what data is provided as input, and (3) how this can potentially influence the output of the algorithmic system, which (4) can affect user beliefs.

In this section, we discussed a number of efforts to improve the transparency of algorithmic systems. Our review of related work shows that these methods can help study algorithmic systems and thus increase the transparency and mitigate the bias. This enables researchers and laypeople to leverage algorithmic systems, produce valid knowledge, and make valid truth claims despite the indeterminacy of algorithmic systems that rely on data. However, these methods still face challenges and limitations that we discuss in the next section.

Challenges of Transparency

Transparency, while beneficial, is not an unmitigated good—as Ananny and Crawford (2018) discussed, transparency has various limitations, and a transparency mechanism without careful design can turn to "seeing without knowing." This is especially problematic since the right design processes for promoting transparency efforts are missing. One reason for this is the complexity of trust. For example, Kizilcec's (2016) experiment around how transparency affects trust in massive open online courses (MOOCs) showed that users do not trust black box models but that they also do not want too much transparency. Kizilcec particularly showed that even if users do understand explanations, the effect of transparency on trust in an algorithmic system depends on a number of factors. Kizilcec's investigation of the effects of the transparency of grading in the context of a MOOC showed that those whose expectations are violated, e.g., because they receive a lower score, trust an algorithmic system more if they are provided with an explanation of how the system works. Kizilcec's findings imply that people trust a system that they understand and perceive as fair. Surprisingly, he also found that a setting in which users do not only receive information about the process but also get to view the raw scores and information about how the system adjusts the scores, leads to less trust than a setting where users are only informed about the processes. The latter led to significant increases in trust, while the former setting with very high transparency completely erodes trust. In this setting, trust is as low as in the setting without any explanations. This implies that while users do not automatically trust black box models, users also do not need or want too detailed information, either. Therefore, transparency is something that needs to be configured, not something that necessarily needs to be maximized.

The findings by Kizilcec (2016) connect to an interesting tension. Machine learning is commonly sold as a powerful way of automating work previously performed by a human. With automation as the goal, asking users to review explanations and to understand how the system works may be perceived as unnecessary or unwanted. However, as described, machine learning systems may work well for some input and fail unexpectedly for other input. Therefore, users must be able to recognize breakdowns. An understanding of how systems work is also important because it helps people properly process the output of algorithmic systems. If a user is, for instance, only recommended extremist news videos on platforms like Facebook, YouTube, or TikTok, this can have consequences on how this user perceives the world, which in turn could influence the users' beliefs and actions. It is, therefore, important that the user has a certain level of awareness that an algorithmic system exists and that this system co-produces the world of users.

This connects to the important role that the organization plays. As Alvarado et al. (2020) argue, this role of the organization has largely been disregarded in the research communities of the Association of Computing

Machinery (ACM), even though it has an important influence on algorithmic experience. In their investigation of user beliefs around YouTube, Alvarado et al. (2020) identified a number of beliefs that are related to the role of the organization that operates YouTube's ML-based recommendation system. Many of these were quite negatively connoted. These beliefs include the idea that some recommendations are paid for and the potential influence of data-sharing practices between different companies. Participants also referred to "a whole team of psychologists" that YouTube is allegedly employing to make users watch more and to produce "as much profit as possible." This made the participant "feel sad about the world."

Towards Algorithmic Literacy and Public Education and Engagement

Our overview of related work showed what a challenging problem transparency is in the context of algorithmic regimes. The complexity of providing the right level of transparency, especially considering the explanatory gap between what is available to explain ML-based curation systems and what users need to understand such systems, along with lack of incentive for businesses, make demands for transparency seem illusive. However, even if we can provide the right level of and incentive for transparency, the lack of the right placement or right audience of transparency can still result in ineffective transparency mechanisms. For example, social media feeds have started providing "transparency" into why specific ads are shown to users; yet previous work has shown that users are not usually able to find those transparency products (e.g., finding the menu of "Why am I seeing this ad?") in the first place—a phenomenon that we call "when transparency isn't transparent." In this section, we propose mechanisms that provide users with the right knowledge for the right context in algorithmic regimes to complement the existing transparency efforts in helping users to become more informed about the decisions they make day-to-day in the interaction with algorithmic regimes. These mechanisms mainly revolve around providing algorithmic literacy and engagement for users of algorithmic regimes via (1) educating youth and fostering literacy around algorithmic systems in school settings, (2) engaging users of algorithmic systems in understanding and detecting the potential biases and harms algorithmic systems can introduce to their experience, and (3) providing the public with information about the algorithms the public sector uses that impact community members significantly.

AI Education in School Settings

Education about algorithms, and AI in a broader sense, has become a part of college and university programmes (in many majors it features as an addition to computer science degrees). However, there is still little education about AI in school settings, which can result in a lack of knowledge among youth about the potential biases and harms of AI. This is despite the fact that youth are one of the main groups of users of algorithmic systems (such as social media, rating platforms, online streaming websites, etc.), and without the right knowledge about the harms these technologies can cause, they cannot have an informed and safe interaction with these systems. So we ask, If mathematics can be an integral part of the school education curriculum, why not include AI as well? Therefore, we propose the idea of "AI is the new math" in school education, and we need to understand how this concept should be incorporated into kids' education in the long term.

We have started investigating youth's understanding of AI, the concept of fairness, and the potential ways of educating children to cover some of the existing knowledge gaps. For example, in working with middle school girls to understand their perspectives and knowledge gaps on ethics and fairness in AI (Solyst et al., 2022), the first author of this chapter, together with her collaborators, found that members of this age group are more familiar with tangible concepts of AI—such as the physical embodiment of algorithms such as robots—than non-tangible AI systems—such as invisible algorithms being used to make decisions from social media feed curation algorithms to pre-trial risk assessments tools. This is despite the fact that most of the systems that youth work with embed invisible algorithms without any physical embodiment (e.g., social media); therefore, it is critical to cover such gaps of knowledge in educating kids about such systems and their impact on their daily lives. This calls for crafting and evaluating AI curriculums to educate youth in order to empower advocacy and action around inequity in AI systems.

Empowering Everyday Users in Understanding and Detecting Potentially Harmful Algorithmic Behaviours

Another aspect of algorithmic literacy is users being informed about the potential biases and harms algorithmic regimes might inflict on users. Recent years have witnessed a new phenomenon in which everyday users of algorithmic systems investigate, detect, and report harmful algorithmic behaviours. One of the roles of this phenomenon, called "everyday algorithm auditing," is to raise awareness among users and provide transparency about the potential biases algorithmic systems can introduce to users' interaction with the system (Shen et al., 2021). We describe this process below and indicate how it can empower users in having an informed interaction with algorithmic systems.

A growing body of literature has proposed formal approaches to audit algorithmic systems for biased and harmful behaviours. While formal auditing approaches, usually led by AI experts, have been greatly impactful in detecting and mitigating biases and harms, they still suffer major blind spots, with critical issues surfacing only in the context of everyday use once systems are deployed. One recent example is the highly publicized case of Twitter's image-cropping algorithm exhibiting racial discrimination by focusing on White faces and cropping out Black ones. Twitter users began to spot issues around this algorithm and came together organically to investigate. Through online discussions, they built upon one another's findings to surface similar biases or to present evidence or counter-evidence for a pattern discovered by another person. This occurred even though the company stated that "it had tested the service for bias before it started using it" (Hern, 2020). Previous research also showed similar approaches by regular users detecting and reporting biases in rating algorithmic systems such as Yelp.com and Booking.com (Eslami et al., 2019). These examples demonstrate that day-to-day exposure to algorithmic outputs can enable regular users of AI systems to discover harmful biases that AI teams might otherwise miss.

The power of everyday users in understanding and detecting potentially harmful algorithmic behaviour has inspired us to look for ways to support users in this process. As the first step, the first author of this chapter, along with her collaborators, have analysed and characterized the concept of everyday algorithm auditing by analysing the recent cases of algorithm auditing performed by everyday users to understand whether and how we can support users to conduct these audits in the future (Shen et al., 2021). Following this step, we conducted a three-phase study, including (1) interviews with everyday users about their understanding of algorithmic bias and their ability to detect such biases, (2) diary studies to understand how users encounter and interact with potentially harmful algorithmic behaviours, and (3) focus groups to investigate users' collective behaviour in identifying harms algorithmic systems might introduce to their interactions with a system (DeVos et al., 2022). This study led to the creation of a process model that illustrates users' search and sense-making dynamics and influences. For example, we found that a user's lived experience and exposure to specific biases can help them in understanding and finding those types of potentially biased algorithmic behaviours. Our goal is to utilize this process to build mechanisms and tools to aid users gain literacy about algorithmic bias and equip them with the right knowledge to be able to detect such harms in algorithmic regimes.

Public and Public Algorithms

In parallel with AI education in school settings, we need to inform other types of stakeholders (including adults and community members) about the algorithms impacting their everyday lives. One group of such algorithms are algorithms that are deployed in high-stakes public sectors (child welfare, criminal justice, etc.). The potential for discriminatory and harmful algorithmic behaviour has spurred efforts in algorithmic accountability, transparency, auditing, and regulation in the public sector. However, it is not clear to what extent the community members who are affected by these algorithms are aware of their presence and impacts, let alone have a voice in the development (or refusal) of these systems. This is particularly a challenge for public algorithms since those who are affected most by these algorithmic systems' decisions are not usually the primary or direct users of these systems. This is because the direct users of public algorithmic systems are usually public sector workers who interact with these systems directly. Therefore, as the first step, the first author, together with her collaborators, has started working with the Pittsburgh Task Force on Public Algorithms which has the goal to "establish best practices and practical guidance for municipalities seeking to ensure algorithmic accountability and equity for all residents." Together, we conducted (1) a countywide survey of more than 1,500 residents, and (2) a series of workshop engagements across Pittsburgh to illustrate the degree of awareness among the residents about the use of public sector algorithms in their local government context, as well as residents' posture toward digitally mediated governance. The survey showed that community members possessed a very low awareness of the presence of algorithmic tools in use by the local government (only 8% of the residents stated that they had heard of a public algorithm used by the city or county, despite the fact that the county has developed dozens of public algorithms), but it demonstrated a high degree of concern and willingness among the residents to engage in deliberation on the governance and oversight of these systems.

This low awareness of the presence of algorithms in the public sector was despite the fact that local organizations (including the task force itself) and the local government agencies did try to provide transparency in several ways, including holding community workshops and discussions about public algorithmic systems as well as providing explanations about these systems in government websites. So why was the residents' awareness of the presence of these systems very low? We believe one main reason for this is the fact that the provided transparency mechanisms were not placed in the right context—in fact, in our survey, we found that those who were aware of the presence of one or more public algorithms gained their awareness mainly from news and other places that they interact regularly with, not a local government agency website or a community workshop. So we asked, "Why not place transparency into the right context, where people can see and interact with it regularly?" This has informed a new project with the idea of putting physical installations about public algorithms in public places, where the public is. Our goal is to give every resident the chance to interact with such installations to both gain information about the public algorithms being (or are going to be) developed in the city, and also give feedback regarding these systems. We are now in the early stages of working with community members to understand their needs and asks from such engagement processes. Our hope is to see a change in the city, and other cities eventually, in terms of informing and engaging citizens in the design, development, and evaluation of public algorithmic systems.

Conclusions

Algorithmic transparency, even when designed in the right form and for the right context and audience, cannot completely resolve the many challenges users encounter in interacting with algorithmic systems, such as potential harms and misinformed behaviours. In this chapter, we provided a fresh perspective into the topic of algorithmic transparency by revisiting some of the existing transparency efforts, their benefits and challenges, and how providing opportunities for algorithmic literacy and user engagement with algorithmic systems can mitigate some of these challenges. We hope that this review and revisit of algorithmic transparency methods can open new avenues for researchers, developers, and users in creating informed and unbiased interactions with algorithmic regimes.

References

Alvarado, O., & Waern, A. (2018). Towards algorithmic experience: Initial efforts for social media contexts. In *CHI '18: Proceedings of the 2018 CHI Conference on Human Factors in Computing Systems* (paper no. 286). https://doi.org/10.1145/3173574.3173860

Alvarado, O., Heuer, H., Vanden Abeele, V., Breiter, A., & Verbert, K. (2020). Middle-aged video consumers' beliefs about algorithmic recommendations on YouTube. In *Proceedings of the ACM on Human–Computer Interaction, 4*(CSCW2), article no. 121. https://doi.org/10.1145/3415192

Alvarado, O., Vanden Abeele, V., Geerts, D., & Verbert, K. (2019). "I really don't know what 'thumbs up' means": Algorithmic experience in movie recommender algorithms. In D. Lamas, F. Loizides, L. Nacke, H. Petrie, M. Winckler, & P. Zaphiris (Eds.), *Human–computer interaction—INTERACT 2019: Lecture notes in computer science* (pp. 521–541). Springer. https://doi.org/10.1007/978-3-030-29387-1_30

Ananny, M., & Crawford, K. (2018). Seeing without knowing: Limitations of the transparency ideal and its application to algorithmic accountability. *New Media & Society, 20*(3), 973–989.

Angwin, J., Larson, J., Mattu, S., & Kirchner, L. (2016, May 23). Machine bias: There's software used across the country to predict future criminals. And it's biased against Blacks. *ProPublica.* https://www.propublica.org/article/machine-bias-risk-assessments-in-criminal-sentencing

Blanco, R., Ceccarelli, D., Lucchese, C., Perego, R., & Silvestri, F. (2012). You should read this! Let me explain you why: Explaining news recommendations to users. In *CIKM '12: Proceedings of the 21st ACM International Conference on Information and Knowledge Management* (pp. 1995–1999). https://doi.org/10.1145/2396761.2398559

Burrell, J. (2016). How the machine "thinks": Understanding opacity in machine learning algorithms. *Big Data & Society, 3*(1). https://doi.org/10.1177/2053951715622512

Cramer, H. S. M., Evers, V., van Someren, M. W., & Wielinga, B. J. (2009). Awareness, training and trust in interaction with adaptive spam filters. In *CHI '09: Proceedings of the SIGCHI Conference on Human Factors in Computing Systems* (pp. 909–912). https://doi.org/10.1145/1518701.1518839

Chiusi, F., Fischer, S., Kayser-Bril, N., & Spielkamp, M. (2020). *Automating society report 2020.* AlgorithmWatch. https://automatingsociety.algorithmwatch.org/

DeVos, A., Dhabalia, A., Shen, H., Holstein, K., & Eslami, M. (2022). Toward user-driven algorithm auditing: Investigating users' strategies for uncovering harmful algorithmic behavior. In *CHI '22: Proceedings of the 2022 CHI Conference on Human Factors in Computing Systems* (article no. 626). https://doi.org/10.1145/3491102.3517441

Diakopoulos, N., & Koliska, M. (2017). Algorithmic transparency in the news media. *Digital Journalism, 5*(7), 809–828.

Eason, K. D. (1989). *Information technology and organisational change.* CRC Press.

Eslami, M., Rickman, A., Vaccaro, K., Aleyasen, A., Vuong, A., Karahalios, K., ... & Sandvig, C. (2015). " I always assumed that I wasn't really that close to [her]" Reasoning about Invisible Algorithms in News Feeds. In Proceedings of the 33rd annual ACM conference on human factors in computing systems (pp. 153-162). https://doi.org/10.1145/2702123.2702556

Eslami, M., Karahalios, K., Sandvig, C., Vaccaro, K., Rickman, A., Hamilton, K., & Kirlik, A. (2016). First I "like" it, then I hide it: Folk theories of social feeds. In *CHI '16: Proceedings of the 2016 CHI Conference on Human Factors in Computing Systems* (pp. 2371–2382). https://doi.org/10.1145/2858036.2858494

Eslami, M., Krishna Kumaran, S. R., Sandvig, C., & Karahalios, K. (2018). Communicating algorithmic process in online behavioral advertising. In *CHI '18: Proceedings of the 2018 CHI Conference on Human Factors in Computing Systems* (paper no. 432). https://doi.org/10.1145/3173574.3174006

Eslami, M., Vaccaro, K., Lee, M. K., Bar On, A. E., Gilbert, E., & Karahalios, K. (2019). User attitudes towards algorithmic opacity and transparency in online reviewing platforms. In *CHI '19: Proceedings of the 2019 CHI Conference on Human Factors in Computing Systems* (paper no. 494). https://doi.org/10.1145/3290605.3300724

Eubanks, V. (2018). *Automating inequality: How high-tech tools profile, police, and punish the poor.* St. Martin's Press.

German Government. (2022). Künstliche Intelligenz im Geschäftsbereich der Bundesregierung [Artificial intelligence in the business area of the federal government]. https://dserver.bundestag.de/btd/20/004/2000430.pdf

Hern, A. (2020, September 21). Twitter apologises for "racist" image-cropping algorithm. *The Guardian.* https://www.theguardian.com/technology/2020/sep/21/twitter-apologises-for-racist-image-cropping-algorithm

Heuer, H. (2021). The explanatory gap in algorithmic news curation. In *Proceedings of Disinformation in Open Online Media: Third Multidisciplinary International Symposium, MISDOOM 2021, Virtual Event, September 21–22, 2021.* https://doi.org/10.1007/978-3-030-87031-7_1

Heuer, H., Jarke, J., & Breiter, A. (2021). Machine learning in tutorials: Universal applicability, underinformed application, and other misconceptions. *Big Data & Society, 8*(1), 1–13. https://doi.org/10.1177/20539517211017593

Jannach, D., Resnick, P., Tuzhilin, A., & Zanker, M. (2016). Recommender systems— Beyond matrix completion. *Communications of the ACM, 59*(11), 94–102. https://doi.org/10.1145/2891406

Kemper, J., & Kolkman, D. (2019). Transparent to whom? No algorithmic accountability without a critical audience. *Information, Communication & Society, 22*(14), 2081–2096.

Kizilcec, R. F. (2016). How much information? Effects of transparency on trust in an algorithmic interface. In *CHI '16: Proceedings of the 2016 CHI Conference on Human Factors in Computing Systems* (pp. 2390–2395). https://doi.org/10.1145/2858036.2858402

Kroll, J. A. (2015). *Accountable algorithms*. PhD dissertation, Princeton University.

Murray, A., & Giammarise, K. (2020, June 24). Pittsburgh suspends policing program that used algorithms to predict crime "hot spots." *Pittsburgh Post-Gazette*. https://www.post-gazette.com/news/crime-courts/2020/06/23/Pittsburgh-suspends-policing-police-program-algorithms-predict-predictive-hot-spots-crime-data/stories/202006230059

Rader, E., & Gray, R. (2015). Understanding user beliefs about algorithmic curation in the Facebook news feed. In *CHI '15: Proceedings of the 33rd Annual ACM Conference on Human Factors in Computing Systems* (pp. 173–182). https://doi.org/10.1145/2702123.2702174

Rader, E., Cotter, K., & Cho, J. (2018). Explanations as mechanisms for supporting algorithmic transparency. In *CHI '18: Proceedings of the 2018 CHI Conference on Human Factors in Computing Systems* (paper no. 103). https://doi.org/10.1145/3173574.3173677

Ribeiro, M. T., Singh, S., & Guestrin, C. (2016). "Why should I trust you?" Explaining the predictions of any classifier. In *KDD '16: Proceedings of the 22nd ACM SIGKDD International Conference on Knowledge Discovery and Data Mining* (pp. 1135–1144). https://doi.org/10.1145/2939672.2939778

Rosch, E. (2002). Principles of categorization. In D. J. Levitin (Ed.), *Foundations of cognitive psychology: Core readings* (pp. 251–270). MIT Press.

Sandvig, C., Hamilton, K., Karahalios, K., & Langbort, C. (2014). Auditing algorithms: Research methods for detecting discrimination on internet platforms. Paper presented at Data and Discrimination: Converting Critical Concerns into Productive Inquiry, a preconference at the 64th Annual Meeting of the International Communication Association, May 22, 2014, Seattle, WA, USA.

Sharp, H., Preece, J., & Rogers, Y. (2019). *Interaction design: Beyond human–computer interaction*. Wiley.

Shen, H., DeVos, A., Eslami, M., & Holstein, K. (2021). Everyday algorithm auditing: Understanding the power of everyday users in surfacing harmful algorithmic behaviors. In *Proceedings of ACM in Human–Computer Interaction, 5*(CSCW), article no. 433. https://doi.org/10.1145/3479577

Solyst, J., Axon, A., Stewart, A. E. B., Eslami, M., & Ogan, A. (2022). Investigating girls' perspectives and knowledge gaps on ethics and fairness in artificial intelligence in a lightweight workshop. In *Proceedings of the 16th International Society of the Learning Sciences (ICLS) 2022* (pp. 807–814). https://doi.org/10.48550/arXiv.2302.13947

Tintarev, N., & Masthoff, J. (2012). Evaluating the effectiveness of explanations for recommender systems. *User Modeling and User-Adapted Interaction, 22*(4), 399–439.

White House. (2016). *Big data: A report on algorithmic systems, opportunity, and civil rights.* Executive Office of the President.

About the Authors

Motahhare Eslami is an assistant professor at Carnegie Mellon University in Pittsburgh, PA, USA, at the Human–Computer Interaction Institute of the School of Computer Science. Her research investigates the accountability challenges in algorithmic systems in order to empower users to make transparent, fair, and informed decisions in their interaction with these systems.

Dr. **Hendrik Heuer** is a senior researcher at the University of Bremen and the Institute for Information Management Bremen (ifib) in Germany. His research focuses on human–computer interaction and machine learning. Currently, he is working on ways to fight misinformation. He studied and worked in Bremen, Stockholm, Helsinki, and Amsterdam, and was a visiting postdoctoral research fellow at Harvard University.

3. Understanding and Analysing Science's Algorithmic Regimes: A Primer in Computational Science Code Studies

Gabriele Gramelsberger, Daniel Wenz, and Dawid Kasprowicz

Abstract

Developing and using of software has become an increasing factor in the scientific production of knowledge and has become an indispensable skill for research scholars. To examine this algorithmic regime of science, new methodological approaches are needed. We present our method of computational science code studies (CSS), which focuses on the written code of software, and introduce two software tools we have developed to analyse data structures, code layers, and code genealogies. In a case study from computational astrophysics we demonstrate how the translation from mathematical to computational models in science influences the way research objects and concepts are conceived in the algorithmic regime of science. We understand CSS as a method for science studies in general.

Keywords: scientific programming; software; science studies; philosophy of science; code analysis

Introduction

Science has increasingly become an endeavour that takes place *in front of* and *in* computers. The development of computer-based simulations, the impact of software in science, big data analysis, and the arrival of machine learning (ML) methods have provided a new way of doing science and producing scientific knowledge that we call the "algorithmic regime of science." In disciplines like particle physics, geology, or molecular biology, the practice of scientific programming and in general the usage of

Jarke, J., B. Prietl, S. Egbert, Y. Boeva, H. Heuer, and M. Arnold (eds.), *Algorithmic Regimes: Methods, Interactions, and Politics*. Amsterdam: Amsterdam University Press, 2024
DOI 10.5117/9789463728485_CH03

computational methods has become an essential part of everyday work. With computational methods, we mean approaches that not only enhance computing power but generate both new theoretical and experimental knowledge. Herein, programming as a scientific practice represents the connecting link between data, models, and the results of computer-driven simulations as visualizations on the screen. For scholars from philosophy of science and science and technology studies (STS), this ongoing growth of an algorithmic regime of science poses methodological challenges. How can we describe the impact of computational methods in scientific disciplines? How do scientists change their understanding of theories and models due to new practices like scientific programming and data-driven methods? Are there tensions or transmissions between approved scientific practices and computational methods that demand new skills of the scientists?

However, in the philosophy of science most of the questions about the status of computational science deal with epistemological issues. There is a vibrant discussion about the ontological status, in particular, of computer-based simulation: Is simulation "experimenting with theories" or is it another and autonomous form of knowledge production (Dowling, 1999; Gramelsberger, 2010; Winsberg, 2010)? Is simulation- and ML-based knowledge production transparent and reproducible or is its epistemic status "opaque" (Humphreys, 2004; Lenhard, 2019)? The discussions around these epistemological issues barely reach a methodological dimension. We argue that a methodological reflection is necessary, not only for the philosophy of science but for science studies in general.

To do so, we will focus here on scientific code as our primary research object. We call our approach "computational science code studies" (CSS). Our central thesis is that scientific code is more than merely another scientific tool of knowledge production. We conceive programming in science as a complex translation from classical mathematical to computational models[1] that consist of two elements: the material basis of code and computational statements.[2] Understanding and analysing science's algorithmic regimes from the perspective of the philosophy of science as well as STS requires

---

1   With "classical mathematical models" we mean models that are based on differential equations, while "computational models" are based on numerical simulations. The transition from one to the other is initiated when classical models are applied to complex situations that result in equations that cannot be solved analytically. This problem is solved by doing numerical simulations of those equations. These simulations are then the only thing that remains visible in the code. For historical details of this development cf. Gramelsberger, 2010, pp. 33–36.

2   We call the code in general, including the comment lines, the material basis of algorithmic regimes in science. The specific portions of the code that function as statements can be called

new methods and practices to explore the material basis and the execution of code but also the practices and politics which come along with science's algorithmic regimes. While ML methods—expanding and transgressing big data analytics—are currently under exploration in science, computer-based simulations have become a well-established and standardized algorithmic regime for science and technology.

We begin with general reflections about the transformation of scientific concepts into the computational from the point of view of the philosophy of science. We continue this train of thought by conducting a review of past and current methods for studying code in science and cultural studies. This leads to the general idea of CSS: Reading the actual code of scientific projects to extrapolate its scientific content and prepare it for an analysis that is able to keep track of the interweaving of science and programming practices. In this context, we introduce the Isomorphic Comment Extractor (ICE) and the General Isomorphic Code Analysis Tool (GICAT), two code analysis tools currently in development at the CSS Lab of the Chair of Theory of Science and Technology at RWTH Aachen University in Germany. Both tools have been designed to analyse different layers of code (comments, hierarchies, imports, or dependencies) and different temporal stages in the evolution of scientific code.

We illustrate the range of application of these tools with a case study of computational astrophysics. This case study also functions as a primer for exploring the material basis of science's algorithmic regimes and thereby to further illustrate our approach, CSS: We demonstrate how shifting between layers and genealogies of code enables science studies scholars to examine how concepts, measurements, and parameters are transformed with regard to the computational model. As translation processes never copy a model but render it in a different way, we ask with the help of our tools for the reconfiguration of scientific concepts and computational statements in the diverse layers of code. We show that with CSS, a new way of accessing scientific programming as a research object is provided that has yet only been treated marginally. This method of analysing scientific code should be useful for other science studies scholars as well to everybody who has to deal with challenges posed by programming practices that are often hard to examine. We therefore understand our method as combinable and extensible with other approaches from science studies.

its ideal basis, as they set up the translation of the mathematical formulations for the *execution* of software code.

The Formation and Transformation of Scientific Concepts into the Computational

Computers developed from being merely auxiliary tools in scientific endeavours to being essential parts of the practice of scientific research itself. This has led to a transformation of classical scientific methods with their clear-cut distinction between theory and experiment into something that is governed to an increasing degree by algorithmic regimes. An important step in this process is the translation of classical mathematical models into computational models consisting of computable statements. This means that in many cases the mathematical modes of description employed in theories switch from more direct forms of representation like differential equations or statistical methods to numerical simulations. As most of the concepts in science are defined or at least strongly dependent on their articulation by mathematical means, it is hard to imagine that this transformation process does leave the underlying scientific concepts unchanged. Therefore, the following questions arise in the context of CSS: How can we identify existing scientific concepts in the web of statements? How can we track changes of scientific concepts that are due to modifications in the code? Do new scientific concepts arise out of the practice of scientific coding?

The transformation of a scientific concept can be understood as an answer to a specific "problem situation" (Nersessian, 2001). According to this idea, concepts "arise from attempts to solve specific problems, using the conceptual, analytical, and material resources provided by the cognitive–social–cultural context in which they are created" (Nersessian, 2008, p. ix). Such new concepts are in most cases not really new; they are transformations of existing concepts, whereby this transformation can be seen as the integration of existing conceptual mechanisms into a new problem situation. The transformation of scientific concepts in computational sciences can be seen as such a "problem situation." The problems to be mastered are not purely inner-theoretical (like problems of consistency) or primarily caused by empirical data; they are brought about by a change of the very medium in which science is conducted. To understand what is at stake here, let's look briefly at the development of the contemporary framework that determines what a scientific concept is.

According to a now classical point of view in the philosophy of science, the meaning of a scientific concept is defined by its role in a theory (Poincaré, 2017; Duhem, 1914; Feyerabend, 1962). This picture implies two main sources for the change of the content of scientific concepts: The first consists of permanent modifications of a theory, and the second of temporary modifications of some aspects of the theory to make it applicable to a specific situation. The latter kind of modification concerns parametric modifications of parts of the theory in experiments and in real-world applications. Here, the concepts prove themselves by predicting or bringing about specific outcomes from a set of given starting conditions. However, the starting conditions and the outcomes are always interpreted and evaluated in the context of the respective theory. Three developments have undermined this classic perspective.

First, the clear distinction between theory and experiment according to which theory leads and the experiments follow (cf. Popper, 1959) became blurred. This was not (only) done by an intricate philosophical argument but by analysing actual scientific practice (Hacking, 1983, 149ff.). The second development was that the propositional or syntactic view of theories (viewing a theory as a set of axioms) (Carnap, 1937; Hempel, 1965) was gradually replaced by the semantic view. According to the latter, scientific theories are first and foremost models (Suppes, 1960; Van Fraassen, 1980). The idea is that instead of seeing a specific scientific concept determined by one specific theory (implicitly defined by a set of axioms), the content of such a concept can be grasped through the sum of the models it figures in (i.e., the "family resemblance" of the operators that represent it in the respective models) (cf. Van Fraassen, 1980). Based on this picture, scientific concepts, which at the beginning of the 20th century were conceived as paradigms of unambiguity and exactness, became to be seen as evolving entities that not only secure and handle accumulated knowledge, but through their flexibility open up the path for new investigations (Wilson, 2006; Brandom, 2011; Bloch-Mullins, 2020). Third, with the rise of the computer model in science, the content of scientific concepts is spread even further apart. One of the most pressing problems is the translation of mathematical models as used in the semantic view of theories into numerical (computable) models. In more complex cases it is not even clear if the numerical model really instantiates the mathematical model of the underlying theory (Gramelsberger, 2011).

All this can be expected to lead to repercussions on the level of the scientific concepts expressed by the theory. In extreme cases the development of the mathematical model and the development of the computer model can split up into different projects that only occasionally interact. The decoupled development of the computer model can rather be understood as an ongoing series of experiments in silico than as a case of classical model building. In this way, the technical aspects can come to the fore: Modifications that are motivated by purely application-oriented considerations can infiltrate tacitly the core of the model. Difficulties for the tracking of scientific concepts in a web of statements range from unclean coding by the individual scientist to the modularity of modern-day programming and the traceability of the different layers of execution in the code. However, from a well-documented piece of software one can potentially reconstruct more references and cross-references than from a classical scientific paper.

Programming as a Research Object in Science and Software Studies

The rising significance of software in the 21st century resulted in new subfields like software studies (Manovich, 2001; Fuller & Goffey, 2016), leading also to an increased attention on algorithms in the last fifteen years (Kitchin & Dodge, 2011; Christin, 2020; Marino, 2020). Thus, scholars from software studies and STS have dealt with the question of how to access the practices of programming. One important and early claim by software studies was to make software visible and to detach it from the idea of a neutral and functional tool (Chun, 2004). Software—and therefore programming practices—had an impact on people, professions, and institutions (Mackenzie, 2006; Chun, 2011). But software has also been shaped by social relations, it was therefore more a socio-technical object than merely a technical tool. This necessity of making software visible became even more urgent with the technical problems of archiving since older software also needs a special hardware and an operating system that are not always archived as well (Chun, 2011, p. 3; Mahoney, 2008). While these cultural and historical approaches highlighted the impacts of software and algorithms (Seaver, 2017), recent STS works pay attention to the practices of programming and the "dulled and expanse fading of ever evolving bodies of code" (Cohn, 2019, p. 423). This shift of attention from the invisibility of software to the everyday actions of programming comes along with the use of ethnographic methods to follow the software. Following up on Ian Lowrie's statement that no one can directly observe an algorithm since it is always a by-product of multiple social actions and agents (Lowrie, 2017, p. 7), STS scholars use ethnographic methods to lay open not only the dynamics of programming but also the intentions and expectations that arise throughout the development of software. This shift is important with regard to scientific programming, since it raises the question how the practice of programming and the way scientists think of their own concepts and models reciprocally impact each other. As Adrian Mackenzie has shown for the field of machine learning software, the increasing use of statistical computer models in science leads to a state of ongoing testing of predictions as statistical hypotheses—a mode of reasoning he referred to as a "regime of anticipation" (Mackenzie, 2013, p. 393). Further research would have to examine for different disciplines how such "regimes of anticipation" influence the scientific understandings of prediction and probability in the algorithmic regime of science.

Ethnographic methods with qualitative interviews have also been widely used in the social studies of science. Considering, as we argue, the shift to algorithmic regimes of science, a crucial question is the relation of developers and users of code since not every scientist who works with computational methods must be a programmer. As Kuksenok et al. have shown in a qualitative analysis of four oceanographic research groups, the relation of users and developers of scientific code can be summed up in three different groups: (1) Scientists who code, (2) computer scientists who develop code and tools for scientists, and (3) scientific programmers (Kuksenok et al., 2017, p. 665; see also Sundberg, 2010). A methodological challenge for the social studies of science as well as for CSS represents the possible blurring of these distinctions in each discipline (Kelly, 2015; Edwards, 2010). Scientists learn how to program, and they extend their programming skills due to new programming languages like Python, e.g., which has become a widely used language in the natural sciences (Storer, 2017). Additionally, cultures of scientific programming change as well. The availability of libraries in Python, but also the possibility for scientists to add new libraries, was one reason for the popularity of Python in natural sciences. However, functional programming, which has often been used in scientific programming languages like Fortran (Suzdalnitskiy, 2020), is not associated with Python in the first place, although it can be implemented. These developments in scientific programming cultures from functional statements to more and more library-oriented languages have yet to be investigated.

As we will see in the forthcoming sections, tools like GICAT offer here a kind of meta-perspective on scientific programming that enables us to analyse how the translation process of the scientific into the computational model has been exercised in the code. To do that, solid knowledge of the scientific project is needed, especially of the models and the data sets that are used.

Software Tool Development for CSS

Getting access to the *material basis and the execution* of science's algorithmic regimes (computer code of the computational model/scientific computer program) is less an issue of code protection than of the complexity and magnitude of scientific computer programs. For example, an atmosphere model in climate science from 2003 consists of a web of statements of 15,891 declarative and 40,826 executable statements written down in 65,757 code lines of the programming language Fortran90 accompanied by 34,622 comment lines (Roeckner, 2003). The scientific computer program xgaltool, which we will take a closer look at in the next sections, consists of a web of statements of 46 classes and 313 definitions in 9,213 lines of the programming language Python, including comment lines (https://gitlab.obspm.fr/dmaschmann/xgaltool). Furthermore, philosophers as well as researchers from STS usually lack programming skills and expertise. Thus, conducting computational science code studies is not a simple task. How can we make the study of computational sciences more accessible? We argue that one necessary step to answer this question consists in programming software tools designed to facilitate case studies on computational sciences in the subfield of code studies (Schüttler, Kasprowicz, & Gramelsberger, 2019). Our aim is to develop a toolbox for scientific code study based on four rules:

1. File structure isomorphism; i.e., under all circumstances preserving the file structure of a scientific computer program while analysing it, because even in object-oriented programming languages the ordered structure of files is meaningful. Thus, such an isomorphism guarantees structural identity with the scientific program as intended by the scientific programmer.
2. Modularity; i.e., based on the file structure isomorphism we are building up a hierarchy of ever more complex tools. Each tool can be used separately (e.g., Isomorphic Comment Extractor, or ICE), but can also be combined to a CSS toolbox for computational science code study.
3. Visual depth; i.e., the ability to zoom in and out of the structural layers of a program. On the top level only the file structure becomes visible, while zooming in unveils the class structure, its functions, and finally the code and comment lines.
4. Analysis filters; i.e., depending on the specific aim of an analysis a toolbar of filters is increasingly developed, which can be turned on and off in order to analyse scientific computer programs like xgaltool.

While file structure isomorphism, modularity, and visual depth help to organize access to the complex and vast body of scientific code, the analysis filters are doing the job of code analysis from a philosophy of science and

STS perspective. It is obvious that conceiving and successfully implementing interesting analysis filters is basic and ongoing research in CSS.

Case Study of Computational Astrophysics

Computational astrophysics provides interesting examples for a study of a specific algorithmic regime. By the 1970s the use of computers had shifted astronomy from observing the sky by using telescopes (empirical regime) to data visualization analysing images of the sky (representational regime) (Daston & Galison, 1992). Since the 1990s the use of CCD (charge-coupled device) chips in telescopes has shifted astronomy into a data-driven science by generating masses of photometric data (algorithmic regime) (Hoeppe, 2014). CCD chips in cameras not only produce images of the sky, but act as sensors for specific wavelengths of light. Thus, instead of "subjectively" analysing the sky and images of the sky, respectively, analysing data sets with algorithms "objectively" has become central for today's astronomy. However, if the algorithms are as objective as scientists claim is one of the interesting research topics in CSS by analysing the interpretative concepts like threshold settings of a scientific computer program.

One of these computational astrophysicists is Daniel Maschmann, who worked for one year at our Computational Science Studies Lab (CSS Lab) in Aachen, Germany, before he moved in 2019 to the Observatoire de Paris and the Sorbonne Université to start his PhD project. Since 2017, the CSS Lab is located at the Chair for the Theory of Science and Technology at RWTH Aachen University (www.css-lab.rwth-aachen.de) and is devoted to developing concepts, methods, and software tools for studying science's algorithmic regimes, in particular, the material basis of computer code, for example, tools like the Isomorphic Comment Extractor (ICE) or the General Isomorphic Code Analysis Tool (GICAT). Daniel Maschmann used early versions of our CSS tools in order to improve his computer program xgaltool, which he had first programmed for his MA thesis (https://gitlab.obspm.fr/dmaschmann/xgaltool; Maschmann et al., 2020). Xgaltool is an open-source computer program developed on GitLab for detecting merging galaxies in the Reference Catalog of galaxy Spectral Energy Distributions (RCSED)—a huge database containing photometric data on energy distributions of 800,299 galaxies in 11 ultraviolet, optical, and near-infrared bands. These photometric data result from CCD camera-equipped telescopes. CCD telescopes were developed in the early 1990s to conduct the Sloan Digital Sky Survey (SDSS) at the Apache Point Observatory in New Mexico—a gigantic endeavour to scan one-third of the sky. Thus, the RCSED selects data from the SDSS for the spectral energy distribution. Furthermore, the RCSED data decompose the measured light into two components: the light emitted by the stars and the light of the galaxies' gas content, which is described by emission lines.

So-called double peak (DP) emission line galaxies have been extensively explored, because this type of galaxy can be an indication of a galaxy merger. A galaxy merger can occur when galaxies collide. The galaxy merger is one of the states of the evolution of galaxies, as classified by Edwin Hubble in 1926. Astrophysicists are still trying to understand how galaxies and stars form. Today they use computer-based simulation as well as indirect evidence from photometric data. DP emission line galaxies are relevant to empirically inspired galaxy evolution theory as they mostly consist of star-forming galaxies and "the star formation rate (SFR) of galaxies is a well-suited diagnostic to characterize their evolutionary state" (Maschmann et al., 2020, p. 1). Thus, what Daniel Maschmann was seeking with his xgaltool were DP emission line galaxies, whose emission line displays in a characteristic shape in the RCSED data. However, these galaxies are rare and represent only 0.8% of the RCSED data (Maschmann et al., 2020, p. 1). Thus, Daniel Maschmann calibrated xgaltool to the specific emission lines as following:

> We developed an automated three-stage selection procedure to find DP galaxies. The first stage pre-selects galaxies with a threshold on the S/N, and performs successively the emission line stacking, line adjustments and empirical selection criteria. Some emission lines are individually fitted at the second stage to select first DP candidates. We also selected candidates showing no DP properties to be the control sample (CS).... At the third stage, we obtained the final DPS using the fit parameter of each line. (Maschmann et al., 2020, p. 2)

From this cryptic quote the computational model for his xgaltool algorithm can be inferred. S/N describes a ratio between S (signal) and N (noise), which enables a classification of galaxies. For S/N < 10, 276,239 galaxies were selected from the RCSED, for S/N < 5 only 189,152 galaxies. Within the latter data sample complicated filtering methods were applied in order to reduce the number of selected emission lines ≥ 3 for 89,412 galaxies for the control sample. Reducing the number of galaxies further led to 7,479 interesting DP candidates. Finally, stage three sorted the emission lines of the 7,479 interesting DP candidates depending on their S/N ratio into three classes: one DP line (175), two DP lines (269), more DP lines (5,219). "The automated selection procedure selected DP galaxies with an objective algorithm. This means that we did not need any visual inspection, which would have been a subjective factor in the sample selection" (Maschmann et al., 2020, p. 6).

Based on the selected double peak (DP) emission line galaxies the scientifically interesting part of the work could start by exploiting the shape of the emission lines exhibited in BPT diagrams. BPT diagrams were developed in 1981 by John A. *B*aldwin, Mark M. *P*hillips and Roberto *T*erlevich to classify emission-line spectra (Baldwin et al., 1981).[3] In the case of DP emission line galaxies three types of BPT diagrams were explored, which were based on "the relative intensities of the strongest lines, into groups corresponding to the predominant excitation mechanisms" (Baldwin et al., 1981, p. 16). Thus, types of galaxies are classifiable; for instance, star-forming (SF) galaxies, active galactic nuclei (AGN) galaxies, and composite (COMP) galaxies. An important scientific result was that most DP galaxies are SF galaxies and thus intensively contribute to galaxy mergers. In this way, by analysing the data carefully some indirect evidence could be gained about the role of DP emission line galaxies in the process of galaxy formation (Maschmann et al., 2020). Using algorithms for automatically generated data samples of the rare DP emission line galaxies, the astrophysicists provide a software- and statistics-based method to detect galaxy mergers and to classify new morphological types of galaxy formations.

CSS Tools Applied: GICAT and ICE

The above case study provides an example of the algorithmic regime of computational astrophysics. Of course, the scientific concepts involved in xgaltool are quite advanced, combining data analysis methods, filter methods, with many other computationally interpretative methods. For philosophers of science as well as for researchers from STS, it is difficult to grasp how scientific research is conducted under algorithmic regimes. This is simply because observational access to code is difficult. Making such code accessible is an important part of CSS, and the tools we develop are an integral part of this endeavour.

---

3   The BPT diagrams are based on the fundamental 19th-century discovery that different chemical elements produce different types of spectra, e.g., celestial objects like galaxies emitting gas. Based on emission spectroscopy the wavelengths of photons emitted by excited atoms or molecules of a gas can be measured and classified. For instance, hydrogen is characterized by the Balmer lines (Balmer 1885).

The Isomorphic Comment Extractor (ICE)

Many details about a scientific program can be found in its comments. However, software documentation is more an art than a science. Software documentation in the code is laborious, time-consuming, effectless on the performance of the code itself, standards are missing, and so forth. Nevertheless, in computational sciences the software is the basis of research. Thus, a well-documented code is part of responsible science. In particular, in the course of the open science development the transparency of software has become a major topic (Aghajani et al., 2019).

In programming, comment analysers are known tools, but they are usually restricted to the programming language used by the programmer. Our ICE tool can extract comments from various programming languages such as C++, Python, Java Scrips, and Fortran. Extracting comments (if available) from scientific computer programs provides useful insights into the scientific process behind the coding. By "throwing" a scientific computer program in the ICE tool one can easily analyse it in an isomorphic mode the story unveiled by the comments of a well-documented software code.

The General Isomorphic Code Analysis Tool (GICAT)

It is a far more complex endeavour to analyse the execution of a scientific computer program exhibited in the web of statements. To give an example: xgaltool file analysis_tools.py alone consists of eight classes and each class consists of several definitions. For instance, the class EmissionLineTools contains 19 definitions, among these the following:

In Python a function is defined using the *def* keyword (Figure 3.1, line 43) followed by arguments and parameters inside the parentheses. Arguments and parameters pass information into a function. With *r* (line 44) and *return* (line 62), for instance, control flow is organized in Python, i.e., calculations are performed and results are returned. In this case lines 61 and 62 set up the calculation of gas metallicity based on the data called in lines 56 to 58. Python also accepts function recursion, i.e., a function calls itself usually structured by if, else, return loops. Different languages employ different concepts—from variations of the before mentioned to completely different programming paradigms. Based on such programming concepts a web of statements is designed by the scientific programmer forming up the intended behaviour of her/his scientific computer program. Each change in the functionality of the code that modifies its behaviour results in a slightly different computational result. If one is not able to grasp these complex

```
43     def get_gas_met_n2(self, line_shape='gauss'):
44         r"""
45         Calculate gas metallicity following using emission lines [NII] 6585 and Halpha 6565
46         We follow Pettini and Pagel (2004) doi:10.1111/j.1365-2966.2004.07591.x
47
48         :param line_shape: Specified the emission-line fit. For the RCSED catalogue (Chilingarian et al.2017) this
49         can be 'gauss' or 'nonpar' for a gaussian or a non-parametric line approximation respectively.
50         For Maschmann et al. (in prep.) this is dedicated to the double gaussian fit and denotes the blue-shifted
51         ('peak_1') or red-shifted component ('peak_2').
52         :type line_shape: str
53
54         :return metallicity in [Z/H] dex
55         """
56         # get emission line fluxes
57         flux_nii = self.get_emission_line_flux(line_wavelength=6585, line_shape=line_shape)
58         flux_h_alpha = self.get_emission_line_flux(line_wavelength=6565, line_shape=line_shape)
59
60         # Pettini and Pagel (2004) Eq. (2)
61         log_n2 = np.log10(flux_nii / flux_h_alpha )
62         return 9.37 + 2.03 * log_n2 + 1.26 * (log_n2**2) + 0.32 * (log_n2**3)
```

Figure 3.1. Lines 43 to 62 of the analysis_tools.py of xgaltool. Courtesy: Daniel Maschmann.

interactions in the code, one is not able to recognize how the concept of metallicity is articulated in it. Therefore, understanding the functionality and its execution over time is crucial for CSS. Analysing, but also following, the development of a scientific computer program, i.e., carrying out a code genealogy, provides insights into changing scientific concepts.

Following these considerations, we started to develop the General Isomorphic Code Analysis Tool (GICAT). GICAT visualizes different layers of execution of a given software project. From class and inheritance structures in object-oriented languages to complex functional interdependencies in functional programming, GICAT can help to identify and disentangle the scientifically significant layers and threads in the web of statements of a given code. GICAT is not limited to Python. Like and in accordance to ICE, it supports different languages under different programming paradigms. To visualize different layers of execution in a web of statements, GICAT works with a set of preconfigured as well as free-definable analysis filters. The preconfigured filters give the user the means to orient herself in the code and to identify the scientific relevant structures on different levels. Free-definable filters are powerful tools that enable the experienced user to make out where the relevant threads and layers of scientific code condense to a structure that encodes more specific points of interest (especially in the deeper analysis of scientific concepts).

The preconfigured filters are automatically adjusted to the programming language of the targeted software project. We can illustrate how they give a first overview by applying GICAT to xgaltool (Maschmann et al., 2020), which gives us a general idea of the structure of the program. Figure 3.2 depicts the global structure of xgaltool via its class relations, the standard filter set for Python projects. In this context we show the project at two different stages. Comparing the structure from 15.06.2021 to the structure of 23.02.2022, we see that a connection between two classes (EnvironmentTools and PlotBPT)

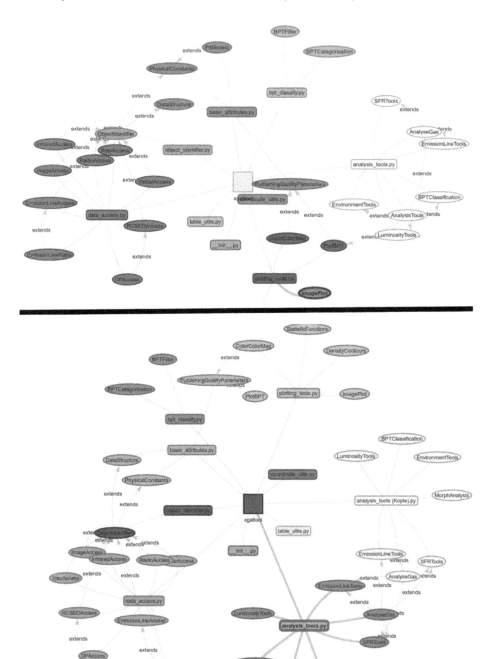

Figure 3.2. GICAT view on xgaltool visualized under the class filter of 15.06.2021 and 23.02.2022, in order to study class relations in two different software versions (code genealogy).

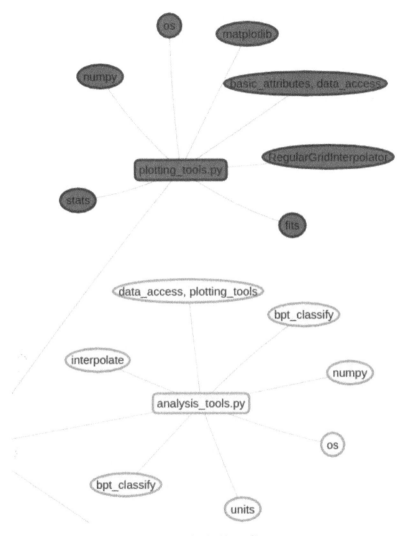

Figure 3.3. GICAT view on xgaltool detail under the library filter.

exists in the 2021 version that does not exist in the 2022 version anymore. This effectively cuts any direct connection between the groups plotting_tools and analysis_tools in the newer version of the program. This illustrates another important feature: GICAT enables the user to do a genealogical analysis, which makes it possible to track the development of different aspects of the scientific structures in the surveyed web of statements over time.

Making relations explicit while being able to place them into the greater picture of a given web of statements can yield important clues for the reconstruction of scientific concepts in a software project. Another example of an advanced filter is shown in Figure 3.3. Here the imports of modules (libraries, in darker circles) and packages (of libraries, in lighter circles) is shown. This is important because as mentioned above one of the main hindrances of getting a clear picture of the structure of a web of statements is the modularity of contemporary programming. With the help of GICAT the user is able to keep track of the different dependencies and gets a synoptic overview of their overall structure.

Following our idea to create a modular toolbox for scientific code study, these features are complemented by ICE. The option to integrate this performant comment extractor and code viewer into the structure of GICAT gives the user direct access to the corresponding parts of the raw code of the visualized structures. This whole package should allow a smooth transition between the visualization of different layers of execution that are hidden in the web of statements as well as between these layers and the corresponding chunks of raw code. Adding the possibility of genealogical analysis, the user can track and reconstruct the evolution of the implementations of scientific models and concepts in the web of statements of a given software. This concerns the modifications that are consciously made by the developers in respect to the scientific content of their project as well as changes that are motivated by purely technical reasons.

Above we have seen that one of the central concepts in Maschmann et al. (2020) is "emission line." The emission line is what appears in a spectrum depending on what specific wavelengths of radiation a source emits. It is one of the primary sources for the astrophysicist to identify and classify galaxies. To reconstruct how this concept is articulated in a web of statements, we have to look at how it is entangled in its different layers of execution. In this regard, we use a GICAT visualization under the filter that depicts the structure of class inheritances (Figure 3.4). If a class inherits from another, this is represented in GICAT by an extension arrow. We see that the class AnalyseGas inherits from the two base classes EmissionLineTools and SFRTools. SFR stands for "star formation rate," which means the total mass of stars formed per year.

This piques our interest for further analysis, because the emission line is normally used to estimate the SFR, while the analysis of a gas is conducted through an analysis of its emission line. Therefore, although it seems natural that the class AnalyseGas inherits from the class EmissionLineTools (as we analyse gas through an analysis of its emission line), it is interesting that the class AnalyseGas inherits from the class SFRTools (as the SFR is estimated through the analysis of a gas via an analysis of its emission line). We have uncovered an important clue how the concept "emission line" is entangled in and articulated by the different layers of the given web of statements.

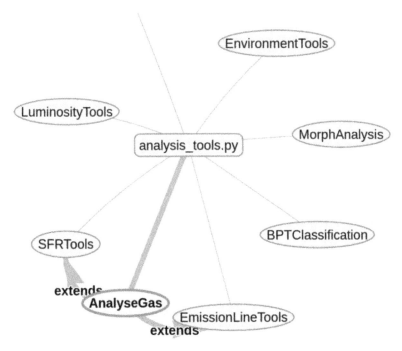

Figure 3.4. Visualization of xgaltool (23.02.2022) under the class-inheritance filter, close up "EmissionLineTools."

Guided by this, we can go on by looking into the relevant code, using ICE, the integrated code viewer, and the comment extractor. Alternatively, or complementary, we could dive deeper into the entangled layers of execution by using a filter that visualizes functional connections and dependencies or explore the structure of libraries our target draws on.

Discussion and Outlook

We have argued that the increasing use of computer simulations in science will reinforce the necessity for science studies to create new methodological approaches. As our case study from astrophysics illustrated, software like xgaltool needs to be analysed to explain the translation of a mathematical into a computational model and the decisions that have to be made during this programming process (as shown by the emission lines with the help of GICAT in 3.4). It should be emphasized that this kind of analysis is not limited to any specific programming paradigm and is also applicable to (seemingly) "indirect" approaches like ML. Machine learning—especially in the context of scientific code—does not happen in a void. Its more specific procedures or preconfigured setups (i.e., a trained neural network) are always embedded in an encompassing architecture (which comprises things like an overarching program, a concrete experimental setup, etc). Reconstructing the scientific relevance of the ML-component consists then (as for any other component) primarily in reconstructing its role in this architecture. For a preconfigured ML setup it may be necessary to look at external sources. If the training is part of the running implementation (like in a program for speech recognition that adjusts itself to its user), then the learning algorithm and the path of the ongoing flow of data can be analysed directly. For such studies in the algorithmic regime of science, our tools offer modes of navigation through file structures and filters for code genealogies to make traceable what changes in the code have occurred, at what time of the project, and conducted by who. As shown in 3.2, this helps also to illustrate the modifications and decisions the scientists had to make during the programming process. These might be routine for scientists who program every day, but for CSS, STS, and also social studies of science, the different ways scientists are influenced recursively by their programming language and the standards how to use it post further research questions.[4] In this sense, how does the shift in scientific programming from functional statements to more and more library-oriented languages like Python influence the theoretical concepts and models of scientific projects? How do these programming practices change the expectations of scientists and their ways to make predictions and classify objects like galaxy mergers?

As mentioned before, our code-oriented approach and the tools we develop do not present the only way to explore algorithmic regimes in science. Additionally, to our perspective from the philosophy of science, methods from STS and the social studies of science can be complementary since both try to describe the role of software in knowledge production as well as the dynamics of scientific programming. Ethnographic methods and tool analysis can serve as in-depth and meta-perspectives, providing ways to zoom into the daily (and dull) work of coding and to zoom out to keep track of longer code genealogies. However, there are still some problems regarding the methodological solutions provided so far. First, it is difficult to generalize from single case studies since coding practices even in one and the same scientific discipline are not yet standardized. We

---

4   See also Kelly (2015) for a comparative approach from software engineering where the characteristics of scientific programmers are compared to guidelines of programming in software engineering.

lack categories and concepts to describe the dynamics in the translation process from knowledge-based scientific to computational models over different disciplines. Second, for science studies scholars not familiar with programming, it is difficult to see how efficiently or how messy the program has been written. What we have shown here is how we can access new artefacts of scientific programming via software tools for non-programming experienced science studies scholars. We have argued that theses artefacts (comment extractions, code genealogies, visualizations of inheritances) allow us to study the question how scientific concepts and models are integrated into computational models via the practices of scientific programming. In this sense, our tools enable the user to identify and study the scientific part of the code and therefore permit to examine the impact of software on the production of knowledge in the algorithmic regime of science.

References

Aghajani, E., Nagy, C., Lucero Vega-Márquez, O., et al. (2019). Software documentation issues unveiled. In *ICSE '19: Proceedings of the 41st International Conference on Software Engineering* (pp. 1199–1210). https://doi.org/10.1109/ICSE.2019.00122

Baldwin, P., Phillips, M. M., & Terlevich, R. (1981). Classification parameters for the emission-line spectra of extragalactic objects. *Publications of the Astronomical Society of the Pacific, 93*(551), 5–19. https://doi.org/10.1086/130766

Balmer, J. J. (1885). Notiz über die Spectrallinien des Wasserstoffs [Note on the spectral lines of hydrogen]. *Annalen der Physik und Chemie, 25*, 80–87.

Bloch-Mullins, C. L. (2020). Scientific concepts as forward-looking: How taxonomic structure facilitates conceptual development. *Journal of the Philosophy of History, 14*, 205–231. https://doi.org/10.1163/18722636-12341438

Brandom, R. B. (2011). Platforms, patchworks, and parking garages: Wilson's account of conceptual fine-structure in wandering significance. *Philosophy and Phenomenological Research, 82*, 183–201. https://doi.org/10.1111/j.1933-1592.2010.00485.x

Carnap, R. (1937). *The logical syntax of language*. Routledge.

Christin, A. (2020). The ethnographer and the algorithm: Beyond the black box. *Theory and Society, 49*, 897–918. https://doi.org/10.1007/s11186-020-09411-3

Chun, W. H. K. (2004). On software, or the persistence of visual knowledge. *Grey Room, 18*(4), 26–51.

Chun, W. H. K. (2011). *Programmed visions: Software and memory*. MIT Press.

Cohn, M. L. (2019). Keeping software present: Software as a timely object for STS studies of the digital. In J. Vertesi & D. Ribes (Eds.), *digitalSTS: A field guide for science & technology studies* (pp. 423–446). De Gruyter.

Daston, L., & Galison, P. (1992). The image of objectivity. *Representations, 40*, 81–128.

Dowling, D. C. (1999). Experimenting on theories. *Science in Context, 12*, 261–274.

Duhem, P. (1914). *The aim and structure of physical theory*. Atheneum.

Edwards, P. (2010). *A vast machine: Computer models, climate data and the politics of global warming*. MIT Press.

Feyerabend, P. (1962). Explanation, reduction, and empiricism. In H. Feigl & G. Maxwell (Eds.), *Minnesota studies in the philosophy of science, vol. 3* (pp. 28–97). University of Pittsburgh Press.

Fuller, M., & Goffey, A. (2016). The obscure objects of orientation. In M. Fuller, *How to be a geek: Essays on the culture of software* (pp. 15–36). Polity Press.

Gramelsberger, G. (2010). *Computerexperimente. Zum Wandel der Wissenschaft im Zeitalter des Computers* [Computer-based experiments: Science in the age of the computer]. Transcript.

Gramelsberger, G. (2011). What do numerical (climate) models really represent? *Studies in History and Philosophy of Science, 42*, 296–302.

Hacking, I. (1983). *Representing and intervening: Introductory topics in the philosophy of natural science*. Cambridge University Press.

Hempel, C. G. (1965). *Aspects of scientific explanation and other essays in the philosophy of science*. The Free Press.

Hoeppe, G. (2014). Working data together: The accountability and reflexivity of digital astronomical practice. *Social Studies of Science, 44*(2), 243–270.

Hubble, E. P. (1926). Extragalactic nebulae. *Astrophysical Journal, 64*, 321–369.

Humphreys, P. (2004). *Extending ourselves: Computational sciences, empiricism, and scientific method*. Oxford University Press.

Kelly, D. (2015). Scientific software development viewed as knowledge acquisition: Towards understanding the development of risk-aversive scientific software. *Journal of Systems and Software, 109*, 50–61. http://dx.doi.org/10.1016/j.jss.2015.07.027

Kitchin, R., & Dodge, M. (2011). *Code/space: Software and everyday life*. MIT Press.

Kuksenok, K., Aragon, C., Fogarty, J., Lee, C. P., & Neff, G. (2017). Deliberate individual change framework for understanding programming practices in four oceanographic groups. *Computer Supported Cooperative Work, 26*, 663–691. https://doi.org/10.1007/s10606-017-9285-x

Lenhard, J. (2019). *Calculated surprises: A philosophy of computer simulation*. Oxford Scholarship Online.

Lowrie, I. (2017). Algorithmic rationality: Epistemology and efficiency in the data sciences. *Big Data & Society, 4*(1). https://doi.org/10.1177/2053951717700925

Mackenzie, A. (2006). *Cutting code: Software and sociality*. Peter Lang.

Mackenzie, A. (2013). Programming subjects in the regime of anticipation: Software studies and subjectivity. *Subjectivity: International Journal of Critical Philosophy, 6*(4), 391–405.

Mahoney, M. S. (2008). What makes the history of software hard? *IEEE Annals of the History of Computing, 30*(3), 8–18. https//doi.org/10.1109/MAHC.2008.55

Manovich, L. (2001). *The language of new media*. MIT Press.

Marino, M. C. (2020). *Critical code studies*. MIT Press.

Maschmann, D., Melchior, A.-L., Mamon, G. A., et al. (2020). Double-peak emission line galaxies in the SDSS catalogue: A minor merger sequence. *Astronomy & Astrophysics, 641*, A171. https://doi.org/10.1051/0004-6361/202037868

Nersessian, N. J. (2001). Conceptual change and commensurability. In H. Sankey & P. Hoyningen-Huene, *Incommensurability and related matters* (pp. 275–301). Kluwer Academic.

Nersessian, N. J. (2008). *Creating scientific concepts*. MIT Press.

Poincaré, H. (2017). *Science and hypothesis*. Bloomsbury. (Original work published 1902).

Popper, K. (1959). *The logic of scientific discovery*. Routledge.

Roeckner, E., et al. (2003). *The atmospheric general circulation model ECHAM5: Model description* (report no. 349). Max-Planck-Institute for Meteorology.

Schüttler, L., Kasprowicz, D., & Gramelsberger, G. (2019). Computational Science Studies. A Tool-Based Methodology for Studying Code. In G. Getzinger (Ed.), *Critical issues in science, technology and society studies: Conference proceedings of the 17th STS Conference Graz 2018, 7th–8th May 2018* (pp. 385–401). Verlag der Technischen Universität Graz.

Storer, T. (2017). Bridging the chasm: A survey of software engineering practice in scientific programming. *ACM Computing Survey, 50*(4), article no. 47. https://doi.org/10.1145/3084225

Sundberg, M. (2010). Organizing simulation code collectives. *Science Studies, 23*(1), 37–57.

Suppes, P. (1960). A comparison of the meaning and uses of models in mathematics and the empirical sciences. *Synthese, 12*, 287–301. https://doi.org/10.1007/BF00485107

Suzdalnitskiy, I. (2020, December 7). These modern programming languages will make you suffer. *Better Programming*.

Van Fraassen, B. C. (1980). *The scientific image*. Clarendon Press.

Wilson, M. (2006). *Wandering significance: An essay on conceptual behavior*. Clarendon Press.

Winsberg, E. (2010). *Science in the age of computer simulation*. University of Chicago Press.

About the Authors

Prof. Dr. **Gabriele Gramelsberger** holds the Chair for the Theory of Science and Technology at RWTH Aachen University in Germany, and is co-director of the Käte Hamburger Kolleg "Cultures of Research." Her research interests include the digital transformation of science; reflective modelling and simulation; and AI in the research and theory of computational neuroscience.

Daniel Wenz is a research assistant at the Chair for Theory of Science and Technology and coordinator of the CSS Lab at RWTH Aachen University in Germany. His research interests include classic epistemology, the theory of science, and the philosophy of mathematics.

Dawid Kasprowicz is a research assistant and fellow coordinator at the Käte Hamburger Kolleg "Cultures of Research" at RWTH Aachen University in Germany. His research fields include philosophy of computational sciences, phenomenology, media theory, and human–robot interactions.

4. Sensitizing for Algorithms: Foregrounding Experience in the Interpretive Study of Algorithmic Regimes

Elias Storms and Oscar Alvarado

Abstract

Investigations of algorithmic regimes benefit from attention to people's experiences. However, when applying methods that involve users and lay people to this topic, particular challenges arise: unequal and low awareness of algorithmic systems, digital inequalities, varied meanings of "algorithm," and the fact that people are often not involved as users in such systems. We propose "sensitizing activities" as a technique to address these challenges: preparatory exercises that subtly foreground the presence of algorithms, thus raising algorithmic awareness and establishing a shared understanding among participants without distorting their experiences and expectations. Drawing on our experience with sensitizing activities in three studies, we provide suggestions to researchers and practitioners who want to deploy this technique in their own investigations.

Keywords: interpretive methodology; co-creation; interaction design; algorithmic awareness

Introduction

As software is eating the world, various kinds of algorithmic systems increasingly play a role in many of our daily activities (Willson, 2017). Algorithms and the technical systems in which they are embedded are no longer the exclusive concern of computer scientists and programmers but have become a relevant topic to many academic disciplines. Due to

Jarke, J., B. Prietl, S. Egbert, Y. Boeva, H. Heuer, and M. Arnold (eds.), *Algorithmic Regimes: Methods, Interactions, and Politics*. Amsterdam: Amsterdam University Press, 2024
DOI 10.5117/9789463728485_CH04

the power they exert over people and societies (Beer, 2017), algorithms become a matter of public relevance (Gillespie, 2014). Considering these developments, "algorithm" is no longer merely a technical term referring to a sequence of computational steps acting on data structures and producing output. The notion of "algorithmic system" refers more broadly to those systems that "operate semi-autonomously, without the need for interaction with, or knowledge of, human users or operators" to which we often delegate everyday tasks (Willson, 2017). In this sense "algorithm" refers to the broader assemblages of which these computational sequences are a part, thus drawing attention to the socio-technical nature of these systems (Burke, 2019). In this chapter, we use "algorithm" and "algorithmic system" to refer to these broader assemblages.

Algorithmic systems become publicly relevant when they select or exclude information, infer or anticipate user information, define what relevant or legitimate knowledge is, flaunt impartiality without human mediation, provoke changes in the behaviour of users, or categorize users or publics according to their preferences (Gillespie, 2014). The increasing importance of such systems in our personal and public lives gives rise to new knowledge regimes which can be called "algorithmic regimes" (see Jarke et al., in this volume). Investigations have highlighted that these algorithmic systems can negatively affect users and society. Findings include biases in penalization outcomes (Bozdag, 2013), increased anxiety among social media users (Bishop, 2018), lack of control and meaningful feedback to users of recommendation systems (Eiband et al., 2019), and an extensive list of ethical issues, such as unjustified actions, opacity, discrimination, and challenges to the autonomy of users (Mittelstadt et al., 2016).

In a previous publication (Alvarado, Storms, et al., 2020), we explored how a co-design approach rooted in participation and co-creation (Sanders & Stappers, 2008; Sanders & Stappers, 2012) can promote the active involvement of users in the design process of user-facing algorithmic systems. More specifically, we identified challenges to end users' involvement in the context of algorithms and how researchers might overcome them, such as low "algorithmic awareness" and the various meanings of the term "algorithm." To address these challenges, we proposed including preparatory activities that "sensitize" participants to the presence of algorithms in their daily interactions with technical systems.

In this chapter, we expand on these ideas to make them useful not just for co-design but for the study of algorithmic systems and regimes more broadly. The leading for this chapter thus is: *How can we subtly prepare participants for active involvement during interpretive research on algorithmic systems?* We first identify two additional challenges to interpretive research on algorithmic systems: digital inequalities and indirect involvement. We then suggest that "sensitizing activities" can help researchers understand how people perceive and experience algorithmic systems. To make our case, we revisit three research projects in which we deployed such sensitizing activities: sensitizing interviews (in research on video recommendations), a sensitizing diary study and workshops (in a project on news recommendations), and sensitizing online questionnaires (in research on tangible interactions with movie recommenders). Reflecting on our experiences, we then provide suggestions for researchers and practitioners who wish to develop and apply similar activities in their projects. Finally, we call for further methodological innovation in the investigation of algorithmic systems from a social sciences perspective. We hope this chapter helps to highlight some of the methodological challenges to the study of algorithmic systems and provides a departure point for further exploration of methods to engage participants in this research context.

Imaginaries and Folk Theories: An Interpretive Approach

Any investigation into how people relate to algorithmic regimes needs to consider how they understand the presence or absence of these technical systems. One tradition in philosophy and the social sciences that puts how people perceive and experience things at the centre of its epistemology, is phenomenology. Phenomenological inquiry pays particular attention to how phenomena appear to individuals (Baert, 2006). Such emphasis on experience and perception is crucial, the argument goes, because how people act is based on how they "make sense" of the world around them. In the context of complex technical systems such as algorithmic systems, a phenomenological lens emphasizes the importance of considering how lay people and experts alike relate to such systems: how they perceive them, which meanings they attach to them, and how their understanding alters behaviour.

Recent research on social media has shown the usefulness of such an approach. Bucher (2017, p. 31) developed the notion of *algorithmic imaginary* to refer to "the way people imagine and experience algorithms [on social media] and what these imaginations make possible." These "imaginaries" have productive and affective power, as peoples' perceptions impact how they interact with and use algorithmic systems.

A related concept is that of *folk theories*. In human–computer interaction (HCI) this notion refers to "the intuitive, informal theories that individuals develop to explain outcomes, effects, or consequences of technological systems" (French & Hancock, 2017). Previous research has explored how these folk theories are formed and how people use diverse sources to form these intuitions, describing their complexity and malleability (DeVito et al., 2018). Others have deployed the concept of folk theories in the context of Twitter (DeVito, Gergle, & Birnholtz, 2017) and Facebook (Eslami et al., 2016) to focus on users' understandings and reactions to algorithmic curation of their feeds and, in turn, how such understandings influence their interactions with these platforms.

The algorithmic imaginary and the folk theory concepts share a "phenomenological sensitivity" as they direct our attention to peoples' perspectives, experiences, and understandings, and how these influence interactions and behaviour. We refer not merely to "experience" in the sense of "user experience" (which is typically the domain of HCI; see the critique by Dourish, 2019), but use it in a broader sense to include tacit and embodied knowledge and emotional affects. Regarding methodology, the phenomenological approach, with its attention to experience, is well represented in interpretive studies in the social sciences (Schwartz-Shea & Yanow, 2012). This methodological framework emphasizes the relevance of local and situated knowledge of those involved and attempts to uncover understandings and experiences through qualitative research techniques such as observations and interviews. While such an interpretive approach is promising for studying algorithmic regimes, there are specific challenges when it comes to involving peoples' experiences with and views on algorithmic systems, which we discuss in the next section.

Methodological Challenges to the Interpretive Study of Algorithmic Systems

The interpretive approach to algorithmic regimes and automated systems discussed in the previous section depends on (some degree of) "involvement" by respondents. In this section, we identify four challenges to such an investigation: (1) limited awareness of algorithms, (2) broader digital inequalities, (3) multiple meanings of the word "algorithm," and (4) indirect involvement.

Limited Awareness of Algorithms

Assessing how knowledgeable people are about algorithms is challenging. Recent work has highlighted the importance of determining how much users understand and are aware of algorithms. For instance, Hargittai et al. (2020) call for more empirical studies into how users approach algorithmic systems and the extent to which they possess the knowledge to use them. Hargittai et al. (2020) note "that there is not necessarily a ground truth to which researchers themselves are privy" since such systems are often proprietary and rarely made public. Such limitations make it challenging to accurately measure people's knowledge about algorithms, yet some assessments exist.

Previous research has exposed how users are often unaware of the presence of algorithmic systems. Hamilton et al. (2014) assessed that less than 25% of regular Facebook users were aware that their news feeds were algorithmically curated. Similarly, Eslami et al. (2015) reported that less than 37.5% of participants in their experiments were aware of algorithmic filtering of their Facebook news feed. Other studies have attempted to measure algorithmic awareness more precisely and in different contexts. Gran et al. (2021) examined awareness of and attitudes towards algorithmic recommendations across 1,624 participants in the highly digitised country of Norway, concluding that 61% of the Norwegian population has no to low awareness of algorithmic intervention in recommender systems. Similarly, Swart (2021) notes that algorithmic awareness among highly educated young people in the Netherlands varies significantly. "Some had never heard of the word 'algorithm' at all," she writes, pointing to crucial gaps in their knowledge (Swart, 2021). Likewise, Koenig (2020) focused on young technical and professional communication students, confirming that they possess some essential yet superficial algorithmic awareness.

Furthermore, researchers have found that becoming aware of algorithmic intervention often involves strong negative emotions (Koenig, 2020) and can provoke feelings of anger, betrayal, and discomfort among participants (Eslami et al., 2015). Crucially, when people become aware of previously hidden algorithmic processes, this consciousness impacts how they behave (Rader & Gray, 2015; Bucher, 2017).

Consequently, algorithmic awareness varies considerably among different populations (as discussed further in the next section). At the same time, it is essential to remember that awareness is not merely "measured" but also "co-constructed" through interactions between researchers and participants when the former presents design scenarios and questions to the latter. Regardless of the "actual" level of awareness among the general population and while being cautious of generalizing all too easily, it is evident that researchers and designers cannot take for granted that users are aware of the algorithms in the technological systems they interact with.

Digital Inequalities

The limited and varied awareness of algorithms is related to broader digital inequalities. Various investigations have highlighted how knowledge about digital infrastructure, including algorithmic systems, differs according to demographic characteristics.

Knowledge and awareness of the presence of algorithms on online platforms seem to vary according to socio-economic characteristics. Such differences reflect the long history of structural, digital, and information inequalities that are related to socio-economic disparities: those with more resources experience more significant opportunities for education and the development of digital skills, create and belong to social networks that sustain more pertinent technical insights and possess greater autonomy of access to digital technologies. They are, therefore, more likely to have experience with, learn how to use, and understand algorithms they interact with (Cotter & Reisdorf, 2020). As a result, knowledge about algorithms "remains the domain of a select few users" (Klawitter & Hargittai, 2018).

For example, people with higher socio-economic status in the United States seem to possess more knowledge about how algorithms work. A high level of education is positively associated with knowledge about algorithms, while age could correlate negatively (Cotter & Reisdorf, 2020). Similarly, in Norway, researchers discovered differences in algorithmic awareness related to age, education, and gender (Gran, Booth, & Bucher, 2021). A study in the Netherlands revealed erroneous algorithmic beliefs are more prevalent among older people, people with lower education, and women (Zarouali, Helberger, & Vreese, 2021). The prevalence of such misconceptions is, in sum, related to the broader digital divide within contemporary society.

These findings underscore that researchers studying algorithmic systems need to be aware that not everyone has equal access to these systems or can relate their experiences to the presence (or absence) of algorithms. Any investigation into the role or impact of algorithmic systems on daily life needs to take such disparities into account, and when people are involved in such research, scholars need to pay attention to socio-economic and demographic diversity.

The Multiple Meanings of "Algorithm"

Besides the low level of algorithmic awareness and the related digital inequalities, a more profound challenge is related to the concept of "algorithm" itself. It is particularly difficult to adequately define what algorithms are to "fully grasp their influences and consequences" (Beer, 2017). Moreover, previous research has proven how terminological differences can affect people's perceptions of algorithmic systems (Langer et al., 2022).

Gillespie (2016) distinguishes different understandings and uses of the term. "Algorithm" can be a concept used by computer programmers to refer to a model that achieves a particular goal. It can also be a synecdoche that refers to its broader socio-technical implications (similar to how we use the concept in this chapter). Sometimes it is used as an adjective to describe a type of phenomenon, as in "algorithmic journalism" or "algorithmic experience." Sometimes the term is used as a "talisman," for example, when companies refer to it to avoid responsibility. These varied uses of the concept point out that "the algorithm" can have different meanings for different contexts or groups, an aspect to consider when investigating algorithmic regimes.

Even people with expert technical knowledge conceptualize algorithms in many ways. Paul Dourish (2016) proposes to approach algorithms as a "term of technical art" used by members of a specific profession to explore how these actors use the word. He suggests an ethnographic approach, considering algorithms as a term used within a particular professional culture. Responding to this call, anthropologist Nick Seaver (2017) emphasizes that algorithms are not technical objects embedded *in* culture but are *themselves* culture. Seaver points out that even among technical experts and practitioners, "the algorithm" does not appear as a singular technical object. It is enacted in different ways, causing the algorithm to become "multiple" (Seaver, 2017). He underscores that even at the level of engineering, the algorithm is everywhere and nowhere at the same time. Algorithms, Seaver concludes, are "composed of collective human practices" and thus do not "heed a strong distinction between technical and non-technical concerns" (Seaver, 2017). Algorithms are thus best approached as "sociotechnical systems, influenced by cultural meanings and social structures" (Seaver, 2019).

This diffuseness and heterogeneity of the term "algorithm," even when used by technical experts, presents a significant challenge when researchers and designers aim to involve participants in their studies of algorithmic regimes. As participants understand the term radically differently, comparing and synthesizing their ideas and experiences becomes difficult. In addition, researchers must be aware of the broader contexts within which participants share and reflect on their experiences, keeping in mind that a single, technical understanding of "the algorithm" fails to account for these multiple meanings of the concept.

Indirect Involvement in Algorithmic Systems

A fourth challenge is related to the multiple ways in which people can be involved in algorithmic systems. While both the algorithmic imaginaries and the folk theories refer to ideas held by users directly interacting with algorithmic systems, we need to look *beyond* the conceptualization of "the user" to identify how algorithms affect people, precisely because people are involved in different capacities than simple "users."

Fields such as human–computer interaction traditionally conceptualize human subjects as users of computer systems. Such emphasis on direct interaction obfuscates the many other ways people are implicated in digital infrastructures (Baumer & Brubaker, 2017). There are subject positions beyond simple use, such as when someone uses a system on behalf of someone else or when a system impacts people who do not directly interact with it. It is therefore vital to consider "subject positions other than that of the classical user" (Baumer & Brubaker, 2017).

This idea is fundamental in the context of algorithmic systems, for example, when they filter job candidates, assign credit scores, calculate insurance fees, or identify people based on their facial characteristics (O'Neil, 2016). While these systems are obviously "used" by someone, these users are not the same as those subjected to and affected by automated decisions. These examples emphasize how people can be unwillingly or unwittingly involved in algorithmic systems.

Consequently, investigations into algorithmic systems need to consider more people than just users. To investigate how those that are "indirectly involved" in algorithmic systems relate to them, it is crucial to include these people in research and design initiatives. Involving them as stakeholders, however, requires careful consideration of their position and the types of knowledge they possess. Moreover, they might not even recognize algorithmic systems, might be unaware of them, and have difficulties conceiving them. In this context, we argue that *sensitizing activities* can be helpful.

Addressing the Challenges: Introducing Sensitizing Activities

With digital inequalities, limited and varied levels of algorithmic awareness, the multiple meanings of the concept algorithm, and the indirect involvement, we have at least four specific challenges that can hinder the active contribution of participants in the research on these systems. To address these challenges, we argue that it is helpful in subtly guiding participants' knowledge, attention, and understanding during the research process. Importantly, researchers need to do this without directly affecting users' personal experiences and understandings of these systems.

In this context, the notion of "sensitizing" can help us develop such strategies. We use the term "sensitizing" similarly to how sociologist Herbert Blumer (1954) used it in the context of social theory. For Blumer, theoretical concepts first and foremost guide the attention of researchers. He used the term "sensitizing concepts" to highlight that they do not provide direct descriptions of phenomena but "suggest directions along which to look" (Blumer, 1954). This approach to theoretical concepts has been very influential in interpretive methodologies and qualitative research in the social sciences and related fields.

In the field of human–computer interaction, researchers have used "sensitizing" to refer to concepts that can foster attitudes and sensibilities in designers, practitioners, and other researchers. For instance, researchers have applied "sensitizing concepts" to consider the consequences of proxemics in interaction design (Krogh et al., 2017), to inform the design of systems that promote playful interactions with children (Rennick Egglestone et al., 2011), or to help designers consider the diversity of human needs when conducting user experience research (Krüger et al., 2017). Other human–computer interaction practitioners have used the term "sensitizing" to actively define activities involving specialists and end users in the design process. For example, researchers have devised role-playing scenarios to sensitize different design teams and introduce them to complex theories about museology (Waern et al., 2020), deployed "sensitizing techniques" to involve children in the design of serious games (Sim et al., 2016), or used sensitizing terms to guide participants who experience, evaluate, and report on open-ended interactive art (Morrison et al., 2011).

Departing from these examples, we use "sensitizing" to denote a similar idea. In the context of algorithmic systems, we use "sensitizing activities" to refer to the *subtle efforts and exercises* via which researchers, designers, or practitioners can sensitize participants to the existence of these algorithmic systems and suggest a shared understanding of what the algorithm is concerning the research context or goal. Such activities should prepare participants for more elaborate reflection on their experiences and more direct engagement with "the algorithm" in subsequent research activities.

For our purposes, *sensitizing* is not focused on theoretical concepts used by researchers (as used by Blumer). Instead, we focus on the participants who are sensitized and who become receptive to algorithmic regimes and their specific qualities via hands-on activities. Sensitizing activities are small tasks and exercises that participants carry out in preparation for research activities and involve them in further reflection on their experiences and perceptions of algorithmic regimes.

Without calling them "sensitizing activities," previous research in HCI has employed these kinds of preparatory exercises before exploring algorithmic regimes. In the context of algorithmic curation on Facebook, Alvarado and Waern (2018) applied "priming tutorials" before a co-design workshop. This tutorial explained to participants "how algorithms are used in several common apps," focusing on Facebook. According to the authors, this explanation improved the awareness and understanding of the participants on how algorithms produce recommendations and select specific information, facilitating subsequent co-design workshops. Follow-up studies also applied similar techniques highlighting the challenges of low algorithmic awareness, one in the context of movie recommendations (Alvarado et al., 2019), and the combination of priming tutorials with group discussions to explore tangible algorithmic imaginaries (Alvarado et al., 2021). Similarly, Swart did not mention "sensitizing activities" explicitly but asked participants "to move through two to three social media apps as they usually would while thinking aloud about the context these platforms presented to them and theorising why these platforms would display these stories" (Swart, 2021). The author mentions this exercise "proved extremely helpful for having interviewees reflect on algorithmic curation and provided plenty of avenues to probe for algorithmic awareness, experiences, and tactics" (Swart, 2021).

It is important to note that the directness of sensitizing activities increases the risk of directly influencing or distorting the original insights and experiences of participants regarding algorithmic systems. Researchers, designers, and practitioners should therefore try to reduce this influence, mainly when we consider that the actual everyday experiences of participants are a crucial ingredient for fruitful research on algorithmic regimes (Willson, 2017; Bucher, 2017).

In the paragraphs below, we share our experiences developing and using sensitizing activities. We do so by discussing three case studies: an investigation of algorithmic video recommendations, a study on algorithmic news recommendations, and research on tangible interactions with movie recommendations. Without claiming a definitive methodological solution for the challenges outlined above, we hope these insights provide a starting point for further reflection and methodological discussion on sensitizing activities and similar approaches.

Sensitizing Interviews

In a study carried out in 2019, we explored how middle-aged consumers of YouTube videos understand their video recommendations and which interactive solutions they would suggest in such an interface (Alvarado, Heuer, et al., 2020). We interviewed 18 participants aged 37 to 60 years, with a mean age of 43.88. Since these participants belong to a generation that did not grow up with these technologies, they possess a high risk of low algorithmic awareness. As discussed above, research has highlighted how algorithmic awareness generally decreases as age increases. To address this issue, we attempted to sensitize participants as part of the research activities. To this end, we opted to start our research with what we called a "sensitizing interview." These sensitizing interviews were applied individually and consisted of common questions about YouTube to trigger reflection on the video recommendation system. Questions were: "Do you know you have video recommendations on YouTube?," "Do you watch the recommended videos that appear on the landing page?," "To what extent do you feel you understand why specific videos are included in your recommendations and others are not?," and "How much control do you think you have over the content that appears on your YouTube recommendations?" After these initial questions, we continued with the semi-structured interviews to explore how participants believed the recommender system on YouTube works and decides what to recommend. We allowed participants to visit and check their YouTube accounts during both parts of the interview.

These sensitizing interviews and complementary preparatory activities proved helpful. It reduced the effects of possible digital inequality in this middle-aged population, ensured algorithmic awareness among participants, helped provide a similar understanding of what to look at when referring to "algorithm" during the study, and thus improved our data collection process. During the interviews, participants felt secure and willing to provide their ideas about algorithmic regimes without restrictions, expressing questions, criticisms, and doubts about the system.

Sensitizing via a Diary Study and Workshops

In 2019, we participated in an interdisciplinary research project on algorithmic news recommendations. Together with legal scholars, we set out to investigate the extent to which news recommender systems are transparent about the data they collect and use, and how we might use co-design methods to develop an interface prototype that would make such algorithms more understandable to everyday users. Here, we focus on the second goal of this research project. We organized co-design workshops where we invited users to reflect on their experiences and subsequently ideate new interface elements that could help increase the transparency and legibility of algorithmic news curation (Storms et al., 2022).[1]

As we know that only a minority of users are conscious of the algorithmic curation of social media feeds, we decided to take extra effort to sensitize participants before they participated in the research and co-design activities. To this end, we opted to (1) include a diary exercise for participants in preparation for the workshops and (2) organize two workshops with the same participants.

During the recruitment process and in the written invitation, we considered avoiding terms such as "algorithms" or "recommender systems" because we wanted to reduce the chances of recruiting overly critical participants about algorithmic regimes. Instead, we said we were looking for participants in a study focused on increasing transparency on how news spreads on social media. In total, 11 people participated in the workshops with various professional backgrounds such as finance, information technology, engineering, the cultural and social sector, and with ages from 18 to 65 years old.

Five days before the first workshop, the principal researcher assigned participants a diary exercise. The exercise aimed to sensitize participants to the algorithmic ranking of their news feeds. We took inspiration for this approach from previous research that explained how people became aware of algorithmic selection and ranking on Facebook by noticing that items were not shown in chronological order (Eslami et al., 2015). In their short, daily diaries, we asked participants to take note of the news they encountered in their Facebook feeds. They filled out a brief questionnaire via Google Forms for the first five items they saw in their feeds, and were asked about the position of each item in the feed, how old the item was, whether friends had previously interacted with it via likes or comments, and how closely it was connected to their interests. By asking participants to look at the time of publication of an item and its position in the news feed, we subtly encouraged them to reflect on the (algorithmic) selection process behind the system.

Feedback from the participants showed that we were successful in this regard. At the end of our study (after the workshops), we sent out a short

---

1   More information about the "Algorithmic Accountability and Transparency in Practice" project is available in Storms et al. (2022), in the format of a poster (https://lirias.kuleuven.be/retrieve/651017) or in the work package reports (https://www.law.kuleuven.be/citip/en/research/atap/reports).

survey to learn from their experiences. Overall, participants found the diary helpful and the exercise informative. One participant mentioned that it caused them to "think more consciously, for once" about what they encountered on Facebook. Another stated that it was "interesting to focus on which news appeared on Facebook and why [it appeared] in this particular order." Other participants mentioned that it helped them prepare better for the subsequent workshop.

We paid additional attention to sensitizing during the first of the two workshops. We provided participants with printed versions of their diary entries and asked them to pick three items that stood out to them. Next, the workshop moderator explained that Facebook has a ranking system that determines how items appear in their news feed. We did not go into technical detail and only mentioned that Facebook has a ranking system that uses many factors to calculate a "relevancy score" for each item. To convey this message, the moderator used simple visuals from the Facebook press website.[2]

The workshop continued with a brainstorming exercise during which our research moderator instructed participants to reflect on their news feeds and write down factors that Facebook might consider when ranking the items. Under the guidance of the moderator, participants then combined these insights into a single diagram via a collaborative affinity mapping activity (Lucero, 2015). During this exercise, the research moderator invited the participants to comment and reflect on the ranking factors they thought were influential. This exercise served both as a complementary sensitizing activity and a way to explore the "algorithmic imaginaries" (Bucher, 2017) of the participants. The resulting insights were used later in the co-design activities during the second workshop.

In this phase, the moderator gave the participants co-design exercises. They presented their designs, shared and discussed goals and motivations, and voted on their ideas. The participants collaboratively proposed possible interface elements that could improve the transparency of personalized news recommender systems. Later in the research project, these ideas served as input for low-fidelity prototypes that we qualitatively evaluated with potential users.

In the end, the earlier sensitizing activities combined with a diary study and a collective brainstorming exercise during the first workshop proved

2   We used screenshots from a video from the Facebook Newsroom, titled "News Feed Ranking in Three Minutes Flat" (https://newsroom.fb.com/news/2018/05/inside-feed-news-feed-ranking/). The screenshots did not show any of the factors considered, but only suggested that a "relevancy score" is generated for each item.

fruitful in making these co-design exercises work. These activities encouraged participants to reflect on the algorithmic curation of their news feeds without directly asking them about their opinions. The activities also helped foreground the algorithms in the participants' daily experiences in a subtle manner, to avoid steering their opinions. Moreover, the first workshop's collective nature helped unify the understandings and notions about algorithmic regimes among the participants prior to their co-design contributions.

Sensitizing via Online Questionnaires

In 2020, we studied tangible interface alternatives for movie recommender systems to investigate how to achieve better transparency, control, and awareness among users (Alvarado et al., 2022). In this study, we wanted to follow a co-design approach, inviting participants to propose their considerations for tangible user interfaces meant to interact with such recommender algorithms. Unfortunately, the COVID-19 pandemic created extra difficulties: actively exploring tangible alternatives requires meeting with participants to try and use various interfaces was impossible, as it would have increased health risks for researchers and participants. Given this context, and considering the digital inequalities, low awareness, and multiple meanings of algorithms, we created an online sensitizing activity to prepare our participants for a later study. For the current chapter, we will describe the sensitizing part of the study because of its pertinence, omitting the collaborative design, evaluation, and tryout of our tangible interfaces.

Considering our previous suggestions on sensitizing activities (Alvarado, Storms, et al., 2020), we created an online questionnaire that participants filled out at home that encouraged self-reflection in preparation for later steps in the study. The online questionnaire invited the participants to log into their favourite movie streaming platform and navigate the system briefly to find a movie they would like to watch next weekend. The questionnaire then asked participants what they knew about the movie recommendations, whether they knew that the recommendations were personalized, and whether they considered these recommendations to decide between movies. We also included questions in line with the design for algorithmic experience in movie recommendation systems (Alvarado et al., 2019), such as the perceived level of transparency and control, awareness about profiling, and opinions on various features and usefulness of the system.

After the questionnaire, we invited participants to a study session. With a moderator, participants revisited their answers to the online questionnaire so that they could expand on them. This step served to "refresh" their experiences and allowed them to include more insights, thus reinforcing the sensitizing effect. We then proceeded with the design exercise.

These activities ensured that participants had some level of awareness of the recommendation algorithm in the movie platforms and provided a departure point for further discussion of their understanding of the algorithmic processes behind the recommendation system. While we did not intend to analyse the results of this sensitizing activity, a cursory analysis of the questionnaires yielded similar results to those from previous studies on movie recommendations (Alvarado et al., 2019, 2021). These similarities suggest that the sensitizing activity was effective in eliciting participants' experiences.

Learning from Our Experiences

The value of sensitizing is that it combines users' situated experiences and general understanding of the presence of the hidden, more technical aspects of computing. In the context of algorithms, people develop "intuitive theories" (Rader & Gray, 2015) and "folk theories" (DeVito, Gergle, & Birnholtz, 2017; DeVito et al., 2018), which implies that any reflexive preliminary exercises can foreground the perceptions of algorithmic systems in the participants. However, sensitizing activities and similar techniques require careful deliberation by the researchers: the activities need to be subtle and not directly influence the original algorithmic imaginaries of participants. The focus needs to be on guiding attention without direct interference.

In the context of video recommendations, the sensitizing interviews we conducted resulted in an effective preparatory exercise to introduce an "algorithmic mindset" among participants, with questions that triggered their own and previously hidden experiences and understandings of the algorithmic system. After the study, participants shared that the interviews focused their attention on the "recommender systems [they] encountered almost every day." The sensitizing interviews thus seem adequate to prepare participants for design exercises later in the study.

In contrast with organizing a diary study and two-phase workshops, sensitizing interviews require less preparation and are more comfortable and faster to organize. As Hargittai et al. (2020) remark, in-depth discussions and interviews with users can also help assess the understandings and awareness of algorithms among users. Consequently, we consider sensitizing interviews a practical, lightweight approach when it is more convenient to meet participants individually.

Similarly, online questionnaires were effective in guiding participants to reflect on the movie recommendations they encountered. From our experience, this approach is even more lightweight and quickly applicable, as it does not require researchers to meet participants individually before data collection or workshop activities. Moreover, this technique allows participants to do the sensitizing activity at a time that best suits them while keeping the researchers' time investment to a minimum. These characteristics can also be weaknesses, as researchers cannot assess whether participants take their time to fill out the questionnaires. Therefore, we suggest that researchers revisit the answers to the online questionnaire during subsequent meetings with participants.

By comparison, combining a diary exercise with a two-phase workshop is more time-consuming. Asking participants to keep a diary and answer short questions daily about their interactions with the algorithmic system encourages close attention to their experiences but also requires time and effort from researchers and participants. Conducting workshops in two phases, while time-consuming, has an additional benefit. In our case, the two weeks separating the two workshops proved fruitful for additional sensitizing, as we asked participants to further reflect on the algorithmic system during their regular social media use.

We consider that sensitizing techniques such as interviews, diary studies together with two-stage workshops, and online questionnaires are approaches that deserve more exploration and application. To be sure, we do not claim these are the best or even the only approaches. We wish to inspire other researchers and encourage further exploration and experimentation with sensitizing activities that help elicit participants' experiences without directly influencing them.

Deploying Sensitizing Activities: Suggestions for Researchers, Designers, and Practitioners

To conclude this chapter, we share some points of attention when applying sensitizing activities when researching algorithmic systems. We hope these suggestions are relevant for researchers, designers, and practitioners interested in this design context.

The Challenges of "Already Sensitized" Participants

Some researchers might consider recruiting participants who already know about algorithms or are already aware of their inner workings to avoid the challenge of low algorithmic awareness. For instance, previous studies investigated expressions about algorithms found on Twitter to recruit this kind of population (DeVito, Gergle, & Birnholtz, 2017; Bucher, 2017). Similarly, Klawitter and Hargittai explicitly mention that they investigated creative entrepreneurs selling their creations online because this section of the population is highly motivated to understand and pay attention to the algorithms that significantly impact their business (Klawitter & Hargittai, 2018).

Nevertheless, we argue that applying sensitizing activities can still be necessary when participants have already expressed some level of algorithmic awareness. As explained earlier in this chapter, the multiple meanings of the word "algorithm" could result in problems when engaging the participants in studies of algorithmic regimes. Consequently, we consider it essential to ensure that participants also understand the algorithm in terms of the research and design goals. Sensitizing activities can help achieve this.

Avoid the Term "Algorithm" during Recruitment

Since the term "algorithm" is fraught with connotations, partly because of increased media attention, it is a good idea to avoid using it during recruitment. Research indicates that the terminology used to describe algorithmic systems (such as "algorithm," "artificial intelligence," "robot," or "computer") can strongly affect how people perceive and evaluate such systems (Langer et al., 2022). Moreover, including technical concepts such as "algorithm" explicitly in the recruitment call, for example, might attract overly critical participants or can bias participants' ideas. Recent literature also mentions this suggestion: both Swart (2021) and Hargittai et al. (2020) did not use the term "algorithm" in conversations with participants to avoid steering their opinions.

The sensitizing activities must focus on the authentic experiences of the participants rather than on the possible preconceptions they might have. Therefore, we recommend avoiding the term in all communications with possible participants, such as emails, posters, or other types of recruitment calls.

Be Aware of Potential Biasing

Even if the general population might not be aware of the algorithmic systems around them, they are still very likely to encounter and engage with them in their daily lives regularly. Likely, they have already heard about algorithms in the context of scandals about platforms collecting data, the ethical dilemmas with self-driving cars, or other related topics that commonly appear in social media or traditional media. Depending on the research and the algorithmic regime context, it can be essential to avoid influencing (and significantly enlarging) such preconceptions as much as possible.

We want to emphasize that the only goal of sensitizing activities is to foreground participants' "algorithmic experiences." They should not steer those experiences towards a specific perception of algorithms. Sensitizing activities should focus on heightening the sensibilities of the participants without interfering with their original and natural conceptions of algorithmic systems.

Attune the Level of Sensitizing to the Research Goal

The required level of sensitizing will depend on the research goal in question. For instance, when the goal is to explore existing algorithmic imaginaries or folk theories, sensitizing should merely guide the attention of the participants to their experience of automated systems. Moreover, researchers might even need to avoid any sensitizing activity in some conditions. When evaluating an interface from a behavioural perspective, for example, or when a quantitative approach with self-answered surveys is used, any form of priming participants, including sensitizing, is undesirable. If, on the other hand, researchers require the participants to engage directly with algorithmic systems during co-design activities or when they are required to actively reflect on previous experiences so that they can provide inputs, sensitizing activities can play an essential preparatory role.

Be Creative

Developing and implementing sensitizing activities implies a reflection during which researchers and practitioners think of ways to make participants sensitive to their own experiences, thus foregrounding algorithms in preparation of further participation during research activities. Consequently, sensitizing activities are inherently creative, opening new and unexpected ways to provoke the same effect on participants. We hope this chapter inspires readers to create similar techniques and share their experiences with others.

This chapter does not present formal methodological guidelines to follow when sensitizing participants to the presence of algorithms. To the best of our knowledge, these do not exist in previous literature. We therefore want to encourage researchers and practitioners to explore and develop different sensitizing techniques, taking the above case studies as examples.

There are various methodological innovations in the existing literature that can inspire future research. Eslami et al. (2015) have developed prototypes with a "seamful design" philosophy, showing traces of algorithmic ranking to elicit participants' experiences with and opinions of algorithmic systems. Other researchers have deployed focus groups to exchange experiences in a collective setting (Siles et al., 2019), used card sorting as an elicitation technique (DeVito et al., 2018), or assigned drawing exercises (Hargittai et al., 2020). While we have no firsthand experience with these techniques, these promising and creative approaches might inspire the development of future sensitizing activities (and might benefit from such an exchange).

Conclusion and Further Opportunities

This chapter explored the challenges of researching algorithmic regimes proposing a question: *How can we subtly prepare participants for active involvement during interpretive research on algorithmic systems?* We used the concept "sensitizing activities" to refer to exercises or questions that subtly guide the attention of participants so that they can more easily reflect on their experiences with algorithmic systems. We do not claim, however, that such sensitizing activities are the single definitive answer to these methodological challenges. On the contrary, we are convinced that methodology can only advance through continued reflection and conversations between researchers.

We wish to conclude this chapter with suggestions for the further development of methodological tools for interpretive research of algorithmic systems. Recent initiatives have attempted to develop ways to measure people's algorithmic awareness, for example, with an "algorithmic literacy scale" (Dogruel, Masur, & Joeckel, 2021), or an "algorithmic media content awareness scale" with different dimensions (Zarouali, Boerman, & Vreese, 2021). Such scales and measures can serve as complementary tools that help prepare participants. One potential use is the measurement before and after sensitizing activities to determine their effectiveness. These measures work via questionnaires, however, while merely asking questions can already produce "sensitizing effects" on participants. Both possibilities and potential effects of such questionnaires are thus relevant areas for future research.

Previous studies have proposed different theories and frameworks related to algorithmic awareness that could inform sensitizing activities. While we have not discussed these studies exhaustively, we want to emphasize their relevance to the creation of future sensitizing activities. Promising examples are Koenig's (2020) levels of algorithmic awareness and the framework by Zarouali, Helberger, and Vreese (2021) of algorithmic misconceptions. These and similar theoretical structures can be useful when devising sensitizing interviews, diary studies, workshops, or questionnaires and can help with the "be creative" guideline we suggested earlier.

Finally, we want to return to the digital inequalities mentioned earlier in this chapter. As research has pointed toward lower algorithmic awareness among women, older age groups, and people with lower income and less education, it is essential to emphasize that disadvantaged social groups are often disproportionally affected by the ethical issues associated with algorithmic decisions. Involving them more actively in research and design could result in more inclusive and publicly beneficial algorithmic systems. While we did not have the opportunity to specifically research intersections between algorithmic systems and disadvantaged populations in our case studies, we would like to encourage future research projects to take economic and power disparities into account to combine interpretive research with a more critical aim.

As outlined above, we consider sensitizing activities to deal with some of the diverse challenges to interpretive research and participatory design of algorithmic systems. We want to invite researchers to continue exploring the methodological issues raised in this chapter, move beyond sensitizing activities as needed, and, above all, aim for more active inclusion of a variety of people when designing algorithmic systems, particularly those populations that are more heavily affected by algorithms and their decisions.

References

Alvarado, O., & Waern, A. (2018). Towards algorithmic experience: Initial efforts for social media contexts. In *CHI '18: Proceedings of the 2018 CHI Conference on Human Factors in Computing Systems* (paper no. 286). https://doi.org/10.1145/3173574.3173860

Alvarado, O., Heuer, H., Vanden Abeele, V., Breiter, A., & Verbert, K. (2020). Middle-aged video consumers' beliefs about algorithmic recommendations on YouTube. In *Proceedings of the ACM on Human–Computer Interaction, 4*(CSCW2), article no. 121. https://doi.org/10.1145/3415192

Alvarado, O., Storms, E., Geerts, D., & Verbert, K. (2020). Foregrounding algorithms: Preparing users for co-design with sensitizing activities. In *NordiCHI '20: Proceedings of the 11th Nordic Conference on Human–Computer Interaction: Shaping experiences, shaping society* (article no. 95). https://doi.org/10.1145/3419249.3421237

Alvarado, O., Vanden Abeele, V., Geerts, D., & Verbert, K. (2019). "I really don't know what 'thumbs up' means": Algorithmic experience in movie recommender algorithms. In D. Lamas, F. Loizides, L. Nacke, H. Petrie, M. Winckler, & P. Zaphiris

(Eds.), *Human–computer interaction—INTERACT 2019: Lecture notes in computer science* (pp. 521–541). Springer. https://doi.org/10.1007/978-3-030-29387-1_30

Alvarado, O., Vanden Abeele, V., Geerts, D., & Verbert, K. (2022). Towards tangible algorithms: Exploring the experiences of tangible interactions with movie recommender algorithms. In *Proceedings of the ACM on Human–Computer Interaction, 6*(CSCW2), article no. 337. https://doi.org/10.1145/3555757

Alvarado, O., Vanden Abeele, V., Geerts, D., Gutiérrez, F., & Verbert, K. (2021). Exploring tangible algorithmic imaginaries in movie recommendations. In *TEI '21: Proceedings of the Fifteenth International Conference on Tangible, Embedded, and Embodied Interaction* (article no. 12). https://doi.org/10.1145/3430524.3440631

Baert, P. (2006). Phenomenology. In B. S. Turner (Ed.), *The Cambridge dictionary of sociology*. Cambridge University Press.

Baumer, E. P. S., & Brubaker, J. R. (2017). Post-userism. In *CHI '17: Proceedings of the 2017 CHI Conference on Human Factors in Computing Systems* (pp. 6291–6303). https://doi.org/10.1145/3025453.3025740

Beer, D. (2017). The social power of algorithms. *Information, Communication & Society, 20*(1), 1–13.

Bishop, S. (2018). Anxiety, panic and self-optimization: Inequalities and the YouTube algorithm. *Convergence, 24*(1), 69–84.

Blumer, H. (1954). What is wrong with social theory? *American Sociological Review, 19*(1), 3–10.

Bozdag, E. (2013). Bias in algorithmic filtering and personalization. *Ethics and Information Technology, 15*(3), 209–227.

Bucher, T. (2017). The algorithmic imaginary: Exploring the ordinary affects of Facebook algorithms. *Information, Communication & Society, 20*(1), 30–44.

Burke, A. (2019). Occluded algorithms. *Big Data & Society, 6*(2). https://doi.org/10.1177/2053951719858743

Cotter, K., & Reisdorf, B. C. (2020). Algorithmic knowledge gaps: A new dimension of (digital) inequality. *International Journal of Communication, 14*, 745–765.

DeVito, M. A., Birnholtz, J., Hancock, J. T., French, M., & Liu, S. (2018). How people form folk theories of social media feeds and what it means for how we study self-presentation. In *CHI '18: Proceedings of the 2018 CHI Conference on Human Factors in Computing Systems* (paper no. 120). https://doi.org/10.1145/3173574.3173694

DeVito, M. A., Gergle, D., & Birnholtz, J. (2017). "Algorithms Ruin Everything": #RIPTwitter, Folk Theories, and Resistance to Algorithmic Change in Social Media. In *CHI '17: Proceedings of the 2017 CHI Conference on Human Factors in Computing Systems* (pp. 3163–3174). https://doi.org/10.1145/3025453.3025659

Dogruel, L., Masur, P., & Joeckel, S. (2021). Development and validation of an algorithm literacy scale for internet users. *Communication Methods and Measures, 16*(2), 115–133.

Dourish, P. (2016). Algorithms and their others: Algorithmic culture in context. *Big Data & Society, 3*(2). https://doi.org/10.1177/2053951716665128

Dourish, P. (2019). User experience as legitimacy trap. *Interactions, 26*(6), 46–49.

Eiband, M., Völkel, S. T., Buschek, D., Cook, S., & Hussmann, H. (2019). When people and algorithms meet: User-reported problems in intelligent everyday applications. In *IUI '19: Proceedings of the 24th International Conference on Intelligent User Interfaces* (pp. 96–106). https://doi.org/10.1145/3301275.3302262

Eslami, M., Karahalios, K., Sandvig, C., Vaccaro, K., Rickman, A., Hamilton, K., & Kirlik, A. (2016). First I "like" it, then I hide it: Folk theories of social feeds. In *CHI '16: Proceedings of the 2016 CHI Conference on Human Factors in Computing Systems* (pp. 2371–2382). https://doi.org/10.1145/2858036.2858494

Eslami, M., Rickman, A., Vaccaro, K., Aleyasen, A., Vuong, A., Karahalios, K., Hamilton, K., Sandvig, C. (2015). "I always assumed that I wasn't really that close to [her]": Reasoning about invisible algorithms in news feeds. In *CHI '15: Proceedings of the 33rd Annual ACM Conference on Human Factors in Computing Systems* (pp. 153–162). https://doi.org/10.1145/2702123.2702556

French, M., & Hancock, J. (2017). What's the folk theory? Reasoning about cyber-social systems. Social Science Research Network (SSRN). https://doi.org/10.2139/ssrn.2910571

Gillespie, T. (2014). The relevance of algorithms. In T. Gillespie, P. J. Boczkowski, & K. A. Foot (Eds.), *Media technologies: Essays on communication, materiality, and society* (pp. 167–193). MIT Press.

Gillespie, T. (2016). Algorithm. In B. Peters (Ed.), *Digital keywords: A vocabulary of information society and culture* (pp. 18–30). Princeton University Press.

Gran, A.-B., Booth, P., & Bucher, T. (2021). To be or not to be algorithm aware: A question of a new digital divide? *Information, Communication & Society, 24*(12), 1779–1796.

Hamilton, K., Karahalios, K., Sandvig, C., & Eslami, M. (2014). A path to understanding the effects of algorithm awareness. In *CHI EA '14: CHI '14 Extended Abstracts on Human Factors in Computing Systems* (pp. 631–642). https://doi.org/10.1145/2559206.2578883

Hargittai, E., Gruber, J., Djukaric, T., Fuchs, J., & Brombach, L. (2020). Black box measures? How to study people's algorithm skills. *Information, Communication & Society, 23*(5), 1–12.

Klawitter, E., & Hargittai, E. (2018). "It's like learning a whole other language": The role of algorithmic skills in the curation of creative goods. *International Journal of Communication, 12*, 3490–3510.

Koenig, A. (2020). The algorithms know me and I know them: Using student journals to uncover algorithmic literacy awareness. *Computers and Composition, 58*, 102611.

Krogh, P. G., Graves Petersen, M., O'Hara, K., & Groenbaek, J. E. (2017). Sensitizing concepts for socio-spatial literacy in HCI. In *CHI '17: Proceedings of the 2017 CHI*

Conference on Human Factors in Computing Systems (pp. 6449–6460). https://doi.org/10.1145/3025453.3025756

Krüger, A. E., Kurowski, S., Pollmann, K., Fronemann, N., & Peissner, M. (2017). Needs profile: Sensitising approach for user experience research. In *OzCHI '17: Proceedings of the 29th Australian Conference on Computer–Human Interaction* (pp. 41–48). https://doi.org/10.1145/3152771.3152776

Langer, M., Hunsicker, T., Feldkamp, T., König, C. J., & Grgić-Hlača, N. (2022). "Look! It's a computer program! It's an algorithm! It's AI!": Does terminology affect human perceptions and evaluations of algorithmic decision-making systems? In *CHI '22: Proceedings of the 2022 CHI Conference on Human Factors in Computing Systems* (article no. 581). https://doi.org/10.1145/3491102.3517527

Lucero, A. (2015). Using affinity diagrams to evaluate interactive prototypes. In J. Abascal, S. Barbosa, M. Fetter, T. Gross, P. Palanque, & M. Winckler (Eds.), *Human–computer interaction—INTERACT 2015* (pp. 231–248). Springer.

Mittelstadt, B. D., Allo, P., Taddeo, M., Wachter, S., & Floridi, L. (2016). The ethics of algorithms: Mapping the debate. *Big Data & Society, 3*(2), 1–21.

Morrison, A., Viller, S., & Mitchell, P. (2011). Building sensitising terms to understand free-play in open-ended interactive art environments. In *CHI '11: Proceedings of the SIGCHI Conference on Human Factors in Computing Systems* (pp. 2335–2344). https://doi.org/10.1145/1978942.1979285

O'Neil, C. (2016). *Weapons of math destruction: How big data increases inequality and threatens democracy*. Broadway Books.

Rader, E., & Gray, R. (2015). Understanding user beliefs about algorithmic curation in the Facebook news feed. In *CHI '15: Proceedings of the 33rd Annual ACM Conference on Human Factors in Computing Systems* (pp. 173–182). https://doi.org/10.1145/2702123.2702174

Rennick Egglestone, S., Walker, B., Marshall, J., Benford, S., & McAuley, D. (2011). Analysing the playground: Sensitizing concepts to inform systems that promote playful interaction. In P. Campos, N. Graham, J. Jorge, N. Nunes, P. Palanque, & M. Winckler (Eds.), *Human–computer interaction—INTERACT 2011* (pp. 452–469). Springer.

Sanders, E. B.-N., & Stappers, P. J. (2008). Co-creation and the new landscapes of design. *CoDesign, 4*(1), 5–18.

Sanders, E. B.-N., & Stappers, P. J. (2012). *Convivial toolbox: Generative research for the front end of design*. BIS Publishers.

Schwartz-Shea, P., & Yanow, D. (2012). *Interpretive research design*. Routledge.

Seaver, N. (2017). Algorithms as culture: Some tactics for the ethnography of algorithmic systems. *Big Data & Society, 4*(2).

Seaver, N. (2019). Knowing algorithms. In J. Vertesi & D. Ribes (Eds.), *digitalSTS: A field guide for science & technology studies* (pp. 412–422). Princeton University Press.

Siles, I., Espinoza-Rojas, J., Naranjo, A., & Tristán, M. F. (2019). The mutual domestication of users and algorithmic recommendations on Netflix. *Communication, Culture and Critique, 12*(4), 499–518.

Sim, G., Horton, M., & Read, J. C. (2016). Sensitizing: Helping children design serious games for a surrogate population. In C. de Carvalho, P. Escudeiro, & A. Coelho (Eds.), *Serious games, interaction, and simulation* (pp. 58–65). Springer.

Storms, E., Alvarado, O., & Monteiro-Krebs, L. (2022). "Transparency is meant for control" and vice versa: Learning from co-designing and evaluating algorithmic news recommenders. *Proceedings of the ACM on Human–Computer Interaction, 6*(CSCW2), article no. 405. https://doi.org/10.1145/3555130

Swart, J. (2021). Experiencing algorithms: How young people understand, feel about, and engage with algorithmic news selection on social media. *Social Media + Society, 7*(2). https://doi.org/10.1177/20563051211008828

Waern, A., Rajkowska, P., Johansson, K. B., Bac, J., Spence, J., & Løvlie, A. S. (2020). Sensitizing scenarios: Sensitizing designer teams to theory. In *CHI '20: Proceedings of the 2020 CHI Conference on Human Factors in Computing Systems*. https://doi.org/10.1145/3313831.3376620

Willson, M. (2017). Algorithms (and the) everyday. *Information, Communication & Society, 20*(1), 137–150.

Zarouali, B., Boerman, S. C., & De Vreese, C. H. (2021). Is this recommended by an algorithm? The development and validation of the algorithmic media content awareness scale (AMCA-scale). *Telematics and Informatics, 62*.

Zarouali, B., Helberger, N., & De Vreese, C. (2021). Investigating algorithmic misconceptions in a media context: Source of a new digital divide? *Media and Communication, 9*(4), 134–144.

About the Authors

Elias Storms is a sociologist, lecturer, and postdoctoral researcher. He lectures in sociology at the University of Antwerp and research methods at the AP University College of Antwerp, both in Belgium. Previously, he was a human–computer interaction researcher at Mintlab, KU Leuven, Belgium, involved in research on algorithmic recommender systems.

Oscar Alvarado is an HCI researcher and professor at the Department of Mass Media Communication, University of Costa Rica. He lectures on technology interaction design. Previously, he was an HCI researcher at the Augment and Mintlab Research Groups at KU Leuven, Belgium, where he obtained his PhD.

5. Reassembling the Black Box of Machine Learning: Of Monsters and the Reversibility of Foldings

Juliane Jarke and Hendrik Heuer

Abstract

Research on algorithmic fairness, accountability and transparency promotes a view on algorithmic systems as black boxes that need to be "opened" and "unpacked". Understanding the black box as a mode of inquiry and knowledge making practice (rather than a thing), this chapter explores what exactly scholars and practitioners aim to unpack when they examine algorithmic black boxes, what they consider to be constitutive elements of these black boxes, and what is "othered" or perceived as "monstrous". The chapter reviews three distinct modes of assembling black boxes of machine learning (ML)-based systems. Encounters with the outer limits of these ML black boxes explore how social actors, temporalities, places, imaginaries, practices, and values are *enfolded* in knowledge making about algorithmic regimes.

Keywords: data; algorithm; critical data studies; algorithmic regime; knowledge, transparency

Introduction

> *There are monsters on the prowl, whose form changes with the history of knowledge.*
> —Michel Foucault (1971, p. 16)

> *You will find in the complex of ordinary, mundane accounts that there are practices for locating monsters but that there are also practices for burying them.*
> — Harold Garfinkel (1968 cited in Munro 2001, p. 473)

Jarke, J., B. Prietl, S. Egbert, Y. Boeva, H. Heuer, and M. Arnold (eds.), *Algorithmic Regimes: Methods, Interactions, and Politics*. Amsterdam: Amsterdam University Press, 2024
DOI 10.5117/9789463728485_CH05

Research on algorithmic fairness, accountability and transparency promotes a view on algorithmic systems as "black boxes" that need to be "opened" and "unpacked" and as something whose inner workings ought to be made visible to outside observers and auditors (e.g., Bucher, 2018; Pasquale, 2015). Referring to black boxes in these instances covers two aspects: (1) an understanding of algorithmic systems as devices that produce and record data for further use, similar to data-monitoring systems in planes, trains, or cars; and (2) an understanding of algorithmic systems that are—to some extent—unknown or "unknowable" (Seaver, 2017, p. 5) and can only be grasped in relation to their inputs and outputs. Hence, the trope of the black box figures what is unknown and opaque about algorithmic systems as an epistemological problem: We need to open the black boxes of algorithmic systems in order to "understand how they may be exerting power on us, and to understand where they might be making unjust mistakes" (Diakopoulos, 2018, cited by Straube, 2019, p. 177).

The opening or unpacking of algorithmic systems has a long tradition in software studies and code studies through methods such as reverse engineering or code analysis (e.g., Fuller, 2008; Manovich, 2013; Kitchin, 2017; Bucher, 2018; see also Gramelsberger et al., in this volume). However, these types of methods are not useful for algorithmic systems based on machine learning (ML), a novel software development paradigm. Unlike software explicitly programmed in formal languages, rules in ML-based systems are inferred from data (see also Jarke et al., in this volume). Amongst the proposals to "unpack" and "open" the black box of ML-based systems, we find ethnographic approaches of ML design processes (e.g., Mackenzie, 2017; Christin, 2020), practical interventions, and action research (e.g., D'Ignazio & Klein, 2020; Thylstrup et al., 2019).

In this chapter, we complement these approaches by understanding black boxes of ML-based systems not as "a *thing* that we can encounter out there in the field" (Straube, 2019, p. 178, emphasis in original), but as a *mode of inquiry* and boundary-making *knowledge practice*. We demonstrate how generative the notion of the black box is as a concept and methodological approach for the critical inquiry of algorithmic regimes, that is, how knowledge *about* algorithmic systems is produced. To do so, we explore how different understandings of ML-based systems as black boxes produce different assemblages of what is constitutive of the black box (and hence needs to be researched) and what resides outside. Those entities that are considered constitutive elements of the inner workings of an algorithmic black box can be understood through the notion of the "fold" (Introna, 2007; Latour, 2002; Lee et al., 2019). The fold describes the ways in which algorithmic systems produce proximities between social groups, times or locations by relating (*folding*) them algorithmically—how social actors, temporalities, places, imaginaries, practices, and values are *enfolded* in algorithmic regimes. However, those entities and foldings that are considered to reside outside the black box are "othered" and perceived as "monstrous" (Bloomfield & Vurdubakis, 1999; Law, 1991). In this understanding,

> [t]he monstrous is [...] what lies beyond the outer limits of legitimate knowledge; that which has been expelled by the normalizing judgments of a given episteme. [...] The monstrous is [...] what Foucault calls the "unthought": the banished Other of orderly knowing. It constitutes its unseen double, a constant source of outrages against epistemic and ontological propriety. It is, in other words, that which has to be refused and contained by a given organization of truth. (Bloomfield & Vurdubakis, 1999, p. 629)

The monstrous is hence what is considered irrelevant for the constitution and inner workings of an algorithmic black box. It is what consciously or unconsciously excluded from the researchers' attention and escapes the analysis of the algorithmic enfolding. This however limits a critical analysis into algorithmic regimes. We argue therefore that researchers need to examine how black boxes of ML-based systems come to be assembled technically, socially and politically. In so doing, we follow Suchman's (2023) call to challenge the "thingness of AI, its status as stable and agential entity [... and] treat the existence of AI itself as controversial" (p.1). As we will demonstrate below, understanding algorithmic black boxes not as a thing, but as a mode of inquiry enables critical scholars to examine how ways of relating, connecting, and folding spaces, times, and (social) actors through algorithmic systems transform knowledge regimes.

The chapter is structured in the following way. First, we review how science and technology studies (STS) scholars have conceptualized *the black box as a mode of inquiry* into the ways in which socio-technical systems are designed and operate. We then review how machine learning has been understood as a black box and reconstruct *three distinct modes of assembling the black box of machine learning*: (1) the black box of ML data, (2) the black box of ML algorithms and trained models, and (3) the black box of ML-based systems in practice. We conclude with a discussion of how black boxes as a method prescribe certain understandings of what is considered a legitimate and constitutive element of an algorithmic system and what is othered. This means we reflect on the ways in which particular understandings of

ML black boxes afford specific understandings of what kinds of entities, practices and foldings need to be researched. This questions the boundary making practices of black boxes: Which entities and foldings are considered legitimate constitutive elements of algorithmic knowledge production and which are perceived as monstrous.

Black Boxing and Its Monsters as a Mode of Inquiry

The trope of the black box has been widely used by scholars in critical algorithm studies as well as practitioners and legal scholars to describe, conceptualize, and research algorithmic systems (e.g., Burrell, 2016; Bucher, 2018; Pasquale, 2015; Kitchin, 2017; Innerarity, 2021). The idea of the black box is derived from cybernetics where (complex) technologies or social organizations are depicted as little (black) boxes with an input and output (Latour, 1987). Understood as a black box, a technology or social organization does not require an understanding of its inner workings. A black box "brackets them as instruments that perform certain valuable functions" (Winner, 1993, p. 365). The term "black box" hence allows to conveniently describe a technology "solely in terms of its inputs and outputs" (ibid.). For example, in many social science studies, technologies are conceived as black boxes that have some kind of social impact (e.g., economic analyses of technological innovation). This was criticized by Pinch and Bijker (1984) in their now seminal text on the social construction of technology. Along with Layton (1977), they argue:

> What is needed is an understanding of technology from inside, both as a body of knowledge and as a social system. Instead, technology is often treated as a "black box" whose contents and behaviour may be assumed to be common knowledge. (Layton, 1977, p. 198, cited in Pinch & Bijker, 1984, p. 404)

What subsequently became one of the main modes of inquiry in STS was to "unpack" or "open" these black boxes of technologies and the processes of their design. An important aim was to "carefully [look] at the inner workings of real technologies and their histories to see what is *actually* taking place" (Winner, 1993, p. 364, our emphasis).

Winner (1993) raised two critical points with respect to early STS work on technological black boxes: (1) an overemphasis on the ways in which technologies come to be designed (the origins of a technology) rather than the ways in which this technology impacts on society (the consequences of technological choices); and (2) a focus on "relevant social actors" that overlooks those groups "that have no voice but that, nevertheless, will be affected by the results of technological change" or that have been deliberately excluded from the design process. What is needed, in order to develop a productive critique of a technology is to create a "comprehensive account" of the "structures, workings, and social origins" (Winner, 1993, p. 365).

A useful analogy for how to consider the various black boxes of machine learning was presented by Law (1986) in his analysis of a novel navigation system developed by Portuguese scientists towards the end of the 15th century. This new knowledge regime allowed the Portuguese fleet to explore unknown waters and return home safely. The navigation system was a black box to naval navigators who simply had to provide input (the position of the sun) and received actionable output (the position of the ship). In his analysis, Law unpacks how and through which actor networks the navigation system was designed and how it subsequently became embedded into knowledge practices (navigation at sea) and afforded new ways of seafaring (ultimately providing the basis for the "discovery" of the "New World"). A black box, Law argues in his discussion, "if placed within the appropriate envelope of other elements, was capable of generating the kind of answers that were needed" (Law, 1986, p. 255) and allowed the vast expansion of Portuguese seafaring.

In Law's account, Portuguese seafaring is constituted through different instances of black boxing (or black boxes), from scientific knowledge that became encoded into the navigation systems which in turn became embedded into the knowledge practices of Portuguese seafarers. While the navigation system remained a black box to naval navigators, the whole socio-technical system of seafaring presented a black box to the Indigenous people who were the ones to bear the dire consequences of the successful embedding of this new technology into seafaring. Likewise, the ways in which the navigation system came to be embedded as part of Portuguese seafaring and subsequently afforded its reconfiguration and new ways of governance, remained a black box to those Portuguese scientists who developed the system in the first place. Their positionality, however, was vastly different from the Indigenous peoples who were affected by the output of the system in incomparable terms. There is hence no one black box to be opened in Law's case study, but many, since different social actors experience technologies as black boxes differently, always through their situated lived experiences, relations and knowledges.

This impossibility of tracing and unpacking something as a fixed black box was further elaborated by Bloomfield and Vurdubakis (1999) who argued that Law's study of the black box of the Portuguese expansion "relies upon a conventional (modernist) ontology *and* a conventional mode of social science accounting" (p. 631, emphasis in original). They ask: "What about the religious artefacts, symbols and acts of worship and prayer which would have been part and parcel of a Portuguese voyage at that time?" and conclude that the actor networks that Law identified were those that are relevant and recognizable to modern social theory but not necessarily to the 15th-century Portuguese mariner. Bloomfield and Vurdubakis hence argue that the opening (and hence assembling) of a black box must be understood as a boundary making knowledge practice. The opening of a black box is hence not merely a process of "unpacking" but of defining what is a constitutive element of the black box and what is not.

Understanding black boxing as such allows us to ask for the "outer limits" and "monsters" (Bloomfield & Vurdubakis, 1999) of algorithmic systems, and to consider those entities, aspects, and practices that are othered and contested. As we will demonstrate below, the fact that such machine learning-based systems are based on statistical inference has implications for what critical algorithm studies scholars as well as ML practitioners consider to be part of the black box of ML and what they implicitly or explicitly perceive as outside. Reconstructing the ways in which different social actors assemble a technology as a black box uncovers their knowledge making practices within algorithmic regimes.

The Black Boxing of Machine Learning: From Technical Understandings of ML Black Boxes to Black Boxes and Their Foldings

First, we need to state that the black box is a necessary element of any software development process. Software libraries and application programming interfaces (APIs) are black boxes that allow software developers to integrate code written by others into their own code. Such black boxing reduces the cognitive load of programmers and allows them to develop new features or functionalities "without having to think about every little detail of how the systems work" (Bucher, 2018, p. 45). Hence, without black boxing, it would not be possible to conceive and develop complex algorithmic systems. In this respect, a "black box contains that which no longer needs to be reconsidered, those things whose contents have become a matter of indifference" (Callon & Latour, 1981, p. 285).

A first way to define the black box of machine learning is hence to assemble the different technical components. For example, Veale (2019)

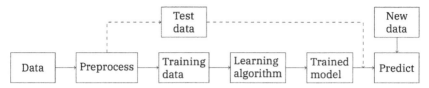

Figure 5.1. The machine learning pipeline according to Veale (2019, p. 35).

differentiates between data, preprocessing, training data and test data, the learning algorithm, the trained model, and the prediction based on new data (Figure 5.1). In any ML-based system following this supervised learning paradigm, the ML algorithm turns input and output data into a trained model. This trained model is at the heart of machine learning. Since the trained model is not based on instructions specified in formal languages, it is not possible to study machine learning systems as instructional text (e.g., as was done in traditional software studies or code studies methodologies). Figure 5.1 visualizes that the data used to train (or infer) a model can be very different from the data that a model will receive to make predictions in practice. The figure also highlights the difference between a machine learning algorithm (ML algorithm) and the trained model: The machine learning algorithm is used to train (or infer) the model used to make predictions and can itself be comparatively simple (see also Heuer et al., 2021).

Such an account understands technology as something that "operates in a more or less uniform manner in different social settings" (Introna, 2007, p. 12). It supports a "tool view" that distinguishes between "technical means" and "social ends" (Introna, 2007; Latour, 2002). Here, the methodological problem of opening the black box of machine learning is one that requires access to the ways in which the algorithmic systems *operates*. This account of machine learning assumes an ontological separation between the technical and the social world. What is invisible in such accounts is how the "technical" and the "social" are co-constitutive: How time, space, and actors come to be *folded into algorithmic systems*, how values, politics and ethics come to *be folded into algorithmic regimes* is of no concern to the opening of a "purely technical" black. However,

> folded into—or enclosed in—the ongoing co-constitutive horizon or nexus of human and technology relationships are (un)intentions, (im) possibilities, (dis)functions, affordances/prohibitions that renders possible some ways of being and not others, that serves the (il)legitimate interests of some and not others. (Introna, 2007, p. 15)

The notion of the fold suggests that we should think about algorithmic relations as "becoming folded or torn, like a handkerchief, to encourage thinking in alternative topologies" (Lee et al., 2019, p. 3). Algorithmic systems are not stable entities with fixed properties but *fold* different social actors, places, objectives, and temporalities . As a result, algorithmic systems may produce proximities of social groups or locations by relating (folding) them algorithmically (Lee et al., 2019). For example, the COMPAS system sorts individuals into categories of high or low risk of recidivism based on folding 135 attributes from criminal records, an individual questionnaire, and population records (Angwin et al., 2016; Dressel & Farid, 2018). Similarly, other algorithmic systems fold together data from different places, temporalities, and social actors related to different social settings, practices, imaginaries, and intentions.

Understanding the opening of a black box as a methodological approach, we are interested in exploring what exactly critical algorithm studies scholars aim to unpack when they examine the "black box" of machine learning, what they consider to be folded within the boundaries of this black box, and what is othered. In the following, we identify and discuss three instances of black boxing machine learning: (1) the black box of ML data, (2) the black box of ML algorithms and trained models, and (3) the black box of ML-based systems in practice. In so doing, we demonstrate that concepts of ML black boxes are not merely a critique of algorithmic systems per se but allow us to ask different types of questions. They each forefront different socio-technical foldings of machine learning and how they come to be constitutive of algorithmic regimes.

The Black Box of ML Data

A first understanding of the term "black box" is in relation to how algorithmic systems create, record and process data (e.g., Houben & Prietl, 2018; Hepp et al., 2022). For example, Ajunwa (2020) explores "the 'black box' at work," relating back to the notion of algorithmic systems as both (1) devices for recording and collecting increasingly personal data about workers, and (2) opaque algorithmic systems that determine hiring decisions or the degree of a workers' productivity. This notion is also prominent in Smith's (2020) account of the "black box city" in which an ever-increasing surveillance infrastructure records our movements and everyday life. Noble and Roberts (2017) similarly point to "black-boxed technologies that amass and commercialize data on students, often without their knowledge" (p. 56). Pasquale (2015) has described this „black box" as a "one-way mirror" through which "[i]mportant corporate actors have unprecedented knowledge of the minutiae of our daily lives, while we know little to nothing about how they use this knowledge to influence the important decisions that we—and they—make" (p. 9). What these accounts of ML black boxes have in common are the ways in which the extent of data collection as well as the further processing and related aims remain opaque to those individuals who leave these "digital traces" (Breiter & Hepp, 2018) and have become digital "data subjects" (Lupton, 2016).

A second understanding of the black box of ML data relates to the ways in which training data sets represent a black box to those developing machine learning-based systems (ML practitioners) (e.g., Hutchinson et al., 2021). In an analysis of ImageNet, one of the most important ML data sets for training image recognition systems, Denton et al. (2021) observe that the data set is used to train a variety of image recognition systems without adequate recognition of the contingencies in which it was developed: "[T]he more naturalized ML datasets become, the more likely they are to be treated as value-neutral scientific artifacts and unquestioningly adopted by ML practitioners. In this manner, they come to resemble black boxes" (p. 2). Denton et al. (2021) trace the genealogy of how ImageNet sourced its over 14 million images, how the 20,000 categories for structuring the data set were derived from WordNet—a lexical database of semantic relations that combines a dictionary and a thesaurus—and how 49,000 crowd workers from 167 countries performed the task of assigning categories to images. To date, many of the problematic contingencies of the process have become enfolded into algorithmic systems and "black boxed," relating, for example, to (1) a strong bias in terms of sourcing the images from social networking sites (e.g., representing the world through the emergence of digital photography and image-sharing practices of the late 2000s), (2) some of the problematic categories that WordNet uses to represent concepts about the world (e.g., bad person, slut), and (3) a naïve understanding that such categories could be assigned to pictures without difficulty (e.g., assuming a self-evident relationship between the world and WordNet). Denton et al. highlight that:

> By failing to account for the particularities of this view—particularities that largely reflect a white gaze—Western, male and wielding a naturalistic rhetoric in popular scientific discourse, the subjective nature of meaning formation and the presence of acts of unreflective interpretation is obfuscated and hidden from view. (Denton et al., 2021, p. 9)

This connects to a concern that we have demonstrated in earlier work: the importance of data and related data preparation and data-labelling practices is vastly understated in ML self-educational resources (Heuer et al., 2021). Similarly, Denton et al. (2021), citing Goodfellow (2016), argue that ML textbooks and curricula offer little guidance on how to construct ML data sets. Sambasivan et al. (2021) likewise, support this claim, stating "everyone wants to do the model work, not the data work" (p. 1). They argue that "data is the most under-valued and de-glamourized aspect of AI." This may result in serious negative consequences, so-called "data cascades" (Sambasivan et al., 2021), in which data sets are used to train models that are not appropriate, representative, and lack data quality.

However, as Gebru et al. (2021) argue, despite their importance, there are no standardized processes for documenting machine learning data sets. They propose "datasheets for datasets" that document the "motivation, composition, collection process, recommended uses, and so on" (p. 86). These data sheets could then be used by data set collectors and data set consumers and maintain what Latour (2002) called "the reversibility of foldings" (p. 258). That does not mean to go back to an imagined original position, but "an ideal of putting into practice the conditions that will facilitate openness rather than closure" (Introna, 2007, p. 16). The purpose is for data set collectors to "encourage careful reflection on the process of creating, distributing, and maintaining a dataset, including any underlying assumptions, potential risks or harms, and implications of use" (Gebru et al., 2021, p. 86–87). For data set consumers, the aim is to ensure "they [the consumers] have the information they need to make informed decisions about using a dataset" (ibid., p. 87). Other social actors such as policymakers, activists, or journalists may also be interested in the genealogy of data sets. In so doing, the foldings of machine learning (understood as black boxes of ML data) become more open and transparent.

The Black Box of ML Algorithms and Trained Models

To many—ML practitioners and critical algorithm studies scholars alike—not only the data sets but also the ways in which ML algorithms create trained models pose a black box, even when they try to educate themselves through self-education resources (Heuer et al., 2021). According to Mackenzie, rendering the "production of prediction visible" remains a challenge (p. 436).

Machine learning is applied to "problems" for which imperative programming—the kind of programming where rules are explicitly encoded—does not perform well. Under the paradigm of imperative programming, a programmer explicitly formulates computational rules of the system in a programming language. ML systems, in contrast, infer rules from data. "Training" an ML model means formulating a mathematical model and defining a cost function. The parameters of this mathematical model are then minimized for this cost function and the available data. Hence, in contrast to systems based on imperative programming, ML-based systems are not explicitly programmed by software developers. While they are still "trained" by somebody, the process is very different (see also Mackenzie, 2013). The ways in which technologies such as machine recognition approach their tasks cannot "follow the path of human intuition" (Chun, 2021, p. 212). Instead, such systems have to determine "invariant characteristics" that distinguish one class of phenomena from all others. This, however, is influenced by a number of factors, e.g., by the ways in which the data is preprocessed and represented. Text, for instance, can be represented in a number of ways, e.g., as a mere dictionary (bag of words), a weighted dictionary (term frequency–inverse document frequency, or TF-IDF), as groups of words (n-grams), or as so-called word vectors that mathematically represent the distributional semantics of a word. These modelling decisions have implications for the inferred model and the predictions of the system. Hence, as Chun (2021) notes, the "nontransparency" of machine learning extends to "how the continuous nature of signals and persons alike is made discrete and molded; how patterns are recognized and fostered" (pp. 153–158).

> [The] machine learning literature has principally retold a kind of romance, in which, after many trials and tribulations with unruly, messy, mixed or 'dirty' data, epistemic order and predictive power prevail over error and the unexpected. (Mackenzie, 2015, p. 436)

Finding a specific function that establishes order and an intelligible prediction is what "allows machine learning practitioners to claim that the algorithm *learns*" (Mackenzie, 2015, p. 436, emphasis in original). Mackenzie continues to ask how anyone may know that a given predictive model is meaningful or valid; that "what a given model has found in the data applies to subsequent events?" (p. 439).

ML practice has developed a number of metrics to measure how well a trained model performs, including accuracy, precision, and recall on data in practice (Müller & Guido, 2016). This is supposed to evaluate how well the model "generalizes." A prime example for an ML algorithm and trained model as a black box is provided by Wu and Zhang (2016), who published a paper titled "Automated Inference on Criminality Using Face

Images." The paper tries to predict whether somebody "is" a criminal or not from his or her face alone. Wu and Zhang (2016) claim to have trained a convolutional neural network that can distinguish criminals and non-criminals from photos of their faces with 89.51% accuracy. For this, they collected 1,800 photos of Chinese adults between 18 and 55 years. All people had no facial hair and no tattoos or scars. The criminals were sourced from 700 photos of convicted criminals provided by the police. The non-criminals were sourced from a data set of 11,000 photos from various sources on the internet.

The paper is noteworthy in that the authors performed a thorough evaluation of the system, e.g., by combining different established and reliable metrics like accuracy, receiver operating characteristic (ROC) curve, and area under the curve (AUC). The authors claim that discriminating structural features like lip curvature, eye inner corner distance, and the so-called nose-mouth angle are predictive of whether somebody "is" a criminal. This approach is eerily similar to 19th-century pseudoscience like phrenology. If it was possible to predict something so complex from the face alone, this would be remarkable. This discovery would have the potential to revolutionize entire scientific fields like biology, psychology, and sociology. Bergstrom and West (2017), therefore, suggest an alternative hypothesis to the extraordinary claim that facial structure reveals criminal tendencies. They highlight that small, but perceptible differences in photographs from the ML data set that has been publicly shared likely influence the result. For instance, people in the photos provided by the police do not smile and they are photographed in harsh lighting conditions. The faces of the "non-criminals" are also improved using software like Photoshop, i.e., the face has smooth skin. They are well-lit and many wear shirts. Although Wu and Zhang (2016) state that they did ensure that the collar is not visible, this could have affected their posture (see also Lopez, in this volume). Hence it is doubtful that the system can actually make predictions about whether somebody is a criminal or not, but more likely that the system is merely able to distinguish between photos of individuals under different lighting conditions.

The example implies that even though a well-tested and reliable ML algorithm was used to train the inferred model, the available data and the differences between the two classes likely gave away the labels, which probably influenced the results of the prediction system. This shows that even though a certain ML algorithm can work for one task, it can fail for a larger number of other tasks if the available data is limited. This misapplication is a prime example of situations where subtle differences in the available data and the way data collectors sourced data led to an inferred model that fails to capture the concept that the ML system is supposed to learn. The ML system merely excels at a proxy task. Opening the black box of ML algorithms and trained models hence aims to unpack how certain conditions, assumptions, and (subtle) differences in training data sets become enfolded into an algorithmic system.

The Black Box ML-Based Systems in Practice

A third way in which machine learning is understood as a black box concerns ML-based systems in practice. What scholars aim to unpack is how ML-based systems are embedded and become folded into processes of organizational decision-making and governance, and subsequently how ML-based systems impact on the lives and futures of different social actors (e.g., Prinsloo, 2020; Hartong & Förschler, 2019; Hu, 2020; Smith, 2020). Hence, the framing of the ML black box shifts yet again, from opening the black box of a (purely) technical system to unpacking the invisible or invisibilized foldings of infrastructures, (data) practices, social roles, and processes in algorithmic regimes.

For example, Prinsloo (2020) examines algorithmic decision-making that is increasingly used to "admit, steer, predict and prescribe students' learning journeys" as black boxes in higher education institutions. Hartong and Förschler (2019) explore the "black box of data-based school monitoring" and how algorithmic systems increasingly shape and influence the practices in state education agencies. Practices that have so far been hidden from view. In this understanding, ML black boxes comprise of public and private sector organizations whose inner workings (e.g., governance, decision-making) are increasingly opaque and unaccountable (Pasquale, 2015; Smith, 2020).

In addition, scholars are interested in uncovering the "impact" of ML-based systems on different social actors. For example, scholars consider those social actors that are affected by biases induced in ML predictions through ML data sets. Several scholars have hence argued that we need a critical scholarship that goes "beyond trying to 'open up the black box'" of algorithmic systems and also "examine sociocultural processes" (Geiger, 2017). As a case study, Geiger (2017) examines the socialization of newcomers to Wikipedia. In a similar vein, Seaver (2017) argues that we must not approach algorithmic systems as "inaccessible black boxes, but as heterogeneous and diffuse sociotechnical systems, with entanglements beyond the boundaries of proprietary software" (p. 10). Here the boundaries of black boxes shift yet again to include, for example, processes of individual or organizational decision-making (see also Büchner et al., in this volume).

In particular, algorithmic systems that facilitate automated decision-making (ADM) in the public sector have received increased scholarly attention. This spans from education to the judicial system but also our social and healthcare infrastructures and welfare (e.g., Eubanks, 2018; Dencik & Kaun, 2020; Angwin et al., 2016). A well-research algorithmic system in this domain is the one used by the Austrian Public Employment Service (Arbeitsmarktservice Österreich, AMS Austria) (Allhutter et al., 2020; Büchner & Dosdall, 2021; Lopez, 2019). The system predicts the prospects of a jobseeker to find a new job within a certain time frame, by folding available data such as gender, age, childcare responsibilities, health restrictions, and disability. It also includes previous occupation, the extent of employment, and the type of regional labour market activity. This prediction is then used to determine whether somebody qualifies for job training support or not. The available data used to train the inferred model are openly documented. The algorithm that is used is a comparatively simple, old, and reliable logistic regression model invented by Cox (1958). What makes the Austrian system remarkable is how visible the bias in the inferred model is against women, older adults, carers, or migrants. In other words, the system itself is not a black box per se. What presents, however, a black box (to jobseekers and researchers alike) is how the predictions of the system reconfigure the decision-making processes of civil servants (Allhutter et al., 2020; Büchner & Dosdall, 2021). For example, how the predictions of the AMS algorithm become "actionable," how they are folded into the work routines of civil servants. This relates to questions about how difficult it is for civil servants to challenge the predictions of the system: Do they simply skip over the prediction or are they required to complete long forms in which they have to explain to their superiors why they disagree? Is there sufficient training (algorithmic literacy) for civil servants to understand and question the output of the system? How does the professional identity of case workers change if they often disagree with or challenge such a system? To what extent do the biased predictions of the system reinforce existing biases against migrant workers? How do such algorithmic systems reconfigure the roles, relationships, agency, and subjectivities of civil servants and citizens?

In sum, scholars examining the black box of ML-based systems in practice attend to the unfolding agency of ML-based systems in practice, and the ways in which the output of an ML-based system is made actionable; how ML-based systems come to be folded into existing decision-making processes and become constitutive elements of algorithmic regimes.

Reassembling the Black Box of Machine Learning

The three black boxes of machine learning that we reconstructed above do not solely cover the technical aspects that come to constitute an ML-based system, but also the ways in which it is and becomes enfolded into the sociomaterial practices of various social actors. The "inner workings" of ML black boxes are hence not of a purely technical nature (e.g., the way in which Veale [2019] assembles—supposedly—technical elements of ML in Figure 5.1), but include relevant social actors and their (knowledge) practices, which more often than not remain invisible in dominant accounts (e.g., crowd workers, data subjects), but also in social imaginaries, different temporalities, locations, aims, and materialities. Overall, the black box (or black boxes for that matter) of machine learning that we have reconstructed have by no means clear-cut boundaries. While the boundaries shift as the object of study shifts and through the knowledge making practices of those examining and experiencing an ML-based system.

The three distinct black boxes presented here may overlap in specific studies, but we distinguish them here for analytical purposes. Figure 5.2 assembles different elements of these black boxes and differentiates between those social actors who are responsible for the "training" of the machine learning model (*ML practitioners*), as well as those who create and collect the data (*data collectors*), those about whom data is collected (*data subjects*) and those who are affected by such systems in practice (*social actors*).

We describe the first black box of machine learning as the black box of ML data (Figure 5.2, blue background/dashed). Scholars attending to this black box aim to reconstruct the folding of sociomaterial actors and practices in relation to the creation, collection, and pre-processing of data available for developing an ML-based system and data in practice (to run the system). In theory, the available data used to train and test the ML system should be representative of the population that is targeted. In practice, however, it is close to impossible and there is reason to believe that this is rarely the case (Chun, 2021; Denton et al., 2021; Sambasivan et al., 2021). Important social actors in relation to the black box of ML data are those actors responsible for data collection and creation (which can be further distinguished into those who coordinate and supervise data collection, e.g., corporations or states, and those who are responsible for individual data labelling decisions, e.g., crowd workers). Opening the black box of ML data allows us to unpack practices of data extraction, data labelling, as well as labour conditions that remain invisible otherwise. In addition, examining the black box of ML data affords attention to those individuals about whom data are collected and

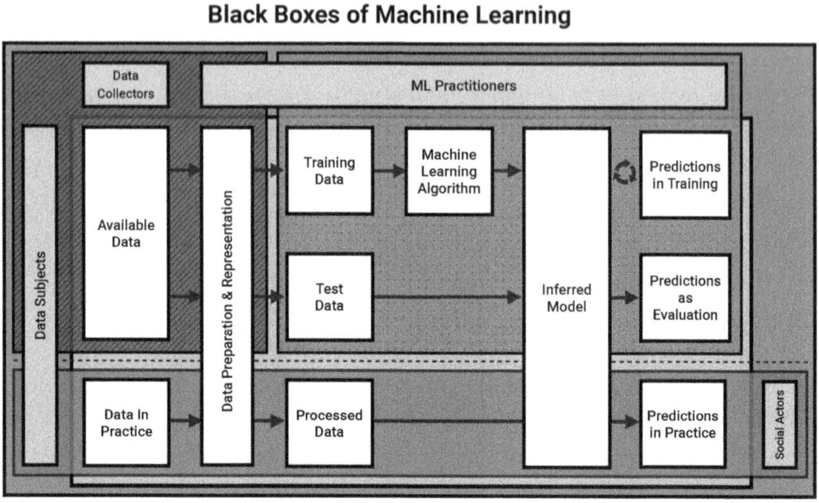

Black Boxes of Machine Learning

Figure 5.2. Three black boxes of machine learning, extending on ML models of Heuer (2020) and Veale (2019).

who are subject of data-based monitoring and surveillance often without their consent and knowledge.

The second approach to opening the black box of ML attends to ML algorithms and trained model (Figure 5.2, green background/dotted). Scholars aim to unpack the use, design, and evaluation of these elements. In these studies, at least three distinct practices and elements in which ML practitioners engage are "opened" through, for example, ethnographic work or participant observation:

1. *Data Preparation and Representation.* To be able to effectively work with different kinds of data, it is necessary to prepare the data and to find suitable representations that machine learning algorithms and inferred models are compatible with. This processing depends on whether data are nominal, ordinal, categorical, or based on audio, video, or images.
2. *The Training–Testing Split.* In this step, the available data is divided into two disjoint subsets. One subset is used for training, i.e., to infer the model, and one subset is used for testing, i.e., to measure the generalization capabilities of the ML model on data in practice.
3. *The Machine Learning Algorithm and the Inferred Model.* The machine learning algorithm is the set of instructions that uses the available training data to infer a model that can make predictions about the task at hand. There are many different supervised machine learning algorithms that follow different paradigms to infer models (Müller & Guido, 2016). To ensure that the algorithmic system can effectively make predictions

about the future, it is important to measure how well the inferred model generalizes beyond the training data, a process called evaluation. For this, several different metrics like accuracy, precision, and recall are used. As explained, since the data in practice may be different from the available data to train the ML-based system, the so-called generalization error between the evaluation and the predictions in practice is expected.

The third black box of ML goes beyond the analysis of the "inner workings" and design of ML-based systems to unpack the ways in which such systems come to be enfolded in practices and infrastructures of knowledge making, circulation, and decision-making (Figure 5.2, pink background/no pattern). To open this black box includes examinations about the ways in which algorithmic systems are made actionable in organizations; how agency and subjectivities, roles, and relations are reconfigured. This is important because algorithmic systems do not have any power or agency per se. Rather, the ways in which they come to be enfolded in and reinforce existing power structures very often remain a black box to those social actors about whom such systems claim to produce knowledge. Attending to the black box of ML-based systems in practice then requires unpacking the subjectivities, relations, and practices of different social actors (e.g., those using a system or those serving as data subjects). This relates, for example, to the question of how different social actors work with, in opposition to, or mediated through algorithmic systems in order to achieve specific goals (e.g., Zakharova & Jarke, 2022) or how newcomers come to be socialized with an algorithmic system (e.g., Geiger, 2017).

   In sum, our analysis of the three instances of black boxing machine learning suggests that by setting out to open "the" black box of machine learning, scholars not only consider the technical elements of an algorithmic system as those in need of illumination but also how and which social actors come to configure and contest, use and refuse ML-based systems. To quote Winner (1993), black boxes allow us "to come to terms with ways in which our technology-centred world might be reconstructed" (p. 376). They allow to examine how different social actors are implicated in the design, implementation, and running of algorithmic systems as constitutive parts of algorithmic regimes. In our analysis, we demonstrated that concepts of ML black boxes are not merely a critique of algorithmic systems per se but allow to ask different types of questions and reassemble machine learning differently. They each forefront different socio-technical foldings of machine learning; different visibilities are produced (e.g., Are only the dominant social actors such as ML practitioners considered? Who remains silent or silenced?). Examining the black box metaphor demonstrates that we must go beyond considerations of single technical artefacts that can be placed and moved between social contexts, but rather consider the ways in which algorithmic regimes are cascades or foldings of black boxes.

Of Monsters and the Reversibility of Foldings in Machine Learning

In this chapter we have demonstrated that black boxing serves as a specific knowledge and boundary-making practice in the emergence and stabilization of algorithmic regimes. Once an algorithmic system comes to be perceived as a black box, it is not only its computational inner workings that remain opaque but a whole nexus of human and technology relationships such as (un)intentions or affordances that are *folded* into the ongoing co-constitutive socio-technical relationships of algorithmic regimes. The black box, as a methodological and conceptual approach to reconstruct these foldings, offers a way to organize and order the heterogeneous entities, times, places, practices, and actors that come to constitute algorithmic regimes. This approach, in particular, defines a black box as those things that are understood as constitutive of algorithmic systems and those things that are outside its limits, that are "monstrous" and a "disruption of institutionalized knowing" (Bloomfield & Vurdubakis, 1999, p. 629).

What comes to be perceived as monstrous differs across socio-cultural settings and between different social actors. One example is the recent paper by Emily Bender, Timnit Gebru, and colleagues (2021) about the dangers of large-scale natural language processing (NLP) models, a specific type of ML model. They calculate the environmental impact of these models and ask: "How big is too big?" Guiding this question is the consideration of whether it is fair that residents in the Maldives or Sudan who will be disproportionately affected by the climate crisis pay the "environmental price of training and deploying ever larger English LMs [language models], when similar large-scale models aren't being produced for Dhivehi or Sudanese Arabic" (p. 613). Bender et al. argue that it's "past time" that those developing large scale language models (or other types of ML systems) need to prioritize the environmental impact and inequitable access to resources. In the acknowledgements the authors state that some of the original authors "were required by their employer to remove their names" because of claims made in the paper that were misplaced—monstrous—to their employers. After the publication of the paper, some of the authors were fired from their employment at Google. In interviews and through social media, those authors said that the paper and their framing of ethical ML systems led to the termination their contracts (e.g., Simonite, 2021). Reading their paper through the analytical lens of our chapter, we can see that the authors assemble the black box of NLP by reconstructing the folding of different places (Maldives, Sudan), interests (environmental impact on marginalized communities), calculations (financial versus environmental costs), and temporalities. These foldings are monstrous in the eyes of Google and other large tech companies which seek to tame the ways in which the *outer limits*, relations and entanglements of "their" algorithmic systems come to be understood. We suggest hence that one way of researching algorithmic regimes is to look out for the *monstrous*.

The outer limits of black boxes can however also become "hopeful monsters" that is "places where the necessary incompatibilities, inconsistencies and overlaps come gently and creatively together" (Law 1991, p.19). By extending the limits of what we take the black box of ML to be, we can reconstruct and re-imagine different ways in which our social and technical realities come to be enfolded into algorithmic regimes. We can question which entities get granted agency within black boxes and to which entities' agency is denied. For example, who gets to be a "relevant social actor" in the constitution of a black box of ML and who not? Who gets to decide this? The ways in which these presences and absences are negotiated are grounded in different epistemic and power regimes. Opening black boxes of machine learning and allowing for encounters with the outer limits enables us to "maintain the reversibility of foldings" (Latour, 2002, p. 258), that is, to question how specific ideas, objectives, places, imaginaries, practices, temporalities, and actors came to be folded into algorithmic regimes.

References

Ajunwa, I. (2020). The "black box" at work. *Big Data & Society, 7*(2). https://doi.org/10.1177/2053951720938093

Angwin, J., Larson, J., Mattu, S., & Kirchner, L. (2016, May 23). Machine bias: There's software used across the country to predict future criminals. And it's biased against Blacks. *ProPublica.* https://www.propublica.org/article/machine-bias-risk-assessments-in-criminal-sentencing

Bender, E. M., Gebru, T., McMillan-Major, A., & Shmitchell, S. (2021). On the dangers of stochastic parrots: Can language models be too big? 🦜. In *FAccT '21: Proceedings of the 2021 ACM Conference on Fairness, Accountability, and Transparency* (pp. 610–623). https://doi.org/10.1145/3442188.3445922

Bergstrom, C., & West, J. (2017). *Criminal machine learning.* https://callingbullshit.
org/case_studies/case_study_criminal_machine_learning.html

Bloomfield, B. P., & Vurdubakis, T. (1999). The outer limits: Monsters, actor networks and the writing of displacement. *Organization, 6*(4), 625–647. https://doi.
org/10.1177/135050849964004

Breiter, A., & Hepp, A. (2018). The complexity of datafication: Putting digital traces in
context. In A. Hepp, A. Breiter, & U. Hasebrink (Eds.), *Communicative figurations:
Transforming communications in times of deep mediatization* (pp. 387–405). Springer.

Bucher, T. (2018). *If... then: Algorithmic power and politics.* Oxford University Press.

Büchner, S., & Dosdall, H. (2021). Organisation und Algorithmus: Wie algorithmische
Kategorien, Vergleiche und Bewertungen durch Organisationen relevant gemacht
werden. *KZfSS Kölner Zeitschrift für Soziologie und Sozialpsychologie, 73*(S1),
333–357. https://doi.org/10.1007/s11577-021-00752-0

Burrell, J. (2016). How the machine "thinks": Understanding opacity in machine learning algorithms. *Big Data & Society, 3*(1). https://doi.org/10.1177/2053951715622512

Callon, M., & Latour, B. (1981). Unscrewing the big Leviathan: How actors macro-
structure reality and how sociologists help them to do so. In K. Knorr-Cetina
& A. V. Cicourel (Eds.), *Advances in social theory and methodology: Toward an
integration of micro- and macro-sociologies* (pp. 227–303). Routledge.

Christin, A. (2020). The ethnographer and the algorithm: Beyond the black box.
Theory and Society, 49, 897–918. https://doi.org/10.1007/s11186-020-09411-3

Chun, W. H. K. (2021). *Discriminating data: Correlation, neighborhoods, and the
new politics of recognition.* MIT Press.

Cox, D. R. (1958). The regression analysis of binary sequences. *Journal of the Royal
Statistical Society Series B: Statistical Methodology*, 20(2), 215-232.

Dencik, L., & Kaun, A. (2020). Datafication and the welfare state. *Global Perspectives,
1*(1), 12912. https://doi.org/10.1525/gp.2020.12912

Denton, E., Hanna, A., Amironesei, R., Smart, A., & Nicole, H. (2021). On the genealogy of machine learning datasets: A critical history of ImageNet. *Big Data &
Society, 8*(2). https://doi.org/10.1177/20539517211035955

D'Ignazio, C., & Klein, L. F. (2020). *Data feminism.* MIT Press.

Dressel, J., & Farid, H. (2018). The accuracy, fairness, and limits of predicting
recidivism. *Science Advances, 4*(1), 1–5. https://doi.org/10.1126/sciadv.aao5580

Eubanks, V. (2018). *Automating inequality: How high-tech tools profile, police, and
punish the poor.* St. Martin's Press.

Foucault, M. (1971). Orders of discourse. *Social Science Information, 10*(2), 7–30.
https://doi.org/10.1177/053901847101000201

Fuller, M. (Ed.). (2008). *Software studies: A lexicon.* MIT Press.

Gebru, T., Morgenstern, J., Vecchione, B., Vaughan, J. W., Wallach, H., Daumé III,
H., & Crawford, K. (2021). Datasheets for datasets. *Communications of the ACM,
64*(12), 86–92. https://doi.org/10.1145/3458723

Geiger, R. S. (2017). Beyond opening up the black box: Investigating the role of algorithmic systems in Wikipedian organizational culture. *Big Data & Society, 4*(2). https://doi.org/10.1177/2053951717730735

Hartong, S., & Förschler, A. (2019). Opening the black box of data-based school monitoring: Data infrastructures, flows and practices in state education agencies. *Big Data & Society, 6*(1). https://doi.org/10.1177/2053951719853311

Hepp, A., Jarke, J., & Kramp, L. (Eds.). (2022). *New perspectives in critical data studies: The ambivalences of data power.* Palgrave Macmillan.

Heuer, H. (2020). *Users & machine learning-based curation systems.* PhD thesis, Universität Bremen. https://doi.org/10.26092/elib/241

Heuer, H., Jarke, J., & Breiter, A. (2021). Machine learning in tutorials: Universal applicability, underinformed application, and other misconceptions. *Big Data & Society, 8*(1), 1–13. https://doi.org/10.1177/20539517211017593

Houben, D., & Prietl, B. (Eds.). (2018). *Datengesellschaft: Einsichten in die Datafizierung des Sozialen.* transcript. https://doi.org/10.1515/9783839439579

Hu, M. (2020). Cambridge Analytica's black box. *Big Data & Society, 7*(2). https://doi.org/10.1177/2053951720938091

Hutchinson, B., Smart, A., Hanna, A., Denton, E., Greer, C., Kjartansson, O., Barnes, P., & Mitchell, M. (2021). Towards accountability for machine learning datasets: Practices from software engineering and infrastructure. *FAccT '21: Proceedings of the 2021 ACM Conference on Fairness, Accountability, and Transparency* (pp. 560–575). https://doi.org/10.1145/3442188.3445918

Innerarity, D. (2021). Making the black box society transparent. *AI & Society, 36*(3), 975–981. https://doi.org/10.1007/s00146-020-01130-8

Introna, L. D. (2007). Maintaining the reversibility of foldings: Making the ethics (politics) of information technology visible. *Ethics and Information Technology, 9*(1), 11–25. https://doi.org/10.1007/s10676-006-9133-z

Kitchin, R. (2017). Thinking critically about and researching algorithms. *Information, Communication & Society, 20*(1), 14–29. https://doi.org/10.1080/1369118X.2016.1154087

Latour, B. (1987). *Science in action: How to follow scientists and engineers through society.* Harvard University Press.

Latour, B. (2002). Morality and technology: The end of the means. *Theory, Culture & Society, 19*(5/6), 247–260.

Law, J. (1986). On the methods of long-distance control: Vessels, navigation and the Portuguese route to India. In J. Law (Ed.), *Power, action, and belief: A new sociology of knowledge?* (pp. 234–263). Routledge. http://journals.sagepub.com/doi/10.1111/j.1467-954X.1984.tb00114.x

Law, J. (1991). Introduction: Monsters, Machines and Sociotechnical Relations. In J. Law (Ed.), *A sociology of monsters: Essays on power, technology and domination.* (pp. 1–23). Routledge.

Lee, F., Bier, J., Christensen, J., Engelmann, L., Helgesson, C.-F., & Williams, R. (2019). Algorithms as folding: Reframing the analytical focus. *Big Data & Society, 6*(2), 205395171986381. https://doi.org/10.1177/2053951719863819

Lopez, P. (2019). Reinforcing Intersectional Inequality via the AMS Algorithm in Austria. In G. Getzinger & M. Jahrbacher (Eds.), *Critical issues in science, technology and society studies: Conference proceedings of the STS conference Graz 2019, May 6th–7th* (pp. 289–309). https://doi.org/10.3217/978-3-85125-668-0-16

Lupton, D. (2016). Personal data practices in the age of lively data. In J. Daniels, K. Gregory & T. M. Cottom (Eds.), *Digital sociologies* (pp. 335–350). Policy Press.

Mackenzie, A. (2013). Programming subjects in the regime of anticipation: Software studies and subjectivity. *Subjectivity: International Journal of Critical Philosophy, 6*(4), 391–405. https://doi.org/10.1057/sub.2013.12

Mackenzie, A. (2015). The production of prediction: What does machine learning want? *European Journal of Cultural Studies, 18*(4–5), 429–445. https://doi.org/10.1177/1367549415577384

Mackenzie, A. (2017). *Machine learners: Archaeology of a data practice.* MIT Press.

Manovich, L. (2013). *Software takes command.* Bloomsbury.

Müller, A. C., & Guido, S. (2016). *Introduction to machine learning with Python: A guide for data scientists.* O'Reilly Media.

Munro, R. (2001). Calling for accounts: numbers, monsters and membership. *The Sociological Review,* 49(4), 473-493.

Noble, S. U., & Roberts, S. T. (2017, March 13). Out of the black box. *Educause Review.* https://er.educause.edu/articles/2017/3/out-of-the-black-box

Pasquale, F. (2015). *The black box society: The secret algorithms that control money and information.* Harvard University Press.

Pinch, T. J., & Bijker, W. E. (1984). The social construction of facts and artefacts: Or, How the sociology of science and the sociology of technology might benefit each other. *Social Studies of Science, 14*(3), 399–441. https://doi.org/10.1177/030631284014003004

Prinsloo, P. (2020). Of "black boxes" and algorithmic decision-making in (higher) education—A commentary. *Big Data & Society, 7*(1). https://doi.org/10.1177/2053951720933994

Sambasivan, N., Kapania, S., Highfill, H., Akrong, D., Paritosh, P., & Aroyo, L. M. (2021). "Everyone wants to do the model work, not the data work": Data cascades in high-stakes AI. *CHI '21: Proceedings of the 2021 CHI Conference on Human Factors in Computing Systems* (article no. 39). https://doi.org/10.1145/3411764.3445518

Seaver, N. (2017). Algorithms as culture: Some tactics for the ethnography of algorithmic systems. *Big Data & Society, 4*(2). https://doi.org/10.1177/2053951717738104

Simonite, T. (2021, June 8). What Really Happened When Google Ousted Timnit Gebru. *Wired.* Retrieved from https://www.wired.com/story/google-timnit-gebru-ai-what-really-happened/

Smith, G. J. (2020). The politics of algorithmic governance in the black box city. *Big Data & Society, 7*(2). https://doi.org/10.1177/2053951720933989

Straube, T. (2019). The black box and its dis/contents. In M. de Goede, E. Bosma, & P. Pallister-Wilkins (Eds.), *Secrecy and methods in security research* (pp. 175–192). Routledge. https://doi.org/10.4324/9780429398186-18

Suchman, L. (2023). The uncontroversial 'thingness' of AI. *Big Data & Society, 10*(2). https://doi.org/10.1177/20539517231206794

Thylstrup, N. B., Flyverbom, M., & Helles, R. (2019). Datafied knowledge production: Introduction to the special theme. *Big Data & Society, 6*(2), 1–5. https://doi.org/10.1177/2053951719875985

Veale, M. (2019). *Governing machine learning that matters*. PhD thesis, University College London. https://discovery.ucl.ac.uk/id/eprint/10078626/1/thesis_final_corrected_mveale.pdf

Winner, L. (1993). Upon opening the black box and finding it empty: Social constructivism and the philosophy of technology. *Science, Technology, & Human Values, 18*(3), 362–378. https://doi.org/10.1177/016224399301800306

Wu, X., & Zhang, X. (2016). Automated inference on criminality using face images. *CoRR, abs/1611.04135*. http://arxiv.org/abs/1611.04135

Zakharova, I., & Jarke, J. (2022). Educational technologies as matters of care. *Learning, Media and Technology, 47*(1), 95–108. https://doi.org/10.1080/17439884.2021.2018605

About the Authors

Juliane Jarke is Professor of Digital Societies at the University of Graz, Austria. Her research attends to the increasing importance of digital data and algorithmic systems in the public sector, in education, and for ageing populations. She received her PhD in organisation, work and technology from Lancaster University, UK, and has a background in computer science, philosophy, and science and technology studies (STS).

Dr. **Hendrik Heuer** is a senior researcher at the University of Bremen and the Institute for Information Management Bremen (ifib) in Germany. His research focuses on human–computer interaction and machine learning. Currently, he is working on ways to fight misinformation. He studied and worked in Bremen, Stockholm, Helsinki, and Amsterdam, and was a visiting postdoctoral research fellow at Harvard University.

6. Commentary: Methods in Algorithmic Regimes

Adrian Mackenzie

Abstract

This entry responds to others in its section by situating algorithms and social research into algorithms around one of the core ambiguities in contemporary social research, an ambiguity as to whether we are studying algorithms or what happens through algorithms. The entry situates the chapters in its section on a spectrum of possibilities relating to this to ambiguity. It explores too some of the implications of that ambiguity in terms of methods that are designed to look for changes, render transparent, or otherwise trace the movement of algorithms through platforms and their associated practices.

Keywords: platform; ambiguity; machine learning; experience

Introduction

When I think about my own research and lived experience of algorithms, a cluster of conceptual and methodological concerns resonates. Like many others, I feel the creeping tide of algorithmic processing seeping through life, soaking deeper into work, friendship, family, citizenship, and the rest. Perhaps unlike other people, I take an interest in algorithms as material-semiotic figures of and in widely shared socio-technical imaginaries (Jasanoff, 2015), an interest that has led me to spend a good amount of time both studying them using software studies approaches, ethnography, and digital social methods, and, in fact, tinkering with them in a kind of disorganized mode of participant observation. Much of my work and life more generally has been mired in what the editors of this volume are calling an algorithmic regime.

I wonder whether all interest in algorithms stems from the deep unease occasioned by technical action, and specifically by what Bruno Latour

Jarke, J., B. Prietl, S. Egbert, Y. Boeva, H. Heuer, and M. Arnold (eds.), *Algorithmic Regimes: Methods, Interactions, and Politics*. Amsterdam: Amsterdam University Press, 2024

DOI 10.5117/9789463728485_CH06

theorized as the detour associated with it (Latour, 2013). One framing of an unease concerning algorithmic forms of technical action has been perceptively articulated by Noortje Marres. Discussing "numerate infrastructures" in *Digital Sociology: The Reinvention of Social Research*, she writes: "social media platforms present social enquiry with an inherently *ambiguous* phenomenon" (Marres, 2017, 129). "Numerate infrastructures" are largely algorithmic. According to Marres' account of these infrastructures, social researchers cannot know in advance whether they are researching something that happens because of algorithms or in spite of them. Did the algorithm create the trend or communicate it? The methodological ambiguity holds beyond social media platforms. Is it the algorithm that we study or what happens through the algorithm?

The chapters in this section of the book approach algorithmic action on different levels. They range between systematic work on computer code and its crafting in scientific research (Gramelsberger, Wenz & Kasprowicz) through to public installations for civic engagements with algorithms (Eslami & Heuer). They move between methods based on talking with people about algorithms (Storms & Alvarado) to ways of understanding how algorithms are framed as things that can be talked about (Jarke & Heuer). Each of the chapters follows a conceptual concern through algorithmic regime: black boxing, transparency, awareness, and algorithmic concretizations of scientific models. Methods appearing in the chapters include interviews, diaries, focus groups, code analysis, software development, and drawing.

Affected by the core ambiguity Marres identifies, I am curious as to whether in following the paths of methodological discussion in the chapters here, the ambiguity is resolved or intensified. Versions of the problems of transparency, awareness, black boxing, and epistemic operations discussed in these chapters certainly relate to this problem. And the ambiguity has long been active in my own trajectory through algorithms, a trajectory that begins with work on Alan Turing's "On Computable Numbers" (Mackenzie, 1996) and runs through software development practices, wireless network infrastructures, genomic science, data science, machine learning, health biosensing, and contemporary image collections and their processing.

Layering of Regimes

In each chapter, the centrality of computation to social order is presented in the light of its regime-defining qualities: certain forms of acceleration, redistribution of epistemic, organizational, economic, and governmental power, and threats to the accountability of government, media, or industry appear there. The ambiguity identified by Marres has its roots in an important modal shift in algorithmic operations over the last few decades. The classic algorithms of computer science include sorting techniques such as bubble sort or sort and searching techniques for strings, graphs, databases and the like, as documented in computer scientist Donald Knuth's *The Art of Computer Programming* (1968–2022). Many such techniques took hold in computer science and software development as they engaged with problems of computational time and space from many different angles, ranging from how disk or memory storage could be used efficiently to reducing the time it takes to draw the graphic elements of a user interface. Indeed, the formal analysis of algorithms, algorithmic complexity theory, is largely focused on estimating how long an algorithm will take to run. The question of how much memory or how long a program would take to run animated much of computer science in the mid- to late 20th century. At the same time, the constant accumulation and refining of these optimized operations has woven the everyday comportments and the layered material orderings of the information age. The orderings of actions in lists, menus, forms, buttons, and other interface elements that frame experiences of interactivity, for instance, depend on a pile of algorithms.

The operational interest in the optimization of computing time has not exactly disappeared from contemporary algorithms. It has been mostly eclipsed by different sets of concerns largely focused on knowledge. As Jarke and Heuer make clear in their chapter, most social research, including these methodology chapters, centres for good reason on versions of machine learning. The algorithms of machine learning are in some ways no different to the classic problem-solving algorithms of the mid-20th century. But the regime has changed in key respects. Unlike the logistic orderings of the classic algorithms, the function of machine learning algorithms is tied up with selected forms of knowing such as prediction, pattern recognition, and classification. It is also increasingly connected to the synthesis of forms of communicative and cultural experience. For instance, if the elevator algorithm in its classical form controlled elevators by always moving in the same direction until all requests were complete, a predictive elevator algorithm would take into account the time of day, past records of movements between floors, and possibly levels of access controlled by key card to move in a more complicated way up and down the building. If classical algorithms were concerned with efficiency and economy of computation (e.g., moving the lift most efficiently up and down), the machine learning algorithms are concerned with states of affairs in the world (e.g., balancing peak demand at certain times of day with short waiting times for some people).

It really does not help here that many of the actual machine learning algorithms have no obvious practical function. I happen to know a bit about the stochastic gradient descent algorithm, for instance, because of my own investments in knowing about certain forms of technical action. This algorithm is central to many machine learning techniques, and especially important in deep learning. But given that I don't work with it all the time, and I'm not a computer or data scientist, I have to pause and think about the conditions under which this algorithm can work to generate classifications and predictions. More importantly, it is not easy to describe the problem that it addresses. The first line of the Wikipedia entry says "optimizing an objective function with suitable smoothness properties (e.g., differentiable)" (Wikipedia, 2022), which hardly helps.

Regime-Changing Practice: Code and Closures

If we envisage the span of practices active in algorithmic regimes, are there practices specific to the regime, and if so, how should social research approach them? Coding is a likely candidate: contemporary algorithms involve software, its development and operation. Gramelsberger and co-authors address the coding practices that lie at the heart of work in algorithmic regimes. Their case study of code for detecting distant galaxies might appear to lie a long way from everyday life of social media or civil society. It may seem that the programming practices of astrophysicists in a French research lab working on the classification of signals from astronomical instruments have little to offer by way of insight in relation to the crowded, hubbub of coders and developers pouring in and out of Silicon Valley, Shanghai, or Cape Town, checking in and checking code on platforms such as GitHub and GitLab. Yet in both places, the same kinds of algorithms for detecting and classifying parts of images can be found. Hence, Gramelsberger et al.'s interest in how to study shifts in the balance of power between experiment and simulation, between theoretical and statistical model, or between time on the instrument and time with the data, is actually highly relevant. The rise of scientific programming, traceable through studies of scientific software development, follows some of the same paths of transformation as the shift from classic logistic algorithms to epistemic predictive algorithms. The fact that astrophysicists have readily found employment in industry research labs working on machine learning is not an accident.

There is much to be learned about how algorithms intersect with existing knowledge practices from code studies: "As translation processes never copy a model but render it in a different way, we ask with the help of our tools for the reconfiguration of scientific concepts and computational statements in the diverse layers of code" (Grammelsberger et al., in this volume).

A second defining practice of algorithmic regimes is detected by Jarke and Heuer. They start from a different practice: ways of talking about algorithmic regimes found in public and academic discussions. Jarke and Heuer work with the central figure of the black box and its problematic opacity. The opacity of algorithms attracts much commentary, and sometimes works to intensify the economic-technical prestige of certain platforms. Rather than treating black boxes as if they exist and must be opened to do social good, their chapter approaches black boxes with heightened sensitivity to both their making and their opening. They shift attention from tightly riveted reinforced strongboxes to folded, provisionally closed cardboard boxes. They write, "Ultimately, reconstructing the ways in which different social actors perceive a technology as a black box tells us much about their own position and the ways in which they make sense of the world." They also say, "This is important for our endeavour to understand algorithmic regimes and the ways in which algorithmic systems refigure knowledge production and circulation" (Jarke & Heuer, in this volume).

In a first step, for instance, they suggest that the very framing of algorithms as a matter of interest relies on the boxes and enclosures that separate algorithms from the preparation of data, or the running of an algorithm from the training of statistical machine learning models. Drawing on science and technology studies (STS), they track some of the foldings that make boxes and leave them open to further folds. The methodological implication here is that—folding in—accompanies every attempt to enclose and purify the operational agency of algorithms. Unboxing an algorithmic regime is more like working out how a sheet of cardboard was creased to form the sides, top, and bottom of a parcel. Effectively, the method they propose is organic to the algorithmic regime. If the operation of the regime requires and relies on black boxing, then a social research method that concerns itself with that black boxing has a chance of negotiating its twists and turns, its folding back and forth on itself.

Sensitizing, Transparency, and Tracing

Like machine learning itself, the mode of knowing algorithms matters. Methods, as John Law and John Urry argue (Law & Urry, 2004), span the

happening of the social and knowledge of the social. Methods make forms
of social life:

> [S]ocial inquiry and its methods are productive: they [help to] make
> social realities and social worlds. They do not simply describe the world
> as it is, but also enact it.... [I]f social investigation makes worlds, then it
> can, in some measure, think about the worlds it wants to help to make.

Law and Urry go on to suggest that many of the standard methods found
in sociology tend to reproduce the nation state forms of social order. The
relevance of social research, its potential to alleviate or better algorithmic
regimes, depends on thinking about the worlds it helps to make.

How do particular methods include not only participants such as citizens,
workers, patients, or users, but the social researchers themselves? Given the
entanglement of social methods with the making of the social, a question
for social researchers in any setting is how they participate. They will also
be citizens, consumers, patients, users, clients, students, or family members.
But their practices of knowing, and the ways they speak about them, their
methodology, are primary enactments of their participation. It is increasingly
common for social researchers to find themselves attached to institutional
forms of algorithmic ordering through participation in interdisciplinary
teams and collaborations, especially in the many research flagship projects
that have run during the last decade around the topic first of "big data"
and now "AI." Researchers participate in algorithmic regimes through the
organizational life of their knowing, as well as in their mundane use of
algorithmic search engines and social media for research.

In their two chapters, Eslami and Heuer, and Storms and Alvarado approach algorithmic regimes from the question of participation not through
coding or talking about machine learners, but via people encountering
algorithmic predictions, recommendations, rankings, and the like in everyday life at home, work, education, or in public. Both chapters concern
methods for intervening in people's experience of the algorithmic regime
by engendering awareness of what happens through the algorithms. In that
respect, they are both concerned with remaking the social. Both have a
concern to use social research methods to allow inhabitants of algorithmic
regime to live differently. Storms and Alvarado concentrate on methods of
sensitizing people to what is already happening all around them. Eslami
and Heuer focus on methods of rendering algorithmic action transparent
so that it can be seen, described, questioned, or contested. The two chapters
could be seen as complementary. If Storms and Alvarado seek to modify

the participants' relation to algorithms, Eslami and Heuer aim to modify the algorithmic system's relation to its direct and indirect users.

Eslami and Heuer's efforts focus on the value of transparency in public sector settings. In such settings, the transparency value has resonances that encompass the procedural ideal of accountability of political actors and states to their citizens and the social-technical-scientific ideal of showing how complicated things work in order to foster analysis of flaws and possible improvements. In algorithmic regimes, where governance is often social-technical, the different senses of transparency coalesce. Eslami and Heuer ask, therefore, the vital question: Transparency for whom?

> An important question in this context is who transparency and awareness are for…. [T]he awareness of algorithmic systems and explanations of how the systems work require human action and, in most cases, both a high level of knowledge about technology and domain expertise. This means that a lot of effort is required to effectively use any transparency intervention in the interface. (Eslami & Heuer, in this volume)

Explanations of how systems work not only rely on expert knowledge but suggest that the making of the algorithms is finished work, and only subject to retrospective review. Transparency is a polyvalent discursive figure. In some respects, algorithmic regime could be said to bring new forms of transparency into existence since they detect patterns in data that would have been difficult or impossible to identify in other epistemic regimes. Their ambitions to render propensities, behaviours, habits, or individual attributes legible and actionable on platforms makes possible new levels of predictive surveillance. The question of when transparency is not desirable, or of the effects of regimes of transparency in generating new forms of marginalization and bias, should be noted. The many data breaches associated with social media and ecommerce platforms in the last decade suggest that accidental transparency.

The idea that transparency is situational, or specific to who or what is affected, is key to crafting effective methods for research in algorithmic regimes. In an algorithmic regime, it is to be expected that many things will work without full transparency. They will become infrastructural most of the time, like the lifts in our apartments or office buildings. Only where social life breaks down or social order is difficult to negotiate will the transparency of the algorithm matter. Many ethnomethodological studies have shown that that achievement of everyday or normal life depends on constant breakdown and repair. Although much of this repair does not require full transparency of the relevant social system, it does entail awareness of what is happening in that situation. If an elevator doesn't arrive quickly, people make decisions about whether to wait or take the stairs without needing to become aware of the elevator dispatch algorithm that controls whether the elevators goes up or down.

The fact that people are situated differently in algorithmic regime also lies at the core of the discussion of sensitizing methods in Storms and Alvarado's chapter. Their practice of sensitizing has elements of diary methods as well as citizen's panel techniques. Some versions of sensitizing focuses on participants' awareness through individual self-observation. Other versions might be organized around group or collective participation.

> We used the concept "sensitizing activities" to refer to exercises or questions that subtly guide the attention of participants so that they can more easily reflect on their experiences with algorithmic systems. We do not claim, however, that such sensitizing activities are the single definitive answer to these methodological challenges. (Storms & Alavado, in this volume)

As the authors put it, the methodological challenge of getting people to reflect on their experience has no "single definitive answer." Experience of algorithmic systems is itself not single or definitive. It is inherently multiple. This is because the various algorithms have specific qualities and are interwoven in the fabric of media-technical-organizational niches and habits. The algorithms themselves vary widely in how they work. More than the sorting and search algorithms often discussed in introductory computer science textbooks, machine learning algorithms, ranging from relatively simple clustering and classification techniques (such as k-means clustering or the k-nearest neighbours algorithm) through to the convolutional, recursive, and adversarial neural network generative algorithms producing novel sounds and images, have many moving parts, and many different ways of traversing data. It is possible to become sensitive to the differences between algorithmic processes. Artists working with deep learning systems (such as CLIP or DALL-E) to generate images report increasing awareness of what configuration of the system produced a certain image.

A second issue, the location of the algorithms within operational ensembles such as platforms, apps, and websites, poses many methodological dilemmas. A single element of an app, say the Explore screen on Instagram, can be the end point of a convoluted pipeline of data gathering, transformation, and algorithmic processing. The predictions used on that page might come from a different pipeline than the predictions that order posts in a timeline. They generate opacity by virtue of their superimposed layering. It is not even clear that engineers and developers have a clear sense of how many different algorithmic systems interact with each other in the platform flow of data and messages. They encounter difficulties in regulating the dynamics of the platform algorithmic regime. These considerations pose some significant design challenges for social research. When we explore an algorithmic regime, how specific should the research become? The authors suggest:

> For our purposes, *sensitizing* is not focused on theoretical concepts used by researchers (as used by Blumer). Instead, we focus on the participants who are sensitized and who become receptive to algorithmic regimes and their specific qualities via hands-on activities. Sensitizing activities are small tasks and exercises that participants carry out in preparation for research activities and involve them in further reflection on their experiences and perceptions of algorithmic regimes. (Storms & Alavado, in this volume)

Sensitizing is understood here as a change in awareness. It is a new experience, or a transformation of an existing experience. Sensitizing is such an interesting term in this respect, with its historical links to chemicals such as silver nitrate used to treat photographic paper so that it responds to light, its biomedical meanings of the effects of allergens such as cat hair on the development of a child's immune system, or the physiological responsiveness of an organ or tissue to drugs or hormones (Oxford English Dictionary, 2022). These figures for a change in receptivity or responsiveness suggest that experience is a complex substrate, and one whose material-corporeal intricacies cannot be understood solely in terms of the familiar tropes of depth, interiority, or intentionality let alone cognition or consciousness. Sensitizing and the consequent sensitivity transforms experience so that it reacts more to and with the algorithmic regime.

Finally, the question of researchers' own sensitization to algorithms looms large here. Does research in algorithmic regimes presuppose sensitizing of social researchers themselves to various aspects of algorithms, including their black boxing, their coding/development, their situated transparencies, and their different accountabilities? By what route do social researchers become sensitive to algorithms? If, like any other citizen/consumer/user/client/player/patient/worker/inmate of the regime, they need to be sensitized in order to effectively engage with them, how do they do that? And if they sensitize, how does that change them?

Conclusion

To live in an algorithmic regime could mean subjection to an authoritarian form of power, it could be a period of time, or a regulated way of doing things. "Regime" has divergent meanings. Regimes range from forms of government to ways of creating health and well-being. Some regimes are state forms of power, particularly authoritarian ones: Putin's Russia. Others relate to periods of time in which a particular government form of held sway; the *ancien régime*. Some regimes are ways of doing things, especially in relation to diet, medical treatment, training, and exercise: "a tough fitness regime." Other relate to coordinated government action: the "global climate regime" or the UN Framework Convention on Climate Change, which most people would not consider a bad thing. In physics, dynamic systems exhibit regimes of behaviour: a chaotic regime, for instance, or a turbulent regime.

The interests of social researchers tend towards the relations and the processes that generate experiences of agency, freedom, connection to others, and the possibilities of collective life. Perhaps they are not concerned with the social life on a grand scale, but with some niche—reproductive kinship, queer gaming, personal finance apps, moral outrage online, urban biodiversity and non-human care, the production of online news, new age spirituality and Instagram influencers, etc. In any of these settings, there will be traces of algorithmic operation, sometimes working in the background, sometimes in the forefront of the research.

Does living in an algorithmic regime produce methodological ambivalence? It is a given in STS that techniques, or what are sometimes misleadingly named technical objects such as platforms or devices, move us in strange or twisted ways (Latour, 2013). The detour, the zigzag, and the labyrinth define technical action in general. So, it is not surprising that algorithms will involve twists and turns. Approaching them, there will be corners around which we cannot see except by turning them. The project of knowing algorithms and their dependencies involves finding ways of following detours or paths around corners and ways of opening doors.

It is a strange time to be a social researcher. The methods on which social sciences have stood during the last century—interview, ethnography, focus group discussion, surveys, document analysis—seem to be overtaken by algorithmic methods of knowing based on relentless testing and refinement of predictions. What it is like to be a social science or humanities researcher living in a regime where algorithms are constantly tested in industrial scale machine learning competitions, with the aim of going beyond the peaks of human performance in cognition, understanding, game playing, recognition, logic, the creation of music or art, and language?

References

Jasanoff, S. (Ed.). (2015). *Dreamscapes of modernity*. University of Chicago Press. https://ebookcentral-proquest-com.virtual.anu.edu.au/lib/anu/detail. action?docID=2130453

Knuth, D. E. (1968–2022). *The art of computer programming* (5 vols.). Addison-Wesley.

Latour, B. (2013). *An inquiry into modes of existence*. Harvard University Press.

Law, J., & Urry, J. (2004). Enacting the social. *Economy and Society, 33*(3), 390–410. https://doi.org/10.1080/0308514042000225716

Mackenzie, A. (1996). Undecidability: The history and time of the universal Turing machine. *Configurations, 4*(3), 359–379.

Marres, N. (2017). *Digital sociology: The reinvention of social research*. Polity.

Oxford English Dictionary. (2022). Sensitize, V. In *OED Online*. Oxford University Press. https://www.oed.com/view/Entry/175996

Wikipedia. (2022). Stochastic gradient descent. In *Wikipedia*. https://en.wikipedia. org/w/index.php?title=Stochastic_gradient_descent&oldid=1110420173

About the Author

Adrian Mackenzie is Professor in the School of Sociology, Australian National University. He works at the intersection of science and technology studies (STS) and media/cultural studies, with a focus on methods, theories, and engagements with algorithms, software, infrastructures, and experience.

II.

INTERACTIONS

7. Buildings in the Algorithmic Regime: Infrastructuring Processes in Computational Design

Yana Boeva and Cordula Kropp

Abstract

Algorithms and their socio-technical environments have entered many aspects of life, including the production of architecture and the built environment. One approach that corresponds to this algorithmic regime is computational design, an umbrella term for combining various digital and computational methods, software and technologies, typically based on data and algorithms. As relational and hybrid arrangements, the algorithmic infrastructures of computational design are subjected to a continuous process of infrastructuring, that is, care and cure coming from social, political, and technological actions. This chapter examines such infrastructuring processes in architecture and construction that have begun to set up a specific form of optimizing design and the built environment according to the calculative rationalities of the algorithmic regime.

Keywords: architecture; infrastructure; software; design technologies; work; built environment

I know the intention is that in 10 years or 20, there will be only 10 per cent of the buildings designed by architects—the special ones. And the rest will be just generated [by software]. Yes, I know, it's just an evil vision.
—Computational designer

Jarke, J., B. Prietl, S. Egbert, Y. Boeva, H. Heuer, and M. Arnold (eds.), *Algorithmic Regimes: Methods, Interactions, and Politics*. Amsterdam: Amsterdam University Press, 2024
DOI 10.5117/9789463728485_CH07

Introduction

Architects, engineers, and the construction sector have been implementing various digital technologies over the last four decades, in the meanwhile resulting in infrastructures of design and construction. Recently, algorithms and their socio-technical environments have entered many physical and material aspects of life, including the production of architecture, construction, and the built environment, thereby giving rise to a new algorithmic regime. One approach that corresponds to this algorithmic regime is computational design, an umbrella term for the combination of various digital and computational methods, software, and technologies, typically based on data, code, algorithms, and artificial intelligence (AI), deployed for calculating geometry, form, simulations, structural performance, or the optimization of building designs. In their multiplicity, algorithms and data have informed the design of many famous iconic buildings through the production of unique software scripts. At the same time, user-generated data derived from algorithms in our personal information and communication technologies is fed into proposals for (future) urban development generated with automated design tools (Kropp et al., 2022). These algorithmic infrastructures, created across different practices and different layers, are not only reconfiguring today's planning practices and standards but also tomorrow's built results.

Algorithmic infrastructures are based on code, data, and software and bear the typical invisibility, heterogeneity, and long-term standard-setting characteristics of infrastructure. At the same time, as relational and hybrid arrangements, they are also subjected to a continuous process of infrastructuring, that is, care and cure coming from social, political, and technological actions. Infrastructuring as a process means contested arrangements and actors struggling for their interests in the implementation of emerging technologies. Research on infrastructures as socio-technical systems has demonstrated their powerful regime effects and social implications (Edwards, 2003; Gillespie, 2014; Introna, 2016; Star, 1999). A central problem of infrastructuring is that its heterogeneity and multiplicity eventually result in an opaque state. In this chapter, we examine such processes in architecture and construction, where infrastructuring processes have begun to manifest and set up a specific form of optimizing design and the built environment according to the calculative rationalities of algorithms. Looking at the corresponding infrastructuring processes in digital and computational design reveals the myriad socio-technical interactions that lead to this distinct algorithmic regime.

Algorithms and data are rarely standalone instances, disconnected from software interfaces and the actors interacting with them (Burke, 2019; Goffey, 2008; Seaver, 2019; Vertesi, 2014). Indeed, "algorithms never exist independently of their use" (Dahlman et al., 2021, p. 3). However, algorithms might be difficult to locate in modern software (Burke, 2019) as software creates "an invisible system of visibility" through the user interface (Chun, 2004, p. 28). Moreover, the idealized textbook algorithm actually appears as many fragments of code dispersed within a larger application (Dourish, 2016). As we will demonstrate, algorithms in computational design take many forms that are often "occluded" (Burke, 2019). As assemblages with design software, algorithms provide bounded manipulation options for many designers who may not be aware of their presence when interacting with them, thus revealing an infrastructural character (on sensitizing methods for making algorithm-aware, see Storms & Alvarado, in this volume). A newer generation of AI-enabled design automation software submerges algorithms deeper into the tools and practices of design production. Interaction with them via dashboard-like interfaces is beginning to shift the production of buildings towards the interests of other stakeholders, such as urban planners, investors, and real estate developers, stressing how the algorithmic regime and its "actuarial logics" begin to reduce built environment to numbers that can be crunched (Burrell & Fourcade, 2021; Kitchin, 2014; Powell, 2021).

We argue that the infrastructuring of computational design impels such an algorithmic regime, which reconfigures practices and decision-making with increasing inscrutability, and reorganizes design work and how buildings are conceived. Introducing new digital and computational technologies to design and architecture has consistently been accompanied by conflicts and shifts in how valid knowledge is produced or who will control the design process (Loukissas, 2012; Neff et al., 2010). The algorithmic regime of computational design calls up such tensions, particularly in moments of heterogeneous infrastructuring through interactions with "algorithmic systems" (Seaver, 2019) and the wider socio-technical assemblages. The chapter spotlights how decisions are made in these hybrid assemblages of algorithms, data, software, technology, standards, and, across organizations, work practices and human actors. Their sovereign application, as we illustrate, requires not only technical skills but an understanding of how a technology-related reconfiguration involves sociocultural, regulatory, and economic aspects (see Jarke & Heuer, in this volume). The chapter draws upon an empirical study of digital architecture and computational design, the practices, skills, and knowledge requirements, and their material manifestations in technologies. It combines interviews with computational designers (architects and engineers) and software developers, field observations from coding classes for architecture students and design studio reviews, a document analysis of promotional material by software providers, webinars, and academic literature on coding skills and training methods in computational design.

In what follows, we first provide context by introducing computational design and how it differs from "mainstream" design practice, then set out the theoretical grounds of infrastructuring. We then illustrate three heterogeneous but interconnected infrastructuring processes of computational design identified in our study. We conclude by reflecting on what the infrastructuring of computational design conveys about architectural practices' present and future conditions and our built environment as the algorithmic regime takes hold.

Computational Design: Buildings Created with Code and Algorithms

Architecture still evokes dreamy images of architects sketching their initial ideas on paper, drafting blueprints, and building physical models. While some of this continues to be practised by contemporary architects, the tools, methods, and practices have not only expanded but they have been reconfigured with the computer and, more recently, on the level of algorithms. As ethnographic research of architectural offices has shown, analogue-based practices continue to exist alongside their digital counterparts, as each allows different forms of exploration and expression (Yaneva, 2009; Yarrow, 2019). Architecture and its adjacent areas of engineering and construction have a long history of using digital technologies, widely associated with computer-aided design (CAD) software packages and the ways these translate the drafting table and drawing conventions into the user interface on the screen (Cardoso Llach, 2015; Gardner, 2018). For instance, instead of drawing a floor plan by hand, a few mouse clicks and using a standardized layout template included in the software can give a faster start to the design of a building. Working with CAD software as the presiding mode of design production is not limited to that aspect only. More recent extensions such as building information modelling (BIM) and parametric modelling have introduced semantics and managerial aspects such as costs, budgets, building materials, logistics, and their relations within 3D models and design software. A detailed account of architectural technologies as well as their differences is beyond the scope of this chapter. However, what is relevant to mention is how these advanced technologies in architectural practice have been and are persistently debated along the tension of creativity and control, foregrounding the infrastructuring processes in the background, as can also be observed with computational design (Cardoso Llach, 2015; Loukissas, 2012).

Computational design approaches in their present forms have been around since the 1990s, though envisioned and experimented with for much longer (Cogdell, 2018; Steenson, 2017). They include a wide range of data-based, algorithmic techniques and software technologies mainly applied to generate and "calculate" design solutions with complex geometries and form, simulate performance and environmental criteria, explore, optimize, and evaluate them, or their combination all at once (Aish & Bredella, 2017; Wortmann & Tunçer, 2017). In a computational designer's words (see Figure 7.1),

> we have it all in here [computational design program]. For example, like, we do this roof, and then I can segment that into elements, and then I get the curves. And in the same program, I have the simulation of the robots and how they fabricate, and I can generate the data for the CNC [computer numerically control] milling through the same program.

Computational design is envisioned by architects as a "categorically different approach to the design, delivery and production of architecture" (Gardner, 2019, p. 109). A substantial difference to mainstream digital design comes from the opportunities of including computer coding and algorithms in design practice that allow one "to escape the strictures inherent in any [design] software" (Burry, 2011, p. 9). Conventional design software already includes some algorithms, mainly in the form of specific software functions, for instance, for automating repetitive portions of design work such as drawing lines, identical floor plans, walls, or other recurring elements. However, as Matthew Fuller notes, proficiency in software generally entails "a more inventive engagement with software's particular qualities and propensities" (2008, p. 3). It is also necessary for writing much needed scripts for application programming interfaces (APIs) to third-party software (ibid.).

Coding in design and architecture, which means using programming languages, takes two forms: a textual one, often being the all-rounder Python, and a visual one in the form of Grasshopper, running within the Rhinoceros 3D design application (typically abbreviated as Rhino). Grasshopper is used for creating algorithms as partially reusable components that can help specify and explore visually different technical design parameters and their relations in so-called nodes. As one computational designer explained, "that's the key to the parametric model; it's not about the physical thing

Figure 7.1. Simulation of the motion planning of a robotic arm in the computational design
software environment Grasshopper/Rhino. Photo: Yana Boeva.

you produce, but it's about the relationships between it all." For example,
this so-called parametric modelling can be applied to the architecture
and fabrication of components, structural engineering, lighting, or wind
performance of a design, or to simulate the energy consumption of a building
(see Figure 7.2). The Grasshopper/Rhino environment is said to provide "an
intuitive way to explore designs without having to learn to script" (Day,
2009). Coding and algorithms are also portrayed as empowering architects
and engineers to engage in the independent production of their own design
tools instead of being just software users (Peters, 2013).

The efforts around the generation of data-based, algorithmic design
options and their assessment mainly oscillate between automating and
assisting designers' actions (Bernal et al., 2015). For instance, the adoption of
machine learning (ML) algorithms in Grasshopper/Rhino can assist designers
by integrating and calculating massive amounts of building data to handle
heterogeneous complexities, ascribed to the matter that each building
design needs to fulfil human and more-than-human requirements (Boeva
et al., 2022). On the other hand, recent ML/AI-enabled, cloud-based design
applications automate the generation of design options, and perhaps with
that, the designers out, by using large amounts of building data derived from
multiple (public) sources such as urban planning, 3D models, or regulatory
data. As our analysis will illustrate, the boundary between automation and
assistance is never clearly demarcated due to the hybrid arrangements
of algorithms, software, human decisions, and interests at play and the
infrastructuring processes that this new algorithmic regime instigates.

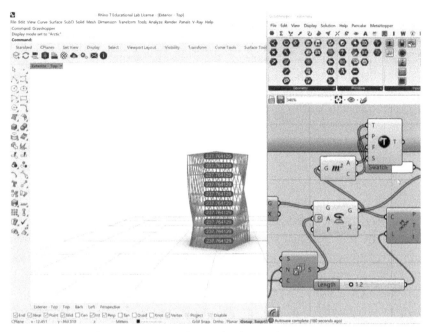

Figure 7.2. An exemplary parametric model created with a Grasshopper script in Rhino showing the algorithmic blocks and nodes. Source: Interviewed computational designer, permission to reproduce image granted.

From Infrastructure to Infrastructuring Digital Technologies

Scholarship in science and technology studies (STS) and studies on computer-supported cooperative work have emphasized that infrastructures are rarely fully stabilized due to their relational and ecological characteristics (Karasti & Blomberg, 2018; Niewöhner, 2015; Vertesi, 2014). Digital information technologies are intentionally left incomplete in a state of being-in-the-making that allows for further extensions, connections, and repurposing, but also to strengthen the dependence upon and control over them (Edwards, 2003). Information infrastructures are temporary and multiple as technologies often get translated from one context to another, modified, expanded, and blended into existing structures, routines, and organizations (Niewöhner, 2015). Researchers of information technologies Helena Karasti and Jeanette Blomberg refer to these "ongoing and continual processes of creating and enacting information infrastructures" as infrastructuring (2018, p. 234). Infrastructuring draws attention to the more processual qualities and helps to understand "the social and ethical implications of choices that are often made as technical choices in the here and now but that have significant consequences far beyond the present" (Niewöhner, 2015, p. 8). These are "complex, spatially and temporarily extended phenomena that simply cannot be studied 'as wholes'" (Karasti & Blomberg, 2018, p. 234), not the least due to their heterogeneity and simultaneity. As Susan Leigh Star and Karen Ruhleder have argued, infrastructures are relational and become ones "for people in practice, connected to activities and structures" (1996, p. 379). The quality of information infrastructures as emerging and transforming in extended processes means that "they never fully exist in an absolute sense" (Karasti & Blomberg, 2018, p. 239) but for specific purposes and needs of a community of practice.

For our analysis of advanced technologies in architectural practice, we focus on two intersecting characteristics of infrastructuring processes. The first one relates to how knowledge defines not only the awareness of infrastructures regarding their implementation and use but also how to adequately adapt them. "Belonging to a given culture means, in part, having fluency in its infrastructures. This is almost like having fluency in a language: a pragmatic knowing-how, rather than an intellectual knowing-that," remarks Paul N. Edwards (2003, p. 189). In surfacing the invisible work behind computational design, we noted that putting algorithms to work in architecture and design requires fluency in the community's information infrastructures, which means grafting onto existing ones and understanding their relevance and limitations simultaneously (Star & Ruhleder, 1996). The second aspect, closely intertwined with knowledge and community membership, refers to the further development and per-formativity of infrastructures over time and scale and the implications on epistemic practices and work relations. Infrastructures are often designed with a centre in mind, where they disappear as the community of practice behind their creation shares a common understanding of how they should be deployed. However, in the periphery, where infrastructures are to be implemented at large, there are struggles and ruptures. The imagination from the centre may not match with the periphery, and shifting arrange-ments begin to pervade the hybrid human–algorithm design processes and practices. In our case, we observed that a relatively small "coding elite" (Burrell & Fourcade, 2021) consisting of some architects, engineers, and software developers fluently manoeuvres the emerging algorithmic regime of computational design by putting coding and algorithms to use. However, they find themselves having to adapt their technological creations according to other forces such as design software preferences of project collaborators, developed routines in practice, high investment costs for retraining and technology, or legally binding regulations. The fit between plan, infrastructure, and social practices needs permanent reproduction in situated actions (Suchman, 2007).

Therefore, the ongoing infrastructuring of computational design as an emerging algorithmic regime simultaneously informs social practices—how architects design with code, algorithms, and software as well as apprehend them—as it designs technical artefacts, that is, the algorithmic technologies in use. As we illustrate below, this produces both consequences for architects' work and opportunities for analysis. In the following, we present three heterogeneous but intersecting infrastructuring processes behind computational design identified in our empirical study. Through different interactions with algorithms, coding practices, and design software, we reveal how multiple digital infrastructures are being adapted by different actors and how that informs building design. The first infrastructuring process introduces the distinctive practice of visual coding in architecture, used for producing small algorithmic scripts and tailored software solutions for particular design requirements. The implementation of these specific scripts and tools is repeatedly formed by the current actuality of the building sector with its different organizations, actors, practices, and technology preferences. This means that actors need to "muddle through" software technologies as the second infrastructuring process at play. The algorithmic possibilities to capture and connect data through various software interfaces make automation an aspiring goal not only for computational designers but other software producers and the users of their products. The third infrastructuring process through design automation then reveals how the emerging algorithmic regime in computational design begins to amplify an optimization of the built environment according to techno-economic rationalities.

"Little Algorithms": Visual Scripting as Infrastructural Practice

Grasshopper, embedded in the Rhino design software, is the most used design optimization tool, as surveys among architects and building engineers reveal (Gardner, 2018, 2019; Wortmann et al., 2022). Many of the interviewed designers confirm that Grasshopper creates distinct coding practices to extend across hybrid systems of software and technologies due to its visual form. The visual representation enables more intuitive interaction with the elements and provides immediate feedback to one's design, which seems closer to the visually based design thinking of architects than textual-based programming languages. A typical algorithmic design interaction in Grasshopper may look like this detailed example provided by a computational designer (the description refers to Figure 7.2):

> If you look at this, what it's really all about is *how you manipulate data through the process.* So, I have a point in space here, and then I want to have it in these particular three boxes here. What I'm doing is [defining] points in space, and I want to sort them along the X, Y, and Z [axes], and then remove one [of them]. Imagine this as the ground floor [of a building] and then level one. These points here are where the column is in space. So, I've set the zero point, and then *what this component does, is it moves in objects.* And then at this point, I've then assigned a rectangle. And then in the *rectangle* [i.e., the algorithm], it *has a parameter of the dimensions,* so I've put in the dimensions. And then from that, I kind of *connect between the two* and now I've got my volumes.... Grasshopper works in kind of *little logics that you kind of stitch together.* And because they're all stitched together, if I change something here in this point, I will end up changing the end thing here.... It's kind of a *flow of information through these manipulations* of kind of *little algorithms.* (Emphasis added)

The practice of building "little algorithms" with Grasshopper is broadly referred to by actors as scripting. This practice of visual scripting facilitates quick iterations of design options of, for example, a specific element to open up the opportunities for decision-making in a team. As one computational designer explained, "When [the architects] would send hand sketches, I would ... integrate these ideas into the parametric model. And then we can move them around and try different options and things like this." Design options created with algorithms are also welcomed in building design competitions for their "wilder," "very own aesthetics," which expands the spectrum of traditionally derived designs, as another computational designer elaborated.

   This kind of scripting of a "little algorithm" with Grasshopper is also distinct from the conventions of software engineering. While underneath Grasshopper components are actually Python code, their enclosure in a visual interface ensures easier interaction in the absence of Python coding skills. Understanding an algorithm's actual semantics and syntax can become redundant, as the components already provide the pre-programmed functions in the form of the nodes, as the illustrative example above suggests. The interaction is bound to understanding how to connect the visual components to each other and what are the minimal parameters, input and output that need to be defined. The visual representation of algorithms as Grasshopper nodes, thus, means that these scripts can become "algorithmic black boxes." Computational design scholar Nadja Gaudillière-Jami observes that, "[o]ver the decades, from tailor-made algorithms to ready-made software solutions, the thickness of interfaces is increasing more and more, and the parameters on which an algorithmic model is based are not always easily accessible" (2020, p. 154). Designers do not need to understand how they are programmed as long as they can manipulate and control the visual user interface:

> You have each of these little [algorithmic] components, [of] which you have an input and you have an output, and then you of kind do some sort of manipulation of the data. And then through bundling all these little manipulations, you kind of get a bigger picture. (As shown in Figure 7.3)

On the other hand, creating algorithms through visual programming in the Grasshopper/Rhino environment has limitations compared to standard textual programming as it increases their inscrutability for others. "[I]t's really unclear what object is coming out of the [Grasshopper] component if it's not well documented and if it's well tested," remarks a software developer. Hence, Grasshopper components representing algorithms can quickly become opaque objects and difficult to debug for others. Asking a designer whether they develop these "little algorithms" themselves, they gave the following reply: "No, these are kind of pre-existing things.... It's pretty much open source, so you can do whatever you want with these components." In addition, interviewed designers and software developers point out that these Grasshopper-based algorithms are often developed for one-off projects with little flexibility and robustness unless actors know how to adjust and repurpose them. Documentation then matters as they get primarily distributed openly on online platforms so that other designers and engineers may use and test them.

The emerging algorithmic regime of computational design pushes architects to adopt such novel practices of designing that are distinctive from the still prevailing practice in CAD. As an infrastructuring process, the visual scripting with Grasshopper creates standards for temporary and relational infrastructures, "helpful for architects to understand how to design their own scripts and their own software" (software developer). This part of scripting allows the production of software plug-ins to interoperate with different software technologies already in use, a way of "muddling through" infrastructure, as we show in the next section.

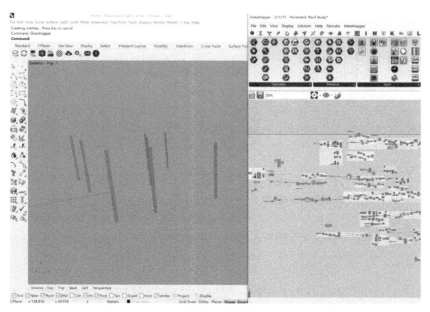

Figure 7.3. A sample Grasshopper script for column placing (3D model, left side) that shows the entirety of connected algorithms through nodes (right side). Source: Interviewed computational designer, permission to reproduce image granted.

Muddling through Software Infrastructures

The ability to transform algorithms into components, document and test them, and establish a robust data exchange workflow to digital libraries and databases requires advanced proficiency levels. Currently, a few architects have been successful in transferring their mostly academically obtained coding skills into professional practice. In contrast, the opportunity to acquire and employ these in office work appears far more challenging. Architectural practice is prone to intense workloads and delegating self-training requirements to after work hours reduces the number of people adopting advanced practices (Gardner, 2019). This, we posit, restricts the comprehensibility of the algorithmic regime of computational design. As a computational designer indicates:

> It is almost standard that there is at least someone in every team who knows a little bit about it [computational design]. They may have seen our tools in training or heard about them,... [but] that they can really use it themselves in a productive way, that's a very, very small proportion.

It results in a "muddling through" existing information technology infrastructures for those with computational design skills if they want to integrate them into existing practices and workflows. Janet Vertesi refers to that as "ad-hoc patchwork": "a sort of lay practice of heterogeneous engineering (Law, 1987) that produces fleeting alignment or misalignment of infrastructures to accomplish local, mundane tasks" (2014, p. 269). Architecture and construction work is abundant in temporal and relational routines. Scripting algorithms in the Grasshopper/Rhino environment such as plug-ins is regularly used to create seamless application programming interfaces (APIs) as part of an infrastructuring into existing "technical structures, routines of work, wide scale organizational and technical resources" (Niewöhner, 2015, p. 3). In particular, commercial design software is perceived by many interviewed experts as being restricted when it comes to complex requirements or problems:

> We model them [Grasshopper scripts] manually and they are somewhat parametric, and then we put them together manually, and then export it into CATIA [design software],... export that into some manufacturing or CAD/CAM plug-in that can produce some code, then translate that code into robot code. You could put together [a] stack of commonly used programs, but they are extremely tedious to work with. They are extremely big black boxes that have so much functionality, but not exactly the one that we want. (Computational designer)

These algorithmic scripts as software fragments are patched together with widespread design software programs used by most stakeholders involved in the building process. Repeatedly, our interviews make clear that the scripts not only intermediate between diverging IT systems to ensure the data flow and their communication but to reassure that an algorithmic regime in architecture and construction is viable. Another computational designer explained that their daily business at present mainly consists of creating APIs for commercial design software, which they do not use to work with but their clients do, or to enterprise resource planning (ERP) systems containing their clients' entire data.

As temporary infrastructures, algorithmic scripts seem plausible and achievable for a few computational designers. However, they may cause frictions among the majority of practitioners involved in the design and construction of a building. At the same time, they still allow for the mutual co-existence of different (including non-digital) practices of designing and building. However, AI, automation in software, and the convergence of design tools into cloud platforms pushed by large IT providers increasingly work towards reducing the need for such kind of algorithmic scripts that "muddle through" digital infrastructures (Boeva et al., 2023; Braun et al., 2022). As this specific infrastructuring process starts taking hold in architecture and construction, what counts as valid knowledge and how it is produced may considerably be challenged by the algorithmic regime behind that.

Design Automation

Imaginaries of automation are proliferating widely across sectors, processes, and human actors and are not missing out on architectural design practice. Different technological producers are pursuing the vision of design automation based on data and defined parameters, a reality with their so-called generative design applications. Exemplary tools and organizations are, among many other examples, the ML/AI-based Spacemaker by Autodesk, Delve by Sidewalk Labs/Alphabet/Google, or Hypar, a start-up by former Autodesk and WeWork employees. For some experts, the reasons behind (more) design automation are not only the technological possibilities, but rather the specific practice of coding and the high-stakes skill requirements that are difficult to obtain in day-to-day work, as this computational designer considers:

> When I started to work for BigArchFirm, that was 2011, everybody told me that in five years everybody will be able to use Grasshopper.... And, it's not the case.... [T]he wish for many people [is] to just have a software that would generate the building for you based on an Excel sheet.

The new tools and their producers, on the contrary, make algorithms and AI "seamless" infrastructures for their potential users. They are mostly advertised as an AI-based assistance to architects that handles rote tasks or complex computations requiring a large number of human resources and time (Leach, 2021). Design automation tools promise to deliver a large number of computationally derived design options according to set parameters and boundary conditions, such as the size of the building plot, the upper limit of the building height, the position of neighbouring buildings, environmental criteria such as sunlight and wind direction, and many more, from which designers, urban planners, investors, and real estate developers can choose (O'Hear, 2019).

Design automation presents a stepping up of the computational design practice of visual scripting with Grasshopper/Rhino. From an outsider's perspective, the process of creating many design options through visual scripting may seem instantaneous compared to modelling them by hand as some of the practices of the interviewed experts implied. In reality, building the script requires more time than the ML/AI algorithms incorporated into these novel design automation tools require to perform the operation. As a result, the process of "adjusting the script" gets delegated to ML/AI, capable of calculating not a few but millions of design options—eventually also implausible ones—in a fraction of a second or minute. The options generated with ML/AI algorithms promise not only to assist designers but to present the decision-makers mentioned above with seemingly reliable and "objective" data-based building designs. A precondition is that there is a clearly quantifiable design goal, as a computational designer remarked with regards to generative design tools. Otherwise, it could be impossible to calculate the results, as their example of an application suggests:

> And what they've [software company] done is that they simply incorporate such ready-made problem-solving things directly into Revit [design software], where I select the room or the floor space of the room and a few tables, for example. And this program then looks for good layout options depending on various factors.

While promising to empower designers' creativity and free them from tedious tasks and calculations, these tools are largely meant for real estate developers, investors, and urban planners to arrive quickly at a design that meets primarily economic objectives. These algorithmic tools are beginning to shift how building design is imagined and also justified. Hence, design automation virtually might make some designers and architects dispensable. According to Spacemaker's founders, the tool was envisioned with real estate developers as core users becoming instrumental in the future of the built environment: "It [Spacemaker] is a requirement from their clients" (Leach, 2021, p. 137). Despite promoting Spacemaker as empowering architects through AI, in their fleeting comments, Spacemaker's CEOs point out that in the future, architects using AI will replace those who don't (ibid., p. 141). This suggests that AI and design automation software are more likely to be used for generating cost-efficient and performance-based solutions rather than complex or socially attractive designs once real estate developers and clients start to consent to this algorithmic regime promising more revenue for less investment. Research on the governmental and industrial push to implement another set of digital design practices and technologies has demonstrated that client demand for the use of specific design technologies changes how buildings are conceived, by whom, and the individual results (Braun et al., 2022; Cardoso Llach, 2017).

The infrastructuring of design automation is not left solely in the hands of large software corporations and start-ups but can also become advantageous for all-in-one construction providers for the same reasons. As an architect working for a large timber construction company evidences,

> The planners get in shock, and they tell us, "Are you planning to get us out of the market?" Because there's a structural algorithm working behind them [generative design tools], and it's optimizing structural frames based on a real set of components [that] you can buy from us today.

Nonetheless, the impact of tech companies and their technologies is foreseeably expected to be more significant, as critical research on algorithmic technologies has demonstrated (Burrell & Fourcade, 2021; Sadowski, 2020). Moreover, design automation opens the inroads toward data extraction and accumulation of architecture and construction's "idle assets" (Langley & Leyshon, 2017). It reaffirms that the algorithmic regime of computational design has woken up the interests of domain outsiders such as large IT companies and software developers who want to train their ML and AI technologies with real data sets in the future. These infrastructuring processes, which disguise different kinds of algorithms as well as AI, are likely to have significant implications for architects and their professional future, the design practice, and sooner or later the kind of buildings we dwell in.

Design under the Algorithmic Regime: Discussion and Conclusion

A premise of this chapter has been that the infrastructuring processes of advanced architectural technologies and approaches set up an algorithmic regime for designing and producing our built environment. Attending to the technical, social, and ideological work in imagining, constructing, and maintaining digital infrastructures to which algorithms belong reveals "the 'when' of complete transparency," the moment an infrastructure emerges (Star & Ruhleder, 1996, p. 132). We adopted the perspective of infrastructuring to uncover the interactions of actors, communities, practices, and algorithmic technologies involved in making computational design a new standard on multiple scales (Edwards, 2003; on comparable analytical perspectives to uncover algorithmic regimes, see Jarke & Heuer and Storms

& Alvarado, in this volume). This perspective reveals how interactions configure and become configured by not one but many algorithmic regimes, as the authors of the introduction to this volume emphasize (Jarke et al.). In Dourish's words, "our experience of algorithms can change as infrastructure changes" (2016, p. 6). Similarly, the infrastructuring processes we presented shows how the algorithmic presence and its effects begin to vary as soon as computational design technologies and their related practices evolved around specific project requirements and practices as well as professional conventions. While we cannot foresee all the effects and changes, we can identify some observable ones from our analysis.

First, the algorithmic regime gives the impression that bringing computational design into action, especially regarding novel and spectacular forms, becomes possible with little effort. The practice of visual scripting with Grasshopper, based on plug-and-playing a few algorithmic design components distributed in online repositories, appears compelling to many designers, as shown in the above examples. Although visual scripting of "little algorithms" provides a solution to some limitations of design software for the smaller expert community of computational designers, it comes as an additional set of skills and knowledge practice distinct from the architectural design thinking and methods of most architects. Those as well as engineers and construction workers use various commercially available software products and have developed their user routines around them in day-to-day work. Changes to other programs become laborious and cost actors and organizations time for retraining and routine development that is rarely provided. At the same time, infrastructuring computational design through visual scripting and the effort to accommodate some of the challenges around skills development within the user interface can reinforce the inscrutability of algorithms and algorithmic systems. As shown, visual scripting demands translational and intermediary work between the algorithmic principles of computer science and those of designing a building. It remains to be seen whether the algorithmic principles of visual scripting will adapt to the ones of architecture and construction, thus enacting an algorithmic regime or the other way around. We hold that this will depend on the design parameters and criteria being optimized in the building process and who gets to set them and choose the design approach.

In addition, our analysis showed that computational design infrastructures used in professional architecture and construction work entail coping with multiple existing standards and solutions. As Star and Ruhleder rightfully have pointed out, "[t]hey begin to interweave themselves with elements of the formal infrastructure to create a unique and evolving hybrid"

(1996, p. 132). Computational designers create algorithmic scripts to enable a data flow and the interoperation of different digital infrastructures used by further actors involved in the design and construction process rather than set out how buildings are being designed. As a result, computational design equally integrates external expectations and intentions, thereby suggesting that its implementation cannot be realized independently of existing infrastructures, practices, and the driving forces behind them. That said, computational design is not the standard of practice yet. If it ever becomes one at all, we contend, it will not be set by the small community of computational design experts.

Finally, the infrastructuring processes in computational design reveal that the domain-internal actors and their attempts to reconfigure design production algorithmically are frequently confronted by influential players such as the tech industry and their ambitions for constituting an algorithmic regime. More so, in the case of larger construction companies, the interests and practices eventually ally with tech rationalities in how they employ the calculative possibilities of algorithm systems. In that case, more attention is needed to how the interstices of technological practices and organizational demands interact with the algorithmic regime of computational design. The selection of building data, their points of entry into and exit from the algorithmic assemblages, and the algorithmic control and evaluation could pivot decisions in building design exclusively around economic interests. Design automation tools, cloud-based services and their providers—"organizations that can deal with complexity and create stories form data" (Powell, 2021, p. 55)—give the means to this nascent algorithmic regime. More and more design tools may rely on ML and AI as "rendering devices" (Egbert, in this volume) to calculate design options and make predictions based on data fed into them. Design software companies such as Autodesk have been investing in research on deep learning algorithms that mine previous building designs, which then gets included in the generative design tools described earlier. Buildings created based on data from previous designs may reproduce the known and stereotyped, not questioning failures and problems, thereby also perpetuating "the algorithmic regime."

The implementation of commercially driven technologies foregrounds that design choices follow values and parameters inscribed in them through older data and categories that algorithms capture and reproduce. This may prove to lead once again to marginalizing what deviates from the standard and established, that is, diversity, sustainability, and justice (Bowker & Star, 1999; Kitchin, 2014; Noble, 2018). Research on algorithms used in credit scoring (Fourcade & Healy, 2016; Rona-Tas, 2017) suggests that these aspects not only co-relate but that those different algorithmic regimes interact with each other. The location of a person's home, the building's design, structure, and architectural quality, but also a person's income and social opportunities become entangled through the calculative predictions of algorithmic regimes. These contingencies need more attention as subjects of analysis in studies of design, technology, and society.

Acknowledgements

This research was supported by the Deutsche Forschungsgemeinschaft (DFG, German Research Foundation) under Germany's Excellence Strategy, EXC 2120/1–390831618.

References

Aish, R., & Bredella, N. (2017). The evolution of architectural computing: From building modelling to design computation. *Architectural Research Quarterly, 21*(1), 65–73. https://doi.org/10.1017/S1359135517000185

Bernal, M., Haymaker, J. R., & Eastman, C. (2015). On the role of computational support for designers in action. *Design Studies, 41*, 163–182. https://doi.org/10.1016/j.destud.2015.08.001

Boeva, Y., Braun, K., & Kropp, C.. (2023). Platformization in the built environment: The political techno-economy of Building Information Modeling. *Science as Culture*. https://doi.org/10.1080/09505431.2023.2237042

Boeva, Y., Wortmann, T., Kropp, C., & Menges, A. (2022). Architectural computing for healthful ecotopian built environments? In M. Kanaani (Ed.), *Routledge companion to ecological design thinking in architecture & urbanism* (pp. 367–379). Routledge. https://doi.org/10.4324/9781003183181-33

Bowker, G. C., & Star, S. L. (1999). *Sorting things out: Classification and its consequences*. MIT Press.

Braun, K., Kropp, C., & Boeva, Y. (2022). Constructing platform capitalism: Inspecting the political techno-economy of building information modeling. *arq: Architectural Research Quarterly, 26*(3), 267–278. https://doi.org/10.1017/S135913552200046X

Burke, A. (2019). Occluded algorithms. *Big Data & Society, 6*(2). https://doi.org/10.1177/2053951719858743

Burrell, J., & Fourcade, M. (2021). The society of algorithms. *Annual Review of Sociology, 47*(1), 213–237. https://doi.org/10.1146/annurev-soc-090820-020800

Burry, M. (2011). *Scripting cultures: Architectural design and programming*. Wiley.

Cardoso Llach, D. (2015). *Builders of the vision: Software and the imagination of design*. Routledge.

Cardoso Llach, D. (2017). Architecture and the structured image: Software simulations as infrastructures for building production. In S. Ammon & R. Capdevila-Werning (Eds.), *The active image: Architecture and engineering in the age of modeling* (pp. 23–52). Springer.

Chun, W. H. K. (2004). On software, or the persistence of visual knowledge. *Grey Room, 18*(4), 26–51.

Cogdell, C. (2018). *Toward a living architecture? Complexism and biology in generative design*. University of Minnesota Press.

Dahlman, S., Gulbrandsen, I. T., & Just, S. N. (2021). Algorithms as organizational figuration: The sociotechnical arrangements of a fintech start-up. *Big Data & Society, 8*(1). https://doi.org/10.1177/20539517211026702

Day, M. (2009, June 2). Rhino grasshopper. *AEC Magazine*. https://aecmag.com/news/rhino-grasshopper/

Dourish, P. (2016). Algorithms and their others: Algorithmic culture in context. *Big Data & Society, 3*(2). https://doi.org/10.1177/2053951716665128

Edwards, P. N. (2003). Infrastructure and modernity: Scales of force, time, and social organization in the history of sociotechnical systems. In T. Misa, P. Brey, & A. Feenberg (Eds.), *Modernity and technology* (pp. 185–225). MIT Press.

Fourcade, M., & Healy, K. (2016). Seeing like a market. *Socio-Economic Review, 15*(1), 9–29. https://doi.org/10.1093/ser/mww033

Fuller, M. (Ed.). (2008). *Software studies: A lexicon*. MIT Press.

Gardner, N. (2018). Architecture–Human–Machine (re)configurations: Examining computational design in practice. *eCAADe, 36*, 139–148.

Gardner, N. (2019). New divisions of digital labour in architecture. *Feminist Review, 123*(1), 106–125. https://doi.org/10.1177/0141778919879766

Gaudillière-Jami, N. (2020). *AD* Magazine: Mirroring the development of the computational field in architecture 1965–2020. In B. Slocum, V. Ago, S. Doyle, A. Marcus, M. Yablonina, & M. del Campo (Eds.), *ACADIA 2020 Distributed Proximities: Proceedings of the 40th Annual Conference of the Association of Computer Aided Design in Architecture* (pp. 150–159).

Gillespie, T. (2014). The relevance of algorithms. In T. Gillespie, P. J. Boczkowski, & K. A. Foot (Eds.), *Media technologies: Essays on communication, materiality, and society* (pp. 167–193). MIT Press.

Goffey, A. (2008). Algorithm. In M. Fuller (Ed.), *Software studies: A lexicon* (pp. 15–20). MIT Press.

Haley, M. (2018). *Autodesk, humans + AI = Future of designing & making*. Autodesk. https://www.youtube.com/watch?v=NSJwq9CVoIk

Introna, L. D. (2016). Algorithms, governance, and governmentality: On governing academic writing. *Science, Technology, & Human Values, 41*(1), 17–49. https://doi.org/10.1177/0162243915587360

Karasti, H., & Blomberg, J. (2018). Studying infrastructuring ethnographically. *Computer Supported Cooperative Work (CSCW), 27*(2), 233–265. https://doi.org/10.1007/s10606-017-9296-7

Kitchin, R. (2014). The real-time city? Big data and smart urbanism. *GeoJournal, 79*(1), 1–14. https://doi.org/10.1007/s10708-013-9516-8

Kropp, C., Braun, K., & Boeva, Y. (2022). Echo chambers of urban design: Platformization in architecture and planning. In A. Strüver & S. Bauriedl (Eds.), *Platformization of urban life: Towards a technocapitalist transformation of European cities* (pp. 237–255). transcript. https://doi.org/10.14361/9783839459645-015

Langley, P., & Leyshon, A. (2017). Platform capitalism: The intermediation and capitalization of digital economic circulation. *Finance and Society, 3*(1), 11–31.

Law, John. (1987). Technology and heterogeneous engineering: The case of the Portuguese expansion. In W. Bijker, T. Hughes, & T. Pinch (Eds.), *The social construction of technological systems* (pp. 111–113). MIT Press.

Leach, N. (2021). *Architecture in the age of artificial intelligence: An introduction for architects*. Bloomsbury Visual Arts.

Loukissas, Y. A. (2012). *Co-designers: Cultures of computer simulation in architecture*. Routledge.

Neff, G., Fiore-Silfvast, B., & Dossick, C. S. (2010). A case study of the failure of digital communication to cross knowledge boundaries in virtual construction. *Information, Communication & Society, 13*(4), 556–573. https://doi.org/10.1080/13691181003645970

Niewöhner, J. (2015). Infrastructures of society, Anthropology of. In *International encyclopedia of the social & behavioral sciences* (pp. 119–125). Elsevier. https://doi.org/10.1016/B978-0-08-097086-8.12201-9

Noble, S. U. (2018). *Algorithms of oppression: How search engines reinforce racism*. New York University Press.

O'Hear, S. (2019, June 9). Spacemaker scores $25 million series A to let property developers use AI. *TechCrunch*. https://techcrunch.com/2019/06/09/spacemaker/

Peters, B. (2013). Computation works: The building of algorithmic thought. *Architectural Design, 83*(2), 8–15. https://doi.org/10.1002/ad.1545

Powell, A. B. (2021). *Undoing optimization: Civic action in smart cities*. Yale University Press.

Rona-Tas, A. (2017). The off-label use of consumer credit ratings. *Historical Social Research, 42*(1), 52–76. https://doi.org/10.12759/HSR.42.2017.1.52-76

Sadowski, J. (2020). The internet of landlords: Digital platforms and new mechanisms of rentier capitalism. *Antipode, 52*(2), 562–580. https://doi.org/10.1111/anti.12595

Seaver, N. (2019). Knowing algorithms. In J. Vertesi & D. Ribes (Eds.), *digitalSTS: A field guide for science & technology studies* (pp. 412–422). Princeton University Press.

Star, S. L. (1999). The ethnography of infrastructure. *American Behavioral Scientist, 43*(3), 377–391. https://doi.org/10.1177/00027649921955326

Star, S. L., & Ruhleder, K. (1996). Steps toward an ecology of infrastructure: Design and access for large information spaces. *Information Systems Research, 7*(1), 111–134. https://doi.org/10.1287/isre.7.1.111

Steenson, M. W. (2017). *Architectural intelligence: How designers and architects created the digital landscape.* MIT Press.

Suchman, L. A. (2007). *Human–machine reconfigurations: Plans and situated actions* (2nd ed.). Cambridge University Press.

Vertesi, J. (2014). Seamful spaces: Heterogeneous infrastructures in interaction. *Science, Technology, & Human Values, 39*(2), 264–284.

Wortmann, T., & Tunçer, B. (2017). Differentiating parametric design: Digital workflows in contemporary architecture and construction. *Design Studies, 52*, 173–197. https://doi.org/10.1016/j.destud.2017.05.004

Wortmann, T., Cichocka, J., & Waibel, C. (2022). Simulation-based optimization in architecture and building engineering: Results from an international user survey in practice and research. *Energy and Buildings, 259*, 111863. https://doi.org/10.1016/j.enbuild.2022.111863

Yaneva, A. (2009). *Made by the Office for Metropolitan Architecture: An ethnography of design.* 010 Publishers.

Yarrow, T. (2019). *Architects: Portraits of a practice.* Cornell University Press.

About the Authors

Yana Boeva is a postdoctoral researcher at the Institute for Social Sciences and the Cluster of Excellence "Integrative Computational Design and Construction for Architecture (IntCDC)" at the University of Stuttgart, Germany. Her research explores the transformation of design, architectural practice, and different user expectations of computation and automation.

Cordula Kropp holds the Chair of Sociology of Technology, Risk and Environment at the Institute for Social Sciences, University of Stuttgart, Germany. She is director of the Centre for Interdisciplinary Risk and Innovation Research (ZIRIUS) and PI at the Cluster of Excellence "Integrative Computational Design and Construction for Architecture (IntCDC)".

8.   The Organization in the Loop:
     Exploring Organizations as Complex
     Elements of Algorithmic Assemblages

Stefanie Büchner, Henrik Dosdall, and Ioanna Constantiou

Abstract
Organizations are a highly relevant contexts for understanding the interactions of algorithmic assemblages and the unfolding of algorithmic regimes. We argue that organizations must be understood as social systems that enable and restrict how algorithmic regimes unfold. We make this conceptual argument by analysing the algorithmic assemblage in the case of predictive policing in Germany and subsequently compare our insights with the case of hospitals which serve as our secondary case. Our analysis focuses on three crucial organizational dimensions: goals, differentiation, and goal conflicts. We argue that taking these dimensions into account sensitizes researchers not only to how organizations empower algorithmic regimes, but also to the frictions and breaks they cause.

Keywords: goal conflicts; differentiation; predictive policing; hospitals

Introduction

Algorithmic regimes unfold their social relevance not only in private settings like online shopping, fitness tracking, streaming, or dating, but also in organized settings, meaning in organizations. They operate in and between organizations by supporting how tasks are carried out, by optimizing organizational processes, or by enabling new forms of interorganizational collaboration. Hence, organizations become important contexts that shape how algorithmic regimes unfold—in the focal organizational settings themselves and by the same token in society at large (see Jarke et al. and Egbert, in this volume).

Jarke, J., B. Prietl, S. Egbert, Y. Boeva, H. Heuer, and M. Arnold (eds.), *Algorithmic Regimes: Methods, Interactions, and Politics.* Amsterdam: Amsterdam University Press, 2024
DOI 10.5117/9789463728485_CH08

Despite their pivotal role for and in algorithmic regimes, though, organizations are not currently receiving much scholarly attention. The observation that it is not only humans and algorithms "in the loop" (Danaher, 2016), but also organizations, constitutes our point of departure and informs our main research question: What is the role of organizations as elements and contexts of the embeddedness of algorithmic systems? To elucidate this question, we explore two different empirical settings which both present prominent yet sufficiently different cases of organizations embedding algorithmic systems. Our primary case is predictive policing in Germany. Predictive policing algorithms are designed to support the police in their task of preventing crime by directing organizational attention to geographical areas of heightened risk of burglaries. Our secondary case, which we primarily use as a contrast, involves algorithmic systems in hospitals that support different organizational tasks such as accounting and diagnosis.

Drawing on empirical data from the literature and our current research, we use these two cases to make the conceptual argument that organizations are active contexts deeply affecting how algorithmic systems unfold by both enabling and restricting this unfolding. To build this argument, we first demonstrate that current research does not pay sufficient attention to organizations when discussing algorithmic systems. Next, we depict organizations as social systems that decide upon their formal processes and structures (Luhmann, 2018). In particular, we highlight organizational dimensions that are important for understanding the interplay of algorithmic systems and organizations: organizational goals, organizational structure, and goal conflicts. The focus on organizational goals allows us to identify the tasks algorithmic systems are supposed to support, while focusing on organizational structure raises a question of which organizational unit is using them. Considering goal conflicts reveals how algorithmic systems compete for organizational resources that are also relevant for fulfilling other tasks. We analyse our primary case by means of these analytical dimensions before turning to our secondary case. In both cases, we demonstrate the organizational impact on algorithmic regimes. In the conclusion we reflect on our analysis in this chapter before pointing to directions for future research.

The Problem of Omnipresent but Conceptually Opaque Organizations

In critical algorithm studies, the meso-level of organizations is not a central point of interest. Rather, prominent scholars argue that we may be witnessing a shift towards the decentring of organizations as "digital data objects ... become central reference points of organizational knowledge making and action" (Alaimo & Kallinikos, 2021, p. 3). However, this tendency does not lead to the dissolution of organizations as complex structures (ibid., p. 15; Kallinikos & Hasselbladh, 2009). Scholars studying algorithms often share a lively interest not in organizations, but in the politics put forward and enforced by algorithmic systems, as in the influential work of Virginia Eubanks, who has analysed the connection between digital tools and their consequences for dealing with and overcoming poverty. Her call for "dismantling the digital poorhouse" (Eubanks, 2018, p. 204) remains paradigmatic for the strong focus on the policy level when studying algorithms (Allhutter et al., 2020; Amoore, 2013; Bucher, 2018; Crawford, 2021; Gillespie, 2010; Hansen & Flyverbom, 2015). When organizations are more explicitly addressed, the focus often falls on certain types of organizations, especially on platforms (Egbert, 2019; Gillespie, 2018; Plantin & Punathambekar, 2019). Platform organizations, though, represent a technology-focused type not easily comparable to more traditional but societally crucial organizations such as bureaucracies or businesses.

Current research demonstrates that organizations are producers as well as users of algorithmic systems. Organizations assume these roles when firms like Amazon use algorithms to optimize the storage of products in their warehouses (Danaher, 2016), when states automate the calculation and payment of benefits (Eubanks, 2018), when architectural offices use computational design to model their buildings (Boeva & Kropp, in this volume), or when courts use algorithmic systems like COMPAS to assess the likelihood of recidivism risk among defendants (Christin, 2017).

Despite this omnipresence of organizations as users and producers, at a conceptual level they remain opaque in their functioning, as they are often reduced to mere sites or "settings" (Schubert & Röhl, 2017, p. 2) for algorithmic systems in use, mainly when algorithms are analysed ethnographically (Christin, 2020; Kitchin, 2017, p. 24f.). In this way, it is less the organized nature of courts, planning and construction companies, Amazon's storage centres, or the bureaucratic organization of welfare states that is of interest when the embedding of algorithmic systems and the interactions in the algorithmic assemblage are being analysed. Instead, these empirical studies focus primarily on specific social fields or working areas (e.g., journalism, justice, police, commerce, architecture) and the types of algorithmic technologies in use (e.g., audience analytics, predictive analytics, decision support and recommender systems, computational design). In sum, organizations are "backgrounded" (cf. Zerubavel, 2015, p. 86) by such an approach as they only appear as layers, sites, or settings of the algorithmic assemblage.

We take issue with reducing organizations to mere background settings or simple contexts for three reasons. The first reason to foreground instead of background organizations is that algorithms operate as elements of algorithmic systems in complex socio-technical arrangements or, as Kitchin (2017, p. 18) puts it, in socio-technical assemblages. For understanding algorithms, it is thus crucial to understand them as

> relational, contingent, contextual in nature, framed within the wider context of their socio-technical assemblage. From this perspective, "algorithm" is one element in a broader apparatus which means it can never be understood as a technical, objective, impartial form of knowledge or mode of operation. (ibid.)

Such a *relational understanding* necessitates exploring the interactions between the elements of the apparatus and therefore depends on separating them analytically (Jarke & Zakharova, forthcoming). Omitting such an analytical separation may lead to problematic cause and effect attributions to the whole assemblage. From an organizational perspective, there is a need to study organizations as specific and complex elements of the algorithmic assemblage.

The second reason for foregrounding organizations is that algorithmic regimes are, in a Foucauldian sense, powerful socio-technical assemblages of knowledge production and circulation that share particular characteristics (see Jarke et al., in this volume). Taking the notion of assemblages and algorithmic regimes into account then means that a careful analysis of assemblages must pay attention not only to the *enabling* forces of algorithmic regimes but also to the *breaks, restrictions, and barriers* of these regimes. Such a *bidirectional sensitivity* demands an analytical frame conducive to avoiding the risk of overestimating the transformative powers of algorithmic assemblages and regimes. As many algorithmic regimes are embedded within and between organizations, this state of research also requires considering the role of organizations as active contexts (Büchner, 2018; Büchner & Dosdall, 2021).

Third, foregrounding organizations offers an analytical point of reference for comparing the complex social embeddings of algorithmic technologies called for by Christin (2020, p. 907), among others. We therefore agree that practical strategies like that of "a similarity-and-difference approach to identify the specific features of algorithmic systems" (ibid.) are fruitful and necessary, for example, in an analysis of how the police and legal professionals use predictive algorithms (Brayne & Christin, 2021). We add to this, though, that such an approach additionally requires attention to organizations, as such a meso-level focus supports cross-case comparisons, thereby opening up a mid-level for studies between micro practices and policies.

Organizations as Complex Elements of Algorithmic Assemblages and Algorithmic Regimes

Early in the debate on the power of algorithms (see also Milan, Lopez, and Egbert, in this volume) and following Latour (2005), Neyland and Möllers (2016, p. 3) proposed to "understand the algorithm-in-action as situated." They further argue that algorithms possess an "associational life" and derive their social power "through algorithmic associations" (ibid., p. 1). To investigate these "algorithmic associations," metaphors play an important role for scholarly thinking about the embeddedness and the relational character of algorithms. In this line of thought, Neyland (2015) suggests associative metaphors such as "algorithmic account" to understand the algorithm in relation to the organizational work putting it to use. Christin (2020, p. 906), on the other hand, proposes the metaphor of "algorithmic refraction" for "paying close attention to the changes that take place whenever algorithmic systems unfold in existing social contexts—when they are built, when they diffuse, and when they are used."

We agree that metaphors play an important role to "bypass algorithmic opacity and tackle the complex chains of human and non-human interventions that together make up algorithmic systems" (ibid., p. 907). At the same time, concepts from organizational sociology also hold great promise and offer more clarity for analysing the complex relations of algorithmic assemblages. In particular, this is the case as they allow us to see that organizations are *active contexts* shaping digital transformation (Büchner, 2018; Büchner & Dosdall, 2021). This theoretical approach directs our attention to the variegated and heterogeneous ways in which organizations inscribe themselves into algorithmic assemblages.

Organizations, Decisions, and Agency

Organizational sociology has undergone a change of focus, with work now being the dominant point of scholarly interest (Barley & Kunda, 2001; Orlikowski & Scott, 2016). This has led to a situation in which scholars no longer treat organizations as a "distinct layer of social life" (Besio et al., 2020, p. 413). Recently, though, scholars such as Du Gay (2020; Du Gay & Vikkelsø, 2017), Besio and colleagues (2020, p. 413), or Schwarting and Ulbricht (2022) have demanded more analytical attention to the characteristic social form of organizations. Their call is echoed by researchers who point out that AI and digitalization are constrained by socioeconomic and organizational factors that shape their implementation (Fleming, 2019, p. 9).

We follow organization-sensitive works by understanding organizations as social systems that differentiate themselves from their environment by taking decisions (Luhmann, 2018; March & Simon, 1958). Among other things (cf. Luhmann, 2018), organizations decide about their goals, their members, and their structure. Understanding organizations as decision-making systems emphasizes that organizations are not just passive objects but have an agent-like quality; they are active entities, after all (Brunsson & Brunsson, 2017; King et al., 2010). However, emphasizing the ability to make decisions implies neither that organizations are deterministic nor that they are fully autonomous. Formal structures come with informality (Barnard, 1938), that organizational rules inform only a part of the decisions required to be made in organizations (Reynaud, 2005) and that attempts at implementing formal control structures often lead to nothing other than unforeseen processes of change (Chown, 2021). With regard to autonomy, organizations follow societal institutions (Meyer & Rowan, 1977) and their logics (Ocasio, Thornton, & Lounsbury, 2017) as they are important sources of legitimacy—a fact increasingly recognized by research on algorithms (cf. Caplan & boyd, 2018). The high variety of organizational forms is testament to the agentic quality of organizations.

Overall, we argue that organizations are active and complex, not passive and one-dimensional contexts—an insight that directly impacts the analysis of algorithmic regimes. For the analysis of algorithmic regimes, this means that organizations and their ability to take decisions influences how algorithmic regimes unfold—just as algorithmic regimes, in an iterative process, influence organizations. However, due to the lack of research on the former, we focus on the question of how organizations bear upon algorithmic regimes. We now turn to our analytical dimensions.

Structure, Goal, and Goal Conflicts as Analytical Dimensions

To elucidate the role of organizations in the algorithmic assemblage, we focus on three dimensions of organizations which we subsequently discuss in their relation to algorithmic regimes. In this section we present our three analytical dimensions leading our conceptual argumentation. First, we focus on the structure of organizations before, second, we turn to the role of organizational goals. Third, we discuss goal conflicts in organizations. While organizations are social orders with more than these elements (Ahrne & Brunsson, 2011), structure, goals, and goal conflicts are near-universal characteristics of organizations and thus should be generally applicable for future analysis.

Our first point of analytical interest focuses on organizational goals as all organizations pursue certain goals. To operationalize their goals, organizations usually define subgoals for which they assign responsibility to specialized units (Cyert & March, 1963; March & Simon, 1958). This already indicates that goals also bear upon organizational structure. What is of relevance here, though, is that defining these subgoals is necessary because abstract goals like providing security in the case of police organizations or providing public health in the case of hospitals need to be put into practice. Consequently, organizations do not just pursue one but *multiple (sub)goals*. The multiplicity of goals is amplified by a high degree of institutional complexity (Greenwood et al., 2011), which requires organizations to conform to an increasing number of external and, at times, contradictory demands (Bromley & Powell, 2012; Brunsson, 1985; Meyer & Rowan, 1977). Taking organizational goals into account thus sensitizes us to ascertain for which goals organizations implement algorithmic systems—and for which goals they do not do so.

Our second point of analytical interest is the differentiated order of organizations (Luhmann, 2018; March & Simon, 1958). While the extent of differentiation depends on the characteristics of the focal organization, almost all organizations differentiate in line with their internal division of labour. Organizational differentiation allows for processes of specialization, which, in turn, make it possible to designate responsibilities and subsequently delegate tasks and responsibilities to specific units. Taking differentiated organizational structures into account, thus, sensitizes us to ascertain which organizational unit is algorithmically supported—and which is not.

Our third and last point of analytical interest are goal conflicts. Due to the existence of complex environments and multiple goals, goal conflicts often are unavoidable. This is the case if pursuing different goals requires drawing on the same pool of resources. Thus, organizations with more resources are less afflicted by goal conflicts than organizations with fewer resources (Nohria & Gulati, 1996). However, what exactly counts more or less depends, among other things, crucially on the number of duties an organization is tasked with and its ability to defer these tasks to future handling. This indicates that the type of organization also matters. For example, organizations like the police or hospitals must often respond immediately to emergencies, requiring the triage of existing resources to address some goals, all the while postponing other goals to a time when the required resources are free again (Faraj & Xiao, 2006; Geiger et al., 2021). However, multiple or even contradictory goals do not necessarily need to become problems, as organizations must *not actively pursue all their goals simultaneously* (Greve & Teh, 2018). Furthermore, they have different means of easing the tensions resulting from contradictory goals, i.e., by prioritizing specific goals for some time at the expense of others (Ramus et al., 2021), by relying on a loosely coupled structure (Weick, 1976) or by resorting to symbolic actions (Brunsson, 1989). Another popular means to solve conflicts are projects (Button & Sharrock, 1996; Midler, 1995) as they often come with their own resources and therefore tend to ease resource tensions; this is an effect that even holds in the case of digitization projects, which often underestimate the resources necessary for successful digital innovations (Büchner et al., forthcoming).

Introducing the Leading and Contrasting Cases

We develop our conceptual argument by two reference cases. For the purposes of our analysis, we refer to both cases intentionally in an uneven manner. We focus on the case of predictive policing as our primary case and turn only occasionally to the secondary and mainly contrasting case of hospitals. The following introduction to our cases mirrors this analytical focus by describing predictive policing in more detail than the case of hospitals.

Predictive policing has gained prominence over the last decade as it uses algorithms to detect increased risks of criminal actions (Brayne, 2017; Egbert & Leese, 2021; Wilson, 2019). For the police, detecting these risks is attractive as it enables patrolling areas at risk of higher criminal activity. This, in turn, holds the promise of preventing criminal activity before it even happens. In Germany, the police use predictive policing technology primarily to detect areas with a higher-than-usual risk of burglaries (Egbert, 2020). Unlike the police in the United States, for example, predictive policing technologies are hence not used to surveil and detect individuals (Brayne, 2017); they are confined to flagging areas subject to an increased risk of burglaries. Another difference between the United States and Germany is that in the past, private companies like Palantir played only a minor role in providing the algorithmic infrastructure for predictive policing. Instead of buying surveillance software, most *Länderpolizeien* (state police forces) have opted to develop their own, even though there are some notable exceptions like the police of Hesse which early on cooperated with Palantir.

Predictive policing relies on the premise of "near-repeat" (Bernasco, 2008). Near-repeat is a behavioural heuristic assuming that some criminal activities entail an increased future risk of the same criminal activity occurring again. In the case of theft, this is due to successful burglaries flagging certain quarters for other burglars as a rewarding area or because perpetrators gain a boost from previous burglaries as they can parlay their gained knowledge to burgle similar targets (ibid.). In any case, *only professional* and not one-time perpetrators are expected to repeat their criminal activities. What follows from this for predictive policing technologies is that the *ascribed professionalism* of a criminal act is a major factor in determining the risks of future burglaries for certain areas (Kaufmann et al., 2019). Once the data on burglaries detected and identified as professional are fed into the database, the risk for future near-repeat burglaries is algorithmically determined. The police can then allocate their patrol forces to prevent future burglaries. Summing up, the algorithmic system of predictive policing is embedded into the police as an organization to predict the likelihood that a specific type of crime will occur. Its output of flagged high-risk areas enables actions to be taken to prevent the forecasted repetition of this crime from happening.

To analyse the case of predictive policing, we primarily use published studies on the subject but view and reinterpret them through our organizational lens (Büchner & Dosdall, forthcoming; Egbert, 2020; Egbert & Leese, 2021; Sandhu & Fussey, 2021). For our contrast case, we use selected empirical illustrations from an ongoing ethnographic study ("Digital Cases," funded by VolkswagenStiftung, 2020–2023) that analyses the role of digital infrastructures in treating patients in a German university hospital. As in many other hospitals, this hospital has a long tradition of being quantified and highly datafied (Reilley & Scheytt, 2019) and of using algorithms for different purposes, ranging from accounting to monitoring and supporting diagnosis (cf. Maiers, 2017; Bossen & Markussen, 2010). We conducted fieldwork by accompanying and interviewing physicians and nurses in day and night shifts for 12 months while also talking to specialized staff with key positions in off-patient work, such as in-house staff from medical informatics

Zooming into Organizational Embeddings

In this section, we draw on the notion of "zooming in" (Nicolini, 2009) to analyse the organizational situatedness of the assemblages of algorithmic systems. Our analytical premise is that organizations empower algorithmic systems and regimes by formally deciding upon their use and the intended area of application. Thereby, organizations endow these algorithmic regimes with agency as they are now part of organizational decision-making processes. This process, though, also creates frictions and tensions for how algorithmic regimes unfold.

In the following, we identify these frictions and tensions along the outlined dimensions of organizational structure, goals, and goal conflicts. First, we show how organizational differentiation engenders a compartmentalization of predictive policing, thereby restricting a full unfolding of the transformative powers of the algorithmic regime, and then we compare this to the case of hospitals. Second, we relate predictive policing to the different goals police organizations pursue before turning to hospitals. Third, we demonstrate how algorithmic systems are affected by goal conflicts and how emerging new goals can influence the unfolding of algorithmic regimes. Here, too, we subsequently refer to selected illustrations from the ethnography of a hospital. Before we begin our analysis, we note that in both our cases, algorithmic regimes are not limited to temporally bounded projects as found in the building sector, where they influence design, planning, and monitoring of construction work (Boeva & Kropp, in this volume). Instead, they are part of the continuous organizational activity.

The Role of Multiple Organizational Goals for the Algorithmic Assemblage

Our point of departure is that organizations have multiple goals, as we have argued in the theoretical part of this chapter. *Two main goals* characterize police organizations. First, the police are responsible for *fighting crime*. Formally, this involves enforcing the law by apprehending offenders as well as ensuring public safety by dealing with imminent dangers threatening the public. The latter includes but is not tantamount to fighting crime as it includes broader yet concrete dangers. A second goal lies in the *prevention of crime* and thus in inhibiting criminal activity from occurring in the first place. Regarding this organizational goal, the police assume a sentinel role different from its apprehension role (Nagin, 2013), which is characteristic of police work related to apprehending offenders.

If we relate these organizational goals to each other in terms of organizational significance, it is well documented that, while important and effective (Weisburd et al., 2017), *prevention work plays a minor role* in most police organizations when compared to crime fighting. One of the reasons is that prevention "lacks glamour; apprehensions offer the excitement of the chase" (Sherman & Weisburd, 1995, p. 646). The case of the police, hence, underscores that organizations do not necessarily assign equal significance to all their organizational goals all the time (Audia & Greve, 2021), as some goals align for some groups more convincingly than others with what is perceived to be the organizations' main goal.

The cited lack of glamour characteristic of prevention work is exacerbated by the ambiguous nature of prevention. By definition, prevention is only successful in the case of a non-event. What remains unknown in the case of a non-event, though, is whether anything would have occurred anyway, or whether actions actually prevented criminal activity. As a result, it is hardly possible to measure the success or failure of prevention. The low visibility and, by the same token, inability to measure the organizational goal of prevention, underscores its more minor role for the organization.

Relating predictive policing to the goals of police organizations thus reveals that predictive policing as used in Germany is related to an organizational goal that in most police organizations is subordinate to the deeply ingrained primary goal of crime fighting. This is undoubtedly one of the reasons why numerous studies show that algorithmic regimes in the field of predictive policing, at least for now, fall short of their predicted transformative potential (Egbert & Leese, 2021; Sandhu & Fussey, 2021). However, our main point is a conceptual one: organizations implement algorithmic systems to support some goals but not necessarily others. This bears upon how the algorithmic assemblage is constituted and how algorithmic regimes unfold in organizations—in the case of predictive policing in Germany, in a somewhat limited way.

In contrast to the police, hospitals use various algorithmic systems for more central and prominent organizational goals, primarily for the diagnosis and treatment of patients and the billing process. Early warning systems and algorithm-based diagnosis suggestions are institutionalized elements of hospital work in many fields. They are used to identify patterns indicating abnormalities in visual representations such as X-ray scans and MRT images or to count, identify, and categorize medical materials, such as analyses of blood samples. In our case, medical staff, therefore, avoided the buzzword "algorithms" when describing concrete algorithmic assemblages used in various devices measuring medical data as a physician in the researched hospital states:

What we do is, you look at the summary from the machine and these machines that have already been the normal practice when I was trained as a doctor: The machines suggest an indication. That's what they do at the end of the day; they suggest an indication.

In a second regard, we mentioned that hospitals use algorithmic systems for the billing process. In Germany, public hospitals can only charge predefined treatments and services laid down in the diagnosis-related groups (DRGs). The classifications include primary and secondary diagnoses, procedure codes and demographic factors. Many hospitals provide coding staff with algorithmic support systems integrated in broader software systems. These systems suggest specific codes and thereby aim to increase hospital income.

In the case of the hospital, the organization uses algorithmic support not only to support diagnosis but also for the billing and coding of nearly all illnesses and treatments as well as for the support of diagnosis. Here, algorithms suggest clusterings and groupings of diagnosis and treatments. In comparison, algorithmic systems in the hospital case are tied to more central and highly relevant goals than in the case of the algorithmic system of predictive policing in Germany. This is particularly clear regarding billing, which is not a relevant goal for the police that is not burdened with acquiring funding for its operation.

The Role of Internal Differentiation of Organizations in the Algorithmic Assemblage

For many authors, predictive policing holds the promise of fundamentally changing how police work is done (Brayne, 2017; Flyverbom & Hansen, 2019; Wilson, 2018). Upon closer inspection through an organizational lens, the German case showcases that predictive policing is much more confined in its organizational outreach than these claims suggest, especially when paying attention to the internal differentiation of the police.

The German police is differentiated according to a combination of regional and functional principles (Frevel & Groß, 2016). Functionally, the organization is differentiated between the uniformed *Schutzpolizei* (uniformed police), who are primarily but not solely responsible for dealing with imminent dangers and thus providing public security, and the plain-clothes *Kriminalpolizei* (criminal police), who are primarily but not solely responsible for criminal investigations and thus with apprehending offenders. Both organizational parts are further differentiated according to particular tasks. In the case of the uniformed police, which is the part of the organization that uses predictive policing, the overall goal of ensuring public safety includes a broad spectrum of tasks, such as dealing with traffic accidents, patrolling areas, receiving complaints, testifying in court, finding and logging evidence, reacting to emergencies, and documenting all of these activities. Furthermore, a variety of other specialized units exist to police waterways, demonstrations or highways.

We do not need to delve deeper into the differentiation of police organizations to make clear that preventing burglaries is just one among various other tasks the uniformed police must deal with. Thus, while the term "predictive policing" gives the impression of organization-wide change, in fact, predictive policing bears primarily upon a relatively small part of organizational activity.

Relating this insight to the algorithmic regime of predictive policing reveals two essential aspects. First, the algorithmic system of predictive policing is directed to support and change the work of only one part of the German police, the *Schutzpolizei*. Second, within the *Schutzpolizei*, predictive policing is relevant for only a minor part of the activities the police are engaged in: preventing burglaries. This is not to say that it is unlikely that the technology diffuses to other task areas in the organization, as some authors predict (Egbert, 2020; Egbert & Leese, 2021; Wilson, 2018). We surmise, though, that such a diffusion process will unlikely be broad and homogeneous. Rather, we expect that such a process would affect the police heterogeneously due to its differentiated structure.

To contextualize this point with regard to the case of hospitals, we return to the coding process mentioned above. This process defines what a hospital can charge for a specific treatment. Here, organizational differentiations also influence the algorithmic assemblage as the algorithm is not used at the ward itself but by a specialized coding department operating separately from the ward. Thus, the data work involved in the coding process does not lie with the doctors but is outsourced to a specialized department. The coding staff in the department we researched was formerly part of the ward, but is now exclusively responsible for this coding work.

The point we want to stress regarding the coding department is that *functional differentiation is not neutral to the algorithmic assemblage*; the specialized unit is not only another setting in which the algorithmic system is applied, but is also detached from the work of frontline operatives. If the coding were to take place on the ward, it would likely influence the doctor's work more directly, for example, by impacting decisions about necessary or profitable medical treatment. Accordingly, the functional differentiation between the coding department and the frontline doctors buffers any direct effects on the medical practice of the ward.

The Role of Existing Goal Conflicts in Organizations and New Goal Conflicts in the Algorithmic Assemblage

In this section, we discuss the role of goal conflicts in the algorithmic assemblage of predictive policing. Our starting point is that, as we have seen above, both police and hospital organizations serve not only one but multiple purposes, which also differ in their relevancy. We have seen that multiple goals can engender goal conflicts when organizations have to draw on a limited pool of resources to meet these goals. This is exacerbated when multiple goals need to be addressed simultaneously and thus cannot be brought in a sequential temporal order to decrease the pressure on the organizational pool of resources.

Predictive policing promises to render police work more efficient. The claim of higher efficiency is grounded in the idea that police work is no longer informed by unreliable experience or officers' whims but by a dense data basis. Paradoxically, while *promising higher* efficiency due to the datafication of police work, predictive policing requires considerable *additional data work*, especially *documentation work*, that in itself exerts considerable stress on organizational resources. The reason for this additional data work is that predictive policing requires police officers to meticulously document burglaries to feed these data back into the database used by the algorithmic system to enable future prognosis. Not doing so can lead to detrimental vicious circles; bad data (Richardson et al., 2019) can spiral through the system and reduce the quality of future prognosis, which, in turn, can lead to a loss of acceptance in the organization for using the technology. Furthermore, the increased data work is not offset by additional organizational resources. Not surprisingly, the time requirements of ensuring a sufficient data basis for predictive policing often conflict with other duties.

Closely related to the data-intensive nature of predictive policing is another source of goal conflicts that stems from the necessity that the police often must rapidly respond to emergencies and thus must reassign resources on short notice. From the perspective of police officers, this means that the same organizational unit responsible for patrolling areas which are algorithmically flagged as having a higher risk of burglaries is also responsible for responding quickly to a broad range of emergencies ranging from domestic violence to car accidents. The resulting conflict between the goals of prevention and dealing with emergencies is regularly resolved in favour of responding to emergencies. The result, as a recent study notes, is that officer attention is often redirected by the demand for immediate intervention (Egbert & Leese, 2021, p. 105). This, however, results in algorithmic prognosis not being followed through systematically due to the interference of goal conflicts.

The entanglement of algorithmic systems in goal conflicts and their influence on the unfolding of algorithmic regimes also becomes virulent in the hospital, especially regarding algorithm-based early warning systems. Early warning systems aim to support the detection of critical changes in a patient's condition (Maiers, 2017). Many of these systems combine different vital signs of patients and set off an acoustic and visual alert if conditions deteriorate, which allows staff to react immediately. However, the goal of improving the monitoring of *single patients* stands in contrast to the goal of ensuring that *all patients on a ward are sufficiently monitored in a given shift.* Therefore, the doctors and nurses on the intensive care unit (ICU) hospital underlined the importance of learning not only to "read the alerts correctly," but to learn to move and act in a calm and concentrated way in the ecosystem of constant visual and auditive signals characteristic of an ICU.

This mode of semi-attention indicates that the omnipresence of goal conflicts in organizations makes frictions in the embedding of the algorithmic assemblage likely and a simple unfolding of an algorithmic regime less likely. Just as in the case of the police, the goal of optimizing the monitoring of single patients in the hospital is challenged by parallel and conflicting tasks that often occur in an unplanned manner and call for situated actions. In the worst case, this goal conflict may cause more "algorithmic work," including checking if the alarm is indeed a warning to be taken seriously or merely an effect of the unavoidable over- and underfitting of these systems (Bailey et al., 2020).

We pointed out the extensive data work of manual documentation for police officers through the introduction of the algorithmic system. We also see indications that this kind of data work done by regular staff alongside the regular workload (Büchner & Jarke, 2022) will intensify goal conflicts in organizations. This is highly likely for administrations which cannot easily grow areas of activity or successfully compete for specialized and highly paid data professionals on the market. Due to resource constraints, we expect that organizations which have to produce data alongside their routine practices will accumulate increasingly problematic data in terms of data quality and will also challenge professionals' core tasks and motivation (Hoeyer & Wadmann, 2020).

In conclusion, we offer a conceptual question. The notion of goal conflicts due to limited resources may appear as a general and unspecific aspect at first glance. Resources are generally rather scarce than munificent, regardless of whether we look inside organizations or outside of them. However, when analysing algorithmic assemblages and the unfolding of algorithmic regimes, we should reflect that the plentiful investments in various digitization projects we witnessed in the last years cannot be taken for granted in the future. Especially in light of multiple societal challenges and crises, a continuation of this trend seems rather unlikely. In effect, manifest and latent goal conflicts that do not appear to influence algorithmic assemblages in the present might make a difference when compensation and resource flows for digital innovation projects decrease or even stop.

Rethinking the Algorithmic Assemblage with Organizations as Active Contexts: Enablement and Frictions for Algorithmic Regimes

Starting from a situated understanding of algorithms as part of a broader and complex assemblage (Kitchin, 2017, p. 18), we used an organizational sociology perspective to elucidate the interplay of organizations and algorithmic systems. To this end, we focused on the role of organizational goals, structures, and goal conflicts for the algorithmic assemblage and the according unfolding of the algorithmic regime.

Our analysis showed that organizations play a complex role that can hardly be condensed to one principle or one direction of influence. Instead, organizations enable *and*, simultaneously, restrict, break, and relativize the power of algorithmic regimes. In the case of predictive policing in Germany, we have argued that the unfolding of predictive policing is limited by the peripheral status of the goal of prevention for the police, which only informs a part of the task set of the uniformed police and goal conflicts stemming from increased data work as well as the need to react to emergencies. In a second step, we related these insights to our contrast case, a hospital. We pointed out that how algorithmic regimes are embedded and how they unfold differs between organizations and that these differences can be analysed by attending to general characteristics of organizations as complex social systems.

Reflecting upon our analysis, we conclude by identifying three challenges resulting from paying closer attention to the role of organizations in the algorithmic assemblage. First, the elaborated conceptual lens enables a bidirectional perspective by demonstrating that organizations not only empower but also restrict algorithmical associations in assemblages. This perspective challenges researchers to *systematically integrate these breaks, frictions, and relativizations* into the study of algorithmic assemblages and regimes instead of reducing their significance, e.g., by placing their hopes in future generations of algorithms which will supposedly overcome current limitations. While we agree that such processes of optimization will likely happen to a certain extent, we emphasize that the clarity of analysis of algorithmic assemblages and regimes does benefit from differentiating between future possibilities and actual configurations of algorithmic assemblages. Taking the complexities of organizations in the assemblage into account does not hinder researching future imaginaries and analysing the strong discursive powers in play (Jasanoff, 2015; Kitchin, 2014). In contrast, it might sensitize us to the importance of organizational changes and organizational alliances for algorithmic regimes to unfold their social power (Hanseth, forthcoming).

The second challenge is to rethink how we *cluster and lump together algorithmic systems and assemblage elements* for analysis. In this chapter, we chose an approach for studying our main case, which paid attention to the rather confined algorithmic systems of predictive policing for the prevention of burglaries. Others might opt for a broader understanding of predictive policing that includes a variety of phenomena outside of algorithmically enabled burglary prevention. How we cluster our phenomena creates systematic tensions; the tension between paying attention to the situatedness of an algorithmic assemblage, on the one hand, and the aim of identifying overreaching patterns or similarities of algorithmic assemblages and regimes, on the other hand. Although the latter is promising, this tension cannot easily be solved. This presents a disadvantage of "zooming out" when more and broader algorithmic systems are lumped together for analysis: our understanding of organizational (dis)embeddings becomes blurry.

The third challenge is also an invitation. We used our shared interest in the role of organizations in algorithmic assemblages and regimes to zoom into the problem of understanding the relation between algorithmic systems and organizations, not from a metaphorical, but from a conceptual angle. However, it also became clear that there is no lack of theoretical challenges when thinking along the lines of Latour about associations and analysing organizations as social systems at the same time. Since this analysis of the complex role of organizations will create some resonance and inspiration, these debates will most likely also do so. Such a dialogue would allow us to use the conceptual arsenal of organizational sociology more comprehensively, e.g., by paying attention to organizational and data culture, the logics of informality, or the reduction of complexity with the aim of inspiring future analyses and contributing to a better understanding of algorithmic regimes.

References

Alaimo, C., & Kallinikos, J. (2020). Managing by data: Algorithmic categories and organizing. *Organization Studies, 1*–23. https://doi.org/10.1177/0170840620934062

Alaimo, C., & Kallinikos, J. (2021). Organizations decentered: Data objects, technology and knowledge. *Organization Science, 1*–19. https://doi.org/10.1287/orsc.2021.1552

Allhutter, D., Cech, F., Fischer, F., Grill, G., & Mager, A. (2020). Algorithmic profiling of job seekers in Austria: How austerity politics are made effective. *Frontiers in Big Data, 3*, article 5. https://doi.org/10.3389/fdata.2020.00005

Amoore, L. (2013). *The politics of possibility: Risk and security beyond probability.* Duke University Press. http://site.ebrary.com/lib/alltitles/docDetail.action?docID=10797305

Ahrne, G., & Brunsson, N. (2011). Organization outside organizations: The significance of partial organization. *Organization,*18(1), 83–104. https://doi.org/10.1177/1350508410376256

Audia, P. G., & Greve, H. R. (2021). *Organizational learning from performance feedback: A behavioral perspective on multiple goals.* Cambridge University Press. https://doi.org/10.1017/9781108344289

Bailey, S., Pierides, D., Brisley, A., Weisshaar, C., & Blakeman, T. (2020). Dismembering organisation: The coordination of algorithmic work in healthcare. *Current Sociology, 68*(4), 546–571. https://doi.org/10.1177/0011392120907638

Barley, S. R., & Kunda, G. (2001). Bringing work back in. *Organization Science, 12*(1), 76–95. https://doi.org/10.1287/orsc.12.1.76.10122

Barnard, C. I. (1938). *The functions of the executive.* Harvard University Press.

Bernasco, W. (2008). Them again? Same-offender involvement in repeat and near repeat burglaries. *European Journal of Criminology, 5*(4), 411–431. http://dx.doi.org/10.1177/1477370808095124

Besio, C., Du Gay, P., & Serrano Velarde, K. (2020). Disappearing organization? Reshaping the sociology of organizations. *Current Sociology, 68*(4), 411–418. https://doi.org/10.1177/0011392120907613

Bossen, C., & Markussen, R. (2010). Infrastructuring and ordering devices in health care: Medication plans and practices on a hospital ward. *Computer Supported Cooperative Work, 19*, 615–637. https://doi.org/10.1007/s10606-010-9131-x

Brayne, S. (2017). Big data surveillance: The case of policing. *American Sociological Review, 82*(5), 977–1008. https://doi.org/10.1177/0003122417725865

Brayne, S., & Christin, A. (2021). Technologies of crime prediction: The reception of algorithms in policing and criminal courts. *Social Problems, 68*(3), 608–624. https://doi.org/10.1093/socpro/spaa004

Bromley, P., & Powell, W. W. (2012). From smoke and mirrors to walking the talk: Decoupling in the contemporary world. *Academy of Management Annals, 6*(1), 1–48. http://dx.doi.org/10.1080/19416520.2012.684462

Brunsson, K., & Brunsson, N. (2017). *Decisions: The complexities of individual and organizational decision-making.* Edward Elgar Publishing.

Brunsson, N. (1985). *The irrational organization: Irrationality as a basis for organizational action and change.* John Wiley & Sons.

Brunsson, N. (1989). *The organization of hypocrisy: Talk, decisions, and actions in organizations.* Wiley.

Bucher, T. (2018). *If … then: Algorithmic power and politics.* Oxford University Press.

Büchner, S. (2018). Zum Verhältnis von Digitalisierung und Organisation. *Zeitschrift für Soziologie, 47*(5), 332–348. https://doi.org/10.1515/zfsoz-2018-0121

Büchner, S., & Dosdall, H. (2021). Organisation und Algorithmus: Wie algorithmische Kategorien, Vergleiche und Bewertungen durch Organisationen relevant gemacht werden. *KZfSS Kölner Zeitschrift für Soziologie und Sozialpsychologie, 73*(S1), 333–357. https://doi.org/10.1007/s11577-021-00752-0

Büchner, S., & Dosdall, H. (2022). Organisation und digitale Technologien: Predictive Policing im organisationalen Kontext. *Soziale Systeme,* 26(1-2), 217–239. https://doi.org/10.1515/sosys-2021-0008

Büchner, S., & Jarke, J. (2022). Data flow or data friction? The ambivalence of organisational data synchronicity. Presented at the "Synchronising Data in Organisations" workshop. University Siegen, September 9, 2022.

Büchner, S., Hergesell, J., & Weber, M. (Forthcoming). Invisible data work. *Historical Social Research.*

Button, G., & Sharrock, W. (1996). Project work: The organization of collaborative design and development in software engineering. *Computer Supported Cooperative Work, 5,* 369–386. https://doi.org/10.1007/BF00136711

Caplan, R., & boyd, d. (2018). Isomorphism through algorithms. Institutional dependencies in the case of Facebook. *Big Data & Society, 5*(1), 1–12. https://doi.org/10.1177/2053951718757253

Chown, J. (2021). The unfolding of control mechanisms inside organizations: Pathways of customization and transmutation. *Administrative Science Quarterly, 66*(3), 711–752. https://doi.org/10.1177/0001839220980015

Christin, A. (2017). Algorithms in practice: Comparing web journalism and criminal justice. *Big Data & Society, 4*(2), 1–14. https://doi.org/10.1177/2053951717718855

Christin, A. (2020). The ethnographer and the algorithm: Beyond the black box. *Theory and Society, 49*, 897–918. https://doi.org/10.1007/s11186-020-09411-3

Crawford, K. (2021). *Atlas of AI: Power, politics, and the planetary costs of artificial intelligence.* Yale University Press.

Cyert, R. M., & March, J. G. (Eds.). (1963). *A behavioral theory of the firm.* Prentice-Hall.

Danaher, J. (2016). The threat of algocracy: Reality, resistance and accommodation. *Philosophy & Technology, 29*(3), 245–268. https://doi.org/10.1007/s13347-015-0211-1

Du Gay, P. (2020). Disappearing "formal organization": How organization studies dissolved its "core object," and what follows from this. *Current Sociology, 68*(4), 459–479. http://dx.doi.org/10.1177/0011392120907644

Du Gay, P., & Vikkelsø, S. (2017). *For formal organization: The past in the present and future of organization theory.* Oxford University Press.

Egbert, S. (2019). Predictive policing and the platformization of police work. *Surveillance & Society, 17*(1/2), 83–88.

Egbert, S. (2020). Datafizierte Polizeiarbeit: (Wissens-) Praktische Implikationen und rechtliche Herausforderungen. In D. Hunold & A. Ruch (Eds.), *Polizeiarbeit zwischen Praxishandeln und Rechtsordnung: Empirische Polizeiforschungen zur polizeipraktischen Ausgestaltung des Rechts* (pp. 77–100). Springer.

Egbert, S., & Leese, M. (2021). *Criminal futures: Predictive policing and everyday police work.* Routledge.

Eubanks, V. (2018). *Automating inequality: How high-tech tools profile, police, and punish the poor.* St. Martin's Press.

Faraj, S., & Xiao, Y. (2006). Coordination in fast-response organizations. *Management Science, 52*(8), 1155–1169. http://dx.doi.org/10.1287/mnsc.1060.0526

Fleming, P. (2019). Robots and organization studies: Why robots might not want to steal your job. *Organization Studies, 40*(1), 23–38. https://doi.org/10.1177/0170840618765568

Flyverbom, M., & Hansen, H. K. (2019). Policing and anticipatory transparency: On digital transformations, proactive governance and logics of temporality. In V. August & F. Osrecki (Eds.), *Der Transparenz-Imperativ* (pp. 171–186). Springer Fachmedien Wiesbaden.

Frevel, B., & Groß, H. (2016). "Polizei ist Ländersache!"—Polizeipolitik unter den Bedingungen des deutschen Föderalismus. In A. Hildebrandt & F. Wolf (Eds.), *Die Politik der Bundesländer* (pp. 61–86). Springer.

Geiger, D., Danner-Schröder, A., & Kremser, W. (2021). Getting ahead of time: Performing temporal boundaries to coordinate routines under temporal uncertainty. *Administrative Science Quarterly, 66*(1), 220–264. https://doi.org/10.1177/0001839220941010

Gillespie, T. (2010). The politics of "platforms." *New Media & Society, 12*(3), 347–364. https://doi.org/10.1177/1461444809342738

Gillespie, T. (2018). *Custodians of the internet: Platforms, content moderation, and the hidden decisions that shape social media.* Yale University Press.

Greenwood, R., Raynard, M., Kodeih, F., Micelotta, E. R., & Lounsbury, M. (2011). Institutional complexity and organizational responses. *Academy of Management Annals, 5*(1), 317–371. https://doi.org/10.5465/19416520.2011.590299

Greve, H. R., & Teh, D. (2018). Goal selection internally and externally: A behavioral theory of institutionalization. *International Journal of Management Reviews, 20*(088), 19–38. https://doi.org/10.1111/ijmr.12138

Hansen, H. K., & Flyverbom, M. (2015). The politics of transparency and the calibration of knowledge in the digital age. *Organization, 22*(6), 872–889. https://doi.org/10.1177/1350508414522315

Hanseth, O. (Forthcoming). When stars align: The interactions and transformations of e-health infrastructure regimes. *Historical Social Research.*

Hoeyer, K., & Wadmann, S. (2020). "Meaningless work": How the datafication of health reconfigures knowledge about work and erodes professional judgement. *Economy and Society, 49*(3), 433–454. https://doi.org/10.1080/03085147.2020.1733842

Jarke, J., & Zakharova, I. (Forthcoming). Data journeys: Considering a conceptual and methodological tool for studying organisational data practices. *Historical Social Research.*

Jasanoff, S. (2015). Future imperfect: Science, technology, and the imaginations of modernity. In S. Jasanoff & S.-H. Kim (Eds.), *Dreamscapes of modernity: Sociotechnical imaginaries and the fabrication of power* (pp. 1–33). University of Chicago Press.

Kallinikos, J., & Hasselbladh, H. (2009). Work, control and computation: Rethinking the legacy of neo-institutionalism. *Research in the Sociology of Organizations, 27*, 267–282. https://doi.org/10.1108/S0733-558X(2009)0000027010

Kaufmann, M., Egbert, S., & Leese, M. (2019). Predictive policing and the politics of patterns. *British Journal of Criminology, 59*(3), 674–692. https://doi.org/10.1093/bjc/azy060

Kelkar, S. (2017). Engineering a platform: The construction of interfaces, users, organizational roles, and the division of labor. *New Media & Society, 20*(7), 2629–2646. https://doi.org/10.1177/1461444817728682

King, B., Felin, T., & Whetten, D. A. (2010). Finding the organization in organizational theory: A meta-theory of the organization as a social actor. *Organization Science, 21*(1), 290–305.

Kitchin, R. (2014). *The data revolution: Big data, open data, data infrastructures & their consequences.* Sage.

Kitchin, R. (2017). Thinking critically about and researching algorithms. *Information, Communication & Society, 20*(1), 14–29. https://doi.org/10.1080/1369118X.2016.1154087

Latour, B. (2005). *Reassembling the social: An introduction to actor-network-theory.* Oxford University Press.

Luhmann, N. (2018). *Organization and decision.* Cambridge University Press.

Maiers, C. (2017). Analytics in action: Users and predictive data in the neonatal intensive care unit. *Information, Communication & Society, 20*(6), 915–929. https://doi.org/10.1080/1369118X.2017.1291701

March, J. G., & Simon, H. A. (1958). *Organizations.* John Wiley & Sons.

Meyer, J. W., & Rowan, B. (1977). Institutionalized organizations: Formal structure as myth and ceremony. *American Journal of Sociology, 83*(2), 340–363. https://doi.org/10.1086/226550

Midler, C. (1995). "Projectification" of the firm, the Renault case. *Scandinavian Journal of Management, 11*(4), 363–375. https://doi.org/10.1016/0956-5221(95)00035-T

Nagin, D. S. (2013). Deterrence in the Twenty-First Century. *Crime and Justice, 42*(1), 199–263.

Neyland, D. (2015). On organizing algorithms. *Theory, Culture & Society, 32*(1), 119–132. https://doi.org/10.1177/0263276414530477

Neyland, D., & Möllers, N. (2016). Algorithmic IF ... THEN rules and the conditions and consequences of power. *Information, Communication & Society, 20*(1), 45–62. https://doi.org/10.1080/1369118X.2016.1156141

Nicolini, D. (2009). Zooming in and out: Studying practices by switching theoretical lenses and trailing connections. *Organization Studies, 30*(12), 1391–1418. https://doi.org/10.1177/0170840609349875

Nohria, N., & Gulati, R. (1996). Is slack good or bad for innovation? *Academy of Management Journal, 39*(5), 1245–1264. https://doi.org/10.2307/256998

Ocasio, W., Thornton, P. D., & Lounsbury, M. (2017). Advances to the institutional logics perspective. In R. Greenwood, C. Oliver, T. B. Lawrence, & R. E. Meyer (Eds.), *The SAGE handbook of organizational institutionalism* (pp. 509–531, 2nd ed.). Sage.

Orlikowski, W. J., & Scott, S. V. (2016). Digital work: A research agenda. In B. Czarniawska (Ed.), *Elgar research agendas: A research agenda for management and organization studies* (pp. 87–95). Edward Elgar Publishing.

Plantin, J.-C., & Punathambekar, A. (2019). Digital media infrastructures: Pipes, platforms, and politics. *Media, Culture & Society, 41*(2), 163–174. https://doi.org/10.1177/0163443718818376

Ramus, T., Vaccaro, A., & Berrone, P. (2021). Time matters! How hybrid organizations use time to respond to divergent stakeholder demands. *Organization Studies, 42*(10), 1529–1555. https://doi.org/10.1177/0170840619900341

Reilley, J., & Scheytt, T. (2019). A calculative infrastructure in the making: The emergence of a multi-layered complex for governing healthcare. In M. Kornberger, G. Bowker, J. Elyachar, A. Mennicken, P. Miller, J. R. Nucho, & N. Pollock (Eds.), *Thinking infrastructures* (pp. 43–68). Emerald Publishing

Reynaud, B. (2005). The void at the heart of rules: Routines in the context of rule-following—The case of the Paris Metro Workshop. *Industrial and Corporate Change, 14*(5), 847–871. http://dx.doi.org/10.1093/icc/dth073

Richardson, R., Schultz, J., & Crawford, K. (2019). Dirty data, bad predictions: How civil rights violations impact police data, predictive policing systems, and justice. *New York University Law Review, 192*, 193–233.

Sandhu, A., & Fussey, P. (2021). The 'uberization of policing'? How Police negotiate and operationalise Predictive Policing Technology. *Policing and Society, 31*(1), 66–81.

Schubert, C., & Röhl, T. (2017). Ethnography and organizations: Materiality and change as methodological challenges. *Qualitative Research, 19*(2), 164–181. https://doi.org/10.1177/1468794117744748

Schwarting, R., & Ulbricht, L. (2022). Why organization matters in "algorithmic discrimination." *KZfSS Kölner Zeitschrift für Soziologie und Sozialpsychologie, 74*(S1), 307–330. https://doi.org/10.1007/s11577-022-00838-3

Sherman, L. W., & Weisburd, D. (1995). General Deterrent Effects of Police Patrol in crime "Hot Spots": A randomized, controlled Trial. Justice Quarterly, 12(4), 625–648. https://doi.org/10.1080/07418829500096221

Weick, K. E. (1976). Educational organizations as loosely coupled systems. *Administrative Science Quarterly, 21*(1), 1–19. https://doi.org/10.2307/2391875

Wilson, D. (2018). Platform policing and the real-time cop. *Surveillance & Society, 17*(1/2), 69–75.

Wilson, D. (2019). Predictive policing management: A brief history of patrol automation. *New Formations, 98*, 139–155.

Zerubavel, E. (2015). *Hidden in plain sight: The social structure of irrelevance.* Oxford University Press.

About the Authors

Stefanie Büchner is Professor for Digital Societies at the Institute of Sociology at the University of Hannover. She leads the Freigeist research group "Digital Cases," which compares datafication and digitization processes in different types of organizations. Her work focuses on the mutual interactions of organizations, professions, and technology.

Henrik Dosdall is an organizational researcher at the University of Applied Sciences for Police and Public Administration in Thuringia in Meiningen, Germany. His work focuses on police organizations and their routines. One of his fields of interest is how police organizations respond to reforms in the area of digitization.

Ioanna Constantiou is a professor in the Department of Digitalization, Copenhagen Business School in Denmark. Her current research work focuses on the impact of digital transformation on traditional industries and especially on how organizations redefine their strategy as well the impact of digital technologies on organizational decision-making.

9. Algorithm-Driven Reconfigurations of Trust Regimes: An Analysis of the Potentiality of Fake News

Jörn Wiengarn and Maike Arnold

Abstract

The aim of this chapter is to better understand the problem of fake news as a manifestation of a new algorithmic regime. The current rise of fake news is closely related to technical changes in news production and dissemination, in particular due to the new relevance of algorithms in this context. The social-epistemic problems of these changes, however, are only insufficiently conceptually understood. We suggest that problematic effects of fake news like generalized mistrust and polarization can be better grasped by focusing on the role trust plays as a medium of orientation for news consumers. The impact of the algorithmic regime behind fake news will be examined in terms of its potential influence on such basic trust structures.

Keywords: values; polarization; disorientation

Introduction

Although many reasons can be given for the recent exacerbation of the problem of fake news, the current algorithm-driven restructuring of the information space must clearly be named as one of the main contributing factors. While the internet and digitalization facilitate the production and dissemination of news in general, it is the specific design of its algorithmic infrastructure that tends to favour the spread of false information (Giansiracusa, 2021). Thus, filtering algorithms as new agents in the information space structure to a considerable extent the way in which information is presented to us today (see also Poechhacker et al., in this volume). Thereby,

Jarke, J., B. Prietl, S. Egbert, Y. Boeva, H. Heuer, and M. Arnold (eds.), *Algorithmic Regimes: Methods, Interactions, and Politics*. Amsterdam: Amsterdam University Press, 2024
DOI 10.5117/9789463728485_CH09

they produce an attention economy that in comparison to traditional mass media channels favours virality and sensationalist content over epistemic values such as truthfulness and factuality (Habermas, 2022; McIntyre, 2018). It is in this technological environment, with its lack of quality filters and incentives for novel and emotional contents, that fake news can thrive and influence the formation of public opinion.

As much as there is agreement that the new prevalence of fake news is driven by technical changes, it is also widely acknowledged that they have far-reaching social-epistemic consequences. Accordingly, the term "fake news" is not only used to refer to a novel kind of deceitful piece of information. Rather, it usually aims to capture some *structural* shift in our news environment and new challenges we face in navigating it. Thus, systemic social-epistemic pathologies like new forms of digital disorientation, digital tribalism, or group polarization are the kinds of associations that the term "fake news" evokes (see, for example, Bernecker et al., 2021)—often mentioned in the same breath with the idea that we are living in a "post-truth" era (see, for example, Habgood-Coote, 2019; McIntyre, 2018). All in all, fake news is associated with a profound restructuring of our lifeworld practices of news consumption, the order of public discourse, and also of basic social interaction forms. It is therefore only logical when Axel Gelfert stresses that fake news captures a "novel kind of social-epistemic dysfunction, arising from systemic distortions of established processes of creating and disseminating newslike content" (Gelfert, 2021, p. 310).

In a nutshell, fake news is an essentially algorithmically driven restructuring of social space and can thus be seen as a manifestation of a new algorithmic regime. To gain a better understanding of this regime, especially with regards to its social-interactive side, is the aim of this chapter. More precisely, we want to illustrate and conceptualize some of its paradigmatic social effects. In doing so, our goal is to provide a conceptual basis that can be used for future detailed studies on the complex interplay between technological changes in news production and the restructuring of social forms of interaction.

To undertake this analysis, we start from the central assumption that the knowledge we acquire through news is fundamentally grounded in trust—trust which is intricately woven within broader networks of trust and structured by what we refer to as trust regimes. Such trust regimes represent an important social-epistemological aspect of the current algorithmic regime in which fake news appears, namely the structuring of basic trust relationships. Our claim is that the far-reaching and potentially disrupting effects of fake news need to be analysed in terms of their impact on the level of such fundamental trust. It is this basic form of trust that fake news not only aims to exploit, but thereby also potentially reinforces, challenges, or undermines. To gain a better understanding of these effects, we will present three ideal-typical model scenarios of the potential social-epistemological impacts of fake news: the robustness scenario, the disorientation scenario, and the polarization scenario.

For that purpose, we focus on fake news rather than more broadly on disinformation, misinformation, or malinformation. The latter may have similar detrimental effects. Fake news, however, explicitly aims to mimic the appearance of news as an allegedly trustworthy type of information in order to benefit from its credibility. It therefore serves as a paradigm case to work out the conceptual logic that lies behind such effects like generalized mistrust that we aim to model.

The chapter is organized as follows: First, we will introduce the notion of trust that lies at the heart of our approach. With a view to the further analysis, we will particularly focus on a specific aspect of trust that becomes relevant for describing the polarizing effects of fake news, namely its value dimension. As we will show, trust partners essentially share relevant values. Second, we will elaborate more specifically on what trust in news amounts to. A core idea we will develop is that trust in news is always embedded in holistic networks of various trust relationships. Such networks serve as a kind of transcendental background against which news consumers determine the trustworthiness of news reports. This idea, combined with the idea that trust consists in sharing values, suggests the conclusion that trust in a news source cannot exist independently from a sense of belonging to a value community. After that, we will propose a definition of fake news and highlight its algorithmic dimension. This will lay the groundwork for introducing the aforementioned three models that aim to capture in a succinct way the disruptive impacts that fake news can have on a deeper social level. We will conclude with a brief outlook on the broader impact of fake news on the complexities of social interactions in the information space.

Trust and Values: A Philosophical Analysis

When it comes to navigating the news world, trust is of the essence. It is essentially in the medium of trust and mistrust that news consumers find orientation and decide which pieces of information to take at face value, which to view with scepticism and which to dismiss as blatantly false. A central assumption of our approach is that the impact of a new algorithmic regime around fake news is essentially to restructure such basic trust patterns. This implies that if we want to understand the full scope of the structure-building effects of this algorithmic regime, we should first gain a comprehensive understanding of what trust actually amounts to. In the following, we will do so by drawing on the philosophical literature.

The concept of interpersonal trust has been at the heart of philosophical debates in recent decades, especially due to an increased interest in testimony and speaker trust. Two questions were central to this debate: First, what does it mean to trust a speaker? And second, how can this trust be epistemically justified? From a historical point of view, the main focus has been on the latter question. In his famous essay "Of Miracles" (Hume, 2007, Section X), for example, David Hume is primarily concerned with the question of whether it is justified to place trust in reports of alleged miracles. To this end, he argues for a general criterion to determine the credibility of an instance of testimony. According to Hume, the justification for trusting other's testimony is based on empirical observation: our reasons for trusting a speaker are "not derived from any connexion, which we perceive a priori, between testimony and reality, but because we are accustomed to find a conformity between them" (Hume, 2007, p. 85). Thus, to the extent that there is an evidential correlation between what people say and what is actually the case, it is reasonable to put our trust in them.

Regardless of how exactly Hume conceived of this inductive evidence-based reasoning,[1] it should be noted that he adopts a rather constrained perspective on the phenomenon of testimony, which Richard Moran later labelled the "evidential view of testimony" (Moran, 2005). This term denotes a view according to which the testimony of another person represents mere potential evidence for what she asserts. From Hume's methodological viewpoint, the fact that a person tells us that so-and-so is the case constitutes nothing more than a piece of evidence from which we can infer, through inductive reasoning, the truth of what they say. However, as Moran argues, this perspective gives a distorted account of trust in a speaker. At best, the evidential view can provide a justification strategy for one's belief in an interlocutor. But it does not provide a phenomenologically adequate description of what it actually *means* to believe them.

Moran's critique sparked a wide discussion regarding the true nature of trust in a speaker. In this context, several authors developed an idea that is particularly instructive for our present purposes, namely the idea that trust in a person implies that relevant values are shared with them (De

---

1   For an overview, see Gelfert, 2014.

Melo-Martín & Intemann, 2018; Goldenberg, 2021; Kaminski, 2020). Among these proponents, Andreas Kaminski developed a detailed conceptual analysis that shows how the notion of trust in a person is intrinsically linked to the idea of a community of shared values between the trust partners. In the following, we want to give a brief sketch of Kaminski's main arguments.

What Moran's discussion of the evidential view has already suggested is that what it means to trust a person cannot be fully fleshed out in terms of a belief *about* them. Just as believing that what a speaker says is true does equate to trusting the speaker, it seems to hold generally that trusting a person for some action p cannot be reduced to a *believing that they do or will do p* (Lahno, 2002). Instead, it appears more plausible that by trusting a person, one does not simply assume that they will perform certain actions, but rather that they will do so *for the right reasons* (Faulkner, 2014). More specifically, trusting a person seems to imply that one assumes that they have a disposition to be value guided in their actions, or to put it another way: a trustor assumes that the trustee manifests a certain virtue, namely the virtue of trustworthiness.

However, this characterization still falls short of fully capturing the essence of interpersonal trust. As Kaminski has argued, trust in a person must be based on the assumption that the trustor *shares* certain relevant values with the trustee (Kaminski, 2020). Merely believing that the other is guided by relevant values does not suffice. Rather, the trustor must assume that they both hold the *same* relevant values dear. That explains, for example, why we would not consider a marriage trickster as trusting their victim: they may *rely on* the disposition of his victim to be guided by certain values. But since they themselves do not share these values, and only have their self-interest in mind, it would be inaccurate to characterize them as trusting (cf. Cogley, 2012; Lahno, 2002).

Moran's analysis is often interpreted as suggesting that once trust is no longer understood in terms of the evidential view, it does not require epistemic justification (cf. Lackey, 2008). However, this would give rise to a problematic dichotomization (Kaminski, 2020). After all, a trustor can only assume to share relevant values with the trustee if they have reasons to believe that this is indeed the case (or has at least no reasons to believe otherwise). Thus, although the reduction of interpersonal trust to a mere epistemic or cognitive phenomenon is flawed, trust always needs an epistemic footing. One cannot trust a person completely "blindly" but must at least assume to have sufficient epistemic reasons that warrant one's trust in her.

The upshot of this brief argumentative sketch is that the notion of personal trust is conceptually linked to the idea of shared values or a community of values between the trust partners. As we will see, this way of conceiving trust opens up the possibility to further explore interactive and emotional patterns related to trust and mistrust dynamics which will turn out to be particularly relevant for analysing the polarizing effects of fake news.

Trust in News

Having clarified the notion of trust in general, we now turn to the analysis of the more specific phenomenon of trust in news. More specifically, we aim to show that trust in this context is irreducibly embedded within a holistic network of trust relationships that provide epistemic orientation to news consumers and serve as a transcendental background to determine the trustworthiness of individual news sources and reports. In this context, we assume that individual news consumers do not autonomously establish relationships of trust from scratch, but always already find themselves within supra-individual structures that organize trust and mistrust. Since such structures also determine what is to be accepted or rejected as knowledge, we refer to them as trust regimes, in reference to Michel Foucault's concept of truth regimes (Foucault, 2000; see also Egbert, in this volume). Such trust regimes thus represent the impact of the algorithmic regime behind fake news with regards to basic trust patterns.

Before we start to develop this idea, it should first be noted that the basic function of news is to convey new information to others about recent events. Therefore, it can be regarded as a special kind of "truth warranting utterances" (Jaster & Lanius, 2021, p. 20), hence as a specific form of testimony (Mößner, 2018). As holds for testimony in general, placing trust in news has the potential to yield knowledge for its audience. Admittedly, while the philosophy of testimony primarily focuses on simplified cases where there are only two individuals—a testifier and an addressee—engaged in face-to-face interactions, things are more complicated when it comes to trusting the news. Here, multiple testifiers are involved in producing or purveying a news report. These reports are usually not addressed to a single individual, but to a larger audience, with both, the creators and the audience, usually remaining anonymous to one another. What is more, the act of communication does not necessarily represent a verbal speech act by the news producer but takes the form of a news report like an article, a TV newscast, or a podcast distributed through various media channels. Finally, the whole communication process is usually embedded in a complex institutional context. When a news report is produced within a larger media company, for example, its production and distribution must proceed according to some standard intra-institutional practices.

If we regard trust in news as a specific form of trust in testimony, the question arises of how such trust can in principle be warranted. What reasons could we in principle name for trusting certain news sources? In a first step, one might be inclined to respond that such trust is warranted by our actual empirical experience. After all, even if trust, as shown above, cannot be reduced to inductive reasoning, such reasoning can nevertheless be assumed to provide a suitable basis for justifying our trust.

However, as C. A. J. Coady points out, such a strategy seems to face a main challenge since for the vast majority of instances of testimony we lack access to empirical evidence to check on them (Coady, 1992). This limitation of our possibilities to directly verify testimony of others is particularly striking in the area of trust in news. It seems that only in exceptional circumstances can we verify what is reported by referring to direct observation. How, for example, can an individual news consumer possibly check whether Emmanuel Macron is in Paris at the moment, how high the global vaccination rate currently is, or that another climate conference is taking place?

Given these limitations, one might propose an alternative path by pointing out that the process of news production and distribution is embedded in an institutional context and practices that broadly ensure that what is reported is not just made up. Such institutions and practices may thus be regarded as a kind of "gatekeeper" or "quality filter" for the truth (Goldman, 1999; McIntyre, 2018). In this vein, Nicola Mößner, for example, states that "by taking the wider context of the news production into account it becomes clear that all comes down to trusting an institution rather than individual people" (Mößner, 2018, p. 9). More precisely, one may assume that journalists have undergone a certified training in which they have acquired good journalistic practices that ensure the truthfulness of what they report. One might also think that conscientious adherence to professional standards is likely to be a prerequisite for success in the journalism profession, while journalists who repeatedly violate ethical guidelines and editorial procedures may struggle to establish themselves. Moreover, one may assume that legal regulations by and large ensure that false reports are not easily published or broadcast. An example of such regulations is Germany's Interstate Media Treaty, which obliges public broadcasters to adhere to journalistic standards and to be "independent and objective" (Interstate Media Treaty, 2020, Article 6, p. 14).[2]

2   What counts as "objective" is, of course, not an objective evaluation but depends on the power and knowledge regime in place.

However, this institution-based approach also has its limitations. Once again, a justification gap becomes apparent that evokes yet another follow-up question, namely: How can one possibly know that the mentioned practices and institutions really exist and that they function sufficiently reliably? It seems that one mostly acquires knowledge about them from the testimony of others, whether it be from people who have direct practical contact with these institutions or from news reports themselves that inform us about them. Therefore, the problem of a limited experience base to justify one's trust reoccurs and it appears that to answer the question of how such trust is warranted, we are forced back to the beginning of our discussion.

What can we learn from this line of thought? It is important to note that our aim was not to argue that our trust in certain news sources ultimately, entangled in some kind of vicious circle, hangs in the air. The above discussion did not show that the trust of news consumers is simply arbitrary. After all, we have seen that in principle one can grab onto at least some evidential anchor points to guide one's trust. In principle, one has, albeit very isolated, empirical evidence to draw on: be it such evidence that directly suggests that a news report is true or evidence that supports the belief in a background institutional system which sufficiently fulfils its function as a kind of quality filter. Thus, it cannot be said that one's trust in news is completely random.

Still, the above discussion makes two points clear: First, from the perspective of an ordinary news consumer, one has only isolated empirical proof at hand to ground one's trust in news reports. The trust attitudes of news consumers are thus strongly underdetermined by evidence. They are not able to linearly deduce from evidence who it is reasonable to trust and who it is reasonable to distrust, if only because evidence itself is always already interpreted in the light of trust (cf. Lahno, 2002). This is precisely why it makes sense to speak of *trust* in news in the first place—if one had overwhelming and unambiguous evidence at hand to determine whether a news source is truthful or not, one would more or less *know* which source is reliable and trusting it would become unnecessary.

Second, the above line of argumentation also demonstrated that an individual's trust in certain news sources is always embedded in a broad network of interwoven trust relationships. One never simply trusts an isolated news source tout court. Things are more complicated for such trust in a particular source is based on and can at the same time fortify trust in other agents. A news consumer's trust in certain news sources is, as we saw, partly based on trust in the institutions that regulate their creation and dissemination. This latter trust is in turn partly based on reports about such institutions. Trust in news, then, does not exist independently of a holistic set of coherent and interdependent attitudes of trust.

As we have indicated, these trust networks provide the backdrop against which one decides who or what is or is not trustworthy. We could therefore say that these trust networks represent a transcendental structure, i.e., a condition of the possibility to trust certain news sources and news content and to distrust others. If, for example, one comes across news content from an unknown source that does not represent a building block of one's trust network, and that also reports in contradiction to the well-known sources of one's trust network, it naturally appears to be untrustworthy. Similarly, if one comes across such a suspicious piece of news, a natural way to verify its accuracy is to have a look at what already trusted sources say on this topic and whether they affirm or contradict its content. On the other hand, sources that occupy a hinge position in one's trust network will rather be taken at face value. Towards these one has formed ingrained practices of trust, such that one usually trusts them without even thinking about it. A person's adopted trust network thus gives her an epistemic footing to assess the trustworthiness of pieces of news.

This trust network model can be extended to include a value-related dimension. Above we have shown that trust in someone is not simply a cognitive attitude, but rather a relationship of shared values. The kind of values that are relevant in the context of trust in news is determined by what the audience in principle expects from a news source: First and foremost, of course, they expect news to report truthfully. Relevant values are therefore epistemic values. Accordingly, trusting a journalist means ascribing to him epistemic virtues such as sincerity and accuracy, which essentially means assuming that they uphold the value of truth (Williams, 2002, pp. 44–45). But it seems that it is not only the value of truth that is relevant for assessing the trustworthiness of a journalist. If news consumers trust journalists, they also ascribe to them a disposition to be guided by certain non-epistemic values: after all, journalists inevitably make choices regarding the events and topics they consider worth reporting on. Trusting journalists thus also means to assume that they make a reasonable value-oriented selection here, i.e., that they prioritize such events that are actually worth reporting.[3] In any case, we can draw the conclusion that since to trust someone means regarding them as sharing certain values with oneself, trust networks ultimately represent specific value communities. The persons and institutions of one's own trust

---

3   This includes that we expect news to report about significant changes in the world, i.e., we rely on the news for "epistemic coverage" (Goldberg, 2010).

network are thus understood, at least from the perspective of the trusting subject, as agents who essentially share one's own values.

In the remainder of this chapter, we will analyse the potential effects that fake news can have within and between such trust networks. As pointed out, trust networks form a transcendental background. However, this background is not set in stone but is contingent. Trust networks not only need to be reproduced and reinforced to stay in place, they can also be challenged and changed. Thus, trust networks are subject to modifications in various ways. The central aim of the remaining analysis is to examine the potential effects of new algorithmic modes of news production and distribution on this deeper level. But before we turn to this endeavour, we first need to get a clearer understanding of what fake news actually is and what role algorithms play in producing and spreading it.

Fake News and the Impact of Algorithms

Following a broad consensus in the literature (cf. Jaster & Lanius, 2018, 2021), we understand by fake news: (1) news-like reports (2) that are either false and/ or misleading and (3) whose creators have an intention to deceive or generally do not care for the truth. In more detail, this means the following: First, fake news mimics common journalism formats to pass itself off as real news. This goes as far as attempts by some fake news websites to copy the logos and URLs of traditional media networks. ABCnews.com.co, for example, was a fake news website which mimicked the URL, design, and logo of the ABC News website (Murtha, 2016). In this way, fake news seeks to exploit the everyday heuristics that news consumers use to identify credible news sources. This is the basis of fake news stories' deceptive effect: precisely because they look like "real," reliable news, they can lead their recipients to false beliefs. Second, despite its appearance as "real" news, fake news is false or misleading by definition. That means that fake news is either false in its literal content or it cleverly communicates falsities, often by omitting relevant facts (Jaster & Lanius, 2021, p. 21). Third, fake news is not just false news. False reports, even by established and all in all trustworthy news institutions, are not uncommon. Unlike fake news, however, these can just represent accidental slips. Behind fake news, however, there is a systematic indifference to the truth on the part of its creators. This does not necessarily have to apply to everyone who shares and spreads fake news, because they may well be convinced of its truthfulness. However, the original producers of fake news either have an intention to deceive (e.g., for political strategic motives) or a mere disregard for the truth.

The latter plays a role especially where fake news is spread for purely financial reasons as a means to generate clicks and views for advertising revenue, like in the case of the infamous Macedonian clickbait farms (Gelfert, 2018, p. 107).

It is important to note that the current surge of fake news is largely due to the design of the algorithmic infrastructure in the information space. Algorithms considerably boost the quantity and effectiveness of fake news on several levels. First, regarding the production of fake news, text generation software like GPT-3 can dramatically accelerate the creation of texts, enabling the mass production of fake news (Giansiracusa, 2021). Second, particularly on social media platforms, recommendation algorithms designed to increase user engagement and the overall number of clicks contribute in several ways to the faster spread of fake news (Vosoughi et al., 2018). These algorithms prioritize content that generates high levels of interaction, regardless of its factual accuracy. As a result, false or misleading information can gain significant visibility and reach a wide audience. Finally, what is presented to individual news consumers is essentially arranged by learning personalization algorithms. These algorithms tailor content to users' preferences and interests, often reinforcing existing beliefs and limiting exposure to diverse perspectives. Consequently, individuals may find themselves confined within filter bubbles (Pariser, 2011; Poechhacker et al., in this volume) and can thus potentially trap individual users in a more or less closed cosmos of fake news.

This describes the technical side of the algorithmic regime that is linked to fake news. The next step of our analysis will be to examine its social impact by looking at how it can potentially modify trust relationships.

An Analysis of Potential Effects of Fake News

In the following, we will introduce and examine three different types of potential effects of fake news, each of which will be explained by means of a model scenario. We call the three scenarios the robustness scenario, the disorientation scenario, and the polarization scenario. It is important to emphasize that we intend to describe the conceptual logic of *potential* effects, that is, we will only explore the space of possibilities of how fake news can affect trust networks. All three scenarios are to be understood as ideal-typical and therefore extreme scenarios. They have a model character and are intended to bring to the fore the working mechanisms of certain paradigm impacts of fake news. Accordingly, we will not discuss the extent to which or under which conditions the described effects actually occur.

For our analysis we will make the following assumptions: First, we will stick to an idealized conceptual opposition between news and fake news according to which they will report in contradiction to each other. Second, consequently, we will assume that news recipients, when repeatedly and persistently exposed to fake news will inevitably encounter conflicting reports—those from fake news source and those from non-fake news sources. Faced with such contradiction a news consumer must find a way to respond. Third, we propose that ideal-typical scenarios can occur regarding how they can adopt their trusting attitudes in light of these conflicting reports. Assuming that their trusting attitudes align with a prevailing trust regime that generally identifies news as credible, this position can either be consolidated, put into question, or overturned.

Robustness Scenario

The robustness scenario is a simplified scenario in which an existing trust regime is not fundamentally challenged. To illustrate this scenario, let's consider a person, A, who generally assumes that news can be trusted. What appears as news counts for A as a central pillar of her trust network, i.e., A has developed the epistemic routine of taking more or less at face value what is presented as news. While occasional false reports may arise, as long as the respective news institution corrects them, they do not significantly disrupt A's trust relationships.

However, if we now assume that A is increasingly confronted with fake news via social media channels that fundamentally and persistently contradicts what other sources report, a profound change occurs. In this scenario, A can no longer rely on their established trust practices, since they are confronted with news claiming that p is the case and news claiming that p is not the case. In light of such conflicting reports, A is confronted with the question of *which* news to trust. One possible option for them would be to draw a simple conclusion and to refine their trust practices: Thus, a possible reaction of A may be to start thinking that messages shared via social media are not necessarily trustworthy.

The described scenario thus exemplifies one possible and paradigmatic reaction to fake news-induced contradictions where a news consumer basically modifies her news consumption practices *from within the framework of her adopted trust network*. In the given example their trust in news-like reports represents a central pillar in A's trust network. And this is basically preserved, as it has in principle only been *added* to the insight that news producers and distributors on social media might not necessarily be committed to truth as a shared value. A can therefore not assume for all sources that there is a self-correcting error culture. Note that this not only removes a contradiction between single pieces of news. Rather, with this principled specification of their attitudes, A would *generally* be shielded from fake news in the described scenario. There is thus no need for a refutation of fake news on a case-by-case basis.

Interestingly, common proposals on how individual news consumers should change their news consumption behaviour in response to fake news similarly tend to suggest modifications within existing trust networks, thereby reinforcing the existing trust regime. For example, the above scenario manifests the same logic as Gelfert's proposal, which advocates for periodic revisions of one's routine news consumption based on learning experiences:

> Just as readers are free to cancel their newspaper subscription, for example, because over time their assessment of the newspaper's biases has changed or its coverage has deteriorated, an agent who is following a certain epistemic routine can, on occasion, choose to revise it. (Gelfert, 2021, p. 329)

It should be noted, however, that this option is only viable if a news consumer trusts what is reported in *some* news—in our example, this would be news beyond social media—and to view these as *benchmarks or criteria* for what is actually true. Only then would the individual news recipient be in position to draw on some standards that can guide them in their evaluation, revision, or fine-tuning of their trust practices. And only then can they reorient themselves *within the framework* of the adopted trust regime. Matters are more complicated, however, when precisely such higher-level criteria are called into question. Such a case is illustrated by our second scenario, the disorientation scenario.

Disorientation Scenario

One of the often pointed out dangers of fake news is that it can create generalized confusion and disorientation (McNair, 2018). Accordingly, a widely shared view is that the rise of fake news has made it increasingly difficult to discern what is true and what is false. By the same token, it is often argued that one of the underlying political motivations behind large-scale fake news campaigns is to foster such disorientation and to create the impression that it is impossible to distinguish truth from falsehood. Again, by appealing to the idea of transcendentally functioning trust networks, we can build a model to make sense of such a process.[4] Suppose again a person, B, is exposed to fake news, resulting in repeated exposure to contradictory reporting. If they are not like A in a position to find a criterion to resolve such contradictions, their situation holds the potential to raise profound questions for them. That is, it not only raises the question of which reports are true. Rather, the potential disruptive effect may run one level deeper, to the level of B's trust network itself. Thus, the question may arise for B: How can I identify a trustworthy source *at all*? What are the appropriate benchmarks for determining the trustworthiness of a source? While A was still able to hold on to trust in certain sources that gave her self-correcting orientation, for B this trust is called into question. In this sense, B would find themselves in a state of higher-order disorientation.

As we have shown above, such disorientation cannot really be resolved by referring to evidence. Neither can it be avoided by simply pointing out to B that there are sources that are trustworthy for institutional reasons. Things are more complicated, because the belief in such background institutions is itself rooted in trust—trust which too is called into question by the emergence of fake news. As discussed above, our ability to verify the existence and effectiveness of institutional safeguards is limited, leaving us no option but to trust respective testimonies such as news reports. If there is generalized doubt about their credibility, however, beliefs in practice-based and institutional precautions might also be undermined as a consequence. This consideration brings to light a kind of cascading effect that can emanate from the phenomenon of fake news. In the end, the scepticism potentially triggered by fake news can, if we push this scenario to the extreme, extend to an entire trust network. All the trust relationships and assumptions described above that embody a certain trust regime can potentially be called into question by the emergence of fake news. Fake news is thus potentially a manifestation of what Petra Gehring calls the "logic of the lie": It may create a whole "medium of mistrust," in which not a single reason for trust can be determined (Gehring, 2001, p. 126).

Such uncertainty does not necessarily mean that a news consumer actually falls prey to fake news; after all, they are exactly sceptical about news in general. An alternative scenario, however, would be where the situation

---

4   For a similar scenario, see Baurmann & Cohnitz, 2021, p. 348.

flips, so to speak, and a news consumer starts to build trust in fake news. Such a case is described in the last scenario we want to discuss.

Polarization Scenario

It is often pointed out as another worrying effect of fake news that it fuels the polarization of public debate. Gelfert even considers this polarizing effect to be a defining feature of fake news (Gelfert, 2021, p. 317). The way such effects work can be conceptualized in a third scenario. To outline the scenario, we again consider a person, C, who is confronted with contradictory news information due to fake news. While the first scenario depicted a case where the contradiction was resolved in favour of already trusted news sources; and the second scenario illustrated an ideal typical case where the contradiction remained unresolved; an obvious third option now is that the contradiction is resolved in the other direction, in favour of fake news. Accordingly, our person, C, may develop trust in fake news and distrust non-fake news, hence "the media."

At this point, we are not concerned with the psychological reasons why a person trusts fake news. Studies suggest that pre-existing biases play a significant role as fake news typically taps into these and reinforces them (Münchau, 2017). Similarly, knowing about biases of news creators and their audiences leads marginalized social groups to distrust media that facilitates their oppression. Leaving these considerations aside, however, we aim to show that with the help of the concept of trust regimes, it becomes visible on a conceptual level what the obvious *consequences* of such misguided trust are. Thus, trust in fake news does not just stop there, but potentially has further cascading effects that result from the transcendental logic of trust networks: As shown above, trust in a news source is always embedded in a broader entanglement of further trust relationships. It follows that trust in fake news naturally reinforces such wider trust contexts: This includes trust in other news sources that report in accordance with the initial fake news source, trust in the institutions and people behind it, and also trust in one's personal network when similar views are affirmed. On the other hand, there are also conceptual implications regarding mistrust in traditional news formats: Against the background of a trust network formed around fake news, non-fake news is to be classified as untrustworthy (cf. Ferrari & Moruzzi, 2021). This in turn has further far-reaching implications: In the end, it implies that the people and institutions behind the allegedly untrustworthy news sources must also be regarded as not sharing the same values and thus as themselves untrustworthy. And, furthermore, those still trusting these news sources appear to be standing on the wrong side. Fake news thus potentially poses the danger of entire regimes of mistrust developing.[5]

Since the flip side of trust in fake news is distrust in the legacy press, it explains how fake news can reinforce polarization tendencies. The concept of trust regimes offers a structural explanation of why such forms of polarization are, as often argued, so persistent and difficult to overcome. As pointed out, news consumers have only limited empirical evidence at their disposal, and if they do, they interpret it in the light of already existing trust networks. In fact, it seems that a whole network of trust relations would have to be replaced in order to overcome deep-rooted forms of polarization.[6] This explains why in a polarized situation it seems so hard to have fruitful debates about the truth or falsehoods of claims. The mere discrediting of the opponent may then seem like the only viable course of action in this helpless situation. Ironically, then, the arbitrary use of the term "fake news" these days, as it is sometimes deplored in philosophical discourse (Coady, 2021), can be seen precisely as an effect of the rise of actual fake news.

It is especially with the polarization scenario that the evaluative dimension of trust relationships becomes apparent. Above we argued that trust relationships represent communities of values. Accordingly, to distrust an agent implies to hold that she does not share crucial values or even undermines them. This perspective highlights that the polarizing effects of fake news are not just to be understood as epistemic effects: The danger of polarization between different trust networks is not only that it undermines a common epistemic ground which could enable mutual understanding. Rather, it follows from the value-oriented nature of trust regimes that polarization entails a tendency to *despise* the other side: agents in this scenario might oppose the dominant trust regime altogether and express their outrage at its representative' lack of trustworthiness by calling them names like the German "*Lügenpresse*" ("Lying press"). More generally, the value dimension can explain not only the emotional tone of fake news, but also the affective reactions to them, as well as the heated tempers when fake news are debated. As our analysis of trust suggests, such emotionality comes into play because questions of trust and mistrust always touch on questions of who shares relevant values and who does not.

---

5   Likewise, fake news often explicitly aims at the delegitimization of traditional sources as well as of state institutions interwoven with them (Bennett & Livingston, 2018).
6   This idea is similar to central ideas of C. Thi Nguyen about echo chambers and why they are so difficult to overcome (Nguyen, 2020).

The Ramifications of Fake News

Our model of polarization effects highlights the far-reaching extent to which an algorithmic regime around fake news intervenes, even at the level of basic social interactions. Admittedly, we were only able to touch on some selected aspects of this complex field, namely trust- and mistrust-driven forms of interaction between news consumers and producers and, especially with regards to polarizing effects, among news consumers themselves. However, it is important to emphasize that since we were primarily interested in developing basic models, we had to disregard many other aspects of the complex influence of fake news on forms of social interaction. One aspect that we could not explore concerns the extent to which news consumers influence each other in their trust and mistrust behaviour and thus have an influence on the impact of fake news. Considering such wider patterns of complex interactions between various agents might also help to better evaluate potential measures to counter the spread of fake news. For example, if we regard measures like fact-checking as interventions by some actors who are themselves integrated within trust networks, it becomes apparent that they must themselves already be trusted to carry out fact-checking in order for their actions to have a positive effect. Such complex issues of the interaction between manifold actors in the information space can only be hinted at here. Nonetheless, we hope that our proposed models serve as a useful conceptual foundation for identifying some of the basic processes that occur within this complex interaction field and provide a starting point for further investigation and analysis of the multifaceted dynamics at play in the realm of fake news and its impact on social interactions.

References

Baurmann, M., & Cohnitz, D. (2021). Trust no one? In S. Bernecker, A. K. Flowerree, & T. Grundmann (Eds.), *The epistemology of fake news* (pp. 334–357). Oxford University Press.

Bennett, W. L., & Livingston, S. (2018). The disinformation order: Disruptive communication and the decline of democratic institutions. *European Journal of Communication, 33*(2), 122–139.

Bernecker, S., Flowerree, A. K., & Grundmann, T. (2021). Introduction. In S. Bernecker, A. K. Flowerree, & T. Grundmann (Eds.), *The epistemology of fake news* (pp. 1–16). Oxford University Press.

Coady, C. A. J. (1992). *Testimony: A philosophical study.* Clarendon Press.

Coady, D. (2021). The fake news about fake news. In S. Bernecker, A. K. Flowerree, & T. Grundmann (Eds.), *The epistemology of fake news* (pp. 68–81). Oxford University Press.

Cogley, Z. (2012). Trust and the trickster problem. *Analytic Philosophy, 53*(1), 30–47.

De Melo-Martín, I., & Intemann, K. (2018). *The fight against doubt: How to bridge the gap between scientists and the public.* Oxford University Press.

Faulkner, P. (2014). The practical rationality of trust. *Synthese, 191*(9), 1975–1989.

Ferrari, F., & Moruzzi, S. (2021). Enquiry and normative deviance. In S. Bernecker, A. K. Flowerree, & T. Grundmann (Eds.), *The epistemology of fake news* (pp. 109–133). Oxford University Press.

Foucault, M. (2000). Truth and power. In J. B. Faubion (Ed.), *Power* (vol. 3, pp. 111–133).

Gehring, P. (2001). Der Zweifel an der Wirklichkeit und die Logik der Lüge: Ein Exempel aus Don Quixote. In K. Röttgers & M. Schmitz-Emans (Eds.), *Dichter lügen* (pp. 107–128). Die blaue Eule.

Gelfert, A. (2014). *A critical introduction to testimony.* A&C Black.

Gelfert, A. (2018). Fake news: A definition. *Informal logic, 38*(1), 84–117.

Gelfert, A. (2021). Fake news, false beliefs, and the fallible art of knowledge maintenance. In S. Bernecker, A. K. Flowerree, & T. Grundmann (Eds.), *The epistemology of fake news* (pp. 310–333). Oxford University Press.

Giansiracusa, N. (2021). *How algorithms create and prevent fake news.* Springer.

Goldberg, S. (2010). *Relying on others: An essay in epistemology.* Oxford University Press.

Goldenberg, M. J. (2021). *Vaccine hesitancy: Public trust, expertise, and the war on science.* University of Pittsburgh Press.

Goldman, A. I. (1999). *Knowledge in a social world.* Oxford University Press.

Habermas, J. (2022). *Ein neuer Strukturwandel der Öffentlichkeit und die deliberative Politik.* Suhrkamp.

Habgood-Coote, J. (2019). Stop talking about fake news! *Inquiry: An Interdisciplinary Journal of Philosophy, 62*(9–10), 1033–1065. https://doi.org/10.1080/002017 4x.2018.1508363

Hume, D. (2007). *An enquiry concerning human understanding* (P. Millican, Ed.). Oxford University Press.

Interstate Media Treaty. (2020, April 14/28). *Interstate Media Treaty (Medienstaatsvertrag).* https://www.die-medienanstalten.de/fileadmin/user_upload/Rechtsgrundlagen/Gesetze_Staatsvertraege/Interstate_Media_Treaty_en.pdf

Jaster, R., & Lanius, D. (2018). What is fake news? *Versus, 47*(2), 207–224.

Jaster, R., & Lanius, D. (2021). Speaking of fake news: Definitions and dimensions. In S. Bernecker, A. K. Flowerree, & T. Grundmann (Eds.), *The epistemology of fake news* (pp. 19–45). Oxford University Press.

Kaminski, A. (2020). *Die verwickelte Einfachheit von Vertrauen und seine spekulative Struktur*. Habilitation thesis, Universität Marburg.

Lackey, J. (2008). *Learning from words: Testimony as a source of knowledge*. Oxford University Press on Demand.

Lahno, B. (2002). *Der Begriff des Vertrauens*. Mentis.

McIntyre, L. (2018). *Post-truth*. MIT Press.

McNair, B. (2018). *Fake news: Falsehood, fabrication and fantasy in journalism*. Routledge.

Moran, R. (2005). Getting told and being believed. *Philosophers' Imprint, 5*(5), 1–29.

Mößner, N. (2018). Trusting the media? TV news as a source of knowledge. *International Journal of Philosophical Studies, 26*(2), 205–220.

Münchau, W. (2017, July 9). From Brexit to fake trade deals: The curse of confirmation bias. *Financial Times*. https://www.ft.com/content/b7d68798-62fb-11e7-91a7-502f7ee26895

Murtha, J. (2016, May 26). How fake news sites frequently trick big-time journalists. *Columbia Journalism Review*. https://www.cjr.org/analysis/how_fake_news_sites_frequently_trick_big-time_journalists.php

Nguyen, C. T. (2020). Echo chambers and epistemic bubbles. *Episteme, 17*(2), 141–161. https://doi.org/10.1017/epi.2018.32

Pariser, E. (2011). *The filter bubble: What the internet is hiding from you*. Penguin.

Vosoughi, S., Roy, D., & Aral, S. (2018). The spread of true and false news online. *Science, 359*(6380), 1146–1151.

Williams, B. A. O. (2002). *Truth & truthfulness: An essay in genealogy*. Princeton University Press.

About the Authors

Jörn Wiengarn is a research associate at the Institute of Philosophy of TU Darmstadt in Germany. His research focuses on the social-epistemological side of scientific and technological developments, with particular emphasis on questions of trust and mistrust in this context.

Maike Arnold is a research associate in the KRITIS research training group and the Institute of Philosophy of TU Darmstadt in Germany. Their research focuses on trust in testimony in the context of critical decision-making, especially concerning critical infrastructures and in the context of the algorithmization of information technology systems.

10. Recommender Systems beyond the Filter Bubble: Algorithmic Media and the Fabrication of Publics

Nikolaus Poechhacker, Marcus Burkhardt, and Jan-Hendrik Passoth

Abstract

The increasing use of recommender systems reorganizes the dissemination of information and can be understood as an algorithmic regime with the potential to splinter the public sphere (Pariser, 2011; Sunstein, 2009). This creates, so the popular narrative goes, an issue for democratic discourse. Yet, this narrative ignores how the audience is always a constructed one (Ang, 1991). Drawing from Dewey's concept of "issue publics," we argue that different algorithmic techniques (Rieder, 2017) for recommendations impact the construction of publics by mediating practices within an algorithmic regime. Analysing how algorithmic techniques are embedded in and mediate between databases, interfaces, and practices sensitizes us to the formation of digital publics. This opens up perspectives for rethinking algorithmic regimes of information distribution for democratic societies.

Keywords: algorithms; democracy; Dewey

Introduction

Debates about network cultures highlighted the democratizing potentials of digital communication and information technologies at the turn of the millennium. Over the course of the past decade, however, digital media have increasingly been seen as a problem for democratic societies, e.g., by enabling and distributing fake news (Wiengarn & Arnold, in this volume)

Jarke, J., B. Prietl, S. Egbert, Y. Boeva, H. Heuer, and M. Arnold (eds.), *Algorithmic Regimes: Methods, Interactions, and Politics*. Amsterdam: Amsterdam University Press, 2024
DOI 10.5117/9789463728485_CH10

and segregating public discourse into filter bubbles (Pariser, 2011) or echo chambers (Sunstein, 2009). Especially the latter has become an issue for political debate, as political theory positions a common public sphere as the prerequisite of modern and reflexive democratic societies (Habermas, 1991) or the stabilization of nation states (Anderson, 2006). Algorithmic filtering systems—i.e., the selection of news feeds, recommendations on media and info sites, or search results—are blamed for segregating the public sphere. Instead of fostering a discussion between a multitude of different positions and world views, it is said that individuals have become prisoners of communicative communities in which only their own opinions and world views are reflected back to them. This, so the argument goes, is an important element in understanding the polarization of contemporary societies. As a result, the democratic dimension of filtering mechanisms such as recommender systems and their impact on the public sphere has become a focus of scholarly and political attention (Gillespie, 2014; Helberger, 2011, 2019; Napoli, 2011; Nechushtai & Lewis, 2019; Pöchhacker et al., 2017; Sørensen & Schmidt, 2016). While the public sphere and publicly available information are often conceptualized in terms of deliberative democracy, legalistic views of democracy are also touched by such conceptions.[1] Open, diverse, and transparent information that allows for public debate is essential for public protest and limiting the state's power over its citizens. Thus, understanding the emergence of new information spheres under algorithmic conditions calls for a deeper understanding of the media systems' infrastructures of media distribution and relevance production. Especially in the field of public broadcasting this was perceived as an issue, as recommender systems seemingly reduce the variety of available information (Helberger, 2019) and therefore undermine the democratic role of public broadcasting services.

And yet, the story is not as straightforward. It is based on two assumptions that hold the narrative together. First, the very idea that filter bubbles exist and, second, that a common public sphere has existed so far. The first assumption has been contested by several scholars (Bruns, 2019; Haim et al., 2018). Such critical inquiries into the existence or non-existence of filter bubble effects have led to a more nuanced discussion about the diversity and contexts of the phenomenon. Whether a filter bubble or echo chamber emerges depends on the contextual and situated interplay of many different actors, including different algorithmic techniques and their utilization. The second assumption implicitly rests on specific ideas of an information space and its infrastructures for contemporary democracies derived from political

1   For a more in-depth discussion of ideal-typical models of democracy, see Held, 2006.

theory and the enacted experience of democratic institutions: the idea of a coherent and monolithic public sphere that is enabled by central institutions as news providers. In such a perspective information filtering is problematic for democratic societies, as it breaks up this common communication space. This assumption ignores the multiple techniques in place to produce the audience that is being addressed by established media systems (Ang, 1991). With the introduction of recommender algorithms, the operation modes of producing publics have changed in a profound way. Instead of constructing the audience as a whole and creating relevance of information for everyone in a comparable way, digital recommender systems introduce a new algorithmic regime in which relevance is individualized. According to Gillespie (2014), digital recommendation algorithms "are now a key logic governing the flows of information" (p. 167), yet the mode in which these publics are constructed shifts. Not at last, as—to Gillespie—the recommendation algorithms invite us to be part of a "calculated public," but do not make transparent what the base public is that has been used to calculate these invitations. Thus, while *the* public is and needs to be constructed via data collection, the resulting calculated publics are fragmented and multiple.

These points both hint towards the socio-technical conditions of possibility to produce and address publics, and how the introduction of new algorithmic regimes are changing the necessary modes of constructing these publics. By taking this perspective, we do not understand algorithms themselves as regimes but rather as one (important) actor in a wider network that follows a specific rational in the nexus of knowledge/power conflation (Ananny, 2016; Bucher, 2018) and that is often embedded in existing forms of organizations (Büchner et al., in this volume; Poechhacker, forthcoming). Algorithmic regimes in that regard are relationally constituted by the arrangement of databases, data production practices, tracking software, media users, signal interpretation, and other socio-technical elements mediated by the specific algorithmic technique applied to calculate recommendations. Classical political theories are, however, often not well equipped to deal with the question of how publics are emerging or are enacted in an algorithmic regime. Instead, these theories are more concerned with how a common public sphere mediates consensus-oriented discourse (Habermas, 1992) or political conflicts (Laclau & Mouffe, 2014). To understand the new media configurations of our democratic societies a different perspective is needed. In this contribution we want to take a first step in this direction by confronting ideal typic techniques of recommender systems with pragmatist ideas of democracy and the public as theorized by John Dewey (2006), asking what role algorithmic regimes and their algorithms have in constituting public(s) as part of a broader information system. We discuss the issue from a theoretical perspective that can inform subsequent empirical investigations and interventions. This allows us to reconstruct ongoing shifts in (public) information systems and anticipate possible reactions in democratic societies. In the following sections, we will discuss how a Deweyan perspective on the public sphere might be helpful in conceptualizing the impact of algorithmic regimes on public discourse. Further, we will take a closer look at two ideal typical recommender techniques to reconstruct how actions are mediated and related in the construction of publics. To do so, we utilize the concept of algorithmic techniques as proposed by Bernhard Rieder (2017). In conclusion, we argue that bringing together an approach of algorithmic techniques and a pragmatist understanding of "issue publics" allows us to understand algorithmic regimes and their impact on information spheres better and even allows us to identify moments of intervention to potentially realize algorithmic regimes that are in line with democratic values and reasoning.

Pragmatics of Filtering

Information, public discourse, and participation in political processes are vital elements in vivid democracies. Especially in recent years, the decoupling of representation, public political communication, and actual political action has been diagnosed. This state has been called post-democracy (Crouch, 2004) and raised the call to democratize democracy (Mouffe, 2005). At the same time, we can observe, especially in times of the diverse ongoing crisis situations, a strong rhetoric of evidence-based politics (Jasanoff, 2005). These trends, while not providing a complete picture, show that debates about democracy are always tied to specific ways of practicing democracy. This also includes practicing the public, as different information spheres cater to different needs of practical democracy. A perspective on these practical issues of doing and making democracy can be found in the pragmatist philosophy of John Dewey (2006). Dewey famously formulated a theory on the production of publics that rests on a bottom-up understanding of the relation between the individual and the collective (see also Marres, 2007). This conception of the democratic public thereby rests on two important assumptions.

First, individuals are competent members of society identifying issues, and, second, publics only exist in the plural. Contrary to other ideas in his time, Dewey argues that people are quite competent in identifying relevant topics by themselves. Public discussion evolves not (just) around topics produced by experts, but around topics, objects, and problems identified as relevant by the people—the public discussion unfolds around different issues, as Dewey calls them. Following the pragmatist philosophy these topics are becoming important as they are emerging out of behaviour that spreads within a given collective or society. Or, in other words, issues become a public issue when enough people are confronted with problems (or reflexive moments) in the unfolding of everyday action and make that a topic of a broader discussion. Whether an issue is private or public is not defined apriori by the content but through communicating patterns that define this outcome in the process. Public issues are defined bottom-up, not top-down. *The* public does not exist in any fixed or predefined manner, but publics become (and cease to exist) a result of self-organizing collectives, reflexively dealing with identified issues.[2]

In this perspective, the filter bubble as such is not a problem but the default. The task for democratic institutions is now to navigate these issue publics and enable other members of the political community to attach themselves to the emerging issues—and as a result become part of the bigger discourse. We can observe this in the setup and mission of public broadcasting. The idea behind the institution is to give a good overview on the social, political, and cultural events within the republic and to enable the informed democratic citizen, an ideal that has been even more discussed in relation to the ongoing digital transformation (Helberger, 2019). In the analogue era of broadcasting this has been realized by central institutions that provide news in a one-to-many model of communication providing information about (1) the existence of selected issues and (2) background information about them. Or in Dewey's conceptual language: through practices of the media providers, selected issues are made available for a broad audience, and each and every individual can decide to engage with them. If enough individuals are engaging with these issues, they become publics in their own right. Thus, established media institutions are not constructing a common public sphere, but mediate between and create the conditions of possibility for different smaller issue publics. In this sense, a recommendation algorithm does not call a public into existence, as Gillespie (2014) formulated it, but rather its potential for existence.

What we can learn from this debate is that recommender systems and their logic of relating information with individuals are ambivalent to the

---

2   There is much more to say about this. Ideal-typically these ideas range in the tension of representative and deliberative democracy. However, they also open up much space for discussion of the role of populism in political debates.

term of democracy—depending on which conception we are following. Recommender systems react to signals from the users and adapt their personalized recommendations accordingly. Algorithmically observed behaviour is what drives the computation of recommendations. This could lead to the conclusion that recommender systems are much more compatible with a bottom-up democracy as envisioned by Dewey. As we will see later on, this distinction is not as straightforward. However, two important conclusions can be drawn from Dewey's conception of a pragmatist account of public discourse that are relevant to understanding how recommender systems impact information spheres. First, it is helpful to conceptualize the singular monolithic public as a special case that was enacted by the imaginary of a centralized media system. Instead, the public reconfigures itself always anew around different issues, forming what Dewey called "issue publics" (Dewey, 2006; Marres, 2007). Most of the time we are dealing with publics in a plural. In that regard the media system serves as an infrastructure for broadening issue publics. Second, in such a conception of public discourse, the bottom-up constructed publics must be taken seriously in a democratic society. While Dewey sees the necessity of experts informing the public, he argues for an integrated and open research, factoring in the problems and experiences of the people involved. The role of experts is therefore a crucial one, but in a radically different way: informing the emerging publics, but also connecting and relating different discussions with the political system and other discussions as well.

As a result of these conclusions, the pressing question in respect to the filter bubble discussion is not whether they exist or not, but how the formation of issue publics is prescribed, transformed, or modulated by an algorithmic regime and how we relate that to a democratic media system. While the ongoing discussion on filter bubbles follows a holistic idea of the public that disintegrates with the introduction of filter technologies, Dewey shifts the focus of attention from the (seemingly) independent public toward the local and practical processes that constitute different publics. This also opens up the possibility to think about the emergence of filter publics in a different form. The contribution of recommender systems to emerging issue publics can—and should—also be read in a media-sensitive way, raising the question how different algorithmic techniques are entangled differently in the making of publics.

A media sensitive perspective on algorithmic regimes requires us to understand the ideas and assumptions that are inscribed into its algorithms. Different algorithms and/or algorithmic techniques realize what Bucher (2018, p. 4) called programmed sociality. Algorithms and software are not determining, but organizing social relationships and prescribe certain meanings that need to be taken up and actualized in subsequent practices. As such they are becoming important elements in a socio-technical structure that interacts with individual agency.[3] For some time now there has been a debate on how to approach algorithms as entities of a socio-technical world (Ziewitz, 2016). The answers range from understanding algorithms as contextual construction of meaning (Seaver, 2018) towards a call to becoming a programmer oneself (Kitchin, 2017; Manovich, 2011). These, however, aim either at the ethnographic reconstruction of specific forms of an algorithm (in its multiplicity) or the full immersion into the field for intervention. A promising approach between these positions has been formulated by Bernhard Rieder (2017). Instead of looking at concrete implementation, we can analyse algorithmic techniques. Algorithmic techniques are abstract formulations of a solution to a given problem. Examples are pseudo code representation of sorting algorithms, or general descriptions of neural networks. They do not represent running code, but are more concrete than a reference to *the algorithm*. This places algorithms in the realm of a professional discourse that travels between sites and represents disciplinary knowledge that exceeds specific situations of implementation but makes algorithms concrete enough to learn something about their socio-technical qualities. While these algorithmic techniques are not working implementations, they provide ideal types of how sorting algorithms, recommender systems, or path finding should work. Especially, as these algorithmic techniques are often transported in academic journals or text books on computer science. Looking at these abstract descriptions of recommender algorithms allows us to reconstruct the basic rational that is inscribed in them and in most implementations. And since these algorithmic techniques do not only travel in space, but also through time, a genealogy of algorithmic techniques also allows us to understand which assumptions have hardened or shifted over time. In the next section, we will have a closer look at the past and present of the algorithmic techniques of two ideal-typical recommender techniques.

Reading Recommender Techniques

Whether knowingly or unknowingly, interacting with recommender systems is an integral part of everyday media use in today's digital media culture.

---

3   With this, algorithmic systems and their conceptualization as structural mediators are touching on the old structure/agency debate (e.g., Giddens, 1984).

And while all recommender systems share the primary purpose of direct-ing the attention of their users to items that could be interesting to them, these systems differ substantially on what information recommendations are based on, how recommendations are evaluated, how individual end users and other actors are entangled in the algorithmic production of recommendations, and what kinds of recommender publics these systems allow to form. Recommendations, for example, can be based on a logic of aggregation or on a logic of personalization. A typical example for aggrega-tion is the "trending topics" feature (as seen on Twitter), where simply the number of interactions per time unit becomes an indicator for calculating relevance. Personalization, on the other hand, seeks to find some form of comparability between different items to create a relation between them (Mackenzie, 2015). Recommendations like these are often found under the heading "people who viewed this item also viewed these: ..." or result in the often counterintuitive genres of Netflix (Koren et al., 2009). However, how comparability is produced in the first place differs, and it changes how recommender algorithms produce collectives of users and items. In the following we discuss the genealogy and inscribed ideas of two ideal-typical techniques of contemporary recommender systems.

The ideas of filter systems to organize information selection and distribu-tion has been around for longer than the discussion on echo chambers. In 1992, the prestigious computer science journal *Communications of the ACM* dedicated an issue to the topic of information filtering. By this time, it had become obvious to researchers and software developers alike that the progressing realization of "[t]he promise of the information age" was a "mixed blessing" (Loeb & Terry, 1992, p. 27). With the expansion of computer networks the availability of digitally networked communication services such as Usenet, and the growing number of users of such services during the 1980s, the challenges posed by the increasing amount of incoming information each individual user has to deal with were framed as a problem of filtering. Here, information filters were not discussed as technologies that establish limits a user cannot or at least shall not surpass as in the case of internet censorship or child protection filters, but as tools for empowering individual users that allow them to "control the potentially unlimited flux of information" (ibid.). In this respect information filtering is aligned with the early ideals of network cultures:

> Open-ended networks such as the internet open up a space of possibili-ties which users can shape for their own purposes. Technical filters as decentralized problem solutions expand their abilities in this respect.

Filter technologies are in the tradition of internet culture because they do not restrict the freedom of information. They give the right not to listen an additional chance of realization. (Hoffmann, 1996, p. 18, authors' translation)

By putting individual users and their informational needs at the centre this form of information filtering is similar to information retrieval which was defined by Calvin Mooers as "[t]he problem of directing a user to stored information, some of which may be unknown" to them (Mooers, 1950, p. 572). While being concerned with similar problems as well as similar entities, information filtering has some unique characteristics. Following Belkin and Croft (1992), information filtering is concerned with enduring information interests as opposed to short-term information needs that information retrieval aims to meet. In this respect filtering addresses a chronic problem rather than an acute one: It is about highlighting certain information for users and bringing it to their attention in a dynamic and ongoing stream of information or media use (or consumption). As computational means for separating the relevant from the irrelevant or the wanted from the unwanted, information filters are technologies for constituting and processing "computer-readable significance" (Becker & Stalder, 2009, p. 8). They are based on profiles which according to Belkin and Croft are considered "to be correct specification of information interests" (Belkin & Croft, 1992, p. 32). By now this assumed correctness of user profiles has to be treated as a problematic presupposition, especially in terms of democratic discourse, which requires also finding solutions to intervene into these emerging algorithmic regimes of information provision. Yet, to do so we have to understand the inscribed ideas of the algorithmic techniques and which practices are mediated in constructing filter results by them.

Content-Based Filtering

In the early 1990s profiles were not primarily preferences assigned to users computationally but sets of rules that users themselves made explicit and which were continuously optimized in order to state their interests or disinterests. Such rules were largely based on criteria related to the content of incoming messages (informational entities) or their metadata, such as the sender of a message or its distribution channel. However, this form of content-based filtering assumes that the user already knows what they are looking for. An assumption that is often found to be problematic—not just in relation to democratic debates. Thus, content-based filtering for contemporary recommender systems (mostly) no longer relies on explicitly formulated rules. Instead, a database of computer-readable descriptions serves as the base from which items similar to those rated high or looked at by a single user are retrieved as recommendations.

A common approach is the TF-IDF (term frequency–inverse document frequency) technique. In it a vector space over all used words describing items is built and similarity is constructed by the relative distance between the vectors describing items. The TF-IDF approach follows an interesting thought, giving terms that are less frequent over all documents a higher priority, as they are seen as more relevant signals. In this approach, very often the description of items is coming from editorial teams writing short texts or applying typical tags and categories to their items to make them identifiable. For example, an item A = {"Zombies," "Romance," "England," "Martial Arts"} would probably be seen similar to B = {"Zombies," "Korea," "Martial Arts," "Romance"} as they would live close in the resulting abstract vector space. This, however, creates issues within the system of the algorithmic regime. To create some ordered and comparable set of item descriptions, the modes of producing them have to be streamlined according to an organizational logic. The algorithmic regime consists not only of the recommender algorithm as a mediator, but also requires the involved actors to standardize their practices of data production. Otherwise, the different items would not be comparable in the lines of a common logic, resulting in surprising and often not helpful results.

A slightly different version of the same principle can be seen in so-called social tagging recommender. Instead of centrally creating tags and descriptions for items, the production of metadata has been externalized to "the crowd," allowing users to upload content and apply tags and descriptions in an open way, i.e., not inside a given classification scheme. Interestingly, this has been called a collaborative classification scheme that is unstructured and also called a folksonomy (Bellogín et al., 2013). The way collaboration works here has shifted from the approach described before (common patterns of usage or centralized production of classification schemes) to a crowd-sourced form of classification, decentring how similarities are being constructed. The relationship between content provider and content consumer has been complicated and multiplied. The configuration of user actions that are put in relation to each other here is not between users and data workers, but with the (emerging) audience and the classification practices of the same group or a subgroup of that. No professional editors or data workers with a pre-given classification scheme are included. Relevance is constructed

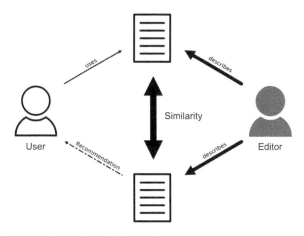

Figure 10.1. Content-based filtering relations.

through a collective effort to identify and classify content. While the logic of the algorithm stays the same, the power to define similar content has shifted dramatically in these applications.[4]

Although the approach is named content based, it represents a form of collaboration between the users, indicating their preferences through consumer behaviour and the editors/data workers producing data descriptions for items to make them comparable in the first place. Potential issues are emerging out of different configurations of actions that are set in relation to each other As shown in Figure 10.1 the algorithm mediates between he consumption patterns of the user and the practices of producing equivalence in metadata descriptions. By mediating these different practices, relevance is constructed in the interactions between those groups, transformed through the logic of the algorithm (e.g., as in this case the TF-IDF logic).

Coming back to Dewey, in this approach different forms of action are made relevant to each other to calculate relevance based on the produced metadata. Instead of relating the actions of users to each other, the algorithmic mediator constructs relevance based by relating the actions of data producers and media consumption of users. A central element in constructing publics and relevance of information items in this algorithmic technique is based on active participation in classifying items and producing meaning by relating "similar" items to each other. Issues arise here in the

4   This is also interesting as processes of consciously producing meaning in such a collaborative process often also create struggles over inclusion and exclusion. See, e.g., Graham et al., 2014.

complex interactions between classification as collective action and its uptake within an interaction order. Classification is (not just here) the power to define what relates to certain topics and what does not, what pieces of information to include, and which to exclude. Classifiers here have the function of floating signifiers and the community of data producers is creating chains of equivalence and can shape political discourse.[5]

Collaborative Filtering

Although content-based methods for filtering information could rely on a large body of research in information retrieval, researchers and practitioners were looking for new and more accurate forms of information filtering. In their article "Using Collaborative Filtering to Weave an Information Tapestry," Goldberg et al. proposed a crucial extension to the content-based filtering approach. They argued for the inclusion of social signals in the evaluation of information flows: "Collaborative filtering simply means that people collaborate to help one another perform filtering by recording their reactions to documents they read" (Goldberg et al., 1992, p. 61).

The intuition behind and explanation of the collaborative filtering approach is the attempt to make use of the knowledge about user behaviour for filtering information: "However, you know that Smith, Jones and O'Brien read all of comp.unixwizards newsgroup material, and reply to the more interesting documents. Tapestry allows you to filter on 'documents replied to by Smith, Jones, or O'Brien'" (ibid., p. 62).

Collaborative filtering relies on the social use of information which implies that significance of informational entities is dynamically changing over time. A message that is filtered out today might be deemed relevant tomorrow because of the attention it received by certain people. Collaborative filtering follows the idea that "people collaborate to help one another perform filtering by recording their reactions to documents they read" (ibid., p. 61). Even though its origins can be traced back at least to the early 1990s, collaborative filtering has been heavily popularized by Netflix and other commercial actors. The idea behind collaborative filtering put forward in modern systems could be summarized as: *similar users like similar things.* Collaborative filtering systems calculate these similarities based on user valuations as well as on user behaviours, which are made comparable subsequently by

---

5   This is, of course, a reference to the political discourse theory developed by Laclau and Mouffe, 2014.

finding patterns in the collected data sets—individual user preferences and behaviours are gathered into a collective "database of intentions" (Battelle, 2006, p. 2).

The notion of helping each other needs a more critical reflection here. What does it mean that someone is helping someone else in the context of collaborative filtering systems? And are users actually aiming to collaborate with each other? It is indeed debatable that the users' (inter) actions with such systems are related to their subjective meaning of helping each other, but simply directed towards other goals—if any. Instead, the actions are made relevant to each other within the logic of the algorithmic regime. Instead of relying on active production of meaning through classification, the algorithmic technique solely rests on the observation of behaviour.

Table 10.1.   User/Item Matrix as Often Used in Collaborative Filtering Recommender

	Item 1	Item 2	Item 3	Item 4	Item 5
User 1	0	3	0	3	0
User 2	4	1	0	2	0
User 3	0	0	3	3	3
User 4	3	0	4	0	3
User 5	4	3	0	5	0

The matrix in Table 10.1 presents this accumulative logic of collaborative filtering in a simplified manner. It contains but one signal for user preferences: explicit ratings assigned to certain items by users. In the given example each user can assign a rating of one to five stars to items. This is then recorded in the matrix. Based on these user–item relations the collaborative filtering algorithm tries to find patterns in the matrix to make users and items comparable to each other. A very common approach to this would be a factorization of the matrix.[6] The remarkable feature of this approach is that the production of data only aims at interactions between users and items. The only recorded metadata is the rating of the items by the users. Potential issues are the product of actions of users that is (made) comparable by the algorithm.

---

6   We are not going into detail here, as this would go beyond the scope of this chapter. For a detailed description, see Koren et al., 2009.

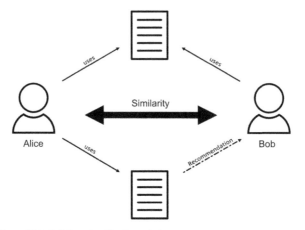

Figure 10.2. Collaborative filtering relations.

The actions of the users are defining how topics and items are being made relevant for a given group without explicitly relying on attached meaning. Coming back to a Deweyan perspective, the collective action making media items relevant—or creating a higher probability of their visibility—and therefore creating (potential) issues is derived from interactions of users with items alone. As shown in Figure 10.2, the algorithmic system relates user actions to the actions of other users to calculate relevance. Practices of editors are, in contrast to content-based filtering, irrelevant to the logic of mediation and the production of publics. This, however, requires the algorithmic regime to install an additional system to create such a database of intentions, which is an (often quite extensive) tracking infrastructure to create the user profiles. The algorithmic regime is not only including the different users, but also needs to install means to make them visible and their interactions with the system machine readable. Instead of providing profiles that describe the recommended items, profiles are now installed for users, linking them to the items that they interacted with in the past. By this, the mediation logic of the algorithmic regime is not based on similarity of items, but of users. An algorithmic regime utilizing collaborative filtering also increasingly includes techniques to control the situation in which the users are consuming the media items. For instance, the interpretation of the (social) signals that are being recorded in these databases of intentions are often a problem. In a process that Poechhacker (forthcoming) has named *algorithmic reflexivity*, the interpretation of these signals and methods to secure these interpretations has to already be resolved during the development of the algorithms for the algorithmic regime. An example of this are implicit ratings of videos in the so-called lean-back mode, i.e., enabling autoplay. A 100% rating could mean that the user really watched the video to the end, but it could also mean that the user fell asleep in front of the computer. In the last years, YouTube and Netflix have addressed this issue by forcing user feedback after some time to ensure that there is still a person in front of the screen watching the video. Thus, the algorithmic regime and its ordering effects are beginning to extend into the actual situation of media consumption.

Algorithmic Regimes and Publics: An Outlook

Recommender systems act as mediators (Morris, 2015) that co-constitute publics according to their modes of programmed sociality (Bucher, 2018). Thus, it is important to have a closer look how these publics are being produced. The focus of attention has been on the question of who is included in the (implicit) negotiations on the constitution of different publics mediated via recommender approaches. What seems to be a purely technical question at first could become an important moment of intervention in the construction of publics by algorithmic regimes. As we argue in this chapter, a media-sensitive approach informed by a pragmatist approach to the constitution of publics allows us to better understand how algorithmic regimes, understood as the ordered relations between different individuals and infrastructural elements mediated by algorithms, enables us to address issues of democratic discourse in a different way.

Two important analytical dimensions must be considered when asking how recommender systems are changing information systems and whether this poses a threat to democracy. The first is the question: Which actors are involved in the construction of equivalence and relevance of information items? (This raises another question: Whose practices are made relevant within the algorithmic regime?) Second, How are these practices are being transformed by the algorithm? This asks for the logic of the algorithm. Inversive term frequency, for example, explicitly values signals higher that are less prevalent. This algorithmic logic is not always directly available to human rationalization. Collaborative filtering produces categories of comparison that are simply not directly available for political discourse. However, by decoding the inscribed assumptions and relations in these algorithmic techniques, we can learn about how political participation and public discourse are realized through these techniques, and where we have possible moments of intervention.

Content-based filtering gives the community or organization that produces labels and classifiers the power to produce chains of equivalence. By doing so, the actions of these coders are defining the margins of the issues, ultimately deciding what to include and what not. The labels and metadata produced for the recommended items act as references to a collection of videos, articles, and other media content that are to be included. The translation of power in such an algorithmic regime is not straightforward, as the logic of the algorithm subverts this linear logic. It is not that a label acts as a signifier to all items relevant to the issue. As pointed out, the discussed rationality of the term "frequency technique" looks for "strong signals." In the applied logic of the term "frequency," this means that labels that are not used often are valued more. This limits an endless extension of the produced equivalence. A label that references everything does not create equivalence in the terms of the algorithm. It just becomes obsolete. However, the conditions of possibility to create issue publics hinges greatly on the coding practices of the data-production community.

Collaborative filtering, on the other hand, does not take the practices of metadata producers into consideration at all. Instead, the technique relies on observed behaviour in terms of implicit or explicit ratings by the users. The algorithmic regime that is based on collaborative filtering mechanisms grants the power to produce equivalence to the same persons that are using the recommender systems. The issues that are arising are self-referential: from the user population for the user population. This could be read as a form of bottom-up democracy, as Dewey was imagining it. Topics and issues are being made relevant through an endless chain of interactions, reaching these people that are (potentially) engaged in them. However, the algorithm is subverting this argument by translating these signals by its very own logic. A logic that is not available to human reasoning—not even to the developers of these algorithms. Translating these issues into political discourse and then potentially action is aggravated by the missing interpretability of these issues. Therefore, a reflexive interpretation of these issues is hardly possible in the system as it is. Again, while the mediation of the algorithm follows the democratic ideal of the bottom-up idea of relevance, the transformation of these relations by the algorithm's logic subverts this alignment.

Both versions of the ideal-typical recommender techniques create issues and publics quite differently. Depending on the used approach, the power to influence the information spheres is granted to different actors. This highlights an important issue. If we want to understand how information spheres for democratic societies are changing, we also have to ask: Based on the actions of whom?[7] The algorithm and its embedded scripts act here as a mediator that relates actors and makes their actions relevant. The second question also related to this is: How are these relations translated by the algorithm? As we have shown, the translation between signals and/or metadata to equivalence and relevance is not straightforward. Quite to the contrary, the algorithm adds here a specific logic of information distribution that needs to be questioned. The algorithm does not just grant the power to define the margins of issues to certain actors but also co-constructs these very issue publics. This, however, brings other actors into the picture: the developers who select and implement algorithmic techniques. This becomes especially important as algorithmic systems are not just implemented, but are optimized and tested in and for the environment in which they should operate (Jaton, 2021). The algorithmic technique mediates between the actors that define the margins (editors or users who give ratings), the users who get recommendations, and the efforts of developers to optimize the algorithmic system.

Understanding algorithms as infrastructure that mediates and transforms algorithmic regimes (see also Boeva & Kropp, in this volume) gives us better awareness how to address issues in relation to democratic societies. But it also raises the question which version of democracy we want to enact with the help of algorithmic systems. The media system, as it functions at the moment, is very much oriented on an analogue definition of relevant topics based on a linear logic of the media system. If we want to keep such a system in place, then recommender systems do threaten that model to a certain degree. Yet, what this really calls for is an adaptation of practices for information provision. With the notion of issue publics we can acknowledge that the media system as it functions so far was a reaction to the socio-technical configuration of its time. But with the introduction of non-linear and often personalized modes of information provision in new algorithmic regimes to the media system, the practices of distributing issues must change accordingly. Content-based recommendation might use new tactics of tagging video or text elements to create a chain of equivalence of what

---

7   This issue of course goes much deeper. Examples from Facebook where users are being tagged by metadata descriptions to make them targetable to specific advertisements or information bits is a big issue. But it is also analytically different from the problem of production of publics. For more on this topic, see Angwin et al., 2017.

we call relevant information. A durable and stable tagging policy, which is then also part of the algorithmic regime, also would allow for formulating machine-readable rules to connect different issue categories with each other with the goal to create diversity. Collaborative filtering is in this respect the bigger challenge, as the very logic is tied to a bottom-up production of relevance. As such, it speaks to an ideal of relevance production by and through the (involved) population. The problem in this regard is that we have to find ways to translate algorithmic logic into the language of political discourse. This would require an ex-post analysis of the calculated data models by experts on the intersection of data science and society. Or, in other words: to fulfil the democratic function of the media system to enable discourse, methods to translate the implicit meaning of emerging issues and their publics into explicit descriptions must be found (see also Jarke & Heuer and Lopez, in this volume).

Recommender approaches and the algorithmic regimes they anticipate show us that in order to include recommender algorithms into information systems that serve democracy requires us to (1) change and adapt the practices in these algorithmic regimes and (2) reflect on the very version of democracy that should be realized through such an algorithmic regime. Starting from an interactionist perspective on digital media and democratic public(s), the filter bubble stops to become a problem in itself. As a basic construction, the filter and the bubble has always been there as a product of collective action in a given society. Instead of framing this as a problem, it calls for (new) ways to mediate issues and to think about democratic inquiry, opening up new possibilities of interaction and integration of issue publics. There are indications that the digital transformation is not the (sole) cause of polarization in contemporary democracy, but instead that these systems could become a way to deal with it in a productive way. This urges us to think which algorithmic regimes we want to install in our democratic societies. A pragmatist account might help us in that regard

Funding

Parts of the work for this contribution were funded by the Deutsche Forschungsgemeinschaft (DFG, German Research Foundation)—Project-ID 262513311—SFB 1187, "Media of Cooperation."

References

Ananny, M. (2016). Toward an ethics of algorithms: Convening, observation, probability, and timeliness. *Science, Technology, & Human Values, 41*(1), 93–117. https://doi.org/10.1177/0162243915606523

Anderson, B. (2006). *Imagined communities: Reflections on the origin and spread of nationalism* (rev. ed.). Verso.

Ang, I. (1991). *Desperately seeking the audience*. Routledge.

Angwin, J., Varner, M., & Tobin, A. (2017, September 14). Facebook enabled advertisers to reach "Jew haters." *ProPublica*. https://www.propublica.org/article/facebook-enabled-advertisers-to-reach-jew-haters

Battelle, J. (2006). *The search: How Google and its rivals rewrote the rules of business and transformed our culture*. Portfolio.

Becker, K., & Stalder, F. (2009). Einleitung. In K. Becker & F. Stalder (Eds.), *Deep search: The politics of search beyond Google* (pp. 7–12). Studien Verlag.

Belkin, N. J., & Croft, W. B. (1992). Information filtering and information retrieval: Two sides of the same coin? *Communications of the ACM, 35*(12), 29–38. https://doi.org/10.1145/138859.138861

Bellogín, A., Cantador, I., & Castells, P. (2013). A comparative study of heterogeneous item recommendations in social systems. *Information Sciences, 221*, 142–169. https://doi.org/10.1016/j.ins.2012.09.039

Bruns, A. (2019). *Are filter bubbles real?* Polity Press.

Bucher, T. (2018). *If ... then: Algorithmic power and politics.* Oxford University Press.

Crouch, C. (2004). *Post-democracy*. Polity.

Dewey, J. (2006). *The public & its problems*. Combined Academic Publ. (Original work published 1927).

Giddens, A. (1984). *The constitution of society: Outline of the theory of structuration*. Polity Press.

Gillespie, T. (2014). The relevance of algorithms. In T. Gillespie, P. J. Boczkowski, & K. A. Foot (Eds.), *Media technologies: Essays on communication, materiality, and society* (pp. 167–193). MIT Press.

Goldberg, D., Nichols, D., Oki, B. M., & Terry, D. (1992). Using collaborative filtering to weave an information tapestry. *Communications of the ACM, 35*(12), 61–70. https://doi.org/10.1145/138859.138867

Graham, M., Hogan, B., Straumann, R. K., & Medhat, A. (2014). Uneven geographies of user-generated information: Patterns of increasing informational poverty. *Annals of the Association of American Geographers, 104*(4), 746–764. https://doi.org/10.1080/00045608.2014.910087

Habermas, J. (1991). The public sphere. In C. Mukerji & M. Schudson (Eds.), *Rethinking popular culture: Contemporary perspectives in cultural studies* (pp. 398–404). University of California Press.

Habermas, J. (1992). *Structural transformation of the public sphere: Inquiry into a category of bourgeois society.* Blackwell. (Original work published 1962).

Haim, M., Graefe, A., & Brosius, H.-B. (2018). Burst of the filter bubble? *Digital Journalism, 6*(3), 330–343. https://doi.org/10.1080/21670811.2017.1338145

Helberger, N. (2011). Diversity by design. *Journal of Information Policy, 1,* 441–469. https://doi.org/10.5325/jinfopoli.1.2011.0441

Helberger, N. (2019). On the democratic role of news recommenders. *Digital Journalism, 7*(8), 993–1012. https://doi.org/10.1080/21670811.2019.1623700

Held, D. (2006). *Models of democracy* (3rd ed.). Stanford University Press.

Hoffmann, U. (1996). Selbstregulierung im Kulturraum Internet Volksentscheid, Cyberangels und Filter. *Das Parlament, 33/34*(6).

Jasanoff, S. (2005). *Designs on nature: Science and democracy in Europe and the United States.* Princeton University Press.

Jaton, F. (2021). *The constitution of algorithms: Ground-truthing, programming, formulating.* MIT Press.

Kitchin, R. (2017). Thinking critically about and researching algorithms. *Information, Communication & Society, 20*(1), 14–29. https://doi.org/10.1080/136911 8X.2016.1154087

Koren, Y., Bell, R., & Volinsky, C. (2009). Matrix factorization techniques for recommender systems. *Computer, 42*(8), 30–37. https://doi.org/10.1109/MC.2009.263

Laclau, E., & Mouffe, C. (2014). *Hegemony and socialist strategy: Towards a radical democratic politics* (2nd ed.). Verso.

Loeb, S., & Terry, D. (1992). Information filtering. *Communications of the ACM, 35*(12), 26–28.

Mackenzie, A. (2015). The production of prediction: What does machine learning want? *European Journal of Cultural Studies, 18*(4–5), 429–445. https://doi.org/10.1177/1367549415577384

Manovich, L. (2011). There is only software. In P. du Gay, S. Hall, L. Janes, A. K. Madsen, H. Mackay, & K. Negus, *Doing cultural studies: The story of the Sony Walkman* (pp. 136–138, 2nd ed.). Sage.

Marres, N. (2007). The issues deserve more credit: Pragmatist contributions to the study of public involvement in controversy. *Social Studies of Science, 37*(5), 759–780. https://doi.org/10.1177/0306312706077367

Mooers, C. N. (1950). Information retrieval viewed as temporal signaling. *Proceedings of the International Congress of Mathematicians, 1,* 572–573.

Morris, J. W. (2015). Curation by code: Infomediaries and the data mining of taste. *European Journal of Cultural Studies, 18*(4–5), 446–463. https://doi.org/10.1177/1367549415577387

Mouffe, C. (2005). *On the political*. Routledge.

Napoli, P. M. (2011). Exposure diversity reconsidered. *Journal of Information Policy, 1*, 246–259. https://doi.org/10.5325/jinfopoli.1.2011.0246

Nechushtai, E., & Lewis, S. C. (2019). What kind of news gatekeepers do we want machines to be? Filter bubbles, fragmentation, and the normative dimensions of algorithmic recommendations. *Computers in Human Behavior, 90*, 298–307. https://doi.org/10.1016/j.chb.2018.07.043

Pariser, E. (2011). *The filter bubble: What the internet is hiding from you*. Penguin.

Pöchhacker, N., Burkhardt, M., Geipel, A., & Passoth, J.-H. (2017). Interventionen in die Produktion algorithmischer Öffentlichkeiten: Recommender Systeme als Herausforderung für öffentlich-rechtliche Sendeanstalten. *kommunikation @ gesellschaft, 18*.

Poechhacker, N. (Forthcoming). *Democratic algorithms*. Meson Press.

Rieder, B. (2017). Scrutinizing an algorithmic technique: The Bayes classifier as interested reading of reality. *Information, Communication & Society, 20*(1), 100–117. https://doi.org/10.1080/1369118X.2016.1181195

Seaver, N. (2018). What should an anthropology of algorithms do? *Cultural Anthropology, 33*(3), 375–385. https://doi.org/10.14506/ca33.3.04

Sørensen, J. K., & Schmidt, J.-H. (2016, September 23). An algorithmic diversity diet? Questioning assumptions behind a diversity recommendation system for PSM. RIPE@2016, Antwerpen, Belgium. http://ripeat.org/library/2016/7015-algorithmic-diversity-diet%C2%A0questioning-assumptions-behind-diversity-recommendation

Sunstein, C. R. (2009). *Republic.com 2.0*. Princeton University Press.

Ziewitz, M. (2016). Governing algorithms: Myth, mess, and methods. *Science, Technology & Human Values, 41*(1), 3–16. https://doi.org/10.1177/0162243915608948

About the Authors

Nikolaus Poechhacker is postdoctoral researcher at the Digital Age Research Center (D!ARC), University of Klagenfurt, Austria. In his work he is researching the relationship between democratic institutions, law, social order, and algorithmic systems in various domains, bringing together perspectives from media theory, science and technology studies (STS), computer science, and sociology.

Marcus Burkhardt is a lecturer in the Media Studies Department, University of Siegen in Germany. His research focuses on the history, theory, and practices of digital media, especially computational media, cultures of coding, and digital methods. He is co-PI of the project "Agentic Media: Formations of Semi-Autonomy," CRC 1187 "Media of Cooperation."

Jan-Hendrik Passoth is Professor of Sociology of Technology in the European New School of Digital Studies of the European University Viadrina Frankfurt (Oder) in Germany. His research focuses on the role of digital infrastructures for democracy and politics, software development as responsible social practice, and the possibilities of intervention in digitization projects through critical design.

11. Commentary: Taking to Machines: Knowledge Production and Social Relations in the Age of Governance *by* Data Infrastructure

Stefania Milan

Abstract

Algorithmic regimes are firmly installed at the core social organization, affecting the way we interact with the world around us. This exercise of "taking to machines," however, raises three critical questions: the opacity of the infrastructure, the potential social costs, and the generative qualities of algorithmic systems able to reshape politics and the polity. These developments are the manifestation of a (relatively new) form of governance—"governance *by* data infrastructure"—capable of moulding social interactions in ways that jeopardize citizen agency. From the vantage point of critical data studies, this commentary describes the main features of governance *by* data infrastructure, exposing what kinds of knowledge are produced by these practices and what publics are evoked—and why we should worry.

Keywords: algorithmic regimes; citizen agency; critical data studies

Introduction

Between 2014 and 2020, the Dutch government deployed an algorithmic system known as SyRI (System Risk Indication) to assess the propensity to fraud or abuse in recipients of child welfare support. SyRI drew sensitive data from 17 databases to assign a "risk score" to the beneficiaries of some form of public assistance. The algorithm, however, unlawfully flagged citizens with a foreign surname, dual citizenship, or residence in low-income districts

Jarke, J., B. Prietl, S. Egbert, Y. Boeva, H. Heuer, and M. Arnold (eds.), *Algorithmic Regimes: Methods, Interactions, and Politics*. Amsterdam: Amsterdam University Press, 2024
DOI 10.5117/9789463728485_CH11

(Bekker, 2021). Those subjected to this algorithmic regime were unaware of being classified. "SyRI is part of a global trend of introducing digital tools in welfare states without taking into account the potentially devastating consequences they may have on a range of internationally protected human rights," warned Philip Alston, United Nations Special Rapporteur on extreme poverty and human rights. "This system can have a hugely negative impact on the rights of poor individuals without according them due process" (UN Office of the High Commissioner, 2019).

The Dutch "risk indicator system" is just one of the many recent examples of how publics and social interactions are evoked and managed through the algorithms. Today, algorithmic regimes are firmly installed at the core of social organization. They mediate anything from shopping to job market selection, from political participation to welfare state service delivery. They have the ability to make and unmake (digital) publics, as demonstrated by Poechhacker, Burkhardt, and Passoth in their analysis of recommender systems. They have social-epistemological effects, as exposed by the examination of the algorithmic structuring of the news environment proposed by Wiengarn and Arnold. They contribute to the ordering of the urban space as Boeva and Kropp describe in their inquiry into the expansion of computational design in the construction and architecture sector. And they do not exist in a vacuum, as Büchner, Dosdall, and Constantiou show in their evaluation of organizational processes in the case of predictive policing in Germany.

This recurrent exercise of "taking to machines" raises at least three critical questions. The first question concerns the opaque nature and inscrutability of these algorithmic forms of governance, which has been amply documented in the literature (see, among others, Pasquale, 2015; Smith, 2020). The scarce transparency and accessibility of algorithmic decision-making is amplified by the fact that they operate in the realm of machine learning, needed to "bring together again" data generated by scattered platforms and mechanisms and make sense of them (Aradau & Blanke, 2022, p. 106). Some have even argued that these developments represent a threat to constitutional democracy in virtue of the power concentration they harbour (Nemitz, 2018).

The second critical question posed by the rapid advance of algorithmic regimes in society has to do with the potential social costs of these mechanisms of generating knowledge and validating it, as the Dutch case exposes. Research has detailed how it is often disadvantaged communities and individuals at the fringe of society that suffer the worst consequences (cf. Lutz, 2019; O'Neil, 2016). A running list of data harms includes the exploitation that might arise from the profiling of people; discrimination; loss of privacy; surveillance, control and physical injury; manipulation (for example, of voting behaviour); exclusion from the necessities for life, such as government subsidies, as well as injustice resulting, for instance, from the use of predictive technologies for politicking (Redden, 2022). Eubanks (2018) goes as far as maintaining that to understand the future of invasive technology, we ought to look at poor communities since it is where expectations are lower that people's rights such as privacy will be upheld.

The third critical question raised by algorithmic mediation as our privileged way of knowing the world has to do with the generative qualities of algorithmic systems: by producing knowledge and truth claims, algorithms influence the likelihood of certain realities above others. In so doing, these new "knowledge regimes" (Jarke et al., in this volume) can reshape our views, including the formation of political opinions, fuelling a sort of "algorithmic governmentality" (Rouvroy & Berns, 2013). Think of the Cambridge Analytica scandal, whereby information volunteered by Facebook users on the platform was appropriated for profiling and microtargeting, with the goal of influencing the outcome of the 2016 US presidential elections. While there is no consensus over the effectiveness of political microtargeting and/or recommender systems (cf. Poechhacker et al., in this volume), this case exposes how this "new mode of 'truth-doing'" results in "knowledge for the government of individuals and populations" (Aradau & Blanke, 2022, pp. 22–31).

Starting from these observations, I hold that the advance of algorithmic regimes in society is to be seen as the manifestation of a (relatively new) form of governance which I term "governance *by* data infrastructure." Governance *by* data infrastructure is capable of moulding social interactions in ways that can jeopardize citizen agency. The commentary is structured as follows. First, it briefly describes the main features of governance *by* data infrastructure. Second, asking what kind of knowledge is produced by these practices and what publics are evoked (and with what consequences), it reflects on the loss of citizen agency associated with this form of governance of the polity.

The Rise of Governance *by* Data Infrastructure

The new modes of machine learning-mediated knowledge production, validation, and dissemination typical of algorithmic regimes are made possible by an array of data infrastructure generating ever-larger quantities of data and setting the conditions for data processing. Examples of data infrastructure include the dashboards that oversee service delivery in the smart city (Coletta et al., 2019), the biometric identification systems adopted by law enforcement agencies across the world (Jansen et al., 2021), and commercial gender classifiers powering consumer facial recognition services (Buolamwini & Gebru, 2018). Intervening in an expansive list of social activities, these data infrastructure produce information that enable "real-time decision-making" (Amoore, 2011, p. 24). Because data inform regulation and regulate human behaviour, these regulatory data infrastructures, as we may call them, increasingly take up functions and roles that were once performed by humans and pertained (almost) exclusively to governments and public administrations. They fuel a form of governance that elevates regulatory data infrastructure to the preferred mode of management of complexity. They intervene in the fulfilment of fundamental state functions in the domains of public safety, health, education—and counting.

This does not happen without friction. The "care and cure" of infrastruc- turing, as noted by Boeva and Kropp (in this volume), entails "contested arrangements and actors struggling for their interests in the implementa- tion of emerging technologies" (p. 142). And because "arrangements of technical architecture are inherently arrangements of power" (DeNardis, 2012, p. 721), the shift to governance *by* data infrastructure marks a sig- nificant transformation. It puts the tech industry in an unprecedented position of power and "fosters novel power relations among public and private actors," not all of them desirable (Bellanova & De Goede, 2020, p. 102). When implemented in state service delivery, for instance, for-profit contractors function as "regulatory agents, turning private centers of power to state purposes" (Braman, 2006, p. 34) and diverting action and control away from the public administration and elected legislators. What's more, this often happens—as the Dutch case well illustrates—outside established mechanisms of democratic scrutiny. Second, data infrastructure contributes to coalesce *a scaffolding of* algorithmic regimes that may last a long time and lends itself to be continuously repurposed to gather more data and generate other knowledge (Milan et al., 2021; see also Büchner et al., in this volume). Digital identity systems are a case in point, as they connect identity authentication to commercial facilities like banking or to welfare state services such as healthcare or food subsidies. In other words, these "foot-in-the-door devices" lay the "groundwork for future adoption of features that might earlier have been rejected as unacceptable or unnecessary" (Pierce, 2019, p. 11). Finally, as the societal dependence on regulatory data infrastructure and the subtending algorithmic regimes get progressively domesticated and normalized, it is increasingly difficult if not impossible to opt out. Education technology is a paradigmatic example: parents and pupils can do little against the introduction of datafication in the school system at all levels (for an overview of problems, see Jarke & Breiter, 2019). I contend that, in the long run, governance *by* data infrastructure will shift power and state-making abilities away from the state and to the private sector, augment inequality, and deeply affect our ability to exercise citizenship.

What Knowledge and What Publics?

What kind of knowledge is produced by all-pervading algorithmic regimes and what kind of publics are evoked—and what and who is, on the contrary, obscured or marginalized? Literature from various disciplines, including science and technology studies (STS), critical data studies, fairness and accuracy in computing but also politics, is awash with critical accounts of incumbent algorithmic regimes in relation to justice, fairness, and inequality. Here I want to refer to two key aspects to speak to the "discursive dimension of public formation and the role of technologies in the shaping of those discourses" (Møller Hartley et al., 2023, p. 3).

The first concerns the power to define realities (and obscure other, competing ones) typical of algorithmic regimes, which I have illustrated above with the example of Cambridge Analytica and that bears a strong connection with the notion of "prediction regimes" explored by Egbert (in this volume). With respect to the civic community, we note how the generative qualities of these systems are potentially transformative of the type of society and polity we live in. This is, among others, because data generated by algorithmic regimes is "fed back to citizens as representations and mirroring of themselves via metrics, such as likes, clicks and shares. In turn, users respond to this mirroring" (Møller Hartley et al., 2023, p. 3). With the technological acceleration of society, things become more complex—towards a change of paradigm (Kitchin, 2014) that subtends to *a systemic change* which is also a point of no return. The introduction of deep learning is "generative of new norms and thresholds of what 'good,' 'normal,' and 'stable' orders look like in the world," claims Amoore (2022, p. 2). This emerging "machine learning political order" is thus not merely about "supplying new instruments and apparatuses of classification or taxonomy for the governing of society, but is *itself* a reordering of that politics, of what the political can be" (ibid., pp. 2–3; original emphasis). Needless to say, citizens rarely have a say in what this "prototypical model of society" (ibid., p. 2) ought to look like. Yet, as Amicelle and colleagues observed, the performative power of technology can redefine the borders between the normal and the abnormal, incorporating substantive forms of inequality along the way (Amicelle et al., 2015).

The second refers to the experimental and trial-and-error approach that often characterizes the design and operation of algorithmic regimes, although this rarely features in the mainstream imaginaries associated with these technologies and discounts its potential detrimental effect on the public debate. This approach, typical of software design, may be at odds with the functioning of liberal democracy, e.g., with respect to the notion of the sovereign people. In addition, the opacity of algorithmic regimes means that affected individuals are typically unable to seek redress (Benjamin, 2019). Often such experimentation goes to the detriment of those it purports to benefit. It is the case of the Colombian SISBÉN, a household targeting system supporting social programmes for the poor and the vulnerable. The various iterations of this algorithmic regime aimed at identifying inconsistencies in population records to reduce the number of people who could access social benefits. It also shifted the focus away from the political problem of poverty, and the state inability to solve it, reducing it to a technical problem of technology design (López, 2020).

From this cursory view, we gather that the formation of (democratic) publics evoked by algorithmic regimes is not only in continuous transformation, but also under threat, for the knowledge algorithmic regimes produce and value, and the way they do it and mobilize said knowledge, eat into the citizens' ability to act in the world—a claim I explore next.

The Erosion of Citizen Agency

The shift to algorithmic regimes as the main mechanism supporting knowledge production and dissemination is "not merely technological, but also social and political, and it therefore confronts us with questions of power, agency and control" (Hintz et al., 2018, p. 2). The move towards governance *by* data infrastructure in the transfer of agency, control, and sovereignty away from the citizens and consumer to non-human agents. The logical "layers"—algorithms, but also standards and protocols—play a key role in determining the intended outcomes of knowledge production, including "ranking" certain types of knowledge over others. Gritsenko and Wood have aptly referred to "design-based governance, with power exercised ex ante via choice architectures defined through protocols, requiring lower levels of commitment from governing actors" (2020, p. 1). Power, therefore, shifts away from users and other entities, such as governmental agencies, towards the designers, standards organizations, and vendors that build and sell algorithmic systems.

Citizen agency is eroded as a result. Citizen agency is here intended as reflexive practice oriented to (political) action, such as our ability to exercise and *enact* citizenship. It is the result of the process of "making sense of the world so as to act within it" (Couldry, 2014, p. 891). Importantly, this process is "interactive and shared," as Melucci observed about a concurrent dynamic, that of collective identity in groupings, which is "constructed and negotiated through a recurrent process of activation of the relations that bind actors together" (1996, p. 70). In other words, citizen agency does not much exist in the guise of individual possibility, as much as it does in its collective nature and the promises (of change) that this collective dynamic holds.

But our interactions today are increasingly mediated by algorithms, with mixed consequences as this section of *Algorithmic Regimes: Methods, Interactions, and Politics* made clear. The collectives that are summoned by algorithms are assembled on the basis of predicted commonalities. As we have seen, these algorithmic regimes are more often than not crystallized in variably stable assemblages that are opaque, unidirectional, and unfair. Elevating algorithmic regimes to the main arbiter of interactions between people and between people and the state, the penetration of governance *by* data infrastructure in society harbours the risk of restricting the boundaries of citizen agency even further. Yet, as there are margins of errors in algorithmic regimes, there are pockets of resistance, creativity, and subversion able to reclaim agency. Meanwhile, methods to foster algorithmic literacy, as explained by Eslami and Heuer (in this volume), and initiatives to promote algorithmic awareness (see the chapter by Storms and Alvarado) have an important role to play as we move towards more and more pervasive algorithmic regimes. The "vanguard" amongst the citizenry—for example, those "data activists" whose data crunching skills are put at the service of the common good—can act as "translators" (Gutiérrez, 2018) of complex socio-technical dynamics, capable of mitigating the disempowerment of laypersons in the face of all-encompassing algorithmic regimes. And promoting "alternative epistemologies" (Milan & van der Velden, 2016) of algorithmic regimes, data activists can contribute to change the way we "talk to machines" in the near future.

References

Amicelle, A., Aradau, C., & Jeandesboz, J. (2015). Questioning security devices: Performativity, resistance, politics. *Security Dialogue, 46*(4), 293–306. https://doi.org/10.1177/0967010615586964

Amoore, L. (2011). Data derivatives: On the emergence of a security risk calculus for our times. *Theory, Culture & Society, 28*(6), 24–43. https://doi.org/10.1177/0263276411417430

Amoore, L. (2022). Machine learning political orders. *Review of International Studies,* 1–17. https://doi.org/10.1017/S0260210522000031

Aradau, C., & Blanke, T. (2022). *Algorithmic reason: The new government of self and other.* Oxford University Press.

Bekker, S. (2021). Fundamental rights in digital welfare states: The case of SyRI in the Netherlands. In O. Spijkers, W. G. Werner, & R. A. Wessel (Eds.), *Netherlands Yearbook of International Law 2019: Yearbooks in International Law: History, Function and Future* (pp. 289–307). T. M. C. Asser Press. https://doi.org/10.1007/978-94-6265-403-7_24

Bellanova, R., & De Goede, M. (2020). The algorithmic regulation of security: An infrastructural perspective. *Regulation & Governance, 16*(1), 102–118. https://doi.org/10.1111/rego.12338

Benjamin, R. (2019). *Race after technology: Abolitionist tools for the New Jim Code.* Polity.

Braman, S. (2006). *Change of state: Information, policy, and power.* MIT Press.

Buolamwini, J., & Gebru, T. (2018). Gender shades: Intersectional accuracy disparities in commercial gender classification. *Proceedings of Machine Learning Research, 81*, 1–15. http://proceedings.mlr.press/v81/buolamwini18a/buolamwini18a.pdf

Coletta, C., Evans, L., Heaphy, L., & Kitchin, R. (Eds.). (2019). *Creating smart cities.* Routledge.

Couldry, N. (2014). A necessary disenchantment: Myth, agency and injustice in a digital world. *Sociological Review, 62*(4), 880–897.

DeNardis, L. (2012). Hidden levers of internet control: An infrastructure-based theory of internet governance. *Information, Communication & Society, 15*(5), 720–738.

Eubanks, V. (2018). *Automating inequality: How high-tech tools profile, police, and punish the poor.* St. Martin's Press.

Gritsenko, D., & Wood, M. (2020). Algorithmic governance: A modes of governance approach. *Regulation & Governance, 16*(1), 45–62. https://doi.org/10.1111/rego.12367

Gutiérrez, M. (2018). *Data activism and social change.* Palgrave Macmillan.

Hintz, A., Dencik, L., & Wahl-Jorgensen, K. (2018). *Digital citizenship in a datafied society.* Polity.

Jansen, F., Sánchez-Monedero, J., & Dencik, L. (2021). Biometric identity systems in law enforcement and the politics of (voice) recognition: The case of SiiP. *Big Data & Society, 8*(2), 20539517211063604. https://doi.org/10.1177/20539517211063604

Jarke, J., & Breiter, A. (2019). Editorial: The datafication of education. *Learning, Media and Technology, 44*(1), 1–6. https://doi.org/10.1080/17439884.2019.1573833

Kitchin, R. (2014). Big data, new epistemologies and paradigm shifts. *Big Data & Society, 1*(1). https://doi.org/10.1177/2053951714528481

López, J. (2020). *Experimentando con la pobreza: El SISBÉN y los proyectos de analítica de datos en Colombia*. Fundación Karisma. https://web.karisma.org.co/wp-content/uploads/download-manager-files/Experimentando%20con%20la%20pobreza.pdf

Lutz, C. (2019). Digital inequalities in the age of artificial intelligence and big data. *Human Behavior and Emerging Technologies, 1*(2), 141–148. https://doi.org/10.1002/hbe2.140

Melucci, A. (1996). *Challenging codes: Collective action in the information age*. Cambridge University Press.

Milan, S., Taylor, L., Gürses, S., & Veale, M. (2021). Promises made to be broken: Digital vaccine certification as hyperrealistic immunity theatre. *European Journal of Risk Regulation, 12*(2), 382–392. https://doi.org/10.1017/err.2021.26

Milan, S., van der Velden, L. (2016). The alternative epistemologies of data activism. *Digital Culture & Society, 2*, 57–74. https://doi.org/10.14361/dcs-2016-0205

Møller Hartley, J., Sørensen, J. K., & Mathieu, D. (Eds.). (2023). *Datapublics: The construction of publics in datafied democracies*. Bristol University Press.

Nemitz, P. (2018). Constitutional democracy and technology in the age of artificial intelligence. *Philosophical Transactions of the Royal Society A: Mathematical, Physical and Engineering Sciences, 376*(2133), 20180089. https://doi.org/10.1098/rsta.2018.0089

O'Neil, C. (2016). *Weapons of math destruction: How big data increases inequality and threatens democracy*. Broadway Books.

Pasquale, F. (2015). *The black box society: The secret algorithms that control money and information*. Harvard University Press.

Pierce, J. (2019). Smart home security cameras and shifting lines of creepiness: A design-led inquiry. *CHI '19: Proceedings of the 2019 CHI Conference on Human Factors in Computing Systems* (paper no. 45). https://doi.org/10.1145/3290605.3300275

Redden, J. (2022). Data harms. In L. Dencik, A. Hintz, J. Redden, & E. Treré (Eds.), *Data justice* (pp. 59–72). Sage.

Rouvroy, A., & Berns, T. (2013). Algorithmic governmentality and prospects of emancipation: Disparateness as a precondition for individuation through relationships? *Réseaux, 177*, 163–196.

Smith, G. J. (2020). The politics of algorithmic governance in the black box city. *Big Data & Society, 7*(2). https://doi.org/10.1177/2053951720933989

UN Office of the High Commissioner. (2019, October 16). The Netherlands is building a surveillance state for the poor, says UN rights expert. https://www.ohchr.org/en/NewsEvents/Pages/DisplayNews.aspx?NewsID=25152&LangID=E

About the Author

Stefania Milan (stefaniamilan.net) investigates the interplay between digital technology, political participation, and governance. She is Professor of Critical Data Studies at the Department of Media Studies of the University of Amsterdam in the Netherlands, Faculty Associate at the Berkman Klein Center for Internet & Society at Harvard University, and Research Associate with the Chair in AI & Democracy at the Florence School of Transnational Governance, European University Institute.

III.

POLITICS

12. The Politics of Data Science: Institutionalizing Algorithmic Regimes of Knowledge Production

Bianca Prietl and Stefanie Raible

Abstract

This chapter studies the rise of *academic* data science in Germany, Austria, and Switzerland. By tracing the institutionalization of this emerging discipline, we endeavour to capture the power dynamics incorporated within current shifts in society's regime of truth. We do so from a discourse analytical perspective, asking how the professionalization of academic data science can be understood as institutionalizing a specific regime of knowledge production, one that is based on algorithmic big data analysis. We understand epistemological questions as inextricably linked to questions of power, and study empirically how data science is structurally implemented, epistemologically positioned, and discursively legitimized within the academic fields in Germany, Austria, and Switzerland.

Keywords: professionalization; knowledge–power analysis

Introduction

This chapter studies the institutionalization of *academic* data science in Europe's DACH region,[1] in order to capture the shifting power dynamics in society's regime of truth prompted by the diffusion of algorithmic modes of knowledge production. We grasp academic data science as playing a crucial role in professionalizing, promoting, and legitimizing these new modes of

---

1   The DACH region comprises the central European countries of Germany (D), Austria (A), and Switzerland (CH).

Jarke, J., B. Prietl, S. Egbert, Y. Boeva, H. Heuer, and M. Arnold (eds.), *Algorithmic Regimes: Methods, Interactions, and Politics*. Amsterdam: Amsterdam University Press, 2024
DOI 10.5117/9789463728485_CH12

knowledge production, as it is where the necessary methods and tools for shaping this new form of knowledge originate and future data scientists are trained, for academia and beyond. Drawing from discourse analytical perspectives on knowledge that understand epistemology as inextricably linked to questions of power, we examine how data science is institutionally structured, epistemologically positioned, and discursively legitimized. In so doing, our overarching goal is to study the new regime of knowledge production that is based on algorithmic big data analysis (Beer, 2019; Thylstrup et al., 2019; Houben & Prietl, 2018; Kitchin, 2014). Empirically, our arguments are based on a research project that provides us with a heterogeneous set of empirical data: the organizational parameters of data science study programmes and chairs at research universities and universities of applied sciences, qualitative interviews with selected scholars in data science, as well as descriptions found in degree programme brochures.

So far, only little is known about the ongoing professionalization and academic institutionalization of data science (Dorschel, 2021a, 2021b; Dorschel & Brandt, 2021; Saner, 2022). Whilst data science has been applied in industrial contexts for quite some time, giving rise to the so-called data analytics industry (Beer, 2019), data science is only just taking root in academia (Ribes, 2019; Saner, 2019; Beaulieu & Leonelli, 2022). In this context, it is mostly established as an inter- or transdisciplinary endeavour at the intersection of mathematics, statistics, and computer science (Slota et al., 2020; Beaulieu & Leonelli, 2022). Science policy actors, but also economic stakeholders, are largely identified as the main drivers behind the professionalization of data science, indicating the defining role of economic rationales and business interests in this development (Saner, 2019; Lowrie, 2017; Ribes, 2019). Proponents of the academic institutionalization of data science point to the supposed economic advantages of data-based knowledge production and the need for nations to develop advanced data analytics expertise in order to compete. Furthermore, data science is described as "domain-agnostic," as it claims to offer a *universal* approach to knowledge production, independent of any discipline, subject, or object (Slota et al., 2020; Ribes, 2019). Commonly described as rooted in the "real world," data science tends to forgo any search for general truths (in the sense of abstract knowledge) and instead focuses on generating useful, applicable findings (Lowrie, 2017; Ribes, 2019). In that sense, data science takes a pragmatic stance on science and knowledge production.

Although these findings hint at some considerable epistemological shifts related to data science, it is rare to encounter literature that questions the links between knowledge and power in this context. Some authors, critical of capitalism, argue that the commodification of data gives rise to a new capitalist logic of accumulation, giving way to "surveillance capitalism" (Zuboff, 2015) or "platform capitalism" (Srnicek, 2016). Applying a perspective critical of the concept of rationality itself, David Beer (2019) analyses the proliferation of a "data gaze" in the data analytics industry, pointing to a drive to expand this form of knowledge (production). He underscores the need "to think about how this knowledge is framed, how it is presented, what type of expertise it evokes and authenticates, and what notions of truth and worth are bound up in these forms of knowledge" (Beer, 2019, p. 6). Heeding Beer's call for analysis, this chapter investigates the organizational as well as epistemological foundations of academic data science, in order to understand the power dynamics incorporated within the current shifts in society's "regime of truth" (Foucault, 1977).

In the following, we briefly sketch the theoretical perspectives and the empirical research and data that build the foundations for our analysis. Then, we present and discuss our empirical findings, and finally draw some overall conclusions.

Theoretical Perspectives

According to Michel Foucault, every society has its own historically specific "regime of truth" (2020, p. 132). Such a regime operates using preferential techniques and procedures for establishing said truth, thus regulating the production of legitimate knowledge. For Foucault, these epistemological questions are inextricably linked to power, which relies on knowledge as a primary vehicle, in that it produces and sustains certain "ordered procedures for the production, regulation, distribution, circulation, and operation of statements" (Foucault, 2020, p. 132). Regimes of truth pre-structure and organize *how* successful claims to truth can be made. They define *who* is granted authority to speak (truth) and who can become the subject of knowledge—or, quite simply, who is in a position to "know." And they regulate *what* can be constituted as knowledge. Foucault therefore argues that power and knowledge must be understood as mutually constitutive, with power regulating how knowledge can come about and knowledge supporting power (relations). Taking up Foucault's concept of a power/knowledge nexus, we look at algorithmic modes of knowledge production, digital data technologies, associated ideas and practices, and data science itself as constitutive for a new *algorithmic* regime of knowledge production. In this sense, data science represents a specific set of knowledge production techniques and, thus, a form of power, as well as an instrument that can promote different interests and support different power relations.

In order to study the power relations incorporated within the academic institutionalization of data science, we furthermore draw on conflict-theoretical perspectives on professionalization (Abbott, 1988, 2001). In doing so, we adopt an anti-essentialist view of professions, dispensing with any assumptions of a core set of professional characteristics. Instead, we apply a processual perspective to understand *how* professions are constituted by claiming and securing the "more or less exclusive right to dominate a particular area of work" (Abbott, 1995, p. 551). In this process, *academic* institutionalization marks an important milestone (Abbott, 1988, pp. 53–54). Following Abbott's elaborations on the "emergence" of professions (1988), we frame the rise of academic data science as a conflict-laden negotiation process aimed at monopolizing a specific area of expertise, especially in relation to established (academic) disciplines.

Whereas Abbott is mostly concerned with studying the emergence of professions on the structural level of actors, organizations, labour divisions, and the distribution of resources, we build upon Tanja Paulitz's (2012) proposal of a genealogical sociology of knowledge in order to capture and study the construction of data science on the *symbolic* level. In our analysis, we delve into the instances in which scholars demarcate the subject and object of their knowing, constitute and profile their epistemological positions, and seek to legitimize their expertise. Following Paulitz (2012), we frame these instances of claiming "epistemic authority" (Gieryn, 1994, 1999) as *discursive practices*. We understand these claims as expressions of and means in the struggle for preferential positions in the social field of academia.

To study "the politics" of algorithmic regimes of knowledge production we inquire as to how data science is *institutionally structured*, *epistemologically positioned*, and *discursively legitimized* in the course of its professionalization and establishment within the academic field in the predominantly German-speaking DACH countries. We take these questions of how knowledge/truth and epistemology emerge in data science to be inherently shaped by power and as a means of power in their own right.

Empirical Research and Data Basis

This chapter is based on an empirical research project conducted by the authors in 2021,[2] combining a range of—mostly qualitative—methods and

2   We would like to thank the Hans Messer Foundation for providing financial support for "The Politics of Data Science" (PoDS) research project.

strategies of data collection and analysis in an iterative-cyclical research process (Strauss & Corbin, 1990).

In a first step, we mapped the structural and organizational institution-alization of data science in the DACH countries in recent years. We collected the following information on data science chairs and study programmes: title/denomination, university type, host department, research/teaching emphases, and desired qualifications. In analysing the data science chairs, we sampled all job announcements between January 2015 and March 2021.[3] From there, we continued to collect qualitative data via the respective university websites. When investigating the data science study programmes, we started with general databases designed for students searching for a major across different universities. Our data collection was again completed on the individual university websites.

After mapping the academic institutionalization of data science in the DACH region on a structural level, we proceeded with a qualitative, discourse-analytical approach by downloading the brochures for all data science degree programmes (n = 92). As these descriptions are by nature advertisements designed to convey a highly positive image of data science, free of any ambiguities, they allow insights into the discursive strategies used to constitute data science and legitimize the necessity for academic training in data science.

In parallel, we conducted in-depth semi-structured qualitative interviews[4] with data science professors from Germany, Austria, and Switzerland (n = 19) who can be understood as key actors in processes of (academic) professionalization (Abbott, 1988, pp. 53–54). As professors, these interview partners are also in the formal position of legitimately representing their area of research and study (Paulitz et al., 2016). Applying the strategy of theoretical sampling (Strauss & Corbin, 1990), we collected data covering

3   We decided on this empirical strategy due to the following reasons: first, in German-speaking countries, all job announcements for professorships are published in the newspaper *Die Zeit*. This blanket access allowed us to gain a complete quantitative overview for the time period in question. Second, in addition to the quantitative numbers of data science professorships, the job announcements also afforded some insights into the formal requirements (especially disciplinary background, desired skills, etc.) as well as how these roles are described and presented in terms of discursive positioning, and finally, their structural positioning seen through the departmental affiliation.

4   Our interview guideline contained questions about the interviewees' professional and disciplinary biography, their understanding of data science, academic careers within data science and doing research and teaching in data science, their research interests, forms of cooperation and academic networks, their stance on critiques towards data science, and their perceptions of the future of their discipline.

the categories of gender (with an over-representation of women), university type (research universities or universities of applied science), (technoscientific and geographic) metropoles or peripheries, academic backgrounds, generalist data scientists or professionals with domain-specific orientation (including dominant domains such as economics as well as niche domains like agriculture). All interviews were conducted via Zoom and transcribed verbatim.

The degree programme brochures and interview transcripts were analysed with the help of MAXQDA, using open and selective coding strategies (Strauss & Corbin, 1990). For both data collection and analysis, our strategies were guided by our research interest in better understanding the positioning, discursive constitution, and legitimization of data science. The empirical findings presented in this chapter mainly draw on our mapping of data science as well as our interviews with data science professors, with some examples referring to descriptions in study programme materials. In both of the latter two data sources, key actors make their discursive claims of epistemic authority directly or indirectly. One crucial difference between study brochures and our interviews that we discuss below is the lack of (critical) self-reflection or (even nuanced) consideration of critical perspectives on data science in the materials for prospective students. This might be due to their advertising character and relatively concise format. Our interviews, in contrast, offered a non-public setting. But the more self-reflexive and self-critical perspectives about data science that we witnessed in those conversations might also be interpreted as their own type of discursive strategy: data scientists may wish to present their discipline as a self-reflexive endeavour, one that is even capable of self-critique and constructive revisions (for the latter, see Prietl & Raible, 2023).

As we did not encounter any systematic country-specific differences, we do not distinguish between the three countries in the following results.

Empirical Findings

Based on our structural and organizational mapping of data science in the DACH region, as well as our qualitative analyses of the study brochures on the one hand and interviews with data science professors on the other hand, we begin by sketching how data science is institutionally structured. Second, we reconstruct its epistemological positioning within the academic field. Third, we present how this positioning is discursively legitimized.

Structural Institutionalization of Data Science

Based on our mapping of the structural implementation of data science chairs and study programmes at universities and universities of applied sciences in the DACH region, we find strong evidence of efforts to professionalize and academically institutionalize data science in these countries. In Spring 2021, there were 92 study programmes in data science, 63 of which were master's degree programmes. At the same time, 80 out of 146 openings for data science chairs advertised between 2015 and 2021 were filled. Of those 80 successful candidates, 71 were men, rendering data science—at this top level—a discipline structurally dominated by men. Looking at the temporal development of job announcements, we can also see a rapid acceleration in the number of open positions in the years observed (2015: n = 8; 2016: n = 17; 2017: n = 28; 2018: n = 26; 2019: n = 35; 2020: n = 32). Thus, there is ample evidence for an academic institutionalization of data science in the DACH region.

Looking at *how* data science is structured within the academic field (see Tables 12.1 and 12.2), we find a strong affiliation with science, technology, engineering, and mathematics (STEM) faculties and departments, especially with computer science. This holds true for both data science chairs and study programmes: out of 146 data science chairs advertised from 2015 onwards, 75 were affiliated with STEM departments, and another 13 with departments focused on STEM *and* economic sciences. A similar pattern can be detected for the study programmes, with 61 out of 92 linked to STEM departments.[5]

Table 12.1. Data Science Chairs

Advertised:	n = 146
Organizational affiliation (faculty, department, or others):	
STEM	n = 75
Economic sciences	n = 13
STEM *and* economic sciences	n = 13
Others	n = 45
Chairs independent from specific domains:	n = 92
Domain-specific chairs:	n = 54
Bio/life science (incl. medicine)	n = 19
Economic science	n = 17
Others	n = 18

---

5   A more detailed classification (e.g., along disciplinary lines) did not appear to be expedient to our analysis due to the largely non-standardized structures of universities and non-standardized processes of naming departments in German-speaking countries.

Required qualifications:	
Background in mathematics, IT/computer science, or statistics (partly with domain focus)	n = 94
Background in domain seen as equivalent	n = 5
No data	n = 47
Positions filled:	n = 80
Male	n = 71
Female	n = 9

Table 12.2.   Data Science Degree Programmes

Total:	n = 92
Degree:	
Master's	n = 63
Bachelor's	n = 29
Organizational affiliation (faculty, department, or others):	
STEM	n = 61
Economic sciences	n = 9
Others	n = 22
General degree programmes	n = 69
Domain-specific degree programmes	n = 26
Economic sciences	n = 11
Bio/life science (incl. medicine)	n = 6
Others	n = 6
Requirements *	
Computer sciences, mathematic, natural sciences	n = 41
Open to others	n = 7
No data	n = 15
Curricular focus**	
Only computer sciences, mathematic, statistics (+ data related topics)	n = 55
Additional: Economic sciences	n = 27
Additional: Bio & life sciences (incl. medicine)	n = 9
Additional: Others	n = 10

* Only for master's degree programmes
** Multiple assignments possible for several designated focuses

The organizational affiliation with STEM and/or computer science is also reflected on a content level, with data science chairs and degree programmes focusing on related skills and competencies. Of the academic positions advertised, 142 out of 146 requested qualifications, skills, and academic experiences clearly linked to a disciplinary background in computer science, mathematics, and/or statistics. These included "combining classic approaches to mathematical optimization with modern methods of data analysis and machine learning"[6] or "predictive modelling,... including computer-driven processes like decision and regression trees, random forests, gradient boosting, but also meta-level approaches, especially model selection, pipeline configuration, Bayesian optimization, and interpretable machine learning."[7] Unsurprisingly, then, a large number of the persons hired as data science professors, whose academic degrees are available via their (institutional) websites, university press releases, public LinkedIn, or similar social media accounts (n = 40), hold a master's (or comparable) degree in computer science or in computer science combined with another STEM subject (n = 19). When it comes to data science study programmes, there is a strong curricular emphasis on computer science content: 55 out of 92 curricula consist *solely* of foundational courses in computer science, mathematics, and statistics as well as some advanced courses in data-related topics (e.g., "data management" or "databases"). Additionally, the master's degree programmes (which currently predominate the overall landscape) request various qualifications and skills in their application formalities, again mainly requiring pre-existing knowledge in STEM fields, especially computer science, with only 15 study programmes *not* asking for prior qualifications and skills in STEM, especially computer science. Hence, data science is closely tied to STEM and, more specifically, to computer science.

Looking at the titles of data science chairs and study programmes, we find two distinct forms in which data science appears: first, as subject in its own right and second, as a subject linked to another discipline or area of research, for example, "business analytics and data science"[8] or "bio data science."[9] The majority of data science chairs (92 out of 146) and study programmes (69 out of 92) are implemented in a generalist manner, independently from specific other domains. Although 55 study programmes do not explicitly list any curricular content from partnering domains,[10] a considerable number still offer domain-specific coursework.[11] The predominant domains are bio and life sciences (including medicine) as

6 Quotation from the advertisement for the chair in data science for engineering at the University of Paderborn, Germany.

7 Quotation from the advertisement for the chair in statistical learning and data science at Ludwig Maximilian University of Munich, Germany.

8 Chair at the University of Graz, Austria.

9 Master's degree programme at the University of Applied Sciences Wiener Neustadt, Austria.

10 Those 14 study programmes, being classified as independent of any domain, list additional teaching content from economic science, ethics, and law.

11 We will return to the term "domain," which plays a crucial role in data science's algorithmic regime, later in this chapter.

well as economic sciences. Out of 54 domain-specific data science chairs, 19 are associated with the bio and life sciences (including medicine) and 17 with economic sciences; out of 26 domain-specific study programmes, 11 are linked to economic sciences and 6 to bio and life sciences (including medicine). Thus, there is a clear tendency for data science to be institutionalized in close alliance with either economic sciences or bio and life sciences (including medicine).

Epistemological Self-Positioning

In study brochures and interviews with data science scholars, data science is predominantly described as *a specific analytical approach to knowledge production*. Instead of referring to distinctive subject areas or objects of research, self-descriptions of data science centre around talk of it being and/or offering a "toolkit," "process," or "method" for data analysis. One data science professor whom we interviewed, for instance, stated: "Well, what is data science? It's really about working with data…. [I]t's work that focuses on the analysis of data" (IV_DE_04, Pos. 41). Following this internal understanding of data science, we searched for elaborations of what might make data science's approach to knowledge production unique. Three aspects stand out in our data: first, data science's approach to knowledge production is seen as *integrating advanced algorithmic methods* for the analysis of large data sets, especially via machine learning, deep learning or, more generally, artificial intelligence, as stated by one data science professor: "If you take machine learning technologies as an example, you'll find them being applied heavily in data science projects" (IV_DE_10, Pos. 21).

Second, data science is presented as *a practical, action-oriented endeavour*, not only generating (abstract and theoretical) knowledge based on data analysis, but providing the foundation for (better) decisions and, thus, directly enabling better measures in academic as well as non-academic fields such as medicine or private companies. The brochure for the master's degree programme in data science at Harz University of Applied Science puts it this way: "Data science pulls insights from data. Practical recommendations can be derived from the findings, and ultimately decisions can be made" (DE_Hochschule Harz_Data Science, Pos. 3).

Third, and strongly connected to this practical, action-oriented approach is a supposed *real-world relevance* of data science. Describing her everyday work, a data science professor, for example, explained: "The problems you deal with aren't those frequently constructed in theory but they actually exist in practice" (IV_DE_12, Pos. 22).

Another professor from a university of applied sciences went a step further by distancing "good" data science from other scientific research—inside and outside of data science—that focuses on complex (theoretical) problems affording several extensive resources (e.g., data or processing power) and not promising a solution. To him, "good" data science means to work on practicable, solvable questions and to achieve practicable, useful solutions for concrete problems of companies:

> The difference is that you won't have completely unrealistic require-
> ments (swallows) and therefore maybe a problem—one that's a real-world
> problem—that can't be solved, because you don't have the necessary
> data, or the technology, or the staff, or something else…. I always like
> being able to keep an eye on industry problems, and producing results
> that can actually be applied by the industry as well. (IV_DE_07, Pos. 110)

Data science is presented here as a specific mode of knowledge production that uses sophisticated algorithmic methods for analysing big data sets to answer questions (and making decisions) stemming from the so-called real world.

From this self-understanding follows that the purported *aim of academic data science* is either to advance data science methods or "merely" to apply them to different research areas. The scholars we interviewed placed themselves along this same continuum. Within our sample, particularly the professors at universities of applied sciences, but not exclusively, tended to describe themselves and their work as close to the latter pole. Many of our interviewees in fact located their daily academic work somewhere between those poles. One data science professor with a strong interest in advancing statistical data analysis methods put it like this:

> Fifty-fifty. Like I said before, there are two basic approaches. I do really
> enjoy taking a methods-driven approach. Because I like sitting back
> and thinking about numbers, formulas, methods—how could they all
> fit together?… But in my everyday work, we have more applied projects.
> (IV_DE_06, Pos. 63)

One central element of data science's understanding of itself as a discipline and as a specific approach to knowledge production is a *special relation with so-called domains* (Ribes et al., 2019; Ribes, 2019; Slota et al., 2020). This connection is not only salient in the literature but also in our empirical data. The term "domain" here refers to other, mostly long-established academic disciplines or non-academic areas of expertise such as specific industries or certain tasks in organizations, such as marketing. While domains are not part of the discipline, they are consistently portrayed as necessary to data science. This relationship of necessity is explained by the fact that it is usually "the domain" that provides the data (sets), the research questions, and the subject matter expertise for data science projects. In other words, domains are the target of data science applications. The following quote from an interview with a data science professor working in cooperation projects with scholars from several disciplines illustrates this crucial role of "domains":

> "So, data science is a combination of statistics and computer science, on the one hand. And domain knowledge is important for its application. Let's say for applications in fields like chemistry, physics, sociology, and others" (IV_AT_01, Pos. 2).

Domains are much more than simply the fields where data science is applied. They also provide the necessary (background) information on the specific object of inquiry. A data science professor who regularly collaborates with medical experts emphasized the crucial nature of domain expertise, making clear the mutual dependence between data scientists and these subject matter experts:

> For example, [a data set] coming from a hospital. So, you sit there and the variables are totally cryptic in some ways. You don't get it at all. Values are missing, but you don't know why—weren't they collected? Did we fail to detect them or were they just not relevant?... So, your best bet is to sit down with someone from the domain to first understand the data together.... This is a give and take that's important to me—an important aspect of data science. (IV_DE_06, Pos. 27)

Other interviewees went as far as to declare that research interests are almost exclusively motivated by domain experts, that is, either scholars from other academic disciplines (e.g., biologists, sociologists) or subject matter experts from other, non-academic fields (e.g., medical doctors, corporate staff) who collaborate with data scientists. From this perspective, data science becomes somewhat of an adjunct discipline: "But the research objectives—or even the questions—always come from the application domain and never from the data scientist. That would be rare. Of course, it can happen, but very rarely" (IV_DE_04, Pos. 41).

Thus, although positioned as external to data science, domains are also presented as constitutive to data science. Likewise, domains play a crucial role in supporting the respective modes of knowledge production.

While data science seems to have penchants for certain specific domains, throughout our data, we also found a palpable *claim to universality*. Its protagonists portrayed data science as offering a universal key to knowledge production. The multiple domains cited as candidates for its application ranged from engineering to the natural sciences, humanities, and social sciences, as well as private or public organizations. In one study brochure, this wide spectrum was presented with virtually boundless enthusiasm: "Applications can be found in almost all areas of human life" (DE_TU Chemnitz_Data Science, Pos. 3). This universal applicability is justified by the "toolkit" qualities that data science brings to the table, as an interviewee explained: "Because the main focus lies on data and methods, not on thematic issues" (IV_DE_09, Pos. 39).

Strongly connected to this claim of universality, we furthermore found an *expansionist tendency in applying data science approaches* in our data. Some data science scholars expressed their hopes that data science methods would eventually become part of other, preferably: all, disciplines. One vehicle for this expansion seems to be the integration of data science into the curricula of other disciplinary degree programmes, like one data science professor outlines for example: "And so, I hope that we get to the point when we are not only teaching robustness, machine learning, and so on in data science study programmes. That we can also, somehow, radiate to other study programmes as well" (IV_DE_13-2, Pos. 119).

To sum up so far, data science is epistemologically positioned as a methodological and mainly *algorithmic toolkit*—or process—for knowledge production. Because of its perceived *universal applicability*, there is a widely held view that data science should be consulted whenever there is knowledge to be produced.

Discursive Legitimization

One key pillar of legitimizing the institutionalization of data science is the idea that data science is fundamentally *beneficial to society*. Reviving techno-utopian visions, one interviewee, for instance, declared wholeheartedly: "And I think that we can give back a great deal to humankind—or in general to society as a whole—without risks" (IV_DE_11, Pos. 2).

This quote does not only postulate data science's benefits for society, but also refers to previously mentioned risks circulating in supposedly techno-dystopian visions, such as the possibility of data misuse (e.g., for manipulating elections). While some interviewees remained rather abstract in contending data science's value to society, others addressed pressing, high-stakes issues such as climate change or the COVID-19 pandemic.

In the material we surveyed, data science justifies its value to society by discursively referring (1) to *informational content* and (2) to the *innovation potential inherent in (big) data (sets) to be extracted via data science methods*. Several interviewees as well as study brochures referred to digitalization and/or datafication as a generalized transformation process—one presented summarily as a given and in no need of explanation. In this rather confident and unquestioned view, data contains the "next generation" of information that is "waiting" to be extracted by data science methods, as stated in a brochure: "This flood of data, as an expression of our behaviour, our preferences and our routines, offers enormous information potential" (AT_Oberoesterreich-FH_Data Science and Engineering, Pos. 3).

In some instances, the information value is directly linked to the innovation potential of data, as exemplified by the following quote from the bachelor's degree programme brochure for data science at FH St. Pölten—University of Applied Sciences, in Austria: "Here, you learn to harness and convert the potential of data for enabling innovation" (AT_St Poelten-FH_Data Science and Business Analytics, Pos. 3).

This idea links data science to innovation, which can be considered a highly desirable goal in its own right in modern societies (Rammert et al., 2018). Taken together, data science is not only presented as possible, but necessary, as one interviewee pointed out:

> The need for people who can deal with complex data types and data sources is already enormous. And it gets bigger every day. And since we will be handling even more types and sources of data in the future, companies, public administration, and research institutions are going to have to find ways to handle these types of data and data volumes. (IV_DE_09, Pos. 103)

Finding innovative ways to harness the informational value of data—with data science leading the way—therefore is postulated as a necessity for society.

The *academic* institutionalization of data science is furthermore legitimized by *linking data science to a strong empiricism* presented as constitutive of science itself. One data science professor linked data science in general and knowledge production in data science specifically to "empirical observation" (IV_DE_03, Pos. 41). The vast majority of interviewees echo this notion in their own statements. Sporadic claims of "neutral" or "objective" observations shined through, for example, when one data science professor primarily interested in progressing methods referred to the usage of a set of data science methods:

> And now it's about gaining … statistically sound … knowledge from data. And statistically sound means again—there are many models, there are many assumptions, there is a lot of mathematics—but in the end we try to gain knowledge from data as objectively as possible. (IV_DE_01, Pos. 42)

Further classic (empiricist) scientific principles like reproducibility or the search for truth[12] are mentioned as criteria for "good" scientific data science. Another data science professor distancing herself—and "good" academic data science—from interest-driven data analytics, cites truth as a primary criterion: "Because it isn't our goal to show that something is this or that way. What we want to do is detect truth" (IV_DE_06, Pos. 81).

This criterion seems to function as a shorthand reminder of the *scientific "nature"* of data science. In legitimizing data science's process of knowledge production, its protagonists lean heavily on existing scientific rationalities, especially empiricism, and present data science as a generalistic version of empirical knowledge production. Data science is therewith situated at the very heart of scientific discovery.

Calls for the expansion of data science are then legitimized by the idea that the application of data science's methods of knowledge production will *advance its collaborating domains as well*. One major reason is the possibility of pursuing so far unanswered questions in the respective disciplines, mainly because new or larger data sets can be accessed through data science's algorithmic methods. For a COVID-19-related research project, one scholar explained why data science enhances research as follows:

> With data, it is possible to answer questions that were unanswerable before. So, for example, for one project we anonymized movement patterns of mobile phones … that we can use to answer concrete questions. For example, questions like, How is the coronavirus spread? And we were able to calculate the answers more precisely than ever before. Just because we had additional—for a third of all mobile phones … we had those patterns and so it was possible to do a calculation and scale it to reflect the entire country. (IV_AT_01, Pos. 2)

12 For discussions about "ground truth" in data science, see Jaton, 2021.

However, our interviewees do not view this progress as disruptive. Instead, they distance themselves from the hype around big data, as well as variations of data science that come with unrealistic promises:

> Ok, are we able to combine that? Are we able to strongly integrate that [data science] in what we actually did before? People are reflecting that it's not about data science replacing everything but supplementing it. I really believe that this higher level is central now. (IV_DE_05, Pos. 44)

In other words, the added value of expanding data science to other disciplines and fields is more likely—and modestly—seen as driven by an integration of data science in existing modes or processes of knowledge production. There is little, if any, talk of substitution. Data science is therefore presented as a catalyst for scientific development and for specific areas of research.

Despite all (techno-utopian) hopes attributed to data science, there were also nuanced and reflective understandings of the field. In our interviews, modes of positioning and legitimizing data science stood in (semi-)stark contrast to study brochures, which showcased positively charged, even rather naïvely techno-utopian motifs driven by the mere existence of "more" data and digital technologies. There are at least two reasons for this presentation gap. First, most scholars were (at least somewhat) aware of (additional) non-technological forces fuelling the rise of data science, such as political funding decisions, and especially, the role of the tech economy, which some see rather enthusiastically while others utter more critical opinions:

> Well, a real driving force for data science is Google. Google is really great, runs great projects ... also Microsoft, but somehow, for most of the projects, I have the impression that Google is on top. (IV_DE_06, Pos. 53)

> And, on the other hand, we have those big players, like Google or Facebook or Amazon, who want to profit from that development. (IV_CH_02, Pos. 52)

Second, several scholars even referred to the potential risks of specific, mostly societal data science applications that they felt warranted consideration in science and society: "From my point of view, it would be important to raise awareness for the risks" (IV_DE_05, Pos. 30).

In most of our interviews, those risks and social threats were elaborated to include algorithmic discrimination or privacy issues. Discussing potential responses to those risks, various (mostly) technological solutions were presented, pointing out the importance of topics like *fairness and transparency in machine learning* (FATML) or *explainable AI*. So, despite all overtly optimistic presentations of data science, there are much more nuanced reflections that do, however, remain within a technocratic frame when searching for technological solutions to the depicted challenges accompanying the use of data science.

Discussion

Looking at the way data science is institutionally structured, epistemologically positioned, and discursively legitimized within the academic fields of Germany, Austria, and Switzerland, we find that the rise of academic data science has some considerable epistemological, and thus political, consequences.

   As data science chairs and study programmes are predominantly affiliated with STEM, and especially computer science, academic data science centres around IT expertise, rendering knowledge production a "problem" to be solved with the help of computer science skills and techniques. Yet these solutions are meant to be applied independent of the object of inquiry, as data science is at once presented as a *universal* approach to knowledge production. This view implies that ultimately all (research) questions can be tackled by submitting them to a data science process, with no need for other research approaches, expertise, or perspectives. Hence, STEM and computer science expertise, approaches, and logics are central to and within data science, and so are the associated actors, practices, and social as well as epistemic cultures dominant within these subfields of academia. With regards to how knowledge and power are related, data science must therefore be considered as fundamentally linked to quantitative research approaches and modes of thinking, more specifically to what has been called a "formal epistemology" (Bath, 2009) with a focus on abstraction, standardization, and formalization. Furthermore, as feminist research on STEM has shown, these fields are not only structurally dominated by men but also symbolically associated with traditional masculinity. Given the fact that the majority of data science professors are men, this does not only pose the question of how data science is itself gendered as a discipline (cf. Paulitz et al., 2015). Going one step further, the growing relevance of data science methods and associated modes of knowing could also lead to a gender shift in currently less male-dominated disciplines (e.g., education science) or "domains," where (male) data scientists are then increasingly recruited as the new "experts."

Wherever data science is implemented as domain specific, it is primarily linked to either economics or bio and life sciences, including medicine. On the one hand, we would thus expect data science and the respective algorithmic modes of knowledge production to have an outsized influence on the epistemic cultures of these disciplines and related societal sectors, such as for-profit industries or medical research. As the emerging discipline enters these fields, it introduces data science rationalities and challenges the role of traditional experts and expertise. On the other hand, data science might become a vehicle for introducing economic and biomedical rationalities into other areas of society, as the training of many data scientists and the body of research the discipline produces draws heavily on economic and biomedical topics and rationalities (for the automated consideration of economic interests in architecture and design through computational design tools, see Boeva & Kropp in this volume).

With regards to data science's epistemological (self-)positioning, we reconstructed that data science is presented as a specific mode of knowledge production with three characteristics: (1) its use of advanced algorithmic methods, associating data science with machine learning and/or artificial intelligence, (2) its practical and action-oriented stance, and (3) its relevance to the "real world." Data science forgoes the longstanding scientific tradition of distancing itself from real-world messiness. On the contrary, data science embraces the "real world" in a pragmatic move, claiming not only to generate knowledge but to shape decisions. Data science's epistemological position is, hence, more in line with the symbolic construction of engineering and the technical sciences (see Paulitz & Prietl, 2022). It balances theory and practice by claiming to be both a scientific endeavour and concerned with "shaping the world."

This (self-)understanding is discursively legitimized by a bundle of arguments that present data science as necessary to society. Recurring to data-solutionist ideas surrounding discourses on big data (cf. Prietl, 2019), such as big data's inherent information value and innovative potential, data science is positioned as beneficial to society. It is especially data science's potential for knowledge production that is held as offering the key to solving humanity's problems. Whilst more nuanced interpretations of data science's potential can be found amongst scholars, such considerations do not systematically question the promises made in the name of data science, but rather reflect upon the related risks and challenges as yet another problem to be tackled by data science and similar technical solutions (for how algorithmic fairness is negotiated within an interdisciplinary team that set out to tackle algorithmic harm "from the inside," see Kinder-Kurlanda & Fahimi, in this volume). Also, data science postulates a strong empiricism and is therefore presented as being at the very "heart of science," implicitly ushering in ideas of a supposed "end of theory" (see Anderson, 2008). According to such views, data could speak for itself, rendering theoretical considerations unnecessary. Theory, on the other hand, is depicted as blurring or obscuring the more immediate message of data as a mirror of the real world.

Conclusion

In this chapter, we set out to study the rise of academic data science in Europe's DACH region, in order to understand the power dynamics incorporated within current shifts in society's regime of truth following the diffusion of algorithmic modes of knowledge production. Based on our analysis of how data science is institutionally structured, epistemologically positioned, and discursively legitimized, we argue that the professionalization of data science gives rise to a new algorithmic regime of knowledge production that has considerable epistemological, and thus, political consequences. At the heart of this algorithmic regime of knowledge production is the idea that advanced algorithmic techniques, especially machine learning and artificial intelligence, are to be used to analyse big data sets to generate knowledge and inform decisions in (almost) every area of society. Taking into account the further ideal of universal applicability, and the related drive for expansion that has already been observed in the data analytics industry (Beer, 2019), the academic institutionalization of data science warrants consideration as an important element of society's overarching regime of truth.

The rise—and spread—of data science might lead to crucial, even all-encompassing transformations in knowledge production that will then be submitted to the affordances—possibilities and restrictions—of data science means and methods, having not only symbolic but also very material consequences. Knowledge production could not only be affected in terms of how data (sets) are analysed (e.g., using machine learning methods), but more fundamentally, even at the research design level. This subsequent shaping of knowledge production starts with which questions are asked, which data are collected by which means, which expertise is considered relevant, and which results are sought. Put differently, with knowledge production being submitted to the affordances of data science (for detailed, yet descriptive insights into the affordances of doing data science, see Beaulieu & Leonelli, 2022, pp. 94–115), the very regime of knowledge production might change, giving rise to serious political questions, such as which topics are no longer studied (e.g., due to a dearth of data or poor data quality), whose expertise is devalued (e.g., sovereign disciplinary experts who become degraded to "mere" domain experts), or whose interests count in knowledge production (e.g., those of third-party partners due to the high relevance of their cooperation and funding in data science, but also due to data science's "real-world orientation").

Building on this analysis, future research should consider the relationship between academic data science and the data analytics industry. Big tech actors such as Google or Amazon are often cited as relevant—sometimes even Goliath-like—forces (see Prietl & Raible, 2023). Another interesting angle would be to look at how power relations are negotiated between academically trained data scientists and data scientists who do not dispose of such objective cultural capital (Bourdieu, 1992), but who have been active in building up the data analytics industry. Moreover, it would be interesting to compare our findings on data science in German-speaking countries to the professionalization of data science in countries like the United States, where big tech companies are located and slightly different professionalization processes seem to take place, either with more autonomous academic data science departments or with industry affiliations to big tech instead of other large corporates (e.g., manufacturing industry) (cf. Dorschel, 2021b, pp. 10–11).

Considering the particular relationship between data science and what are called domains, it would furthermore be of interest to consider the influence that the rise of data science is actually having within these disciplines and areas of knowledge production: How are data science methods of knowledge production integrated (or not) within these disciplines? What is the current academic division of labour in partnerships between domains and data science? Looking into those concrete research practices and the involvement of data scientists and so-called domain experts might also allow us to reflect critically on different axes of power (e.g., gender relations) within those emerging regimes of truth.

References

Abbott, A. (1988). *The system of professions: An essay on the division of expert labor.* University of Chicago Press.

Abbott, A. (1995). Boundaries of social work or social work of boundaries? *Social Service Review, 69*(4), 545–562.

Abbott, A. (2001). *Chaos of disciplines.* University of Chicago Press.

Anderson, C. (2008, June 23). The end of theory: The data deluge makes the scientific method obsolete. *Wired*. https://www.wired.com/2008/06/pb-theory/

Bath, C. (2009). *De-Gendering informatischer Artefakte: Grundlagen einer kritisch feministischen Technikgestaltung*. Dissertation, University of Bremen. http://nbn-resolving.de/urn:nbn:de:gbv:46-00102741-12

Beaulieu, A., & Leonelli, S. (2022). *Data and society: A critical introduction*. Sage.

Beer, D. (2019). *The data gaze: Capitalism, power and perception*. Sage. https://dx.doi.org/10.4135/9781526463210

Bourdieu, P. (1992). *Die verborgenen Mechanismen der Macht*. Schriften zu Politik & Kultur 1. VSA.

Dorschel, R. (2021a). "Data Science." Analyse einer emergierenden Profession mittels einer Verknüpfung von Diskurs- und Feldtheorie. *Soziologie, 50*(1), 94–102.

Dorschel, R. (2021b). Discovering needs for digital capitalism: The hybrid profession of data science. *Big Data & Society, 8*(2), 1–13. https://doi.org/10.1177/20539517211040760

Dorschel, R., & Brandt, P. (2021). Professionalisierung mittels Ambiguität: Die diskursive Konstruktion von Data Scientists in Wirtschaft und Wissenschaft. *Zeitschrift für Soziologie, 50*(3–4), 193–210. https://doi.org/10.1515/zfsoz-2021-0014

Foucault, M. (1977). The political function of the intellectual. *Radical Philosophy, 17*(13), 12–14.

Foucault, M. (2020). *The essential works of Michel Foucault, 1954–1984, vol. 3: Power* (J. D. Faubion, Ed.; R. Hurley et al., Trans.). Penguin.

Gieryn, T. F. (1994). Boundaries of science. In S. Jasanoff, G. Markle, J. Peterson, & T. Pinch (Eds.), *Handbook of science, technology and society* (pp. 393–443). Sage.

Gieryn, T. F. (1999). *Cultural boundaries of science: Credibility on the line*. University of Chicago Press.

Houben, D., & Prietl, B. (Eds.). (2018). *Datengesellschaft: Einsichten in die Datafizierung des Sozialen*. transcript. https://doi.org/10.1515/9783839439579

Jaton, F. (2021). Assessing biases, relaxing moralism: On ground-truthing practices in machine learning design and application. *Big Data & Society, 8*(1), 1–15. https://doi.org/10.1177/20539517211013569

Kitchin, R. (2014). Big data, new epistemologies and paradigm shifts. *Big Data & Society, 1*(1). https://doi.org/10.1177/2053951714528481

Lowrie, I. (2017). Algorithmic rationality: Epistemology and efficiency in the data sciences. *Big Data & Society, 4*(1). https://doi.org/10.1177/2053951717700925

Paulitz, T. (2012). "Hegemoniale Männlichkeit" als narrative Distinktionspraxis im Wissenschaftsspiel. *Österreichische Zeitschrift für Soziologie, 37*(1), 45–64. https://doi.org/10.1007/s11614-012-0013-y

Paulitz, T., & Prietl, B. (2022). Wie männlich ist die digitale Avantgarde? Zum Zusammenspiel von Technik und Männlichkeit im Kontext aktueller Digitalisierungsschübe. In M. Kastein, & L. Weber (Eds.), *Care-Arbeit und Gender in der digitalen Transformation* (pp. 86–102). Beltz Juventa.

Paulitz, T., Hey, B., Kink, S., & Prietl, B. (Eds.). (2015). *Akademische Wissenskulturen und soziale Praxis. Geschlechterforschung zu natur-, technik- und geisteswissenschaftlichen Fächern*. Westfälisches Dampfboot.

Paulitz, T., Kink, S., & Prietl, B. (2016). Analytical strategy for dealing with neutrality claims and implicit masculinity constructions: Methodological challenges for gender studies in science and technology. *Forum: Qualitative Social Research, 17*(3). http://nbn-resolving.de/urn:nbn:de:0114-fqs1603138

Prietl, B. (2019). Die Versprechen von Big Data im Spiegel feministischer Rationalitätskritik. *Gender, 3,* 11–25. https://doi.org/10.3224/gender.v11i3.02

Prietl, B., & Raible, S. (2023). Claiming universal epistemic authority: Relational boundary work and the academic institutionalization of data science. *Swiss Journal of Sociology, 49*(3).

Rammert, W., Windeler, A., Knoblauch, H., & Hutter, M. (2018). Expanding the innovation zone. In W. Rammert, A. Windeler, H. Knoblauch, & M. Hutter (Eds.), *Innovation society today: Perspectives, fields, and cases* (pp. 1–11). Springer.

Ribes, D. (2019). STS, meet data science, once again. *Science, Technology, & Human Values, 44*(3), 514–539. https://doi.org/10.1177/0162243918798899

Ribes, D., Hoffman, A. S., Slota, S. C., & Bowker, G. C. (2019). The logic of domains. *Social Studies of Science, 49*(3), 281–309. https://doi.org/10.1177/0306312719849709

Saner, P. (2019). Envisioning higher education: How imaging the future shapes the implementation of a new field in higher education. *Swiss Journal of Sociology, 45,* 359–381. https://doi.org/10.2478/sjs-2019-0017

Saner, P. (2022). *Datenwissenschaften und Gesellschaft. Die Genese eines transversalen Wissensfeldes*. transcript. https://doi.org/10.14361/9783839462591

Slota, S. C., Hoffman, A. S., Ribes, D., & Bowker, G. C. (2020). Prospecting (in) the data sciences. *Big Data & Society, 7*(1), 1–12. https://doi.org/10.1177/2053951720906849

Srnicek, N. (2016). *Platform capitalism*. Wiley.

Strauss, A., & Corbin, J. M. (1990). *Basics of qualitative research: Grounded theory procedures and techniques*. Sage.

Thylstrup, N. B., Flyverbom, M., & Helles, R. (2019). Datafied knowledge production: Introduction to the special theme. *Big Data & Society, 6*(2), 1–5. https://doi.org/10.1177/2053951719875985

Zuboff, S. (2015). Big other: Surveillance capitalism and the prospects of an information civilization. *Journal of Information Technology, 30*(1), 75–89. https://doi.org/10.1057/jit.2015.5

About the Authors

Bianca Prietl is Professor for Gender Studies with a Focus on Digitalization at the University of Basel in Switzerland. Her main area of expertise is feminist technoscience studies, with her more recent work focusing on the interrelations of knowledge, power, and gender in the context of (digital) datafication.

Stefanie Raible is a research assistant and PhD candidate at the Institute of Sociology of Johannes Kepler University Linz in Austria. Her research is concerned with the relationships between digital technologies, organizations, and society.

13. Algorithmic Futures: Governmentality and Prediction Regimes

Simon Egbert

Abstract

Attempts to generate knowledge about the future and to make it usable for decisions in the present have existed for a long time in human history. Modern societies, however, are characterized by a particularly close relationship to the future and use numerous possibilities of (scientific) foreknowledge production to colonize it. Nonetheless, with recent advances in machine learning fuelled by predictive analytics, approaches to predicting the future in order to optimize strategies and actions in the present are becoming even more important. Before this backdrop, I analyse the application of predictive analytics as "prediction regimes," utilizing the Foucauldian governmentality approach. It is argued that predictive algorithms serve as "rendering devices," making the future calculable and, hence, governable in the present.

Keywords: algorithms; data; calculability

Introduction

Attempts to generate knowledge about the future and to make it usable for decisions in the present have existed for a long time in human history. Whether it was ancient practices of divination by consulting prophets or using oracles, or medieval efforts to foresee future events by asking witches and other soothsayers: the future has always been an important point of reference for human action (e.g., Koselleck, 2004). But modern societies, beginning with industrialization, are characterized by a particularly close relationship to the future and use numerous possibilities of (scientific) foreknowledge production to colonize it (Adam & Groves, 2007). Nevertheless, with recent

Jarke, J., B. Prietl, S. Egbert, Y. Boeva, H. Heuer, and M. Arnold (eds.), *Algorithmic Regimes: Methods, Interactions, and Politics*. Amsterdam: Amsterdam University Press, 2024
DOI 10.5117/9789463728485_CH13

advances in predictive analytics, approaches to predicting the future in order to optimize strategies and actions in the present are becoming even more important (Rona-Tas, 2020; Esposito, 2021).

Predictive algorithms, understood here as deliberately future-related "encoded procedures for transforming input into a desired output, based on specific calculations" (Gillespie, 2014, p. 167) are now a decisive factor when it comes to decision-making, evaluation processes or classification practices in many and diverse social fields—like in policing (Kaufmann, Egbert, & Leese, 2019), credit scoring (Hurley & Adebayo, 2016), public employment services (Lopez, 2019), education (Jarke & Macgilchrist, 2021) or e-commerce (Jannach et al., 2010). In fact, voices can already be heard stating that we live in a "predictive society" (Davenport, 2016, p. xix), underlining the great impact of predictive knowledge in people's lives. Although this diagnosis may seem like an exaggerated (over)generalization, it is not to be denied that predictive methods already have a significant impact—and indeed, will likely have an even greater impact in the future. This impact is closely connected to the capacity of predictive algorithms to provide knowledge for processes of decision-making and to (unwittingly) shape people's behaviour.

Predictive algorithms are always closely connected to the people who program and/or (wish to) implement them and to the societal contexts for which they are planned. At the same time, predictive algorithms are developed and implemented to shape people's practices, both those of operators and of the populations targeted. That is, they are regularly implemented as governing technologies—as technical means aiming directly at shaping the actions of others. Due to this, I propose to make use of the Foucauldian notion of governmentality and the subsequent literature from governmentality studies to analyse the role of algorithmically generated predictive knowledge in practices of governing people. I will analyse predictive analytics as a special, future-related subtype of "algorithmic regimes," namely as "prediction regimes." With this, I mean more or less stable and recognizable algorithmically mediated patterns of thinking and acting on the world that revolve around the explicit production and implementation of predictions.

Before this conceptual backdrop, in this chapter predictive algorithms are grasped as constituting special practices of governing, in which the future plays an important role as a powerful reference, understood as part of "algorithmic governmentality" (Rouvroy, 2011, 2013; Rouvroy & Berns, 2013). Prediction regimes in the algorithmic society are typically heavily influenced by predictive analytics, that is, "the process of extracting information from large data sets in order to make predictions and estimates about future outcomes" (Larose & Larose, 2015, p. 4). Although often big data is—at least implicitly—understood as being closely connected to predictive component (e.g., Mayer-Schönberger & Cukier, 2013, p. 55), I propose here to make a clear terminological and conceptual distinction between algorithmic governmental and algorithmic regimes, respectively, and prediction regimes. Predictions are in fact only one way of utilizing algorithmic big data and we should define the term more narrowly rather than more broadly (see, e.g., Kitchin, 2014, p. 101). Of course, this does not mean that we understand predictive analytics to mean only those methods that actually predict the future in the strict sense of the word—i.e., that depict a future state in all its details in the present. Rather, prediction regimes in this sense include those procedures in which knowledge about possible states and developments in the future is systematically and intentionally produced on the basis of appropriately developed models and statistical procedures and used for decision-making. In doing so, I argue, it becomes possible to study (more) directly the politics of predictive algorithms, including the close nexus of knowledge and power, as well as the important role of technologies in these politics. Hence, such a conceptual background provides us with an analytical lens enabling us to focus on the situatedness as well as socio-technical nature of algorithmically mediated prediction practices and their consequences.

This chapter proceeds as follows: First, I will describe the Foucauldian idea of governmentality. This is followed by a presentation of the role of technologies in governing practices. After that, I will engage with Rouvroy's notion of algorithmic governmentality. Then, I will discuss what I mean by prediction regimes, suggesting some key questions for debate in future research, in order to understand the ramifications and politics of algorithmic regimes in general.

Acting upon Actions: The Power/Knowledge Nexus and Regimes of Governing

Introducing the notion of "governmentality" in his lectures at the Collège de France in 1978 (2007), Foucault designated the multiple, mostly subtle ways in which power is exercised in modern (Western) states. In doing so, Foucault significantly recalibrated his analysis of power and its techniques in relation to his prior studies—most notably with reference to disciplinary power (Foucault, 1977a)—in at least two ways (Bröckling et al., 2011, p. 1f.): (1) the addressees of governmental interventions are conceptualized more comprehensively, focusing not only on their bodies and their formation for the sake of discipline, but also highlighting the active role of subjects in practices of governing, stressing the relational character of power (Foucault, 2000b); (2) the role of the state in governing practices is expanded so that the corresponding analysis is no longer focused only on institutions, like the hospital (Foucault, 1973) or the prison (Foucault, 1977a). The often subtle, day-to-day practices of governing and power come to the fore particularly as a result. Power, as already indicated, is understood as a relational phenomenon, conceptualized as "a mode of action that does not act directly and immediately on others. Instead, it acts upon their actions: action upon an action, on possible or actual future or present actions" (Foucault, 2000b, p. 340). The exercise of power, then, focuses "on the field of possibilities in which the behaviour of active subjects is able to inscribe itself.... [I]t is always a way of acting upon one or more acting subjects by virtue of their acting or being capable of action" (Foucault, 2000b, p. 341). Following this, the term "conduct" comes into play, precisely because of its double meaning of "leading others" as well as "behaviour," facilitating the definition of the exercising of power as "conduct of conduct" (Foucault, 2000b, p. 341; cf. Gordon, 1991, p. 2).

Closely connected to this relational understanding of power, which structures the field of possible actions of others, is the question of government. Understood in a broad fashion, and not one restricted to politics, government refers to ways in which the actions of individuals or groups are structured in different societal fields: "To govern, in this sense, is to structure the possible field of action of others" (Foucault, 2000b, p. 341). Following this understanding, governing is always political, as it entails the creation of distinction, and the structuring of possibilities of actions, crucially implying the inhibition of certain behaviours (Bröckling et al., 2011, p. 13). In this sense, governing always includes repression, albeit often subtly. Before this backdrop, Foucault's uncompleted work on "the history of governmentality" (Foucault, 2007, p. 108), and the related work of "governmentality studies" even more so, was about the analysis of (neoliberal) day-to-day governing practices in the form of indirect guidance by setting the conditions for possibilities of action, especially by focusing on the ways in which the governed could be stimulated to govern themselves (Gordon, 1991). Even far from direct and unmediated practices of coercion or compulsion, individuals and their behaviour can still be influenced, so the idea goes, by creating a framework so that the subjects govern themselves—that is, using "technologies of the self" (Foucault, 2000a, p. 403).

Due to the theoretical re-accentuation of the subjects' active role in governing practices, the perspective of governmentality, from a conceptual standpoint, provides a hinge by mediating, on the one hand, between power and subjectivity and thus enabling a dynamic linking of social demands and the individual ways of dealing with them—in the sense of a heterogeneous and lively social practice; on the other hand, the close nexus of power and knowledge is highlighted, stressing the productive role of the former, which needs to create the world to be governed so that this same world becomes manageable (Bröckling et al., 2011, p. 2). Knowledge, therefore, refers here to the ways in which the world is perceived and made intelligible. How are future-related social problems created? What (predictive) strategies are perceived as solutions to these problems? What kind of categories, on the basis of what indicators, are established? What (algorithmic) instruments are considered necessary and purposeful here? This is why the term "rationality" is so crucial in governmentality studies, referring to "the way or system of thinking about the nature of the practice of government ... capable of making some form of that activity thinkable and practicable" (Gordon, 1991, p. 3).

Following this idea of rationality, the co-productive connection of forms of knowledge and (political) modes of intervention becomes relevant (Bröckling et al., 2011, p. 11), pointing to the "regime(s) of truth" (Foucault, 1977b, p. 13) inextricably linked to power and, hence, governing practices: "There can be no possible exercise of power without a certain economy of discourses of truth which operates through and on the basis of this association" (Foucault, 1980, p. 93). And elsewhere, Foucault writes: "Truth is of the world: it is produced by virtue of multiple constraints. And it induces the regular effects of power. Each society has its regime of truth, its 'general politics' of truth" (ibid.). These regimes consist of several components, ranging from the discourses and institutions which produce them to "the techniques and procedures which are valorised for obtaining truth" (Foucault, 1980, p. 93).

The notion of regime, however, was not only coined by Foucault in reference to truth, it was also used in connection with the term "rationality." In 1978, Foucault said: "It's true that 'practices' don't exist without a certain regime of rationality," pointing to the corresponding constitution of rules, procedures, etc., which codify rationalities as well as the entities and domains of knowledge brought into the world by this means, and about which true or false propositions can be made (Foucault, 1991, p. 79). In this sense, regimes signify a more or less stable and coherent set of thoughts about and actions upon the world; they are more or less organized and, to varying degrees, institutionalized, referring to a certain degree of routinization (Dean, 1999, p. 21). Ultimately, when distinct "patterns of governing" can be observed, it makes sense to speak of regimes (Bröckling et al., 2011, p. 17). Regimes then form one of the basic units of analysis of governmentality studies, guiding analyses of the dominant ways in which people are governed and govern themselves in different societal fields, that is, in which (subtle) ways people's actions are acted upon. Thus, the particular focus of governmentality studies is on the epistemic and practical processes that make these regimes possible in the first place. Governmentality studies are, in other words, systematic studies of the art of rendering the world governable. And this is to a fundamental matter, as we will discuss in the next section, in many cases not only a political but also a profoundly technical affair.

Rendering Reality Governable: Technologies of Government

Practices of governing are inherently productive: they create the reality they are about to govern by "executing the division of the sensible ... and assigning things and people to certain positions" (Bröckling et al., 2011, p. 17f.). To exemplify this, we can take a look at the topos of risk, which, as Ewald (1991, p. 199) famously wrote, has no ontological reality: "Nothing is a risk in itself; there is no risk in reality. But on the other hand, anything can be a risk; it all depends on how one analyses the danger, considers the event." Although lacking ontological reality, risk is nevertheless one of the most prominent foundations for governing practices in modern societies. It opens up a space for intervention by ordering reality in a specific way, rendering it calculable, enabling the manageability of the inherently uncertain future, facilitating the development of societal institutions like insurance (Cevolini & Esposito, 2020, p. 2). Therefore, corresponding governing practices of risk depend on "forms of knowledge that make it thinkable,... the techniques that discover it,... and the political rationalities and programmes that deploy it" (Dean, 1998, p. 25).

Hence, practices of governing are extremely dependent on the support of generative devices, providing means to render the world intelligible. In the course of this, technologies[1] play a crucial role: "If government is to achieve ends, or seeks to realize values, it must use technical means" (Dean, 1999, p. 31; cf. Rose, 1999, p. 52). Consequently, Bröckling et al. (2011, p. 12; cf. Dean, 1999, pp. 21, 36) propose the analysis of technical artefacts and their role in governing practices as one of the five key methodological principles of governmentality studies, focusing on "the procedural devices through

---

1   Technologies, as understood here, not only refer to technological artefacts, but also involve certain procedures, processes, formulas, etc., which are utilized to achieve certain (political) goals.

which individuals and collectives shape the behaviour of each other or themselves." Technologies, in this sense, can be understood as "rendering devices," enabling governmental practices by rendering the world governable.

A widely discussed technology-centred example in governmentality studies, which promises useful insights in the context of studying algorithmic regimes, revolves around the theme of calculability. This refers to practices in which individuals are made governable by creating numbers and charts, by comparing figures and trends, making it possible to render individuals responsible for financial developments (Miller & O'Leary, 1994; Miller, 2001; Miller & Rose, 2008, pp. 66–68). With reference to the progression of sophisticated accounting techniques, Miller (1994) shows how productive calculative techniques are, in terms of creating "calculating selves," that is, in being able to make individuals responsible for the development of economic figures, with special attention to inefficiencies (for example, Miller & O'Leary, 1994). Accounting, in this sense, is about making visible the activities of individuals in relation to certain (economic) goals and norms, rendering their behaviour comparable and, hence, manageable through systematic recourse to quantification practices. Thus, calculability refers to a specific style of "governing by numbers" (Miller, 2001), which is not, however, simply a way of using numbers for documenting reality and using the figures to make the actions of others manageable. Rather, calculation implies a translation of the regime of knowledge with reference to the corresponding governing programme, as it brings along with it attributions of objectivity and neutrality, which are commonly associated with numbers (Porter, 1995). This creates new dynamics of trust, legitimation, and assertiveness (Rose, 1999, pp. 197–199; Miller, 2001, p. 382) but also responsibility for the corresponding decisions, which can then be referred to the calculative procedure (Miller & O'Leary, 1994, p. 112). That is, calculative governing can make use of the "social authority" connected to numbers, distancing itself "from the world of politics and intrigue" (Miller, 1994, p. 246)—making itself appear apolitical, although, of course, being quintessentially political. In addition, calculative governing does not process messy reality as it is; rather, it "abstracts from the quality of things" (Miller, 2014, p. 237), editing the world in a specific way in order to make it governable (Rose, 1999, p. 204). This is also why calculative technologies have a close relationship to decision-making, enabling epistemic foundations for concluding—in the double sense of making conclusions and bringing something to a close.

What is important when studying the role of technologies as knowledge devices in regimes of governing is their capacity to shed light on certain segments of reality only and, by definition, making others disappear (Dean,

1999, p. 30). By making some things thinkable and, hence, visible, regimes of governing always also create disappearances and invisibilities: every visibility regime has or produces blind spots and, in doing so, makes certain things unthinkable (Hempel et al., 2011, p. 8; Flyverbom, 2019). This again highlights the political character of regimes of governing, stressing their capacity to order the world on the basis of rationalities, and in doing so drawing distinctions between people and/or things, hence creating unequal distributions of (in)visibility.

Due to this active as well as momentous participation of technologies of government, as "rendering devices," in regimes of governing, it comes as no surprise that ideas from science and technologies studies and especially actor-network theory are referred to regularly (e.g., Dean, 1999, p. 30; Rose, 1999, p. 36; Miller & Rose, 2008, pp. 65–68). In fact, in several publications, regimes of governing are framed as "assemblages" (Miller, 1994, p. 242; Dean, 1999, p. 22; Rose, 1999, p. 52), highlighting the fact that governing technologies are, like accounting, to which Miller (2014, p. 238) refers here, "simultaneously social and technical," consisting of human and non-human entities, which form a powerful connection with substantial generative capabilities: "Information in this sense is not the outcome of a neutral recording function. It is itself a way of acting upon the real, a way of devising techniques for inscribing it in such a way as to make the domain in question susceptible to evaluation, calculation and intervention" (Miller & Rose, 2008, p. 66; cf. Rose, 1999, p. 204).

Algorithmic Governmentality: The Art of Governing in the Digital Society

As shown, governmentality studies have a clear focus on how governing regimes are inextricably linked to the capabilities of technologies for rendering the world knowable and, hence, governable. Against this backdrop, it is hardly surprising that numerous publications are already available that connect the role of algorithms in contemporary society with ideas and concepts from governmentality studies (e.g., Introna, 2016; Aradau & Blanke, 2017; Flyverbom, 2019; Krasmann, 2020; Flyverbom & Garsten, 2021; Henman, 2021; Peeters & Schuilenburg, 2021). Her analyses of "algorithmic governmentality" place Rouvroy (2011, 2013) at the forefront in this regard. Hence, in this chapter I will discuss her account, and supplement her insights with other ideas from digital governmentality as well as (critical) data/ algorithm studies, respectively.

The notion of algorithmic governmentality is used by Rouvroy and Berns (2013, p. 171) to denote "a certain type of (a)normative or (a)political rationality founded on the automated collection, aggregation and analysis of big data so as to model, anticipate and pre-emptively affect possible behaviours." Algorithmic governmentality, in this sense, consists of three stages: (1) it embraces the collection of massive amounts of data and the constitution of data warehouses; (2) it involves algorithmic data processing, which is to be understood as a process of knowledge production, focusing on machine learning techniques searching for correlations in data in order to enable the real-time production of hypotheses; (3) it includes the exploitation of the processed knowledge in order to act on individual behaviour, especially by associating it with profiles and, in doing so, anticipating it in order to pre-empt it, if necessary (Rouvroy & Berns, 2013, pp. 167–170). Algorithmic governmentality, as distinct rationality and an "unprecedented regime of power" (Rouvroy, 2013, p. 152), implies a new "regime of digital truth" (Rouvroy & Stiegler, 2016, p. 6) at its epistemic centre, pointing to a new way of knowledge production about those entities to be governed, who are made available for the conduct of conduct simply through new digital means.

Following Rouvroy (2013, p. 143), this rationality of algorithmic governmentality refers epistemically to "data behaviourism," a "new way of knowledge production about future preferences[,] attitudes, behaviours, or events without considering the subject's psychological motivations, speeches, or narratives, but rather relying on data." It is not the individuals with their diverse characteristics and structural inscriptions that are the object of knowledge in algorithmic governing techniques, but rather their digital profile. And this does not represent the individual reality with all its messiness and ambivalence, but only certain extracts from it, a "statistical 'double'" (Rouvroy & Berns, 2013, p. 166). This double, a "data derivative" in the sense of Amoore (2011), is channelled and distorted specifically, reflecting the motives and goals of the governing entities (Rouvroy, 2013, p. 144).

By following the approach of data behaviourism, in algorithmic governmentality the crucial role of statistics as a "rendering device" is revived. Yet, the statistical approach does indeed change, since the individuals sought out to be governed are targeted and processed in a new way, by distancing itself from the commensurability-driven and collective-building practices of "state statistics" known from biopolitics (Rouvroy, 2013, p. 149). In fact, the basic promise of machine learning big data analyses is to facilitate a personalized way of conducting the conduct of individuals (e.g., Mayer-Schönberger & Cukier, 2013). That is, the prevailing goal is no longer to grasp the individual as an entity from a certain representative sample, no longer relating the singular cases to a general norm, thus implying a departure from the average—which was, for a long time, one of the most central epistemic devices in statistically based practices of governing (Desrosières, 1998, pp. 67–102). Instead, machine learning algorithms are intended to search for correlations in data in order to refer these directly to the individual. These patterns are still superficial, however, proposing a generalization of individuality, personalizing not the individuals themselves but only their statistical doubles (Krasmann, 2020, p. 2101).

However, data behaviourism is not only about segmenting, simplifying, and decontextualizing individual personality and shaping it according to one's own interests and viability. It is also about seeing humans in a certain way: as behaviouristic entities. In doing so, algorithmic governmentality deploys a "logic of the surface," a mode of governing for which the only thing that counts is what can be found "on the surface of the visible behavior" (Krasmann, 2020, p. 2098). By painting "a 'superficial' picture of human behavior" (ibid.), machine learning algorithms at the same time create new possibilities of making human behaviour manageable and reduce reality to the statistically intelligible, to the world as it is traceable by and visible to algorithms (Rouvroy, 2011, p. 126; Krasmann, 2020, p. 2103). While unable to look inside us, they make use of patterns and profiles with reference to the available data, thereby "scratching the surface of our personality," without in any way understanding it (Rouvroy, 2013, p. 149f.; Krasmann, 2020, p. 2102). Before this backdrop, on an epistemological level, machine learning algorithms imply a "new perceptual regime" on the basis of "a purely statistical observation of correlations" (Rouvroy, 2011, p. 126). Pursuing an "ontology of associations" (Amoore, 2011), this marks a new era of governmental technologies based on statistics, as it does not aim at testing hypotheses and causal knowledge (Kitchin, 2014, p. 103; Aradau & Blanke, 2017, p. 379; Rouvroy, 2013, p. 149). Rather, it looks for correlations in data to find patterns inductively, which in turn can be used to reach certain (mostly business or state security-related) ends (e.g., Amoore, 2019; Krasmann, 2020, p. 2101). Borrowing a conceptual differentiation of Flyverbom (2019, p. 16) regarding transparency regimes, we have to think of machine learning algorithms in general and predictive algorithms in specific not as windows but as prisms, since they do not represent (future) reality as it is or will be, but rather "create extensive and manifold reconfigurations" in terms of the socio-technical production of a space of (in)visibilities.

What will certainly not be new to scholars from data or algorithm studies (e.g., boyd & Crawford, 2012; Kitchin, 2017) is pointed out by Rouvroy (2011, p. 128) with reference to algorithmic governmentality: corresponding processes of knowledge production, although having "an aura of 'pure' knowledge" (Rouvroy, 2013, p. 148; cf. Gillespie, 2014, p. 179f.), are by no means neutral procedures, providing governing entities with objective insights into the governed. Instead, they are interest-driven knowledge devices, targeting only fragments of reality—with the latter also represented in a specific and distorted way. In this context, Rouvroy refers to Rose (1999, p. 204) and his discussion of the role of numbers in governmental practices, stressing that the "reduction of complexity by numbers can be neither ideologically nor theoretically innocent: hence the social enters the statistical through the 'interests' of those who undertake this task." Building on this, unsupervised machine learning algorithms are also to be understood as "human–computer assemblages" (Aradau & Blanke, 2015, p. 6), that is, as contingent and dynamic networks of human and non-human entities, only able in conjunction to produce outcomes capable of governing others by acting upon their actions.

Being part of algorithmic governmentality, the information that results from this algorithmic operation is used to structure the actions of others, to determine their field of possibilities. Then, algorithmic knowledge is performative and, therefore, inventive, enabling certain practices—but also inhibiting others. In doing so, the algorithms manufacture certain assumptions about people, provoking certain decisions about them, in turn making them behave in certain ways, so fostering a style of "governing through feedback loops" (Krasmann, 2020, p. 2101). By "render[ing] everything *actual, present*" (Rouvroy, 2013, p. 129), algorithmically generated profiles provide classifications according to which individuals are acted upon. As a result, the profiles or (risk) categories become real, although virtual. The governed individuals adapt their behaviour due to the classifications and decisions they are confronted with, actualizing the algorithmic outcome, making it real in a performative sense (Flyverbom & Garsten, 2021, p. 5). However, they also adapt their thinking about themselves and the world, precisely in the sense of Foucauldian technologies of the self, by incorporating the technically inscribed norms and values—as far as known—into their own reasoning or by changing their behaviour in a way they believe the algorithms would approve of, in order to get better algorithmic decisions, profiles, scores, etc.—"backwards performativity," according to Rouvroy (2013, p. 153).

To sum up, the socio-technical processes of algorithmic knowledge production and its application, as embedded in algorithmic governmentality, imply questions of power. This is not only because digital truth regimes include tangible consequences for the individuals governed. Rather, at the same time as being subject to algorithmic decision-making and profiling, in most cases individuals are not able to reconstruct the processes behind the results, let alone to contest them (Rouvroy, 2011, p. 121). This is not only due to the reluctance of many vendors and/or operators of profiling algorithms, for example, to make the decisions behind the algorithms transparent (Zarsky, 2013), but also due to the fact that in many cases, the persons concerned do not even know that they are the subject of algorithmic processing. This is why Rona-Tas (2020, p. 901) qualifies (predictive) algorithms as "instruments of power."

Prediction Regimes

After describing what algorithmic governmentality involves in general, we will now turn to a special, yet important element of it: prediction regimes. Referring to what has been written above, I use prediction regimes to denote more or less stable algorithmically mediated patterns of thinking and acting on the world, which revolve around the production and implementation of *explicitly* future-related knowledge devices: predictions. In this sense, prediction regimes systematically and intentionally strive to render the future accessible in order to make it governable in the present. In doing so, they interfere with the lives of the governed, for example, by providing risk scores and future-related profiles of manifold kinds, which are utilized to decide what can (not) be offered to the people concerned. Therefore, predictive knowledge, as the epistemic core of prediction regimes, as well as predictive analytics, as the technological core of prediction regimes, help to structure the field of people's future-related possibilities, making certain behaviours more probable than others. Although governing practices in (nearly) all cases are oriented towards the future in the way that they aim to shape the peoples future behaviour, I argue that it is necessary for analytical purpose to grasp prediction regimes as subgroup of algorithmic regimes, to focus on the technological role in the process of future-related knowledge production on the one hand and on the contexts in which predictions are generated and utilized for decision-making in a systematic and intentional manner. Shedding light on the utilization of predictive analytics for governing practices, I argue, enables us to study closely the inherently political character of the algorithmic society (Peeters & Schuilenburg, 2021), including the close nexus of knowledge and power, as well as the important role of (algorithmic) technologies in these politics. Hence, such a conceptual background provides us with an analytical lens for focusing on the performative as well as socio-technical nature of algorithmically mediated prediction practices and their consequences.

Although the future has always been an important reference for mankind, be it as a predetermined future in the hands of God or as a shapable future open to people's actions and decisions in the present (Adam & Groves, 2007; Koselleck, 2004), with the advent of predictive analytics, the role of the future is once again becoming more dominant (e.g., Siegel, 2016; Agrawal et al., 2018). Predictive analytics promise considerable usefulness for governing practices, as predictive algorithms can exponentiate the capabilities of those in power to conduct the conduct of others (Flyverbom & Garsten, 2021; Peeters & Schuilenburg, 2021). Therefore, it seems necessary to focus more explicitly on the predictive component of algorithmic governmentality, as integrating the realm of the future systematically into practices of governing has crucial implications for the forms and effects of the corresponding politics.

Moving from algorithmic governmentality in general to a focused analysis on prediction regimes is also indicated on a conceptual dimension, as predictive analytics is more or less explicitly the algorithmic reference of Rouvroy's elaboration of algorithmic governmentality. As indicated above, one of the three stages of algorithmic governmentality includes the exploitation of algorithmic knowledge to act on individual behaviour, by making it intelligible through profiles, and, in doing so, anticipating it in order to pre-empt it, if necessary (Rouvroy & Berns, 2013, p. 171). Elsewhere, Rouvroy (2011, p. 121) writes, referring to algorithmic governmentality and automatic computing, that she is focusing on "the 'regimes of truth,' ... the categorization and (sometimes performative) predictions these systems are capable to establish, maintain and propagate" (cf. Rouvroy, 2013, p. 146f.). I will now take up the relevant ideas about predictive analytics written in the context of algorithmic governmentality, combining them with further assumptions on the peculiarities of predictive algorithms, highlighting the analytical productivity of thinking future-generating algorithmic governing assemblages in terms of prediction regimes.

As outlined above, Rouvroy (2011, 2013) analyses algorithmic governmentality with special recourse to the pre-emptive effects of (predictive) algorithms. By using the term "pre-emption," she highlights the capability of algorithmic profiling to close certain futures—in the sense of erasing alternative ways of acting in the future—in the present. In doing so, she refers implicitly to the double meaning of pre-emption as anticipating future states of being as well as preventing future events from happening. In line with this, Rouvroy (2013, p. 156f.) argues that pre-emptive algorithmic governmentality "spares the burden of making persons appear as agents, leave[ing] no occasion for persons to become 'subjects.'"

The pre-emptive effect of predictive algorithms is closely linked to the performative potential of algorithms in general, which is substantially enhanced, however, when thinking about predictive algorithms and the circularity they generate by informing decisions in the present, which in turn have an effect on the future—by changing it. By providing knowledge for certain decisions and actions in the present, the number of "future possibilities for all involved actors" is reduced (Esposito, 2021, p. 536), making certain future events more probable than others or simply making certain future states of being impossible (Henman, 2021, p. 23). In this sense, "algorithmic predictions are instruments of actions" because "the very reason for making predictions is to intervene and change the future" (Rona-Tas, 2020, p. 904; see also Flyverbom & Garsten, 2021). What is important to stress here is that this pre-emptive effect not only holds true for the people who are governed, but also for those governing. For example, when police use crime prediction software, indicating those areas where crime is mostly likely to happen in the near future, the patrol forces sent there to deter soon-to-be criminals from offending not only limit the future possibilities of those offenders. They also reduce their own options, as they can only be in one place at a time: "If the crimes end up happening somewhere else, one will be watching the wrong people" (Esposito, 2021, p. 536).

These performative or "looping effects" (Flyverbom & Garsten, 2021, p. 5) of predictions are, however, not only repressive in the sense that they suppress future-related alternatives and possibilities of acting and thinking. They can have also productive effects in the sense that they create opportunities, for the governed individuals as well. With reference to the development of insurance, Ewald (1991, p. 208) points to its historical role as a "liberator of action." By creating a sense of (social) security, insurance emancipated individuals from paralyzing fear, empowering them to be enterprising although the results of their actions and plans were uncertain and, at times, even risky. When there is an approach of more or less true solidarity to insurance, where all members of a certain group—for example, industry workers—share the risk of future damage together by all paying the same (small) amount in order to be able to compensate those who will actually suffer accidents, this enabling force may indeed be dominant. However, in contemporary times, insurance companies *do* differentiate the risk of insurance holders according to the probability of them having accidents and/or filing claims in the future. This in turn means that the insurance premiums differ among insurance holders, depending on their calculated risk. Due to this, ultimately insurance premiums can be so high for certain individuals that they are not able to afford them, thus being left out of the liberating character of insurance. And since this risk mode is far more dominant in contemporary society, not only in the insurance business, in many cases algorithmic profiling is indeed an "inhibitor of action," discouraging people from doing things because it would be too risky (Cevolini & Esposito, 2020, p. 7).

Besides their performative character, which has a repressive connotation in many cases, predictive regimes are also fundamentally characterized by their socio-technical nature. Firstly, this is due to the need to draw on technical instruments when producing predictive knowledge, in order to be credible. Without technical underpinning, it becomes rather difficult to convince a sufficiently large number of people of a prediction (Beckert, 2013, p. 242). Secondly, the socio-technical peculiarity of prediction regimes originates from the fact that algorithmic predictions alone do not have any effect. They have an effect only when they inform the decision-making practices of their operators (Peeters & Schuilenburg, 2021, p. 4). Thirdly, the idea of prediction in itself is never purely technical, but always dependent on a societal context, which infuses into it a temporal orientation towards the future. Lopez and Eyert (2021; see also Eyert & Lopez, 2023) argue with reference to the technical and mathematical substance of predictive algorithms that time as a parameter is in fact non-existent in this kind of setting and that the "pre" in prediction is a socially stabilized definition, which points to the filling of data gaps with reference to the corresponding function. They conclude that a prediction only emerges "when the purely mathematical-technical system converges to a socio-technical system in which the foresight is believed to be epistemically robust and legitimate." Hence, they highlight the fact that predictions, in many if not all cases, would be better termed "postdictions," as they simply use data from the past for their statistical analysis. A similar argument is made by Rona-Tas (2020, p. 896), who states that "'prediction' ... is a misleading metaphor," as corresponding processes "are not forecasting something yet to happen." Rather, they

> are looking for patterns in the (near) past. The test set is not in the future. It is in the same time block as the training set. We are not predicting change, we are predicting patterns of variation.... The real prediction is not in the algorithmic calculation. It is in the unspoken assumption that the variation will remain the same.

Additionally to this, Mühlhoff highlights another translation step in the doing of predictions, namely the decision to select one alternative from the range of different options suggested by the algorithmic system, which often differ only marginally in their probability (Mühlhoff, 2021, p. 677).

This socio-technical character of algorithmic predictions points to the importance of the users and their goals, and to the power they have to enforce their interests, as well as their definition of a certain algorithm as predictive and their assumptions about its effectiveness, and, if relevant, its fairness. As Kiviat (2019, p. 1151) writes consistently in reference to credit scoring: "Algorithmic prediction is imbued with normative viewpoints—they are viewpoints that suit the goals of corporations"—and the goals of security agencies, one might add.

Before this backdrop, the study of prediction regimes refers directly to the underlying goals, values, and motives of the developers and proponents of the predictive algorithms, and to the (political) circumstances from which they originate. Nevertheless, the role of the utilized algorithmic "rendering devices," as the other relevant part of the socio-technical assemblages of prediction regimes, should also undoubtedly be of key interest. They are the ones that make the future actionable in the first place; and they do so in a specific way—by creating (in)visibility, knowability, and, ultimately, governability (Flyverbom, 2019, p. 43). In a third step, an analysis of prediction regimes, understood as socio-technical assemblages, also needs to systematically address the interaction of humans and algorithms, pointing out the ways in which the predictive algorithms are developed and how their scores and profiles are applied. In particular, this involves the importance of analysing the mutual adaption of predictive technology and governmental practices, which is a fundamental political question per definition, as it entails the selective production of knowledge or visibilities, as well as ignorance or invisibilities, plus the corresponding evaluation, classification, and hierarchization of people, then associated with the enabling or withholding of (future-related) opportunities.

Conclusion

Predictive analytics are becoming increasingly common in contemporary society—a society composed of algorithmic regimes in general and prediction regimes in particular. Before this backdrop, in this chapter I proposed to adopt the Foucauldian approach of governmentality and the subsequent literature from governmentality studies in order to analyse systematically the role of predictive knowledge produced by machine learning algorithms. It has been shown that the art of governing relies considerably on knowledge, which has had a strong relation to scientific and technological instruments from the very beginning. In this sense, governing is crucially about rendering the world governable in the first place. With reference to Rouvroy's analysis of algorithmic governmentality, it has been further presented that such governing practices in the algorithmic age imply certain epistemic features, which refer, for example, to the inherent flat world view of such processes, culminating in a governing approach acting only on the surface. Hence, I suggest an understanding of predictive algorithms as "rendering devices," enabling the occurrence of manifold governing practices that make systematic and intentional use of the future by algorithmic means—and so manufacture the future in a certain, inevitably selective way. As a special type of algorithmic regime, finally I have proposed an understanding of prediction regimes as relatively stable, algorithmically mediated patterns of thinking and acting upon others, which function by making use of the future and interfering with the lives of the governed, ultimately shedding light on the political dimension of the algorithmic society.

Funding

This project has received funding from the European Research Council (ERC) under the European Union's Horizon 2020 research and innovation programme (grant agreement no. 833749).

References

Adam, B., & Groves, C. (2007). *Future matters: Action, knowledge, ethics*. Brill.

Agrawal, A., Gans, J., & Goldfarb, A. (2018). *Prediction machines: The simple economics of artificial intelligence*. Harvard Business Review Press.

Amoore, L. (2011). Data derivatives: On the emergence of a security risk calculus for our times. *Theory, Culture & Society, 28*(6), 24–43. https://doi.org/10.1177/0263276411417430

Amoore, L. (2019). Introduction: Thinking with algorithms: Cognition and computation in the work of N. Katherine Hayles. *Theory, Culture & Society, 36*(2), 3–16. https://doi.org/10.1177/0263276418818884

Aradau, C., & Blanke, T. (2015). The (big) data-security assemblage: Knowledge and critique. *Big Data & Society, 2*(2), 1–12. https://doi.org/10.1177/2053951715609066

Aradau, C., & Blanke, T. (2017). Politics of prediction: Security and the time/space of governmentality in the age of big data. *European Journal of Social Theory, 20*(3), 373–391. https://doi.org/10.1177/1368431016667623

Beckert, J. (2013). *Imagined futures: Fictional expectations and capitalist dynamics.* Harvard University Press.

boyd, d., & Crawford, K. (2012). Critical questions for big data: Provocations for a cultural, technological, and scholarly phenomenon. *Information, Communication & Society, 15*(5), 662–669. https://doi.org/10.1080/1369118X.2012.678878

Bröckling, U., Krasmann, S., & Lemke, T. (2011). From Foucault's lectures at the Collège de France to studies of governmentality. In U. Bröckling, S. Krasmann, & T. Lemke (Eds.), *Governmentality: Current issues and future challenges* (pp. 1–33). Routledge.

Cevolini, A., & Esposito, E. (2020). From pool to profile: Social consequences of algorithmic prediction in insurance. *Big Data & Society, 7*(2), 1–11. https://doi.org/10.1177/2053951720939228

Davenport, T. H. (2016). Foreword. In E. Siegel, *Predictive analytics: The power to predict who will click, buy, lie, or die* (pp. xvii–xix). Wiley.

Dean, M. (1998). Risk, calculable and incalculable. *Soziale Welt, 49*(1), 25–42.

Dean, M. (1999). *Governmentality: Power and rule in modern society.* Sage.

Desrosières, A. (1998). *The politics of large numbers: A history of statistical reasoning.* Harvard University Press.

Esposito, E. (2021). Unpredictability. In N. B. Thylstrup, D. Agostinho, A. Ring, C. D'Ignazio, & K. Veel (Eds.), *Uncertain archives: Critical keywords for big data* (pp. 533–539). MIT Press.

Ewald, F. (1991). Insurance and risk. In G. Burchell, C. Gordon, & P. Miller (Eds.), *The Foucault effect: Studies in governmentality* (pp. 197–210). University of Chicago Press.

Eyert, F., & Lopez, P. (2023). Rethinking transparency as a communicative constellation. In *FAccT '23: Proceedings of the 2023 ACM Conference on Fairness, Accountability, and Transparency* (pp. 444–454). https://doi.org/10.1145/3593013.3594010

Flyverbom, M. (2019). *The digital prism. Transparency and managed visibilities in a datafied world.* Cambridge University Press.

Flyverbom, M., & Garsten, C. (2021). Anticipation and organization: Seeing, knowing and governing futures. *Organization Theory, 2*(3), 1–25. https://doi.org/10.1177/26317877211020325

Foucault, M. (1973). *The birth of the clinic: An archaeology of medical perception.* Pantheon Books.

Foucault, M. (1976). *The history of sexuality, vol. 1: An introduction.* Pantheon Books.

Foucault, M. (1977a). *Discipline and punish: The birth of the prison.* Random House.

Foucault, M. (1977b). The political function of the intellectual. *Radical Philosophy, 17*(13), 12–14.

Foucault, M. (1980). Two Lectures. In M. Foucault, *Power/knowledge: Selected interviews and other writings 1972–1977* (pp. 78–108). Pantheon.

Foucault, M. (1991). Questions of method. In G. Burchell, C. Gordon, & P. Miller (Eds.), *The Foucault effect: Studies in governmentality* (pp. 73–86). University of Chicago Press.

Foucault, M. (2000a). The political technology of individuals. In M. Foucault, *The essential works of Michel Foucault, 1954–1984, vol. 3: Power* (J. D. Faubion, Ed.; R. Hurley et al., Trans.; pp. 403–417). New Press.

Foucault, M. (2000b). The subject and power. In M. Foucault, *The essential works of Michel Foucault, 1954–1984, vol. 3: Power* (J. D. Faubion, Ed.; R. Hurley et al., Trans.; pp. 326–348). New Press.

Foucault, M. (2007). [Lecture] 4. 1 February 1978. In M. Foucault, *Security, territory and population: Lectures at the Collège de France 1977–1978* (pp. 87–114). Palgrave Macmillan.

Gillespie, T. (2014). The relevance of algorithms. In T. Gillespie, P. J. Boczkowski, & K. A. Foot (Eds.), *Media technologies: Essays on communication, materiality, and society* (pp. 167–193). MIT Press.

Gordon, C. (1991). Governmental rationality: An introduction. In G. Burchell, C. Gordon, & P. Miller (Eds.), *The Foucault effect: Studies in governmentality* (pp. 1–51). University of Chicago Press.

Hempel, L., Krasmann, S., & Bröckling, U. (2011). Sichtbarkeitsregime. Eine Einleitung. In L. Hempel, S. Krasmann, & U. Bröckling (Eds.), *Sichtbarkeitsregime. Überwachung, Sicherheit und Privatheit im 21. Jahrhundert* (pp. 7–24). VS Verlag.

Henman, P. (2021). Governing by algorithms and algorithmic governmentality. In M. Schuilenburg, & R. Peeters (Eds.), *Algorithmic society: Technology, power, and knowledge* (pp. 19–34). Routledge.

Hurley, M., & Adebayo, J. (2016). Credit scoring in the era of big data. *Yale Journal of Law and Technology, 18*(1), article 5.

Introna, L. (2016). Algorithms, governance, and governmentality: On governing academic writing. *Science, Technology, & Human Values, 41*(1), 17–41. https://doi.org/10.1177/0162243915587360

Jannach, D., Zanker, M., Felfernig, A., & Friedrich, G. (2010). *Recommender systems: An introduction.* Cambridge University Press.

Jarke, J., & Macgilchrist, F. (2021). Dashboard stories: How narratives told by predictive analytics reconfigure roles, risk and sociality in education. *Big Data & Society, 8*(1). https://doi.org/10.1177/20539517211025561

Kaufmann, M., Egbert, S., & Leese, M. (2019). Predictive policing and the politics of patterns. *British Journal of Criminology, 59*(3), 674–692. https://doi.org/10.1093/bjc/azy060

Kitchin, R. (2014). *The data revolution: Big data, open data, data infrastructures & their consequences*. Sage.

Kitchin, R. (2017). Thinking critically about and researching algorithms. *Information, Communication & Society, 20*(1), 14–29. https://doi.org/10.1080/136911 8X.2016.1154087

Kiviat, B. (2019). The moral limits of predictive practices: The case of credit-based insurance scores. *American Sociological Review, 84*(6), 1134–1158.

Koselleck, R. (2004). *Futures past: On the semantics of historical time*. Columbia University Press.

Krasmann, S. (2020). The logic of the surface: On the epistemology of algorithms in times of big data. *Information, Communication & Society, 23*(14), 2096–2109. https://doi.org/10.1080/1369118X.2020.1726986

Larose, D. T., Larose, C. T. (2015). *Data mining and predictive analytics* (2nd ed.). Wiley.

Lopez, P. (2019). Reinforcing Intersectional Inequality via the AMS Algorithm in Austria. In G. Getzinger & M. Jahrbacher (Eds.), *Critical issues in science, technology and society studies: Conference proceedings of the STS conference Graz 2019, May 6th–7th* (pp. 289–309). https://doi.org/10.3217/978-3-85125-668-0-16

Lopez, P., & Eyert, F. (2021). The logic of post-diction and the predictive paradigm of machine learning [Conference presentation]. 4S 2021, Toronto, ON, Canada.

Mayer-Schönberger, V., & Cukier, K. (2013). *Big data: A revolution that will transform how we live, work and think*. John Murray.

Miller, P. (1994). Accounting and objectivity: The invention of calculating selves and calculable spaces. In A. Megill (Ed.), *Rethinking objectivity* (pp. 239–264). Duke University Press.

Miller, P. (2001). Governing by numbers: Why calculative practices matter. *Social Research, 68*(2), 379–396.

Miller, P. (2014). Accounting for the calculating self. In N. Thrift, A. Tickell, S. Woolgar, & W. H. Rupp (Eds.), *Globalisation in practice* (pp. 236–241). Oxford University Press.

Miller, P., & O'Leary, T. (1994). Governing the calculable person. In A. G. Hopwood, & P. Miller (Eds.), *Accounting as social and institutional practice* (pp. 98–115). Cambridge University Press.

Miller, P., & Rose, N. (2008). *Governing the present: Administering economic, social and personal life*. Polity Press.

Mühlhoff, R. (2021). Predictive privacy: Towards an applied ethics of data analytics. *Ethics and Information Technology, 23*(4), 675–690. https://doi.org/10.1007/s10676-021-09606-x

Peeters, R., & Schuilenburg, M. (2021). The algorithmic society. An introduction. In M. Schuilenburg, & R. Peeters (Eds.), *The algorithmic society: Technology, power, and knowledge* (pp. 1–15). Routledge.

Porter, T. M. (1995). *Trust in numbers: The pursuit of objectivity in science and public life*. Princeton University Press.

Rona-Tas, A. (2020). Predicting the future: Art and algorithms. *Socio-Economic Review, 18*(3), 893–911. https://doi.org/10.1093/ser/mwaa040

Rose, N. (1999). *Powers of freedom: Reframing political thought*. Cambridge University Press.

Rouvroy, A. (2011). Technology, virtuality and utopia: Governmentality in an age of autonomic computing. In M. Hildebrandt & A. Rouvroy (Eds.), *Law, human agency and autonomic computing* (pp. 119–140). Routledge.

Rouvroy, A. (2013). The end(s) of critique: Data behaviourism versus due process. In M. Hildebrandt, K. de Vries (Eds.), *Privacy, due process and the computational turn: The philosophy of law meets the philosophy of technology* (pp. 143–167). Routledge.

Rouvroy, A., & Berns, T. (2013). Algorithmic governmentality and prospects of emancipation: Disparateness as a precondition for individuation through relationships? *Réseaux, 177*, 163–196.

Rouvroy, A., & Stiegler, B. (2016). The digital regime of truth: From the algorithmic governmentality to a new rule of law. *Le Deleuziana, 3*, 6–27.

Siegel, E. (2016). *Predictive analytics: The power to predict who will click, buy, lie or die* (rev. and updated ed.). Wiley.

Zarsky, T. Z. (2013). Transparent predictions. *University of Illinois Law Review, 2013*(4), 1503–1570.

About the Author

Simon Egbert, PhD, is a postdoctoral researcher in the Faculty of Sociology of Bielefeld University, in Germany, working in the research project "The Social Consequences of Algorithmic Forecast in Insurance, Medicine and Policing" (ERC grant agreement no. 833749). His research interests are science and technology studies (STS), algorithm studies, sociology of testing, and the sociology of the future.

14. Power and Resistance in the Twitter Bias Discourse[1]

Paola Lopez

Abstract

In 2020, the machine learning algorithm deployed by Twitter to generate cropped image previews was accused of carrying a racial bias: users complained that Black people were systematically cropped out and, thus, made invisible by the cropping tool. Subsequently, Twitter conducted bias analyses and removed the cropping tool. Soon after, the company hosted an "algorithmic bias bounty challenge" inviting the general public to detect algorithmic harm. This chapter examines in Foucauldian terms the push-and-pull dynamics of the power relations play: Firstly, it studies the algorithmic knowledge production around the cropping tool; secondly, the bias discourse as a vehicle for resistance, and, thirdly, how Twitter as a company effectively stabilized its position—rendering the bias discourse a vehicle for counter-resistance, too.

Keywords: machine learning; saliency-based image cropping; Foucault; bias bounty; computer vision; fairness

Introduction

When a Twitter user includes one or more images in a post, the platform crops the images in order to create a preview in the timeline. In doing that, the built-in algorithmic systems determine what is to be seen in the preview, and what is not. In September 2020, several Twitter users raised accusations of racial bias, claiming that Black persons were being systematically erased.

---

[1]   This paper was accepted at the 2023 ACM Conference on Fairness, Accountability and Transparency.

Jarke, J., B. Prietl, S. Egbert, Y. Boeva, H. Heuer, and M. Arnold (eds.), *Algorithmic Regimes: Methods, Interactions, and Politics*. Amsterdam: Amsterdam University Press, 2024
DOI 10.5117/9789463728485_CH14

Twitter users uploaded images containing faces of White and of Black persons to show that the cropping algorithm centred the preview on the White person and cropped out the Black person (Hern, 2020). One example that got a lot of attention was a vertical picture strip of one photo of Barack Obama and one of Mitch McConnell showing that the Twitter preview always focused on McConnell while cropping out Obama, regardless of how the images were positioned. As a response to the accusations, then-Twitter researchers published an in-depth bias analysis. The bias-prone cropping tool was removed from the platform. Furthermore, Twitter "tr[ied] something radical by introducing the industry's first algorithmic bias bounty competition" (Chowdhury & Williams, 2021). Within this competition, the general public was invited to detect potential harm caused by the cropping tool.

Twitter's image-cropping algorithm is a fascinating case study for exploring the push-and-pull dynamics of power relations between, firstly, algorithmic knowledge production inherent in machine learning systems, secondly, the bias discourse as resistance, and, thirdly, ensuing corporate responses as stabilization measures towards the resistance. In order to account for this three-part narrative of the case study, this chapter is structured along the examination of the following three questions:

1. How is the algorithmic and, especially, data-based knowledge production around the image-cropping tool entrenched in power relations?
2. In what way does the discourse around bias serve as a vehicle for resistance against said power? Why and in what way is it effective?
3. How and to what extent did Twitter as a company stabilize its position within and in relation to the bias discourse?

This chapter explores these questions along the following sections: "Theoretical Perspective" lays out the interdisciplinary theoretical perspective of the analysis, combining, firstly, a mathematical-epistemic perspective that examines the mathematics underlying both machine learning systems and bias analyses with, secondly, Foucauldian concepts that make it possible to view mathematical tools as articulations of societal power relations. The subsequent three sections engage with the three questions posed above: "Power" is concerned with the first question, and it focuses on the algorithmic knowledge production in relation to Twitter's cropping tool and its mathematical-epistemic foundations. "Resistance" addresses the second question, and it examines three bias analyses of the cropping tool, as well as their epistemic limitations, and it continues by conceptualizing the bias discourse in recent academic scholarship and activism as resistance to power. "Stabilization" engages with the third question discussing Twitter's response to the bias accusations, and it explores the bias discourse and its effectiveness as a vehicle for both resistance and counter-resistance. "Discussion" concludes the paper and reflects on limitations of this case study, and on the contribution this chapter makes to studying the politics of algorithmic knowledge production.

The case of Twitter's cropping algorithm reveals the complexity and elucidates crucial aspects of the push-and-pull dynamics of power and resistance that pervade, firstly, algorithmic regimes themselves, and secondly, on a meta level, the study of algorithmic regimes which is, too, a site of knowledge production and, thus, of power.

Theoretical Perspective

This chapter employs a twofold interdisciplinary theoretical perspective: A mathematical-epistemic perspective examines the mathematics underlying quantitative methods, focusing, firstly, on what kind of knowledge is produced, and secondly, on the epistemic limitations of the produced knowledge. By epistemic limitations, I denote limitations to what can be known through a specific quantitative method. This perspective is applied to examine published papers about the saliency-based image-cropping tool itself (Theis et al., 2018; Theis & Wang, 2018), focusing on the underlying training data (Borji & Itti, 2015; Jiang et al., 2015; Judd et al., 2009), as well as papers on three bias analyses of the cropping tool that were conducted (Birhane et al., 2022; Kulynych, 2021; Yee et al., 2021), especially on the concept of bias and its quantification. The focus lies on the question of what can and what cannot be found within the mathematics of a quantitative method. This perspective, thus, can point to intra-mathematical limitations.

As mentioned above, this chapter is interested in the interplay between mathematical tools and their embedding in a specific context. An intra-mathematical perspective alone cannot account for the ways in which the knowledge produced through both the machine learning system and the bias analyses is stabilized and made effective in a social constellation. In order to examine the heterogeneous power relations that are at play and that cannot be grasped by only looking at the mathematics, this chapter employs Michel Foucault's concepts of power, power/knowledge, and discourse. This approach reveals power relations that are in place in the production of knowledge by quantitative methods: Foucault's concept of *power* has many facets, and in the following, I will focus on power as "the multiplicity of force relations immanent in the sphere in which they operate" (Foucault, 1978, p. 92). Power relations make us do things—as such, power "produces reality" (Foucault, 1995, p. 194). Foucault's understanding of power is not one of singular acts of coercion exercised by certain powerful actors. Power is not something to be *had*—it is dispersed, always being negotiated, always being reconfigured.

Power is intrinsically connected to *knowledge*, as "there is no power relation without the correlative constitution of a field of knowledge, nor any knowledge that does not presuppose and constitute at the same time power relations" (Foucault, 1995, p. 27). In the context of this chapter, knowledge includes, e.g., every output of a quantitative method: specific image crops as well as the results of bias analyses. Knowledge, however, does not stand for itself. *Discourses* are ways in which meaningful knowledge and, thus, reality, is created: According to Foucault, power relations are "indissociable from a discourse of truth, and they can neither be established nor function unless a true discourse is produced, accumulated, put into circulation, and set to work" (Foucault, 2003, p. 24). Specifically, by *bias discourse*, I denote the ways in which knowledge about bias in data-based algorithmic systems is produced, the social constellations in which it functions, its (implicit or explicitly stated) definitions, its underlying epistemic and methodical testing assumptions, the claims that can be made on its basis as well as the meaning these claims are endowed with, and the responses that are enabled by it.

Following Foucault's notion of a "regime of truth" (Foucault, 1977, p. 13), I call the ways in which knowledge production via algorithmic machine learning methods infuses, influences, and determines a myriad of aspects of human life (e.g., the image previews on screens of millions of Twitter users)—and the extent to which we allow and invite algorithmic systems to shape crucial aspects of our lives—an *algorithmic regime* of knowledge production.

The combined interdisciplinary perspective aims to address intra-mathematical specificities and limitations, as well as the ways in which specificities are produced and limitations are stabilized through power.

Power

Twitter's Saliency-Based Cropping Algorithm

Twitter has not always used the widely criticized tool for image cropping. Before 2018, the images were cropped using a face detection system that produced a crop around the "most prominent face" (Theis & Wang, 2018). When the face detection system was not able to identify a face in the image, the crop would be focused on its centre. This approach, according to Twitter, often created "awkwardly cropped preview images" (Theis & Wang, 2018) due to technical limitations of face detection and the wide variety of images that were uploaded. In 2018, Twitter introduced a new system that centred a crop on the most "salient" area of an uploaded image: "A region having high saliency means that a person is likely to look at it when freely viewing the image" (Theis & Wang, 2018). Saliency was assumed to be a good indicator for the most interesting and, thus, most important regions of an image (Yee et al., 2021, p. 6). The saliency-based algorithm crops an image in two steps: first, the image is divided into a grid of points, and for each point, a prediction is made about its "saliency score"; then, the image is cropped around the point with the highest predicted saliency, the "focal point" (Yee et al., 2021, p. 7), adhering to a given ratio between height and width.

A supervised machine learning model predicts the most salient areas of an image (Theis et al., 2018). In supervised machine learning, previously labelled data is used during the training phase to find patterns. These patterns are generalized to rules in the form of a mathematical model that can be applied to predict the labels of new, unlabelled input data (see, e.g., Bishop, 2006). In the case of saliency-based image cropping, the training data consists of images and the labels are corresponding saliency maps that are obtained by measuring eye movements of observers who look at the images: The data that was used to train the model is publicly[2] available. Yee et al. (2021) mention three databases of images with corresponding saliency maps: the CAT2000 dataset by Borji and Itti (2015), the MIT300 dataset by Judd et al. (2009), and the SALICON dataset by Jiang et al. (2015). The CAT2000 dataset, for example, contains 20 categories of images, including "Art," "Cartoon," "Indoor," "Line Drawings," "Outdoor Natural," and others (Borji & Itti, 2015, p. 1). This dataset, as well as the MIT300 dataset, were produced in standardized settings in which individuals looked at the images, while their eye movements were tracked and recorded. The CAT2000 dataset collected eye-tracking data from 120 observers in total (and 24 viewers per image), and 4,000 images in total (Borji & Itti, 2015, p. 3), the MIT300 dataset was

2   Birhane et al. pointed out, however, that not all training data is publicly available (2022, p. 4052). In the original blog post by Twitter that announced the new saliency-based approach to image cropping, it says: "These predictions, together with some third-party saliency data, are then used to train a smaller, faster network" (Theis & Wang, 2018). It is not clear whether the "third-party saliency data" mentioned refers to the three publicly available datasets or not.

built using 15 viewers of 1,003 images (Judd et al., 2009, p. 1). The SALICON dataset by Jiang et al. (2015), in contrast, used "a general-purpose mouse instead of an expensive eye tracker to record viewing behaviors" (Jiang et al., 2015, p. 1079). The observers were mostly young and often undergraduate students (see, e.g., Borji & Itti, 2015, p. 3). The datasets were produced to be "use[d] as ground truth data to train a model of saliency using machine learning" (Judd et al., 2009, p. 1).

Regarding the model architecture, Twitter's cropping algorithm is based on the existing model, DeepGaze II, which, in turn, is based on VGG-19, a model that is pre-trained for object recognition (Theis et al., 2018, p. 2). As DeepGaze II is too computationally costly to be used in the context of real-time image uploading, Theis et al. used different techniques to make the model more efficient while not losing too much information (2018, p. 12). According to Twitter, "people tend to pay more attention to faces, text, animals, but also other objects and regions of high contrast" (Theis & Wang, 2018). This, however, is a heuristic *ex-post* observation—the saliency prediction model does not recognize objects or faces but is trained to imitate viewing patterns of the human observers whose eye movements were tracked to produce the training datasets.

Power Becomes Knowledge Becomes Power

From a mathematical-epistemic perspective, supervised machine learning methods are data-based modes of knowledge production. The training data is the epistemic fabric of machine learning models, in that these models can only predict and, thus, provide as output, what they have found as patterns in the training data, in this case: the saliency maps distilled from eye-tracking data of the observers. In Foucauldian terms, quite literally, the observer "and the knowledge that may be gained of him belong to [the] production [of reality]" (Foucault, 1995, p. 194). The observers are themselves "not free in relation to the power system" (Foucault, 1995, p. 27) that shapes the way in which they look at a picture: Looking at an image is a "capillary" (Foucault, 1978, p. 84) bodily act entrenched in societal viewing patterns that, in turn, are infused by the power relations that prevail in society. Applying this machine learning technique to Twitter's image cropping, then, is a way in which the individual bodily acts of shortly looking at a picture are aggregated (via the saliency maps), translated to data-based knowledge, transferred, and multiplied to millions of screens of Twitter users in the form of the produced image previews. In that sense, power becomes knowledge: the power relations that inform the viewing habits of the observers become eye-tracking data. And machine learning-generated knowledge becomes power: the cropping tool determines what millions of people will and will not see on their screens.

A vehicle for this amplification can be found in the very architecture of machine learning systems. One issue raised by Yee et al. (2021)—who, at the time, were researchers at Twitter—in their bias analysis of the cropping tool (see below) is what they termed the "argmax bias." "Argmax" is short for *argumentum maximi*, the mathematical operator defined as the position at which a mathematical function—in this case, the saliency score—reaches its maximal value. Yee et al. (2021) argue that, since Twitter's image-cropping algorithm centres its crop on the one maximum saliency point (i.e., the argmax of the saliency score function), this will amplify issues of erasure: An image might contain several regions with high saliency, e.g., several similarly salient faces, and the very built-in cropping mechanism of choosing the one focal point crops out other faces that might differ only slightly in saliency (Yee et al., 2021, p. 11). This, as Yee et al. (2021) argue, is a general issue with the application of machine learning methods, as the mathematics behind these methods is always probabilistic in nature. Determinate decisions are made afterwards. The mathematics of machine learning methods does know grey areas and nuances—a certain, albeit limited, degree of nuance is built into their very mathematical functionality. It is researchers and practitioners, "subject[s] of knowledge" (Foucault, 1995, p. 27), who place these methods in contexts in which an unambiguous output is being produced.

Resistance

Bias Analyses of Twitter's Cropping Tool

There is potential for harm when the eye-tracking data of few and specific people determine what is to be seen and what remains invisible: The saliency-based cropping tool algorithmically augments the gaze of these few observers to the entire community of millions of Twitter users. In a blog post put up in October 2020, reacting to numerous accusations of bias, Twitter stated that although the cropping system had been tested for bias before its deployment, there was need for more testing, as well as for a change of the technology behind the cropping tool: "We are currently conducting additional analysis to add further rigor to our testing, are committed to sharing our findings, and are exploring ways to open-source our analysis so that others can help keep us accountable" (Agrawal & Davis, 2020).

In the following, I will describe two approaches for bias testing, their methodologies, and the fairness metrics that were applied: a multiple-image approach operationalized by Yee et al. (2021), as well as by Birhane et al. (2022), and a single-image approach by Kulynych (2021). The multi-image approach uses vertical or horizontal concatenations of images in order to analyse the saliency prediction model's behaviour: Will the predicted saliency be highest on the image of person A or person B? The single-image approach makes slight modifications to one image of one person in order to study the saliency prediction model's behaviour with regard to these modifications.

In a paper by researchers of the former META team at Twitter, Kyra Yee, Uthaipon Tantipongpipat, and Shubhanshu Mishra (2021), the authors conduct a broad analysis of different potentially harmful aspects of saliency-based image cropping. They give a definition of representational harm, and they focus on user agency and social responsibility (Yee et al., 2021, p. 3). By providing a broad and interdisciplinary context, as well as by laying out the limits of quantitative fairness analysis to addressing questions of representational harm, they go beyond a purely technical analysis. Quantitatively, they test for "[u]nequal treatment on different demographics" (Yee et al., 2021, p. 2), and for male gaze, which they define as the cropping tool "emphasiz[ing] a woman's body instead of the head" (Yee et al., 2021, p. 3). As a formalized fairness metric for measuring bias with regard to different demographics, they use *demographic parity*, which they define as the tool cropping in a way so that "in cases where the model is forced to choose between two individuals, the rate at which they are cropped out should be roughly equal" (Yee et al., 2021, p. 7). In other words, on average, the model should not crop out more individuals from one demographic group than from another. If it does, then, according to this methodology, the model can be considered biased against one demographic group compared to another.

The authors use the Wikidata API to assemble the WikiCeleb dataset, which consists of "images and labels of celebrities" (Yee et al., 2021, p. 8), and they curate four intersectional demographic subgroup datasets: "Black-Female," "Black-Male," "White-Female," "White-Male." The fairness analysis is conducted on all six pairings of these four subgroups, horizontally positioning one image of each subgroup next to an image of the other subgroup. For example, the fairness analysis on the groups "Black-Male" and "White-Male" would concatenate one image from the "Black-Male" dataset and one image from the "White-Male" dataset, observe on which of the two images the maximum saliency point is positioned (and, therefore, the crop would be centred around), and repeat that process 10,000 times for different combinations of images (Yee et al., 2021, p. 9). Using this approach and statistically evaluating the choosing behaviour of the model, they conclude that the model favours images with the label "Female" over images with the label "Male," and "White" over "Black"—intersectional group comparison shows that the model statistically strongly favours images from the "White-Female" dataset over the "Black-Male" dataset. Thus, according to Yee et al. (2021), the saliency prediction model is biased with regard to gender, race, and the respective intersectional subgroups.

Abeba Birhane, at the time a researcher at University College Dublin, together with Vinay Uday Prabhu and John Whaley, researchers at the company UnifyID Inc., in their paper (2022), use a similar methodology to analyse fairness and bias, as well as potential male gaze in three saliency-based cropping algorithms: the cropping tool used by Twitter, as well as those cropping tools used by Google and by Apple as part of other applications. Aspiring to compare their results with the study by Yee et al. (2021), Birhane et al. (2022) use the same pairings of the same intersectional demographic groups. Birhane et al. curate a dataset consisting of images from the Chicago Face Database (CFD),[3] a publicly available dataset of standardized photographs of volunteers that are self-labelled regarding gender and race (2022, p. 4057). This dataset is smaller in size than the dataset in Yee et al. (2021), but it has the advantage that its images are controlled with regard to "factors such as saturation, size, resolution, lighting conditions, facial expressions, clothing, and eye gaze" (Birhane et al., 2022, p. 4056), which ensures the images within the dataset to be more comparable, and, thus, renders the methodology more robust. The results in Birhane et al. (2022) correspond to those in Yee et al. (2021). In both papers, the authors conclude that there are significant race and gender biases in Twitter's saliency-based cropping tool.

In his winning submission to Twitter's algorithmic bias bounty competition (see below), Bogdan Kulynych, a researcher at the École polytechnique fédérale de Lausanne, uses a different methodology: in his single-image approach he investigates the question of what "make[s] the ... saliency-prediction model more excited" (Kulynych, 2021). Drawing from the concept of counterfactual fairness and counterfactual explanations, he approaches the saliency model by asking what needs to be different about an image in order to increase its maximum saliency score. Kulynych uses StyleGAN2-ADA (Karras et al., 2020), a generative adversarial network (GAN), to create synthetic images. He starts with one synthetic face image and retrieves its

---

3   Available at: https://www.chicagofaces.org/.

maximum saliency score from Twitter's saliency model. Then, by slightly changing the parameter inputs for the GAN, he creates further images that are very similar to the first image, as "the StyleGAN2-ADA model enables smooth interpolation in the space of latent parameters: Small changes to the latent parameters result in semantically 'small' changes to the generated faces" (Kulynych, 2021). Kulynych, then, after optimizing simultaneously for maximum saliency and minimum parameter changes, tries to understand the internal behaviour of the saliency prediction model. The result consists of 16 counterfactuals, i.e., 16 collections of 6 faces each, that look, to a human observer, very similar, but have differing saliency outputs. Kulynych codes the images with labels of qualities that he assigns to the faces. He finds that, in some counterfactuals, the saliency increases as the face becomes apparently slimmer; in others, the saliency increases "through making the face appear more stereotypically feminine, as perceived by the coder [Kulynych]," also by "lightening or warming the skin color," and "changing the apparent age" to a younger apparent age. Kulynych concludes that "the predicted maximum saliency increases by a combination of changes that include making the persons' skin lighter or warmer and smoother; and quite often changing the appearance to that of a younger, more slim, and more stereotypically feminine person" (Kulynych, 2021).

In summary, Yee et al. (2021), Birhane et al. (2022), and Kulynych (2021) found that there are significant biases in the saliency prediction model's behaviour. While Yee et al. (2021) and Birhane et al. (2022) used a multi-image quantitative approach in order to assess the model's average choosing behaviour in terms of demographic groups, Kulynych (2021) used a single-image approach with synthetically created counterfactuals to heuristically infer systematic favouring by the model. All three studies extensively discuss the limitations of their respective approach, and they provide context to the question of bias and potential harm caused by a saliency-based cropping tool.

Epistemic Limitations to Bias Testing

Finding and measuring bias in algorithmic systems, and specifically in computer vision systems, is not an easy endeavour (see, e.g., Cavazos et al., 2021; Glüge et al., 2020). In order to measure bias, one has to define it, and defining bias requires an underlying concept of what is "alike" and what is "different." Bias, then, can be conceptualized as a *differentiation* made by an algorithmic system that is, in some explicitly defined or tacitly implied sense, undesirable: Yee et al. (2021) and Birhane et al. (2022) employ the fairness metric of demographic parity which means that "the model should not be favoring representing one demographic over another" (Yee et al., 2021, p. 6). This fairness metric builds on the following implicit notions of "similarity" and "difference": If two individuals appear in an image in a similar, or rather *in a comparable way*—then the model should not systematically differentiate according to the individuals' race and/or gender. In the testing setup by Yee et al. (2021), comparability is defined as two images of individuals from the WikiCeleb database being concatenated horizontally. In Birhane et al., comparability is defined as two images from the Chicago Face Database being concatenated vertically with a blank square separating them. Being confronted with comparable images (as defined by the respective testing methodology), the saliency prediction model, if it adheres to demographic parity, will, on average, not differentiate in terms of the faces' race or gender. Kulynych creates synthetic images that are supposed to be similar to study the way in which the saliency model differentiates. If the predicted saliency increases as the synthetic images undergo, for example, "skin lightening" (Kulynych, 2021)—in other words, if two images are roughly alike, but differ only in skin tone—Kulynych concludes that the saliency tool favours the lighter face and, thus, differentiates in an undesirable way.

Similarity and difference, though, are concepts that are difficult to robustly define if the underlying data is visual data and, therefore, much more complex than categorical or simple quantitative variables. Human vision does not see the data in the same way computer vision does: an algorithmic system "sees" an image in terms of pixels and their corresponding RGB values. If, for example, "age" is a variable (or feature) in a machine learning model, then there is no aspect of the data input "age = 27" that is hidden from human understanding, nothing that a machine learning model can "see" that a human actor cannot, or vice versa. (In large-scale patterns, of course, there are things that humans cannot grasp or detect.) In visual data, however, human vision and algorithmic image data processing differ starkly.

An example from recent scholarship on adversarial attacks on computer vision systems illustrates the wide gap between human vision and computer vision. Adversarial examples in computer vision are images that are purposely modified in a way that causes a visual system to make a mistake: "It's possible to construct an adversarial example ... which is perceptually indistinguishable ... but is classified incorrectly" (Kurakin et al., 2017, p. 2). By "perceptually indistinguishable," the authors mean indistinguishable by a human observer. A famous example is an image of a panda that, at first, is classified by an object recognition system as "panda" with just under 60% confidence. Then, adding a layer of perturbation pixels that are imperceptible by human vision, the image—which, to human vision, still looks like the same image of the panda—is classified as a "gibbon" with 99% confidence (Goodfellow et al., 2015, p. 3). To a human observer, the two images look alike. To the computer vision system, they differ significantly. What looks similar and what looks different, thus, can vary a lot between human vision and computer vision. This is not to say that malevolent actors will use adversarial examples to manipulate bias analyses. Instead, this example illustrates the large gap between "alikeness" as determined by human vision versus computer vision. This gap will inevitably have some effect on bias testing of visual computing models. This aspect is discussed by Birhane et al., who point out "how trivial it was to change one aspect of the very same dataset (such as the height-to-width ratio or the lighting or the background pixel value) and *radically transform*" (2022, p. 4057) the results. It is, in other words, possible to modify the bias testing images so that human observers consider the resulting images (with the changed lighting, height-to-width ratio, or background pixel value) to be still similar enough to the old picture—the images are still images of the same humans—while the behaviour of the cropping tool changes significantly. In total, the underlying notions of "same-ness" and "difference" that bias testing indispensably relies on, together with the inherent gap between human vision and computer vision, make it methodically difficult (if not, in fact, impossible) to test for bias in a way that provides results that cannot be contested easily.

Another difficulty arises from the saliency-based method itself: returning to the definition by the then-Twitter researchers—that "the model should not be favoring representing one demographic over another" (Yee et al., 2021, p. 6)—this might suggest that the model has a choice *in terms of humans*. However, the Twitter saliency model never chooses between individuals. It does not "see" in terms of individuals, since it is trained on saliency maps, and not on face detection and/or object recognition. It only "sees" contrast and colours (i.e., RGB data values), and its vision (i.e., its analysis of visual data) is structured along a grid. The model has no concept of human, gender, or race. Thus, it cannot actively differentiate in terms of individuals of different demographic groups. Of course, this does not mean that there cannot be systematically different effects on different demographics. De-biasing the saliency-based tool with regard to demographic parity, however, would make no sense conceptually. From a mathematical-epistemic perspective, it would be futile to try to technically force a saliency prediction model to adhere to demographic parity, if the model does not recognize faces or humans. One would have to, in a separate process, add a separate model to detect faces and then to recognize race and gender—with the widely researched limitations and bias pitfalls of face recognition (see, e.g., Buolamwini & Gebru,

2018)—and then to choose according to the metric of demographic parity. Moreover, this approach would implicitly assume that there is a quantifiable difference on the level of pixels between images of humans of different genders and/or races, i.e., measurable criteria of differentiation that can be made machine-readable, whereas critical scholarship has long contested the idea that gender and race can be found in biology (see, e.g., Fausto-Sterling, 2020), or in pixels, for that matter (see also Stark & Hutson, 2022).

The approaches to bias testing discussed above are outcome-based, meaning that the authors first curate an image dataset, and then test the behaviour of the saliency prediction model on that dataset. A different approach would be to conduct some kind of bias analysis on the training data, as Yee et al. (2022) mention at the end of their paper. Of course, this approach entails the underlying assumption that the saliency prediction model does indeed mimic the viewing behaviour encoded in the training data sufficiently well, which it might not even do (see Raji et al., 2022). One could study the images in the training data together with the given saliency heat maps. This can be done for the publicly available datasets—everybody can download the images that were used to measure eye tracking, as well as the respective distilled heat maps.

This approach has similar limitations regarding the methodology as the outcome-based approach. Even the fairness metric of demographic parity that is, in theory, easy to quantify turns out to be complicated: When is the training data set biased, when is it balanced? Should one examine the images, or the images together with the heat maps? Should the humans that are visible in the training dataset exhibit demographic parity, i.e., should there be the same number of people of each (previously defined) demographic that one studies (race, gender, age,...) in all images in total? Or in every single image within the training dataset? What about intersectional groups? How can one account for different positions of individuals in an image, i.e., for individuals who are in the front of the image, versus in the background? At this point, one will return to the question raised at the beginning of this section: How can "alikeness" be defined in visual data? When do two (or several) humans appear in an image in a comparable way? These are questions that will have to be thoroughly thought out if one plans to analyse the training datasets for biases.

The Bias Discourse

Having explored the limitations to bias testing in computer vision, this section examines the power relations that are at play. The mathematical limitations to bias testing discussed in the previous section will play a crucial role. According to Foucault, "[w]here there is power, there is resistance" (1978, p. 95). The bias testing studies discussed above, as well as the individual Twitter users who posted cropping examples and complained about bias (see, e.g., Madland, 2020), and the Twitter users that commented on, re-tweeted, and wrote about the supposedly biased image crops, form "points of resistance" (Foucault, 1978, p. 95) against the power that is exercised by Twitter via the cropping tool. Resistance to power, however, is "never in a position of exteriority in relation to power" (Foucault, 1978, p. 95), rather, it is "inscribed in [power relations] as an irreducible opposite" (p. 96). Thus, the knowledge production about bias in the cropping tool, too, implies and is implied by power (see also Lum et al., 2022). The methodical setups discussed above, the ways in which bias is conceptualized and made quantifiable, the choice of demographic groups that are being tested for, the images that are used, as well as the limitations to bias testing, are "mechanisms and instances which enable one to distinguish true from false statements" (Foucault, 1977, p. 13) regarding the biased-ness of the saliency prediction model—brought forth and stabilized by the bias discourse.

The bias discourse, thus, becomes a focal point of and a vehicle for resistance against algorithmic knowledge production. Research and studies on bias (see, e.g., the well-known works of Angwin et al., 2016; Benjamin, 2019a; Buolamwini & Gebru, 2018; Friedman & Nissenbaum, 1996; see also Kinder-Kurlanda & Fahimi, in this volume), as well as NGOs (see, e.g., Kayser-Bril, 2019; Vervloesem, 2020), international organizations (see, e.g., UN Special Rapporteur, 2019), and works of popular science (see, e.g., Benjamin, 2019b; Noble, 2018; O'Neil, 2016) form, in Foucauldian terms, a "swarm of points of resistance [that] traverses social stratifications and individual unities" (Foucault, 1978, p. 96). In turn, the plurality of resistances exercise power by stabilizing the produced and, in fact, porous, knowledge about bias even throughout its mathematical limitations. Birhane et al. explicitly state that "the brittleness of the cropping frameworks made it worryingly easy to *ethics-wash* the survival ratios in any direction to fit a pre-concocted narrative" (2022, p. 4057). In other words, it is possible to modify aspects of the test images, as mentioned above, to create a different result that would imply unbiased-ness.

Twitter could have pointed out flaws in the bias analyses. Twitter also could have conducted a methodically equally robust bias analysis with the result of unbiased-ness. In fact, Twitter stated in a blog post that there have been previous (non-published) bias analyses that have shown the cropping system to not be biased (Agrawal & Davis, 2020). However, instead of contesting the produced knowledge about bias in the cropping tool, Twitter reacted by removing the tool and establishing a cropping modality that does not deploy machine learning. The bias discourse was effective: Twitter chose to not resist the resistance—at least not in a direct way, as will be elaborated throughout the next section.

Stabilization

The Bias Bounty Challenge

In May 2021, the same month the bias study by then-Twitter researchers Yee et al. (2021) was uploaded to arXiv, Twitter rolled out a new system behind the cropping of images. The major change was that images with standard size would not be cropped at all. If cropping is necessary due to unusual image ratios—if an image is extreme in height or width—the image would be cropped around the centre (Davis, 2021; Yee et al., 2021, p. 18). In July 2021, in a quite novel way of reacting to public criticism, Twitter launched an "algorithmic bias bounty challenge" (Chowdhury & Williams, 2021; Twitter, 2021) as a "community-led approach to build better algorithms" (Yee & Font Peradejordi, 2021). "Bug bounty challenges," usually, are competitions in which companies award "ethical hackers" (HackerOne, 2022) with monetary bounties for finding vulnerabilities in IT security or malfunctioning parts in their software. Platforms that host bug bounty programs for companies advertise that bug bounties are "an effective measure to enhance ... cybersecurity regarding all the weaknesses that might be found and exploited by the eye of a real hacker" (SecureBug, 2021). Twitter adapted the bug bounty format to a competition for finding "algorithmic bias" (Chowdhury & Williams, 2021), a format that is becoming popular (see also Globus-Harris et al., 2022; Kenway et al., 2022; Eslami & Heuer, in this volume). The challenge was open from July 30 to August 6, 2021, and Twitter awarded $7,000 in total as bounties, divided into first, second, third place, as well as one prize for "Most Innovative" and one for "Most Generalizable" (Twitter, 2021). In the challenge prompt, Twitter stated: "You are given access to Twitter's saliency model and the code used to generate a crop of an image given a predicted maximally salient point" (Twitter, 2021). Assuming that this software is used to crop an uploaded image for a preview in the timeline, "[y]our mission is to demonstrate what potential harms such an algorithm may introduce" (Twitter, 2021). Bounty hunters are encouraged to "[l]everage a mix of quantitative and qualitative methods" (Twitter, 2021). To grade the submissions and, subsequently, determine the winners of the competition, Twitter used a point scheme: different kinds of harms were assigned with varying point scores. "Point allocation," it says in the instructions, "is a reflection of the complexity of identification and exploitation of these issues, and does not represent a reflection of the level of importance of the harm" (Twitter, 2021). The types of harm in the point allocation scheme are closely connected to the definition of "representational harm" that Yee et al. (2021) provide in their paper: "denigration," "stereotyping," "under-representation," "mis-recognition," "ex-nomination," "erasure," "reputational harm," "psychological harm," "economical harm," and a "wild card" (Twitter, 2021). Demonstrating "denigration," for example, would be graded with 10 or 20 points, depending on whether the harm could "occur from 'natural' images that a well-intentioned user would reasonably post," or "from doctored images posted by malicious actors" (Twitter, 2021). This base point score would then be multiplied by different factors, depending on the potential "damage or impact," in which the multiplier is highest if the "[h]arm is measured along multiple axes of identity and disproportionally affects multiple marginalised communities or the intersections of multiple marginalised identities" (Twitter, 2021). Other point multipliers are applied according to the number of affected users by said harm, as well as for justification of methodology, and other factors. Bogdan Kulynych's submission discussed above won the 1st prize of the bias bounty. Twitter regarded the bias bounty as a success. In a blog post published after the bias bounty it was emphasized how beneficial it was to "learn from a diverse, global community of ethical AI hackers whose lived experiences make it possible for them to discover unintended consequences we wouldn't have otherwise been able to" (Yee & Font Peradejordi, 2021).

Power as Resistance to Resistance

From a technical perspective, it is to be noted that—contrary to what Twitter's announcement of granting "access to Twitter's saliency model" (Twitter, 2021) might suggest—the saliency-based prediction model was not made transparent. Instead, the bias bounty participants were only able to access the saliency prediction in a black box way via an API: Submitting images as input query, the black box would return saliency heat maps structured in a grid, the maximum saliency scores, and the crop windows for different height-to-width ratios. This grants, in fact, not more meaningful (albeit definitely more practical and workable) access to the cropping model than users had when the tool was in use. Uploading an image and examining the cropped preview was what many Twitter users did when they originally raised accusations of bias in 2020. In his submission to the bias bounty challenge, Kulynych stated that the mere black box access was a "significant challenge" (2021) for his bias analysis.

The bounty prizes were low compared to the average bug bounty prizes awarded in regular bug bounties (Kayser-Bril, 2021). Looking at that through the lens of power, Twitter is still a big tech company, and "[relations of power] are the immediate effects of … divisions, inequalities, and disequilibriums" (Foucault, 1978, p. 94). The imbalance of resources and knowledge between Twitter as a company, on the one hand, and its users and the bias bounty participants, on the other hand, makes it possible for Twitter to claim transparency, yet not grant meaningful access to the inner workings of its saliency-based cropping tool. Further, by designing the bounty challenge in the way they did (with low bounties and only five prizes), Twitter created a constellation in which the company was able to benefit from numerous submissions "from around the world, ranging from individuals, to universities, start-ups, and enterprise companies" (Yee & Font Peradejordi, 2021). All submissions that did not receive one of the five prizes were not rewarded for their work (see also Kenway et al., 2022). In that way, quite literally, "power produces knowledge" (Foucault, 1995, p. 27): Twitter's hosting the bias bounty challenge summoned knowledge that was produced by other people without monetary compensation.

The bias bounty and its surrounding spectacle served as a means of stabilization for Twitter's then-representation of itself as a tech company that, until the Elon Musk era began, aimed to "mak[e] the way we practice ML more fair, accountable and transparent" (Erkan & Pandey, 2019), and "strive to work in a way that's transparent and easy to understand" (Agrawal & Davis, 2020), as stated by Twitter's then-CEO Parag Agrawal and then-Chief Design Officer Dantley Davis in a blog post about the cropping tool. Twitter's self-representation has obviously drastically changed, and the company has become unrecognizable since Elon Musk became Twitter's CEO and, subsequently, shut down Twitter's AI ethics team, META (Knight, 2022). At the time, however, the strategy was effective. The bias discourse, thus, turns out to be not only a vehicle for resistance, but also for counter-resistance: Twitter did not have to contest the bias discourse, or the knowledge produced in and stabilized by the discourse. Instead, the company was able to find a comfortable place within it.

Discussion

This chapter examined the push-and-pull dynamics of the power relations at play in the case of Twitter's saliency-based cropping algorithm. This case study—the development and deployment of the cropping tool, the accusations of bias, the ensuing bias analyses and the therein produced knowledge, as well as Twitter's responsive actions—can be seen as a blueprint of an ever-ongoing "process which, through ceaseless struggles and confrontations, transforms, strengthens, or reverses" (Foucault, 1978, p. 92) the power relations, and with them, the politics embedded in algorithmic regimes. In the production of the cropping tool, power becomes knowledge and knowledge becomes power—a constellation that is rooted in the mathematics of machine learning systems.

This chapter discussed three bias analyses that were conducted, and it was argued that the production of knowledge about bias can be seen as resistance against—and, thus, as a locus of politics within—the truth regime of algorithmic knowledge production. As showed, conceptualizing and measuring bias entails its mathematical-epistemic limitations that potentially render the results porous. Still, the bias discourse provided an effective vehicle for resistance: Twitter succumbed to the criticism and shut down the cropping tool. However, by hosting the algorithmic bias bounty challenge, Twitter stabilized its position within and in relation to the bias discourse and, thus, resisted the resistance, rendering the bias discourse a vehicle for counter-resistance, too.

The choice of material considered in this case study brings with it certain limitations. Having to rely on public statements, papers, and blog posts on the part of Twitter entails a lack of intra-organizational perspective: Twitter appears as a singular actor, and intra-organizational power struggles, conflicts, and collisions of interests or values remain invisible. Especially considering recent developments and the dissolution of Twitter's META team, it is to be assumed that Twitter as a company is not and has never been one homogeneous actor. It would be immensely interesting to conduct structured interviews with then-Twitter researchers to explore intra-organizational power struggles that otherwise can only be speculated about. Moreover, this case study points further research to strategies employed by big tech companies to adapt to bias-related resistance—strategies that can, as in the case discussed here, cost close to nothing. Furthermore, it will be interesting to explore how to productively engage with the inherent mathematical-epistemic limitations of bias testing.

This case study highlights the multidimensionality and interdisciplinarity of the endeavour of studying algorithmic regimes—itself a locus of study—with actors as heterogeneous as users, companies, activists, international organizations, researchers, NGOs, programmers, journalists, legislative bodies, etc., their different discourses, practices of knowledge production, goals, implicit assumptions, explicit conceptualizations, and the "heterogeneous, unstable, and tense force relations" (Foucault, 1978, p. 93) that are at play.

References

Agrawal, P., & Davis, D. (2020, October 1). Transparency around image cropping and changes to come. *Blog.Twitter.com*. https://blog.twitter.com/official/en_us/topics/product/2020/transparency-image-cropping.html

Angwin, J., Larson, J., Mattu, S., & Kirchner, L. (2016, May 23). Machine bias: There's software used across the country to predict future criminals. And it's biased against Blacks. *ProPublica*. https://www.propublica.org/article/machine-bias-risk-assessments-in-criminal-sentencing

Benjamin, R. (2019a). Assessing risk, automating racism. *Science, 366*(6464), 421–422. https://doi.org/10.1126/science.aaz3873

Benjamin, R. (2019b). *Race after technology: Abolitionist tools for the New Jim Code*. Polity.

Birhane, A., Prabhu, V. U., & Whaley, J. (2022). Auditing saliency cropping algorithms. In *Proceedings of the IEEE/CVF Winter Conference on Applications of Computer Vision (WACV)* (pp. 4051–4059).

Bishop, C. M. (2006). *Pattern recognition and machine learning*. Springer.

Borji, A., & Itti, L. (2015). CAT2000: A large scale fixation dataset for boosting saliency research. *ArXiv:1505.03581*. http://arxiv.org/abs/1505.03581

Buolamwini, J., & Gebru, T. (2018). Gender shades: Intersectional accuracy disparities in commercial gender classification. *Proceedings of Machine Learning Research, 81*, 1–15. http://proceedings.mlr.press/v81/buolamwini18a/buolamwini18a.pdf

Cavazos, J. G., Phillips, P. J., Castillo, C. D., & O'Toole, A. J. (2021). Accuracy comparison across face recognition algorithms: Where are we on measuring race bias? *IEEE Transactions on Biometrics, Behavior, and Identity Science, 3*(1), 101–111. https://doi.org/10.1109/TBIOM.2020.3027269

Chowdhury, R., & Williams, J. (2021, July 30). Introducing Twitter's first algorithmic bias bounty challenge. *Blog.Twitter.com*. https://blog.twitter.com/engineering/en_us/topics/insights/2021/algorithmic-bias-bounty-challenge

Davis, D. [@dantley]. (2021). I'm excited to share that we're rolling this out to everyone today on iOS and Android. You'll now be able [Tweet]. *Twitter*. https://twitter.com/dantley/status/1390040111228723200

Erkan, N., & Pandey, S. (2019, January 29). Partnering with researchers at UC Berkeley to improve the use of ML. *Blog.Twitter.com*. https://blog.twitter.com/en_us/topics/company/2019/ucberkeley-twitter-ml

Fausto-Sterling, A. (2020). *Sexing the body: Gender politics and the construction of sexuality* (2nd ed.). Basic Books.

Foucault, M. (1977). The political function of the intellectual. *Radical Philosophy, 17*(13), 12–14.

Foucault, M. (1978). *The history of sexuality*. Pantheon.

Foucault, M. (1995). *Discipline and punish: The birth of the prison*. Vintage.

Foucault, M. (2003). *Society must be defended: Lectures at the Collège de France, 1975–76* (M. Bertani & A. Fontana, Eds.; D. Macey, Trans.). Picador.

Friedman, B., & Nissenbaum, H. (1996). Bias in computer systems. *ACM Transactions on Information Systems, 14*(3), 330–347. https://doi.org/10.1145/230538.230561

Globus-Harris, I., Kearns, M., & Roth, A. (2022). An algorithmic framework for bias bounties. In *FAccT '22: Proceedings of the 2022 ACM Conference on Fairness, Accountability, and Transparency* (pp. 1106–1124). https://doi.org/10.1145/3531146.3533172

Glüge, S., Amirian, M., Flumini, D., & Stadelmann, T. (2020). How (not) to measure bias in face recognition networks. In F.-P. Schilling & T. Stadelmann (Eds.), *Artificial neural networks in pattern recognition* (pp. 125–137). Springer International Publishing. https://doi.org/10.1007/978-3-030-58309-5_10

Goodfellow, I. J., Shlens, J., & Szegedy, C. (2015). Explaining and harnessing adversarial examples. *ArXiv:1412.6572 [Cs, Stat]*. http://arxiv.org/abs/1412.6572

HackerOne. (2022). Your direct line to the masterminds. *HackerOne*. https://www.hackerone.com/product/bug-bounty-platform

Hern, A. (2020, September 21). Twitter apologises for "racist" image-cropping algorithm. *The Guardian*. https://www.theguardian.com/technology/2020/sep/21/twitter-apologises-for-racist-image-cropping-algorithm

Jiang, M., Huang, S., Duan, J., & Zhao, Q. (2015). SALICON: Saliency in context. *2015 IEEE Conference on Computer Vision and Pattern Recognition (CVPR)*, 1072–1080. https://doi.org/10.1109/CVPR.2015.7298710

Judd, T., Ehinger, K., Durand, F., & Torralba, A. (2009). Learning to predict where humans look. *2009 IEEE 12th International Conference on Computer Vision*, 2106–2113. https://doi.org/10.1109/ICCV.2009.5459462

Karras, T., Aittala, M., Hellsten, J., Laine, S., Lehtinen, J., & Aila, T. (2020). Training generative adversarial networks with limited data. *ArXiv:2006.06676 [Cs, Stat]*. http://arxiv.org/abs/2006.06676

Kayser-Bril, N. (2019, October 6). Austria's employment agency rolls out discriminatory algorithm, sees no problem. AlgorithmWatch. https://algorithmwatch.org/en/story/austrias-employment-agency-ams-rolls-out-discriminatory-algorithm/

Kayser-Bril, N. (2021, August 17). Twitter's algorithmic bias bug bounty could be the way forward, if regulators step in. AlgorithmWatch. https://algorithmwatch.org/en/twitters-algorithmic-bias-bug-bounty/

Kenway, J., François, C., Costanza-Chock, S., Raji, I. D., & Buolamwini, J. (2022). *Bug bounties for algorithmic harms? Lessons from cybersecurity vulnerability disclosure for algorithmic harms discovery, disclosure, and redress.* Algorithmic Justice League.

Knight, W. (2022, November 4). Elon Musk has fired Twitter's "Ethical AI" team. *Wired.* https://www.wired.com/story/twitter-ethical-ai-team/

Kulynych, B. (2021). How to become more salient? Surfacing representation biases of the saliency prediction model. GitHub. https://github.com/bogdan-kulynych/saliency_bias/commits/main

Kurakin, A., Goodfellow, I., & Bengio, S. (2017). Adversarial examples in the physical world. *ArXiv:1607.02533.* http://arxiv.org/abs/1607.02533

Lum, K., Zhang, Y., & Bower, A. (2022). De-biasing "bias" measurement. In *FAccT '22: Proceedings of the 2022 ACM Conference on Fairness, Accountability, and Transparency* (pp. 379–389). https://doi.org/10.1145/3531146.3533105

Madland, C. [@colinmadland]. (2020). A faculty member has been asking how to stop Zoom from removing his head when he uses a virtual background [Tweet]. *Twitter.* https://twitter.com/colinmadland/status/1307111822772842496

Noble, S. U. (2018). *Algorithms of oppression: How search engines reinforce racism.* New York University Press.

O'Neil, C. (2016). *Weapons of math destruction: How big data increases inequality and threatens democracy.* Crown.

Raji, I. D., Kumar, I. E., Horowitz, A., & Selbst, A. (2022). The fallacy of AI functionality. In *FAccT '22: Proceedings of the 2022 ACM Conference on Fairness, Accountability, and Transparency* (pp. 959–972). https://doi.org/10.1145/3531146.3533158

SecureBug. (2021, August 16). Bug bounty programs: Benefits and challenges. *SecureBug.se.* https://securebug.se/blog/bug-bounty-programs-benefits-and-challenges/

Stark, L., & Hutson, J. (2022). Physiognomic artificial intelligence. *Fordham Intellectual Property, Media and Entertainment Law Journal, 32*(4), 922–978.

Theis, L., & Wang, Z. (2018, January 24). Speedy neural networks for smart auto-cropping of images. *Blog.Twitter.com.* https://blog.twitter.com/engineering/en_us/topics/infrastructure/2018/Smart-Auto-Cropping-of-Images

Theis, L., Korshunova, I., Tejani, A., & Huszár, F. (2018). Faster gaze prediction with dense networks and Fisher pruning. *ArXiv:1801.05787.* http://arxiv.org/abs/1801.05787

Twitter. (2021, July 30). Twitter algorithmic bias. *HackerOne*. https://hackerone.
    com/twitter-algorithmic-bias?type=team

UN Special Rapporteur. (2019). *Report of the Special Rapporteur on extreme poverty
    and human rights*. https://undocs.org/A/74/493

Vervloesem, K. (2020, April 6). How Dutch activists got an invasive fraud detec-
    tion algorithm banned. AlgorithmWatch. https://algorithmwatch.org/en/
    syri-netherlands-algorithm/

Yee, K., & Font Peradejordi, I. (2021, September 7). Sharing learnings from the first
    algorithmic bias bounty challenge. *Blog.Twitter.com*. https://blog.twitter.com/
    engineering/en_us/topics/insights/2021/learnings-from-the-first-algorithmic-
    bias-bounty-challenge

Yee, K., Tantipongpipat, U., & Mishra, S. (2021). Image cropping on Twitter: Fairness
    metrics, their limitations, and the importance of representation, design, and
    agency. *Proceedings of the ACM on Human–Computer Interaction, 5*(CSCW2),
    article no. 450. https://doi.org/10.1145/3479594

About the Author

Paola Lopez is a mathematician currently working on an interdisciplinary
PhD thesis at the Department of Legal Philosophy at the University of Vienna,
Austria. She is also an affiliated researcher at the Weizenbaum Institute
for the Networked Society in Berlin. She studies algorithmic systems, their
epistemic limitations, and the (in)justice of their deployment by state actors
towards individuals.

15. Making Algorithms Fair: Ethnographic Insights from Machine Learning Interventions

Katharina Kinder-Kurlanda and Miriam Fahimi

Abstract

With a growing number of cases of algorithmic harm being reported, various stakeholders are developing strategies for changing the algorithmic regime for the better. In this contribution we offer ethnographic insights gained when participating in one such effort, a European research and training project. We investigate three dimensions of the algorithmic regime: First, we explore individual, mostly disciplinary interventions to mitigate algorithmic harm and show how interdisciplinary collaborations are activated by attempts to generalize individual accounts of fairness. Second, we demonstrate how a flexibility in the concepts of algorithmic fairness allowed successful collaboration within the project. Finally, we examine attempts to move beyond narrow, disciplinary requirements, and investigate how the algorithmic regime affects such interventions.

Keywords: algorithmic fairness; algorithmic bias; ethnography

Introduction

The current algorithmic regime is being contested. Critics from various academic disciplines, media, and civil society are increasingly reporting on its vain promises: while the use of data-intensive, machine learning-based AI and neural nets pledged better predictions based on scaling, efficiency, and accuracy, a growing number of cases of bias, discrimination, and opaque decision-making are being reported. Consequently, various stakeholders are developing strategies and intervention projects in order to change the

Jarke, J., B. Prietl, S. Egbert, Y. Boeva, H. Heuer, and M. Arnold (eds.), *Algorithmic Regimes: Methods, Interactions, and Politics*. Amsterdam: Amsterdam University Press, 2024
DOI 10.5117/9789463728485_CH15

algorithmic regime for the better. For instance, the European Commission is drafting a novel act on the "regulation of AI" to regulate algorithmic harm (European Commission et al., 2021).

In a similar vein, projects in computer science and related disciplines are emerging around the topics of mitigating algorithmic bias and implementing fairness in algorithmic decision-making. Part of these efforts is the European project that is the object of this chapter and in which a group of scientists is trying to understand and address algorithmic bias combined with the development of better algorithms for use by industry partners. The project involves scholars from computer science and legal studies as well as the authors of this chapter, two social scientists, one acting as a principal investigator (PI) and one as a PhD student.

In this contribution we consider the algorithmic regime from the perspective of those who want to build better algorithms. Doing so requires working sometimes within, and sometimes against the algorithmic regime: as algorithms are gaining importance in many areas of public life and work, efforts to improve them are also gaining attention and recognition—and are thus inextricably linked to the new modes of knowledge production and dissemination offered by the machine learning-based "algorithmic systems" (Seaver, 2019) that are transforming contemporary societies (also see Jarke et al. and Prietl & Raible, in this volume). Based on ethnographic insights derived from interviews conducted for and around the project, email questions distributed among the PhD students in the project, as well as our continuing observations and field notes, we thus study actors and their practices as they are contributing to producing, mobilizing, or (de)stabilizing an algorithmic regime, while also critically challenging it. Individual actors are in this conceptualization influenced by institutions and other structures; but not all of their agency can solely be understood as the effects of structure. Rather, actors reproduce structure, but they also occasionally transform it (Bhaskar, 1979). The algorithmic regime is thus being produced, maintained, and constantly reinvented by many different individual and collective actors. Many of these are working for a transnational network of companies interested in commercial applications, but there are also various algorithms being tested and deployed in other domains, particularly governance, and—as is the case in the project—in academia, albeit often in collaboration with industry partners.

Different collaborative and institutional actors such as universities, big tech companies, and governance institutions are researching, developing, and applying novel algorithms and predictive systems. While these actors shape algorithms (see Büchner et al., in this volume), algorithms also shape social institutions and potential interventions. As such, algorithms have a part in social ordering processes, as they promote certain visions of calculative objectivity and may also be connected to wider governmentalities (Beer, 2017; also see Egbert, in this volume). The interplay of these entanglements of actors and things leads to the maintenance and stabilization of a complex system which is brought into focus by this volume: the algorithmic regime.

While we acknowledge that bias in data-intensive machine learning algorithms may be exacerbated by decisions taken by those who develop and apply the algorithms, it is not the point of this contribution to disentangle where exactly a certain bias may originate. Rather, we put the focus on how those who are working on preventing bias in the current algorithmic regime fare in this undertaking. We show that depending on their specific roles and situations within the project, their negotiation of disciplines, and their strategic considerations at the current stage of their academic career, academics' efforts and practices were motivated by a variety of conflicting reasons—and limited or promoted by specific structures and requirements of the project. We thus explore the politics of the algorithmic regime from the inside, to understand how actors create but also transform the algorithmic regime.

Critics of the Algorithmic Regime

Currently, there is growing criticism from different academic fields highlighting that the algorithmic regime is unfair, biased, and opaque (on opaque algorithms and black boxing, also see Jarke & Heuer, in this volume). Many authors have pointed out that algorithms allowed the extension of control and surveillance by some over others, often in the pursuit of monetary gain (e.g., Kitchin, 2014; Zuboff, 2015; Beer, 2018; Leonelli, 2019). Work on the politics of algorithms has focused on classification, categorization, and standardization (Bowker & Star, 2000), even prior to the recent rise of machine learning algorithms, highlighting how algorithms' functions can be powerfully deployed within the social world (Beer, 2017; Crawford, 2021; DuBrin & Gorham, 2021; Ricaurte, 2019; Schwarz, 2021; West et al., 2019). Beer (2017) has pointed out that the notion of the algorithm in itself is an important feature of their potential power. Feminist, decolonial, and intersectional perspectives have assessed how new forms of colonialism and oppression are created via the promise of objectivity, neutrality, and efficiency of the algorithmic regime, technologized communication, and infrastructure media (Benjamin, 2019; Buolamwini & Gebru, 2018; Criado-Perez, 2020; D'Ignazio & Klein, 2020; Eubanks, 2018; Noble, 2018).

A recent focus both in scientific literature and in public discourse has been on the discriminative effects of the algorithmic regime, especially when data-intensive machine learning methods are applied to assist in decision-making in complex social situations. The algorithmic regime, as its dissenting voices claim, reproduces or even increases inequalities or discriminations (Karimi et al., 2018). It is interwoven with existing (discriminative, e.g., racist or sexist) institutions and structures (Chandler & Munday, 2011), but it may also amplify or introduce algorithmic discrimination as it favours those phenomena and aspects of human behaviour that are easily quantifiable over those which are hard or even impossible to measure (Andrus et al., 2021). Once introduced, the algorithmic regime therefore encourages the creation of very specific data collection infrastructures and policies, often amplifying existing power relations.

Computing within and against the Algorithmic Regime

Harm and discrimination connected to the algorithmic regime is thus a current topic in computer science, human–computer interaction, and data science, mostly referred to as *algorithmic bias* (Baeza-Yates, 2020; Blodgett et al., 2020; Bozdag, 2013; Grimes & Schulz, 2002; Kamar et al., 2015; Kirkpatrick, 2016; Mehrabi et al., 2019; Ntoutsi et al., 2020; Suresh & Guttag, 2019; Torralba & Efros, 2011; Trammell & Cullen, 2021; on algorithmic bias in a Twitter case, see Lopez, in this volume). In general, two types of bias are addressed: One is statistical bias, which refers to systematic differences between what is seen as "truth" or "fact" and the respective results of an algorithmic prediction. For example, "representation bias" refers to a systematic difference between a population and the representation of that population in a data set: certain individuals may be more likely to be selected or to self-select for a study, certain observations may be more likely to be reported, and certain phenomena more likely to be observed for a particular set of subjects. Such biases may be especially difficult to control in big data, where many data sets are the by-product of other activities with different, often operational, goals (Barocas & Selbst, 2016; boyd & Crawford, 2012). However, usually machine learning algorithms are built on the premise that the data from which the model has learned are representative of the data on which it is applied. This means that if misrepresented groups coincide with already disadvantaged social groups, even "unbiased computational processes can lead to discriminative decision procedures" (Calders & Žliobaitė, 2013). Misrepresentation in the data can lead to vicious cycles that perpetuate discrimination and disadvantage (Barocas & Selbst, 2016; O'Neil, 2016).

A second type of bias refers to the historical or social origins of algorithmic bias connected to reflecting and amplifying existing power asymmetries. These biases refer to social conditions, e.g., "gender bias," when the "AMS algorithm" discriminates against women (Lopez, 2021; Allhutter et al., 2020; Criado-Perez, 2020; Hancox-Li & Kumar, 2021; Keyes, 2018), "racial bias," when a "recidivism algorithm" discriminates against Black defendants (Angwin et al., 2016), and "intersectional bias," when the facial recognition algorithm can hardly detect Black women's faces (Buolamwini & Gebru, 2018; Scheuerman et al., 2021). In contrast to clearly defining and distinguishing between different types of bias, science and technology studies (STS) scholars have argued for considering entanglements between different types of bias and have put forward socio-technical understandings of bias (Lopez, 2021; Poechhacker & Kacianka, 2021).

Many scholars in the computer sciences and related disciplines have called for finding solutions to algorithmic bias (Diakopoulos, 2015).[1] Interventions are seen to be possible because there is a potential for social change in computer science, for example, because it allows for the formalization and visualization of social problems from a new perspective (Abebe et al., 2020). Ntoutsi et al. (2020) thus propose de-biasing methods focusing on the data (pre-processing methods), methods focusing on the algorithm (in-processing methods), and methods focusing on the model and applications (post-processing methods). Some computational scholars also call for going beyond de-biasing (Balayn & Gürses, 2021) and propose striving for algorithmic fairness and fairness more generally. Most computer science approaches to the topic of fairness are concerned with the possibilities for implementing different computational fairness approaches in so-called "fairness metrics." Computational fairness notions are, for instance, "fairness through unawareness," which means not including so-called sensitive attributes such as gender/address, etc., in the modelling, or "demographic parity," which means that equal groups should be treated equally (Barocas et al., 2017, 2020; Romei & Ruggieri, 2014; Verma & Rubin, 2018; Žliobaitė, 2017).

---

1   Of course, different approaches to mitigating bias and ensuring algorithmic accountability also exist from a variety of other disciplines, especially law (European Commission et al., 2021; Wachter et al., 2020; Zuiderveen Borgesius, 2020). Still the most discussed publications and the most popular voices come from the computer science communities.

The current interest of many computer scientists in bias and fairness is also connected to the rising awareness of algorithms' discriminative effects in the European Commission that is seeking solutions to the fact that such discrimination may not be adequately captured by current legislation (European Commission et al., 2021). The EU has also recently proposed new rules for a "fair and innovative data economy" in the so-called Data Act,[2] which aims to counteract imbalances in access to digital data which are currently much in favour of big companies. It was in the context of both the increased focus on algorithmic bias in computer science as well as the attention paid to the topic by the EU that our EU-funded Marie Skłodowska-Curie project started in 2020 and set out to tackle the problem of algorithmic bias. Its aim was to contribute to the development of unbiased and fair algorithms. Set up as an innovative training network, the project provides funding for 15 PhD projects on the topic of algorithmic bias and fairness. Training and research are intended to be "multidisciplinary ... in computer science, data science, machine learning, law and social science," but computer science perspectives dominate. The next section specifies the project, its surrounding context, and involved people.

The Project

In line with the computer science approaches discussed in the sections above, the project understood computing research as a new possibility to address the issues of "fairness" and "social good." In the project there was an agreement that algorithms can bring benefits if these issues are further researched and advocated for. The focus was thus "on how bias enters AI systems and how it is manifested in the data comprising the input to AI algorithms. Tackling bias entails answering the question of how to define fairness such that it can be considered in AI systems (Ntoutsi et al., 2020, p. 2). Understanding bias in algorithms from an interdisciplinary perspective was from the start one of the main features of the project (Ntoutsi et al., 2020). The project emerged out of a long-standing, loose collaboration of scholars that had attempted to merge social science and computer science approaches in the building of data-rich technology before (see Berendt et al., 2021). In the job adverts for the PhD student positions, project aims were stated as follows:

2   https://ec.europa.eu/commission/presscorner/detail/en/ip_22_1113.

> [The project] aims at developing novel methods for AI-based decision-making without bias by taking into account ethical and legal considerations in the design of technical solutions. The core objectives of [the project] are to understand legal, social and technical challenges of bias in AI decision-making, to counter them by developing fairness-aware algorithms, to automatically explain AI results, and to document the overall process for data provenance and transparency.

The project thus made certain solutions to the problem of algorithmic power (e.g., building a data set free of a certain bias) seem more obvious than others (e.g., understanding who was gaining power in what domain by deploying what idea of algorithms), but it also enabled us social scientists to work with our more relational perspective of wanting to look at the "enactment" of bias and fairness (Law & Mol, 2008). The text from the job advert was a compromise negotiated by the different project participants—with consequences for possibilities to do research, to recruit, and to publish. After a recruitment process, 15 PhD students were hired between August 2020 and March 2021. Due to the pandemic regulations at that time, personal meetings were not possible for the first one and a half years of the project. While collaborative meetings and events were held remotely as a substitute, everyone in the project started working towards their own ways of making the algorithmic regime fair.

We, as the two social scientists in the project, had a double role as both researchers involved in the specific requirements and objectives of the project, and as participant observers of the building of algorithms. As participating observers, we noticed that everyone seemed to have different understandings of how improving the algorithmic regime might be achieved, not least depending on their specific sub-project and/or PhD programme. While everyone agreed that the instances of algorithmic harm as pointed out in the literature should be addressed, different ways were found of trying to intervene in a specific area of interest, or employing specific tools. Some were studying how law can address algorithmic bias given current anti-discrimination regulations, others were training machine learning models more from the perspective of statisticians rather than that of software users, and some were working on specific parts of fairness such as explainable AI.

Research Question and Methods

Our observations of the multiple and distinct ways of making algorithms fair led to an interest in how the different scientists in the project reflected on their and others' interventional practices. What were their motivations? What did they perceive as highlights, as obstacles or as (possibly necessary) frictions? And what did they think about their achievements, how would they deal with upcoming ambiguities? Our interest was to some degree in finding out whether the intended changes to the algorithmic regime were going to be successful; but mostly we were interested in understanding the practices around these attempts to change algorithms for the better.

In February 2022, we sent out six questions about the incentives, objectives, and struggles of their work to the 14 PhD students in the project by email and received written replies from all of them. Two PhD projects were law related and 12 PhD projects were computer science related. PhD students not only had an academic background in computer science, but many had also other backgrounds, e.g., in mathematics, physics, psychology, or economics. We asked the PhD students why they applied for the PhD position addressing bias in algorithms; what their motivation was for intervening in algorithmic fairness; how they were trying to improve the issue of algorithmic bias, as a problem for science but also as a problem for society; details about how they addressed issues of algorithmic bias and tried to intervene; who they envisioned to profit from the work in the project; and what they thought might change as a result of their work. We received very detailed and prompt answers that overall showed a strong awareness of algorithmic bias as an issue of high importance for our societies and a keen awareness of the limits of the impact one may have as a PhD student on such an important issue. Possibly a reason for some of the voiced frustration with the perceived limited possibilities for intervention, and how PhD students stressed the existence of these limits, was due to our position as the two social scientists in the project—and students' knowledge of some of the critique of simplified "solutionism" in computer science which they thought we might support.

In the next section, we outline the possibilities, constraints, and frictions around what "intervention" could be achieved within the specific positions as PIs and PhD students—and we explore what these interventions looked like from the perspective of the scientists in the project, who only at first glance seemed to have very well-defined and obvious aims and solutions.

Making the Algorithmic Regime Fair

Supporting current criticism, PhD students involved in the project considered the existing algorithmic regime as not acceptable because of its harmful and discriminative effects. As one PhD student wrote: "The world is very often unfair and I believe that already existing unfairness should not be amplified by algorithms, but instead counteracted as best of our knowledge and possibilities" (PhD student, computer science).

The algorithmic regime was not only seen as unfair, it was also seen as something which can, in general, be changed. Being part of the project meant to contribute to this change as the project would advance an exploration and development of novel techniques for an alternative algorithmic regime.

While career advancement and the good job opportunity played a role in the students' decision to apply for the PhD position, so did their interest in advancing algorithmic fairness. All the PhD students explicitly stated that doing *meaningful work* was important to them, with many aiming to overcome inequalities, to support social good, and to address major social challenges. One student stated that they were interested because they saw "the possibility that my research results ... hopefully will do some good to society" (PhD student, computer science), another that their supervisor was "doing something beyond straight technocentric approaches to the topic" (PhD student, computer science), and a third even envisioned themselves being able to "promote human rights in the growing areas where automated decision-making systems are applied" (PhD student, computer science). As yet another PhD student in computer science put it, the "nature of the field combines the traditional sense of working on a machine learning application with the satisfaction of having a positive impact on society." Thus, contributing to a change of the current algorithmic regime was perceived as doing meaningful work and as promoting social good.

In the next sections, we explore three dimensions of changing the current algorithmic regime to make it fairer. In the section titled "Individual Interventions," we show that on an individual level furthering fairness in algorithms "worked," because everyone could accomplish change in the sense of improving a tool or method towards something they considered to be fair. Such individual interventions seemed feasible and doable, but they were also often perceived as limited due to the specificity of disciplinary or technical requirements. Departing from the increasing frustrations with such individual interventions, we next investigate attempts to collaboratively account for fairness and also highlight our own role in this. In "Flexibilities of Algorithmic Fairness," we show that agreeing on a multiplicity of meanings of algorithmic fairness was both a strategic decision that allowed for interdisciplinary collaboration and for positioning work in different communities and was also motivated by the insight that individual fairness accounts were not generalizable.

In "Beyond Bias," we eventually provide insights into the PhD students' attempts to move beyond the pre-structured frame of the project and show how these steps were embedded into the algorithmic regime. While we present these three dimensions in a specific order, related practices did not necessarily happen in this exact chronological sequence.

Individual Interventions

The project laid foundations for an alternative vision of the algorithmic regime and the individual projects made this vision look feasible at the micro-level. As the project started under isolating pandemic restrictions, the PhD students became experts in their respective sub-projects. When we asked students how they "try to improve the issue of algorithmic bias" in a questionnaire, their answers were clearly formulated with regard to specific PhD topics. In line with the logic of such a project, everyone stated something different: One PhD student in computer science said that typical tasks for her were "checking the data set to see if there is any imbalance or putting extra constraints (which are relatively easy to optimization) to the objective functions." Another PhD student recounted that "science-wise, I'm trying to develop methods that formalize how humans can perceive protected attributes so that the algorithms can incorporate this information and arrive at fairer results." PhD students in computer science were investigating different aspects of algorithmic bias such as "the temporal aspects of bias," "bias in visual data," bias in "the documentation of data and models," or bias in "deepfake detection models for different demographic groups." Changing the algorithmic regime for the better resonated well with possibilities for individual interventions as the objective of making the algorithmic regime fair was taken up within different career situations and discipline-specific methods and approaches to generating knowledge. Past research has shown how there is a cultural division in which researchers orient themselves towards their own epistemic communities, which may be separated from other communities by a "complex texture of knowledge as practiced in the deep social spaces of modern institutions" (Knorr-Cetina, 1999, p. 2). Success criteria for publications and projects may be very different across fields, even if similar data or topics are of interest (Weller & Kinder-Kurlanda, 2015; Kinder-Kurlanda, 2020). For example, computer scientists may adhere to simplifying solutionism as computer science tends to decontextualize and abstract the functional capacities of AI technologies and to overstate mathematical correction (Àvila et al., 2020).

In the project, we observed how computer science PhD students questioned and tried to avoid such solutionism. As the project evolved, available approaches to mitigating bias were seen to be "preliminary" although "still beneficial compared to a situation without bias mitigation" as one PhD student said. Concerns and questions arose during remote meetings and in personal exchanges circling around the limitations of technical solutions and fixes: even if all biases in a specific algorithm could be "removed"—was the situation in which the algorithm was being used "fair" in the first place? And considering algorithms' reliance on very specific types of data—what about the fact that algorithms only considered very specific things while others remained hidden?

The individual interventions for algorithmic fairness which we outlined above started being perceived as insufficient to tackle algorithmic harms— especially once one considered how algorithms favoured those phenomena and aspects of human behaviour that were easily quantifiable over those which were hard or even impossible to measure:

> We [computer scientists] sometimes want to measure the un-measurable, detect the un-detectable, and standardize the un-standardize-able.… By working on the problem of FAIR ML from a technosolutionist stance we all continue to perpetuate the harms we think we are trying to mitigate. (PhD student, computer science)

PhD students from computer science felt that the project's intended interdisciplinary approach to algorithmic fairness would not necessarily align with the requirements to develop solutions for industry partners as well as with the narrow requirements of the doctoral programs that they were enrolled in. For example, in these programs, interdisciplinary publications and outcomes might be of little immediate use: "After all, we all will be assessed as computer scientists" (PhD student, computer science). Acting and researching within the project required negotiating the sometimes incommensurable aims of contributing to individual sub-projects and disciplinary understandings of "fairness," of generating specific interdisciplinary publications and outputs, and of completing EU-project-specific deliverables. But it was not only PhD students who considered how to balance the aim of making algorithms fairer with the requirements of their career situation. For example, one PI described in one of our interviews how the logic of projects went against the fact that social situations would change over time, requiring to reassess what counted as fair:

So, the solution cannot be just a fixed thing that we put forward and we say, "Problem solved; let's go to the next one." I'm more interested in the processes that can ensure an ongoing ... fairness of the systems that we do and that involves people.... It's not that simple. (PI, computer science)

Working against frustrations about narrow requirements and quick technological fixes, interdisciplinary collaborations—as desired by the project—seemed a way out of the rabbit hole. One computer science PhD student even located the limitations to solutions in a lacking collaboration between computer science and social science: "The connection between the social science and the computer science needs better bonding to enable for creating better pipelines" (PhD student, computer science).

Thus, would such interdisciplinary collaborations allow us to step closer towards a fair algorithmic regime?

Flexibilities of Algorithmic Fairness

In our field notes from the early days of the project we noted how the claim for a common understanding of fairness sometimes put us at the centre of attention. The social science perspective was perceived as the "most different" from the computer science one. As such, we felt that it was expected from us to contribute to finding a more holistic and ethical fairness definition, which could provide a common ground for the other project partners. This situation led to a reflection of what our own role might be, what computer scientists' expectations of us might be, and whether these matched our own. Even in the proposal, careful consideration had gone into the wording of the social science tasks in such a way that they would allow us to do research that was not predefined by the requirements of one of the technical solutions. This was because we had, in similar settings to this project, already tried out different ways of collaborating as ethnographers with computer scientists: in one past project the ethnographer's role had been to ensure that technologies developed by the project's computer scientists would be useful in the intended target setting. This created difficulties in agreeing on aims of the work performed within the project. The meandering gaze usually present in ethnography and the critical stance of a constructivist epistemology were difficult to align with the predetermined decisions about specific technologies being employed (Kinder-Kurlanda, 2014). In another project the ethnography and the computer science work had been more aligned (Kinder-Kurlanda et al., 2018), eventually leading to conceptual work rather than to a successful technical implementation of a new system emerging as project results (Poller et al., 2014). We wanted to build on these past experiences of collaboration and were excited to be part of the project. We were also conscious of reciprocity issues: What would be useful to others in the project? What would be useful to us? The project promised a possibility of intervention in the algorithmic regime from a position that combined STS scholarship with an opportunity to shape the current version of the algorithmic regime. From our past experiences we knew that collaborating with computer scientists entailed discussing vocabulary, methods, and aims of any activities within the project.

While individual interventions were perceived as both feasible and narrow at the same time, the project indeed became a place of constant negotiation of the meaning of central concepts such as "bias" and "fairness." Negotiations happened in various conversations and meetings involving different people, and, maybe more importantly, the many decisions taken on an everyday basis about how to accomplish the project's objectives. Discussions were not confrontational but rather resulted in agreements about being flexible and open about the multiple meanings of central concepts. This openness and flexibility towards terminologies is in line with a general period of *interpretive flexibility* of fairness in fair machine learning (Selbst et al., 2019, in reference to Pinch & Bijker, 1984). Different interpretations of what a novel technology should and could entail by different social groups inform a complex process of negotiation, where, at the end, a closure of development can be achieved and a technology becomes relatively stable. Applying this perspective to machine learning, Selbst and colleagues (2019) have outlined how the fair machine learning community agrees on the fact that algorithmic bias is a problem that needs to be addressed (or in our words, that the current version of the algorithmic regime can and must be changed). Despite this agreement, the community promotes different, sometimes contradictory, ways and fairness formalizations in order to contribute to solving the problem.

Ávila et al. (2020) argue that exactly because there is little precision or consistency about conceptual and operational understandings of fairness at the interdisciplinary intersection of machine learning, big data, and application domains, this does not lead to a desired outcome such as fairer decisions being produced. Their interpretation seems to be in line with some of the views of the PhDs and PIs involved in the project who are missing fairness standards for computer science: "Still, we can't say there is a fair algorithm applicable to many areas.... Computer science people still can't unite on a unified definition for fairness—maybe really there isn't [one]!" (PhD student, computer science).

However, we observed that it was precisely the interpretative flexibility of meanings of algorithmic fairness that was required in order to be able to negotiate the variety of decisions in the process of changing the algorithmic regime: individual perspectives on how to achieve algorithmic fairness seemed neither to be *generalizable* nor easy to translate into another epistemic community's concepts. Thus, allowing for fairness to be conceptualized differently in one's own sub-project than in others was a prerequisite for collaborations. It also seemed that the complexity of making the algorithmic regime fair required the involved actors to *strategically* allow for different conceptualizations of algorithmic fairness to co-exist. Thus, one person could use gender-just decision-making as her understanding of fairness in one project, while using a technical approach such as mitigating selection bias in visual data for another. The computer scientists, as well as everyone else in the project, could be seen to be trying to find a balance between achieving strategic research goals required for the PhD program while doing something "meaningful"—two aims that were sometimes complementary and sometimes not.

By being required to hold multiple meanings and visions of fairness simultaneously and to strategically work with definitions and concepts that partially went against our *actual* individual research interest, we all had much in common—across all disciplines and career levels.

Beyond Bias

This flexibility of algorithmic fairness definitions and concepts also allowed us, in our discussions in and around the project, to consider fairness beyond the algorithmic system or even beyond its application domain. The fact that intended target settings (whether algorithmically enhanced or not) already may be characterized by inequalities may have been at the heart of many of the project researchers' unease about the impact of their efforts and interventions. Consequently, there was a keen awareness both amongst PIs and PhD students that in order to facilitate change, they not only needed to go beyond the limitations of their methods but also beyond the agreed-upon outline and actions of the already interdisciplinary project. For instance, PhD students were looking for alternative ways to engage with wider perspectives on fairness, ethics, and human rights. One PhD student started a feminist reading group, in which most of the other PhD students became involved after some time. Another PhD student became more engaged in the fairness discourse on social media: "I wouldn't count Twitter as a way of improving societal problems, but I'd like to believe that one day my voice as a researcher will be of value to others." A PhD student in legal studies got involved in transparency issues of corporate actors: "I seek to propose an effective way in which the law can provide guarantees to citizens and protect their rights while increasing trust in AI through greater transparency of the companies and actors that use such systems" (PhD student, law). PhD students as well as PIs were also advocating for the invitation of speakers with critical perspectives to project training events. Thus, decisions such as who to invite to a summer school, what to write in a project report, or what dissemination activities to undertake (and by whom these should be performed) led to *alternative understandings of fairness* to be introduced and others being questioned or allowed to exist in parallel. Algorithmic fairness in such an alternative sense could then also mean to address the unequal distribution of funds and resources between computer sciences, legal sciences, and social sciences or to demand more opportunities for participation and co-determination for early career researchers.

However, even alternative versions and visions of the algorithmic regime were still based on their crucial socio-technical constituents: algorithms. While they aimed to "critically question and reflect around the whole AI ecosystem and its societal implications" (PhD student, computer science) and even questioned whether machine learning-based algorithmic decision-making should be implemented at all, they continued to engage with existing, embedded ML systems and to build respective algorithms. It would be very unusual or even impossible to obtain a PhD degree in computer science in the area addressed by the project without novel algorithms to be tested or applied. It would also have been against the objective of the project itself.

However, the insights gained within the project about the complex relationship between fairness and bias solutions could only be developed out of an understanding that resulted out of the interdisciplinary effort of discussing concepts and building solutions. We see this as an equally valuable result to the more technical solutions and are currently looking for ways to make them useful to other projects in the future.

Conclusion

We approached the algorithmic regime from the inside, namely from the perspective of those researching how to address fairness and bias issues.

We have taken first steps towards finding out where exactly they (and we) were confined or activated by specific approaches, methods, and performed roles within the interdisciplinary process. At the beginning, individual actors had very different ideas about what they considered fair and how to achieve fairness. We especially saw how methods for mitigating algorithmic bias that were available to the computer science PhD students could satisfy their individual goal of achieving what they considered to be "fair" but would not satisfy the demands of collaborative conceptualizations of fairness. Rather, collaborative accounts of fairness required strategically allowing for different conceptualizations of fairness to coexist. Further research could investigate resulting effects of multiple fairness concepts, for instance, from the perspective of democratic processes and values (also see Poechhacker et al., in this volume). We have also described the various attempts of making algorithms fair that moved beyond the project's initial scope. Often, it turned out that these attempts were still being rewarded by the project (so, for example, the self-organized reading group was mentioned in a report deliverable). The project may eventually contribute to building another version of an algorithmic regime—and addressing bias in algorithms may not make this version into something that always enhances social good or human rights but may also allow stabilizing specific domain actors' control over making certain decisions within this domain. Certainly, improving algorithms is a very productive intervention, there are methods, tools, and possibilities for academic success. At the same time, definitions of algorithmic fairness were repeatedly not finalized, proved to be provisional and flawed, and algorithmic fairness has not yet become the solution that had been promised.

From the views we have offered from the inside, we are left with new questions concerning the politics of the algorithmic regime: Are we con-tributing to developing a novel version of the algorithmic regime, which even satisfies its critical voices? Are we maintaining existing algorithmic practices because critics are repelled as we develop fair metrics, tools, and explana-tions of opaque algorithmic decision-making? Would the project—not the regime—be considered a failure because we did not provide one generaliz-able fairness definition? Or, rather, does the impossibility of collaborative fairness prove that there is no fair version of the algorithmic regime at all? Does the divined regime, just as the current one, always remain unfinished and messy in any case (Dourish & Bell, 2011)? Does this mean that the conceptualization of an algorithmic "regime" cannot sufficiently grasp the messiness and ambiguity of actors' complex enactments? Considering and investigating these questions in future research will hopefully shed much needed light on the politics of the regime, its actors, ambiguous practices, and algorithmic constituents.

Funding

This work received funding from the European Union's Horizon 2020 research and innovation programme under the Marie Skłodowska-Curie grant agreement no. 860630.

References

Abebe, R., Barocas, S., Kleinberg, J., Levy, K., Raghavan, M., & Robinson, D. G. (2020). Roles for computing in social change. In *FAT* '20: Proceedings of the 2020 Conference on Fairness, Accountability, and Transparency* (pp. 252–260). https://doi.org/10.1145/3351095.3372871

Allhutter, D., Cech, F., Fischer, F., Grill, G., & Mager, A. (2020). Algorithmic profiling of job seekers in Austria: How austerity politics are made effective. *Frontiers in Big Data, 3*, article 5. https://doi.org/10.3389/fdata.2020.00005

Andrus, M., Spitzer, E., Brown, J., & Xiang, A. (2021). What we can't measure, we can't understand: Challenges to demographic data procurement in the pursuit of fairness. *FAccT' 21: Proceedings of the 2021 ACM Conference on Fairness, Accountability, and Transparency* (pp. 249–260). https://doi.org/10.1145/3442188.3445888

Angwin, J., Larson, J., Mattu, S., & Kirchner, L. (2016, May 23). Machine bias: There's software used across the country to predict future criminals. And it's biased against Blacks. *ProPublica.* https://www.propublica.org/article/machine-bias-risk-assessments-in-criminal-sentencing

Ávila, F., Hannah-Moffat, K., & Maurutto, P. (2020). The seductiveness of fairness: Is machine learning the answer? Algorithmic fairness in criminal justice systems. In M. Schuilenburg & R. Peeters (Eds.), *The algorithmic society: Technology, power, and knowledge* (pp. 87–103). Routledge.

Baeza-Yates, R. (2020). Bias on the web and beyond: An accessibility point of view. In *W4A '20: Proceedings of the 17th International Web for All Conference* (article no. 10). https://doi.org/10.1145/3371300.3385335

Balayn, A., & Gürses, S. (2021). *Beyond debiasing: Regulating AI and its inequalities.* EDRi report. https://edri.org/wp-content/uploads/2021/09/EDRi_Beyond-Debiasing-Report_Online.pdf

Barocas, S., & Selbst, A. D. (2016). Big data's disparate impact. *California Law Review, 104*, 671–732.

Barocas, S., Hardt, M., & Narayanan, A. (2017). Fair machine learning—Limitations and opportunities (June 16, 2021). Nips tutorial 1.

Barocas, S., Selbst, A. D., & Raghavan, M. (2020). The hidden assumptions behind counterfactual explanations and principal reasons. In *FAT* '20: Proceedings of the 2020 Conference on Fairness, Accountability, and Transparency* (pp. 80–89). https://doi.org/10.1145/3351095.3372830

Beer, D. (2017). The social power of algorithms. *Information, Communication & Society, 20*(1), 1–13.

Beer, D. (2018). *The data gaze: Capitalism, power and perception*. Sage.

Benjamin, R. (2019). *Race after technology: Abolitionist tools for the New Jim Code*. Polity.

Berendt, B., Gandon, F., Halford, S., Hall, W., Hendler, J., Kinder-Kurlanda, K., Ntoutsi, E., & Staab, S. (2021). Web futures: Inclusive, intelligent, sustainable: The 2020 manifesto for web science. Dagstuhl Manifestos, Schloss Dagstuhl—LZI GmbH.

Bhaskar, R. (1979). *The possibility of naturalism: A philosophical critique of the contemporary human sciences*. Harvester Press.

Blodgett, S. L., Barocas, S., Daumé III, H., & Wallach, H. (2020). Language (technology) is power: A critical survey of "bias" in NLP. *arXiv:2005.14050* [*cs*]. http://arxiv.org/abs/2005.14050

Bowker, G. C., & Star, S. L. (2000). *Sorting things out: Classification and its consequences*. MIT Press.

boyd, d., & Crawford, K. (2012). Critical questions for big data: Provocations for a cultural, technological, and scholarly phenomenon. *Information, Communication & Society, 15*(5), 662–679.

Bozdag, E. (2013). Bias in algorithmic filtering and personalization. *Ethics and Information Technology, 15*(3), 209–227. http://dx-doi-org.uaccess.univie.ac.at/10.1007/s10676-013-9321-6

Buolamwini, J., & Gebru, T. (2018). Gender shades: Intersectional accuracy disparities in commercial gender classification. *Proceedings of Machine Learning Research, 81*, 1–15. http://proceedings.mlr.press/v81/buolamwini18a/buolamwini18a.pdf

Calders, T., & Žliobaitė, I. (2013). Why unbiased computational processes can lead to discriminative decision procedures. In *Discrimination and privacy in the information society* (pp. 43–57). Springer.

Chandler, D., & Munday, R. (2011). *A dictionary of media and communication*. Oxford University Press.

Crawford, K. (2021). *Atlas of AI: Power, politics, and the planetary costs of artificial intelligence*. Yale University Press.

Criado-Perez, C. (2020). *Unsichtbare Frauen. Wie eine von Daten beherrschte Welt die Hälfte der Bevölkerung ignoriert*. btb Verlag.

Diakopoulos, N. (2015). Algorithmic accountability: Journalistic investigation of computational power structures. *Digital Journalism, 3*(3), 398–415.

D'Ignazio, C., & Klein, L. F. (2020). *Data feminism*. MIT Press.

Dourish, P., & Bell, G. (2011). *Divining a digital future: Mess and mythology in ubiquitous computing*. MIT Press.

DuBrin, R., & Gorham, A. E. (2021). Algorithmic interpellation. *Constellations, 28*(2), 176–191.

Eubanks, V. (2018). *Automating inequality: How high-tech tools profile, police, and punish the poor*. St. Martin's Press.

European Commission, Directorate-General for Justice and Consumers, Gerards, J., & Xenidis, R. (2021). *Algorithmic discrimination in Europe: Challenges and opportunities for gender equality and non-discrimination law*. Publications Office. https://data.europa.eu/doi/10.2838/77444

Grimes, D. A., & Schulz, K. F. (2002). Bias and causal associations in observational research. *Lancet, 359*, 248–252.

Hancox-Li, L., & Kumar, I. E. (2021). Epistemic values in feature importance methods: Lessons from feminist epistemology. *FAccT '21: Proceedings of the 2021 ACM Conference on Fairness, Accountability, and Transparency* (pp. 817–826). https://doi.org/10.1145/3442188.3445943

Kamar, E., Kapoor, A., & Horvitz, E. (2015). Identifying and accounting for task-dependent bias in crowdsourcing. *Proceedings of the AAAI Conference on Human Computation and Crowdsourcing, 3*(1), 92–101. https://doi.org/10.1609/hcomp.v3i1.13238

Karimi, F., Génois, M., Wagner, C., Singer, P., & Strohmaier, M. (2018). Homophily influences ranking of minorities in social networks. *Scientific Reports, 8*(1), 1–12.

Keyes, O. (2018). The misgendering machines: Trans/HCI implications of automatic gender recognition. In *Proceedings of the ACM on Human–Computer Interaction, 2*(CSCW), article no. 88. https://doi.org/10.1145/3274357

Kinder-Kurlanda, K. E. (2014). Ethnography in a computer science centered project. In ICC '14 Workshop, ACM WebSci '14 Conference, Bloomington, IN.

Kinder-Kurlanda, K. (2020). Big Social Media Data als epistemologische Herausforderung für die Soziologie. In S. Maasen & J.-H. Passoth (Eds.), *Soziologie des Digitalen—Digitale Soziologie? Soziale Welt—Sonderband 23* (pp. 109–133). Nomos Verlagsgesellschaft.

Kinder-Kurlanda, K., Sørensen, & E., Kocksch, L. (2018). Troubling the ordering in cybersecurity research. EASST 2018: Meetings: Making Science, Technology and Society Together, Lancaster University, UK, 25–27 July 2018.

Kirkpatrick, K. (2016). Battling algorithmic bias: How do we ensure algorithms treat us fairly? *Communications of the ACM, 59*(10), 16–17. https://doi.org/10.1145/2983270

Kitchin, R. (2014). Big data, new epistemologies and paradigm shifts. *Big Data & Society, 1*(1). https://doi.org/10.1177/2053951714528481

Knorr-Cetina, K. (1999). *Epistemic cultures: How the sciences make knowledge.* Harvard University Press.

Law, J., & Mol, A. (2008). The actor-enacted: Cumbrian sheep in 2001. In C. Knappett & L. Malafouris (Eds.), *Material agency: Towards a non-anthropocentric approach* (pp. 57–77). Springer.

Leonelli, S. (2019). Data—From objects to assets. *Nature, 574,* 317–320. https://doi.org/10.1038/d41586-019-03062-w

Lopez, P. (2021). Bias does not equal bias: A socio-technical typology of bias in data-based algorithmic systems. *Internet Policy Review, 10*(4). https://doi.org/10.14763/2021.4.1598

Mehrabi, N., Morstatter, F., Saxena, N., Lerman, K., & Galstyan, A. (2019). A survey on bias and fairness in machine learning. *arXiv:1908.09635* [cs]. http://arxiv.org/abs/1908.09635

Noble, S. U. (2018). *Algorithms of oppression: How search engines reinforce racism.* New York University Press.

Ntoutsi, E., Fafalios, P., Gadiraju, U., Iosifidis, V., Nejdl, W., Vidal, M.-E., Ruggieri, S., Turini, F., Papadopoulos, S., Krasanakis, E., Kompatsiaris, I., Kinder-Kurlanda, K., Wagner, C., Karimi, F., Fernandez, M., Alani, H., Berendt, B., Kruegel, T., Heinze, C.,... & Staab, S. (2020). Bias in data-driven artificial intelligence systems—An introductory survey. *WIREs Data Mining and Knowledge Discovery, 10*(3), e1356. https://doi.org/10.1002/widm.1356

O'Neil, C. (2016). *Weapons of math destruction: How big data increases inequality and threatens democracy.* Broadway Books.

Pinch, T. J., & Bijker, W. E. (1984). The social construction of facts and artefacts: Or, How the sociology of science and the sociology of technology might benefit each other. *Social Studies of Science, 14*(3), 399–441. https://doi.org/10.1177/030631284014003004

Poechhacker, N., & Kacianka, S. (2021). Algorithmic accountability in context: Socio-technical perspectives on structural causal models. *Frontiers in Big Data, 3.* https://doi.org/10.3389/fdata.2020.519957

Poller, A., Türpe, S., Kinder-Kurlanda, K. (2014). An asset to security modeling? Analyzing stakeholder collaborations instead of threats to assets. In *NSPW '14: Proceedings of the 2014 New Security Paradigms Workshop* (pp. 69–82). https://doi.org/10.1145/2683467.2683474

Ricaurte, P. (2019). Data epistemologies, the coloniality of power, and resistance. *Television & New Media, 20*(4), 350–365.

Romei, A., & Ruggieri, S. (2014). A multidisciplinary survey on discrimination analysis. *Knowledge Engineering Review, 29*(5), 582–638. https://doi.org/10.1017/S0269888913000039

Scheuerman, M. K., Pape, M., & Hanna, A. (2021). Auto-essentialization: Gender in automated facial analysis as extended colonial project. *Big Data & Society, 8*(2), 20539517211053710. https://doi.org/10.1177/20539517211053712

Schwarz, O. (2021). *Sociological theory for digital society: The codes that bind us together*. Polity Press.

Seaver, N. (2019). Knowing algorithms. In J. Vertesi & D. Ribes (Eds.), *digitalSTS: A field guide for science & technology studies* (pp. 412–422). Princeton University Press.

Selbst, A. D., boyd, d., Friedler, S. A., Venkatasubramanian, S., & Vertesi, J. (2019). Fairness and abstraction in sociotechnical systems. In *FAT* '19: Proceedings of the Conference on Fairness, Accountability, and Transparency* (pp. 59–68). https://doi.org/10.1145/3287560.3287598

Suresh, H., & Guttag, J. (2019). A framework for understanding unintended consequences of machine learning. https://www.semanticscholar.org/paper/A-Framework-for-Understanding-Unintended-of-Machine-Suresh-Guttag/61c425bdda0e053074e96c3e6761ff1d7e0dd469

Torralba, A., & Efros, A. A. (2011). Unbiased look at dataset bias. In *IEEE Conference on Computer Vision and Pattern Recognition (CVPR)* (pp. 1521–1528). https://doi.org/10.1109/CVPR.2011.5995347

Trammell, A., & Cullen, A. L. (2021). A cultural approach to algorithmic bias in games. *New Media & Society, 23*(1), 159–174. https://doi.org/10.1177/1461444819900508

Verma, S., & Rubin, J. (2018). Fairness definitions explained. In *FairWare '18: Proceedings of the International Workshop on Software Fairness.* https://doi.org/10.1145/3194770.3194776

Wachter, S., Mittelstadt, B., & Russell, C. (2020). Why fairness cannot be automated: Bridging the gap between EU non-discrimination law and AI. Social Science Research Network (SSRN). https://doi.org/10.2139/ssrn.3547922

Weller, K., & Kinder-Kurlanda, K. E. (2015). Uncovering the challenges in collection, sharing and documentation: The hidden data of social media research? In *Standards and practices in large-scale social media research: Papers from the 2015 ICWSM Workshop. Proceedings Ninth International AAAI Conference on Web and Social Media, Oxford University, May 26, 2015–May 29, 2015* (pp. 28–37). AAAI Press.

West, S. M., Whittaker, M., & Crawford, K. (2019). Discriminating systems: Gender, race and power in AI. AI Now Institute. https://ainowinstitute.org/discriminatingsystems.html

Žliobaitė, I. (2017). Measuring discrimination in algorithmic decision making. *Data Mining and Knowledge Discovery, 31*, 1060–1089. https://doi.org/10.1007/s10618-017-0506-1

Zuboff, S. (2015). Big other: Surveillance capitalism and the prospects of an information civilization. *Journal of Information Technology, 30*(1), 75–89. https://doi.org/10.1057/jit.2015.5

Zuiderveen Borgesius, F. J. (2020). Strengthening legal protection against discrimination by algorithms and artificial intelligence. *International Journal of Human Rights, 24*(10), 1572–1593. https://doi.org/10.1080/13642987.2020.1743976

About the Authors

Katharina Kinder-Kurlanda is Professor of Digital Culture at the Digital Age Research Center at the University of Klagenfurt, Austria. She studied cultural anthropology, computer science, and history in Tübingen and Frankfurt and received her PhD from Lancaster University, UK. Her research interests are algorithms in the everyday, science and technology studies (STS), data practices, and data ethics.

Miriam Fahimi is a Marie Skłodowska-Curie Fellow in an H2020 project on artificial intelligence and a PhD candidate in science and technology studies at the Digital Age Research Center (D!ARC) at the University of Klagenfurt, Austria. Her research interests include feminist and relational approaches to technology and infrastructures.

16. Commentary: The Entanglements, Experiments, and Uncertainties of Algorithmic Regimes

Nanna Bonde Thylstrup

Abstract

This commentary argues that as we engage with the politics of algorithmic systems, we need not only to attend to the ways in which they generate new modes of control, organization, and knowledge production, but also how these new algorithmic regimes are constituted by messes, failures, and uncertainties. This is exactly why critical engagements such as those featured in this section are so crucial. They open small, important windows into the modes of valuation, labour, and aesthetics involved in upholding algorithmic regimes, which also allows us to truly appreciate their temporally sensitive and fundamentally unstable form.

Keywords: power; archives; mess; uncertainty

Introduction

How might we describe the politics of algorithmic regimes? Which organizations should we examine, which theories should we employ, and what methods should we use? As the contributions in this section show, there is not one correct answer: analyses and methods must be as heterogeneous as the territories they examine. But while territories may be heterogeneous, the role of power in shaping them is constant. The chapters in this section therefore also show the saliency of attending closely to the power dynamics at play in the unfolding politics of algorithmic landscapes, especially when it comes to the nexus between power and knowledge. In the following I weave together insights from these chapters to foreground three points

Jarke, J., B. Prietl, S. Egbert, Y. Boeva, H. Heuer, and M. Arnold (eds.), *Algorithmic Regimes: Methods, Interactions, and Politics*. Amsterdam: Amsterdam University Press, 2024
DOI 10.5117/9789463728485_CH16

that speak to and extend the insights offered in them: Thus, I make the point that as we engage with the politics of algorithmic systems, we need not only to attend to the ways in which they generate new modes of control, organization, and knowledge production, but also how these new modes are always also constituted by entanglements, failures, and uncertainties.

Entanglements

The emerging constellations of algorithmic regimes and the multiplicities of politics of knowledge in organizations are becoming increasingly crucial areas of analysis. As the chapters in this section show, while big tech (largely emerging out of Silicon Valley) offers one important nexus of analysis, it is far from the only one. Instead, attention must also be directed towards new knowledge/power assemblages far from the political and geographic reality of Silicon Valley. Such analyses are crucial because they allow us better to attend to not only the political regimes of knowledge that shape future governance infrastructures, but also the potential sites of friction they may generate. As analyses of public–private machine learning projects show, data scientific projects do not unfold in a political vacuum but will always be entangled within—and in negotiation with—surrounding environments (Amoore, 2020; Thylstrup et al. 2022). Yet, data science is often presented as a pragmatic, even miraculous, universal toolbox of Swiss Army knives that can be applied across different contexts (Slota et al., 2020). Bianca Prietl and Stefanie Raible's analysis of the professionalization of data science in universities in Germany, Austria, and Switzerland (in this volume) offers a good example of how such a framing unfolds. In their chapter, we see how institutional structures, epistemological positioning, and discursive legitimization enables the conceptualization of data science to appear as a scientific method that can be applied independent of the object of inquiry, but also why it must always be embedded in a political reality. The insights in Prietl and Raible's chapter exceed educational landscapes because it helps us understand how tech assemblages are depoliticized, even when they are deeply political. Take partnerships such as those Palantir have entered in with the health and police force in Europe and prominent NGOs (such as the World Food Programme). These partnerships were framed as neutral or even as "AI for good." Yet, it matters that Palantir, a defence contractor, is also working on data related to refugees (Martin et al., 2022). Even so, such concerns about spillover are often left unaddressed by involved and adjacent actors.

Rather than accepting the premise of "pragmatic" methods that shy away from engaging with context, then, the chapters in this section show the need to extend our understanding of the wider regimes technologies unfold within, and their entangled nature. Katharina Kinder-Kurlanda and Miriam Fahimi's chapter on the NoBIAS project, which seeks to develop better methods for understanding and mitigating algorithmic bias, shows, for instance, how contingent such engagements are and how dependent they are on different, and changing, vocabularies. They shed crucial light on how efforts to achieve fair AI are conditioned not only by technological knowledge, but also different contextual understandings of what "bias" means (not to speak of a variety of often conflicting reasons for getting involved in such work). Kinder-Kurlanda and Fahimi thus remind us that any analytical attempts at making machine learning systems "fairer" must contend with multiple relationalities and moments of interpretation. Their contribution can be situated within a broader regime of linguistic governance, rich with moments of interpretation that generate cultural spaces of uncertainty and potential instability (Hall, 1997, 1999). And as Kinder-Kurlanda and Fahimi show, rather than stabilizing such spaces through universal definitions of, for example, what is "fair," actors in algorithmic regimes would be better served by being equipped with knowledge about the oscillating meanings of concepts in specific contexts. This is because cultural systems and their meanings change and are contingent. Take content moderation systems, for instance, and their difficulties stabilizing language. While many content moderation system today implement systems that define and detect "toxic" content, these systems often fail because they struggle with the dynamic nature of cultural languages: what was once accepted practice, for instance, can suddenly be considered harmful and socially transgressive (Thylstrup & Talat, 2020). Similarly, content that is taboo in some communities, may be readily accepted in others. These cultural dynamics emphasize that when we talk about "fair," it is often less a question of the "essence" of an expression and more a question of the properties that are attached to the content. To ensure fairness, then, algorithmic regimes should continuously align with actors such as social and digital justice movements instead of taking categories of e.g., fair and "toxicity" for granted.

Experiments

We often ascribe regimes of prediction (see e.g., Egbert, in this volume) a sense of command of everything from trends in culture and thought to potential epidemics, criminal acts, environmental disasters, and terrorist threats. Yet, as outlined above, while algorithmic regimes may seem to generate more mechanisms of control in algorithmic regimes, they are in fact highly messy entities that often even fail more than they succeed. Time and again experts and observers not only question the statistical validity of the diagnoses and prognoses promised by algorithmic regimes, but also warn of the broader implications of the large-scale determination of knowledge by algorithmic regimes. Yet, even in their failures, algorithmic systems often thrive. Thus, rather than undermining the power waged by tech companies, such stories often seem to consolidate and even extend their power. As such the fickle role of failure in algorithmic regimes also indicates a more fundamental clash of scientific paradigms regarding what constitutes knowledge and how best to achieve it. Clashes that are again nested within the deeper politics of how we understand success and failure in experimental algorithmic regimes: who has the power to determine something as a failure, and who is made to endure the consequences of these errors? As Orit Halpern (2021) points out, moments of failure in algorithmic regimes also become embedded in a logic of the experiment where: "experiments … prove which forms of research and technology need to be invoked next; that should exist and must be built." Marres (2020) calls this ongoing experimental implementation of algorithmic regimes exemplary of a new, "experimental" mode of industrial innovation, where experiments and beta testing that would previously occur in a lab, are today located in everyday societal and intimate settings like streets, personal computers, and smart phones. This is the dynamic exposed by Paola Lopez in her analysis of the Twitter crop algorithm. Her chapter thus succinctly shows how, in algorithmic regimes, even failures are routinely turned into a generative possibility and potential value creation.

How might we understand the role of failure in algorithmic regimes as a deeply political one? At the end of his essay "Life: Experience and Science," Michel Foucault concludes,

> at the most basic level of life, the processes of coding and decoding give way to a chance occurrence that, before becoming a disease, a deficiency, or a monstrosity, is something like a disturbance in the informative system, something like a "mistake." In this sense, life—and this is its radical feature—is that which is capable of error. (Foucault, 1998, p. 476)

Foucault's analysis points to the ambivalence of error, or failure, as both a creative event and a moment of power. This understanding of error can help us move out of simplified ideas of error as an either purely productive process or as technical glitches that can be "corrected" to instead repoliticize error as fundamentally tied to questions of power. Contemporary feminist engagements with the failures of algorithmic regimes offer crucial perspectives on this. Relevant to the feature of the crop function, for instance, Catherine D'Ignazio (2021) has shown how the historical positioning of certain bodies as more anomalous than others also means that there is often uncertainty as to whether an outlier is an error in the recording of data or represents a true variation in the population. D'Ignazio thus reminds the reader that rejecting outliers as errors in data sets has serious implications for data subjects and notes that these implications also tend to reproduce gendered and racialized discriminations. In their work on (mis)gendering, Os Keyes (2021) moreover shows how these lines of oppression also remain lodged within the binary imaginary of data science, which at once excludes, for instance, trans experience from its organization of information, and at the same time continually reinserts trans people into static gender narratives drawn from archival material from pretransition lives.

The paradoxical role of failure in algorithmic regimes also places new demands on critical engagements with them. A default mechanism of algorithmic critique is often to expose its errors and make visible how regimes of power/knowledge built around algorithms are not so knowledgeable after all. Yet, in algorithmic regimes, this mode of engagement is in fact often challenged, because they seem to thrive on uncertainty and disruptive moments. Thus, moments of breakdown can both be viewed as moments of potential critique in the form of error, glitch, and subversion, and as a conceptualization of failure as a creative process that is easily co-opted as ventures. In the worst cases, failures can even be mobilized by platforms to deflect state and corporate accountability because uncertainty and experimentation is endogenous to digital-age capitalism.

As such the fickle role of failure in algorithmic regimes also indicates a more fundamental clash of scientific paradigms regarding what constitutes knowledge and how best to achieve it. Clashes that are again nested within the deeper politics of how we understand failure in digital knowledge regimes, who has the power to determine something as a failure, and who is made to endure the consequences of these errors. As such, phenomena of failure such as the one explored by Lopez (in this volume) are in fact symptomatic examples of how major tech companies reconfigure errors into what Orit Halpern (2021) calls demos: "experiments that prove which forms of research and technology need to be invoked next; that should exist and must be built." Indeed, as Noortje Marres (2020) points out in relation to the ongoing experimental implementation of self-driving cars, such approaches are exemplary of a new, "experimental" mode of industrial innovation, where experiments and beta testing that would previously occur in a lab, are today located in everyday societal and intimate settings like streets, personal computers, and smart phones.

Uncertainty

As the above paragraphs show, the politics of algorithmic regimes are sites of knowledge retention and production fraught with failures and messes. This section suggests that we can meaningfully understand these conditions as expressions of an uncertainty, and that this uncertainty is endemic to algorithmic regimes, enhanced further by their complicity in systems of neoliberal global governance, authoritarian regimes, and dispossessions caused by wars and climate change. The uncertainty of algorithmic regimes is thus as much a function of disruption complicit with, rather than resistant to power as it is a dynamic that challenges power structures. This begs the question: if today's algorithmic regimes are constituted as much by entanglements and failures, how might we understand the knowledge production that takes place in the knowledge/power nexus, and how might we critically engage with it without reifying existing power structures?

Along with my co-authors (Thylstrup et al., 2021) I have previously argued that critical archival theory offers one rich analytic approach to the power/knowledge nexus in algorithmic regimes because it foregrounds both its profoundly political constitution as well as its speculative openings that may offer refuge for new critical engagements. Derrida (1995) famously traced the etymology of the term "archive" to *arkhe*, the Greek noun signifying beginning and commandment, and drew attention to the related noun *arkheion*, designating the homes where ancient magistrates (archons) stored the documents of the law (2). This perspective allows us to view archives as profoundly authoritative: as the origins "from which order is given" (Derrida, 1995, p. 1). Like Derrida, Foucault (2018) mobilizes the archive as a theoretical concept bound up with power. He locates this power in what he calls "the system of discursivity," that is, the system of possibility of what can be said (Foucault, 2018). Michel Rolph Trouillot similarly describes archives not only as neutral sites of knowledge retrieval but also as cultural sites of world-making where archivists are interpreters as much as guardians of archival content (Trouillot, 1995). These "hermeneutic operations" (Ring, 2015) involve the selection, preservation, and destruction of material and the obstruction of access, and they are often entangled within colonial, gendered, and racialized power structures that manifest as moments and principles of exclusion (Chaudhuri et al., 2010; Onuoha, 2021; Taylor, 2020).

The lessons learned from poststructuralist and more recent critical archival theory can be productively harnessed in the field of algorithmic regimes to look at the new knowledge regimes in which the crucial methods of appraisal, storage, and classification are once again being performed by a small group that exercises White patriarchal power over the rest of the world, with disproportionate impact. As Safiya Noble (2019) states, "Political struggles over the classification of knowledge have been with us since human beings have been documenting history. The politics of knowledge plays out in whose knowledge is captured, in what context and how it gets deployed." Current practices of algorithmic production, collection, distribution, and consumption both build upon and draw from the history of theorizing the archive, even as they raise pertinent new questions that exceed the horizon of analogue archives. To think about the politics of knowledge regimes in this way also allows us to recognize the historical roots of current practices of data gathering, hoarding, storing, leaking, and wasting while also remembering that today's seemingly streamlined interaction between human beings and our digital files and folders is every bit as messy, porous, and generative as archival encounters have always been (Thylstrup et al., 2021).

Crucially, while algorithmic regimes may function as archival power/ knowledge nexuses, cultural archival theory also reminds us of the impossibility of total control within these regimes. Foucault (2018) identified archives as making up a "web of which they [the holders of the archive] are not the masters" (p. 143). Today's seemingly streamlined interaction between human beings and our digital data and storage is arguably every bit as messy, porous, and generative as the archival technologies and practices Foucault described. Recognizing the structural instability of archives can help nuance approaches to the power of algorithmic regimes, for instance, of prediction, because it shows that the power of algorithmic regimes lies just as much in their performative nature as in their actual capacity for prediction—and that governors of algorithmic regimes also battle their own archival instabilities and vulnerabilities. Foucault (2018) thus identified archives as making up a "web of which they [the holders of the archive] are not the masters" (p. 143). And in Derrida's (1995) feverish archives, there is an "aggression and destruction drive" (p. 19) that renders "the violent patriarchive ... less authoritative by the haunting impossibility of its own totalizing desire" (Ring, 2015, p. 398). The structural uncertainty that haunts (an)archival regimes thus both demands an acknowledgement of the structural injustice of the politics of algorithmic regimes and also creates openings for new forms of critique that resist reifying their powers.

Algorithmic Regimes as Gimmicks

So far, I have sought to foreground the ways in which algorithmic regimes are constituted by messes, failures, and uncertainties, and how these characteristics are both part of their power and their Achilles heel. Think of self-driving cars, which still fail to deliver on their promises. Or machine learning models such as Midjourney, whose aesthetic success stories are constantly also accompanied by horror stories of racialized, gendered, and colonial biases. To conclude, I want to offer a question and a perspective: if algorithmic regimes are messy, full of failures, and highly uncertain, why are they still so powerful? One potential answer is that it is exactly because they overperform and underperform at the same time. My final proposal, then, is to understand algorithmic regimes as *gimmicks*. My interpretation of algorithmic regimes as organized around gimmicks draws on Sianne Ngai's (2020) wonderfully provocative theory of the gimmick as "a miniature model of capitalism itself":

> The gimmick is thus capitalism's most successful aesthetic category but also its biggest embarrassment and structural problem. With its dubious yet attractive promises about the saving of time, the reduction of labor, and the expansion of value, it gives us tantalizing glimpses of a world in which social life will no longer be organized by labor, while indexing one that continuously regenerates the conditions keeping labor's social necessity in place. (p. 2)

I think Ngai's description deftly encapsulates how algorithmic regimes are premised on an aesthetic specific to a mode of production that binds value to labour and time. And, more importantly, it also opens to a new form of critical engagement that may help us understand not only how algorithmic regimes extract surplus value from living labour but also how they—through their gimmicks—"encod[e] the limits to accumulation and expanded reproduction that expose capitalism to crisis" (Ngai, 2020, p. 4). This is exactly why critical engagements such as those featured in this section are so crucial. Because they open small, important windows into the modes of valuation, labour, and aesthetics involved in upholding algorithmic regimes, which allow us to truly appreciate their temporally sensitive and fundamentally unstable nature.

References

Amoore, L. (2020). *Cloud ethics: Algorithms and the attributes of ourselves and others*. Duke University Press.

Chaudhuri, N., Katz, S. J., & Perry, M. E. (2010). *Contesting archives: Finding women in the sources*. University of Illinois Press.

Derrida, J. (1995). *Archive fever: A Freudian impression* (E. Prenowitz, Trans.). Diacritics.

D'Ignazio, C. (2021). Outlier. In N. B. Thylstrup, D. Agostinho, A. Ring, C. D'Ignazio, & K. Veel (Eds.), *Uncertain archives: Critical keywords for big data* (pp. 377–387). MIT Press.

Eliassen, K. O. (2010). The archives of Michel Foucault. In E. Røssaak (Ed.), *The archive in motion: New conceptions of the archive in contemporary thought and new media practices* (pp. 29–52). Novus Press.

Foucault, M. (2018). *The order of things: An archaeology of the human sciences*. Routledge.

Foucault, M. 1994. "Life: Experience and Science." In: M. Foucault. *Aesthetics, Method and Epistemology* (pp. 465–479). The New Press.

Hall, S. (1997). The spectacle of the "Other." In S. Hall, J. Evans, & S. Nixon (Eds.), *Representation: Cultural representations and signifying practices* (pp. 223–290). Sage.

Hall, S. (1999). Race, the floating signifier: Featuring Stuart Hall [Transcript]. Media Education Foundation. https://www.mediaed.org/transcripts/Stuart-Hall-Race-the-Floating-Signifier-Transcript.pdf

Halpern, O. (2021). Demo. In N. B. Thylstrup, D. Agostinho, A. Ring, C. D'Ignazio, & K. Veel (Eds.), *Uncertain archives: Critical keywords for big data* (pp. 133–140). MIT Press.

Keyes, O. (2021). (Mis)gendering. In N. B. Thylstrup, D. Agostinho, A. Ring, C. D'Ignazio, & K. Veel (Eds.), *Uncertain archives: Critical keywords for big data* (pp. 339–346). MIT Press.

Marres, N. (2020). Co-existence or displacement: Do street trials of intelligent vehicles test society? *British Journal of Sociology, 71*(3), 537–555.

Martin, A., Sharma, G., Peter de Souza, S., Taylor, L., Van Eerd, B., McDonald, S., & Dijstelbloem, H. (2022). Digitisation and sovereignty in humanitarian space: Technologies, territories and tensions. *Geopolitics, 28*(3), 1362–1397. https://doi.org/10.1080/14650045.2022.2047468

Ngai, S. (2020). *Theory of the gimmick: Aesthetic judgment and capitalist form.* Harvard University Press.

Noble, S. U. (2019). The ethics of AI. Paper delivered at Digital Democracies Conference: Artificial Publics, Just Infrastructures, Ethical Learning; Simon Fraser University, May 16, 2019.

Onuoha, M. (2021). Natural. In N. B. Thylstrup, D. Agostinho, A. Ring, C. D'Ignazio, & K. Veel (Eds.), *Uncertain archives: Critical keywords for big data* (pp. 353–357). MIT Press.

Ring, A. (2015). *After the Stasi: Collaboration and the struggle for sovereign subjectivity.* Bloomsbury Academic.

Slota, S. C., Hoffman, A. S., Ribes, D., & Bowker, G. C. (2020). Prospecting (in) the data sciences. *Big Data & Society, 7*(1). https://doi.org/10.1177/20539517209068

Taylor, D. (2020). *The archive and the repertoire: Performing cultural memory in the Americas.* Duke University Press.

Thylstrup, N. B., & Talat, Z. (2020). Detecting "dirt" and "toxicity": Rethinking content moderation as pollution behaviour. Social Science Research Network (SSRN). http://doi.org/10.2139/ssrn.3709719

Thylstrup, N. B., Agostinho, A. Ring, C. D'Ignazio, & K. Veel (Eds.). (2021). *Uncertain archives: Critical keywords for big data.* MIT Press.

Thylstrup, N. B., Hansen, K. B., Flyverbom, M., & Amoore, L. (2022). Politics of data reuse in machine learning systems: Theorizing reuse entanglements. *Big Data & Society, 9*(2). https://doi.org/10.1177/20539517221139785

Trouillot, M. R. (1995). *Silencing the past: Power and the production of history.* Beacon Press.

About the Author

Nanna Bonde Thylstrup is Associate Professor on the Promotion Programme at the University of Copenhagen. Her research focuses on the politics and ethics of data and machine learning and the interplay between digital developments and cultural, social, and political change. Her most recent book is *Uncertain Archives: Critical Keywords for Big Data* (MIT Press, 2021).

Index